Understanding economic policy

For most of the post-war period, economic policy has been the battleground on which elections have been won or lost. Issues like unemployment, inflation and prosperity remain at the centre of political debate and for this reason neither of the major political parties has determined its economic policies on economic grounds alone. Economic policy is determined by the interaction of both political and economic factors, and for that reason is best understood through an interdisciplinary approach.

In *Understanding Economic Policy*, Maurice Mullard provides a framework for understanding the nature of economic policy making. In an accessible and non-technical way he outlines two models of economic policy: a laissez-faire, liberal approach of the kind associated with recent Conservative governments, and the type of managed economy normally identified as 'Keynesian'. Both the micro and macro implications of both approaches are considered at length. The aim of the text, therefore, is to examine the relationship between economic events and political change; that is, between political autonomy and economic constraints in the making of economic policy.

The text proceeds to discuss both models in the context of economic policy since the war. The Labour governments of 1945–51 are seen to lay the foundations for the years of consensus which preceded the Thatcher era. The book concludes by considering the prospects for economic policy in the 1990s in the wake of events, including ERM entry.

Maurice Mullard is Senior Lecturer in Politics and Economics at Bradford and Ilkley Community College. His previous publications include *The Politics of Public Expenditure* (Routledge, 1987) and *Local Government and Thatcherism*, with H. Butcher, I. G. Law and R. Leach (Routledge, 1989).

Understanding economic policy

Maurice Mullard

London and New York

First published 1992
by Routledge
11 New Fetter Lane, London EC4P 4EE

Simultaneously published in the USA and Canada
by Routledge
a division of Routledge, Chapman and Hall, Inc.
29 West 35th Street, New York, NY 10001

Typeset in Garamond by
Michael Mepham, Frome, Somerset
Printed and bound in Great Britain by
Mackays of Chatham PLC, Chatham, Kent

British Library Cataloguing in Publication Data
Maurice Mullard 1946–
    Understanding Economic Policy
    1. Great Britain. Economic conditions
    I. Title
    330.941
    ISBN 0–415–06881–9
    ISBN 0–415–06882–7 (pbk)

Library of Congress Cataloging in Publication Data
Mullard, Maurice, 1946–
    Understanding economic policy/ Maurice Mullard
    Includes bibliographical references and index
    ISBN 0–415–06881–9
    1 Great Britain – Economic policy – 1945–   2 Great
    Britain – Politics and government – 1945–   3 Economic
    Policy   I Title
    HC256.5.M85   1991
    338.941–dc20

In memory of
Ursula, Frederick and Carmena Brown
the people who cared and looked
after me

Contents

Figures

Prologue

The making of economic policy represents a continuing tension between the dimensions of political choice as much as the process of responding to economic pressures and events which are not in direct control of government. The major concern for the student of economics and politics is to explore the changing relationship between the autonomy of government, that is the ability of governments to give direction to the economy and constraints imposed by economic events which are not within the immediate control of government. The making of economic policy points to the process where the divisions as to what is 'politics' and 'economics' become less transparent. While politics is associated with government policy, political priorities, choice, political judgement and political calculation, economics is concerned with the analysis of economic events and how the economic context both restricts and facilitates the political process.

While governments do have limited autonomy to influence economic events either by reducing interest rates to gain favour with households with mortgages or increasing pensions, there are other events which the government do not have the autonomy to influence. The decision by the UK government in October 1990 to enter the EMS has already imposed new limits on the autonomy of the government in the conduct of monetary policy. Despite warning that EMS entry has been at a level which is not sustainable to maintain UK competitiveness and the recent increases in unemployment, the government no longer has the option to use interest rates to devalue the currency to help exports and reduce unemployment. Within the new discipline of the EMS, UK firms and trade unions have to learn new ways of conducting industrial relations if competitiveness and employment are to be protected. At present the government seems to have limited itself to exhortations about the needs of more discipline in wage bargaining. In the meantime trade union members who do not feel directly threatened by unemployment have no incentive to moderate their wage demands and allow for productivity to reduce prices which means that unemployment will continue to rise until better ways of settling wages within the EMS can be found.

The unemployed are once again to bear the consequences of myopic British pay-bargaining. Employers and unions remain unwilling to recognise that wage settlements based on last year's price inflation are a recipe for disaster.

(Financial Times editorial, 7 December 1990).

In the conduct of economic policy governments do have certain policy options. The responses to economic events always involve choice. However, while it is correct to argue that economic policy reflects political choice it would also be misleading to imply that governments have to complete control over economic policy. The unification of Germany and the implications for German policies to deal with the new deficits are likely to influence UK interest rates as are the decisions on Britain joining the EMS and the responses by employers and trade unions to the new bargaining context. Both these external and internal constraints reflect the limits of the UK government's ability to influence interest rates. In this context the government has limited autonomy in responding to the problems of recession and unemployment.

The study of economics has often meant that students have had to restrict themselves to the understanding of economic principles, economic techniques and economic models. In this context the attempt to construct policy options as derived from the study of economics seemed to indicate that the role of economists should be restricted to explaining economic events without looking at the competing policy options which were available to government. The resignation of Nigel Lawson as Chancellor of the Exchequer in October 1989 was to an extent attributed to the influence of Sir Alan Walters as economic adviser to the former Prime Minister Margaret Thatcher. Mr Lawson argued that while it was within the brief of Sir Alan to advise the Prime Minister on economic issues he did not have the right to criticise or question the Chancellor on the economy – advisers were there to give advice while politicians had to make the decisions. Mr Lawson in this instance felt that Sir Alan had crossed the boundary of economics and politics.

It would seem that while the classical economists including Adam Smith, Keynes and more recently Samuel Brittan have had no problem in seeing themselves as political economists, the teaching of economics and the influence of econometrics have become so specialised that economists increasingly seem to draw a line between what was seen as being the issues of concern to economists as distinct from the process of government and policy-making. This text attempts to recapture some of the ground of classical political economy by seeking to show that economic modelling, econometrics and economic data are themselves built on principles and assumptions which are implicitly political in the sense that the principles and assumptions are constructed around specific views of the individual or government.

In seeking to re-generate the language of political economy the text seeks to combine principles from economics arguing that these principles are essential tools for both economic analysis but also for the construction of political principles. These principles are outlined in the first part of the text. The second part is then devoted to exploring UK economic policy since 1945 and seeks to explain the changing relationships between economic events, government, public institutions and vested interests and how these both shaped and influenced economic policy-making.

In the first part the concern has been, first, to develop market liberal and Keynesian principles at three levels so that chapters are directed towards evolving an overall view of each model; second to utilise the tools as derived from these models to both explain and explore policy options on dealing with specific issues including unemployment and inflation; and third to outline the political dimensions of each model. In following this logic therefore there are three chapters devoted to developing the principles, the policies and the politics for the market liberal model and likewise three chapters directed to a Keynesian model.

In the discussion of the market model it is argued that the concepts of the individual, rational choice, markets and competition are perceived to be the core assumptions and that analysis of how both the micro- and macro-economy works are founded on these assumptions. Furthermore in the context of a market model a role for government can be derived around issues of market failure including the problems of externalities, spillover effects, public goods and income re-distribution. Hence in developing the market model it will be argued that market economists can provide a framework for government policies within the principles of market liberalism and suggests that for market economists there are spaces where government intervention in the provision of public goods could actually advance both the interests of the individual and the community without restricting individual freedom or undermining the central tenet of market liberalism, namely that individuals should be treated as ends rather than means to an end.

In developing these tools it is then argued that market liberal economists seek to deal with issues of unemployment and inflation in the context of markets and the dynamics of supply and demand. Within the context of markets it will be argued that unemployment is explained in terms of the presence of rigidities in the labour market either because of rigidities within the supply side including trade unions, social security benefits and discrimination within labour markets or that problems arise on the demand side such as the cost of labour and national insurance. Within a market liberal context therefore government should seek to influence the demand and supply side of the labour market either through trade union reform, the reform of social security, taxation and legislation against race and sex discrimination. In dealing with inflation market economists also emphasise the problem of demand which is caused mainly by increases in the money supply, bank lending and government expenditure.

The third chapter in this section then deals with the issue of politics and suggests that there are two models of politics which can be derived in the context of market principles. There is the model which can be described as the representing the moral political economy of market liberalism and which has its roots in the views of thinkers such as Cobden and Bright who argued against imperialism and for free trade as the mechanism for achieving prosperity and world peace. In contrast there is the Hobbesian view of the individual in relation to the sovereignty of the state which argues that while individuals should pursue self interest in the context of markets there is a need for government to provide discipline and social order. In contrast to the market liberal vision of spontaneous individualism there is also the view that markets and individuals need to be contained within a strong and centralising state. While market liberals argue that the principles which guide state intervention should be guided be market principles, Hobbesians would argue that, while markets are the concern of civil society, issues of discipline and social order continue to be the concern of the sovereign state.

Chapters 5, 6 and 7 concentrate on Keynesian economics and adopt a similar approach to the chapters dealing with market liberalism. As with the market model the concern is to provide tools which are seen as belonging to a Keynesian model and to show how these tools are utilised in dealing with issues such as unemployment and inflation but also to outline the elements of what can be defined as the politics of Keynesianism Chapter 5 deals with what are perceived to be the core principles of Keynesian economics and how these differ from the key concepts associated with the market model. The view that Keynesianism represented more than just an adjustment to the market model but actually constituted a Kuhnian paradigm shift is then pursued in Chapters 6 and 7. The theme to be emphasised here is that Keynesianism represents an alternative form of politics which can be categorised as the politics for a civilised economy where the discipline of the labour market is replaced by the ethics of dialogue and the search for a politics of consent involving governments, employers and employees. Within this context Keynesianism becomes more than a set of economic techniques confined to demand management and becomes a wider political agenda in which governments set their macroeconomic policy with the aim of maintaining a fully employed economy but where trade unions and employers contribute directly to economic policy.

Keynesianism therefore represents the search for a politics of consent between government and strategic economics groups. In this the Keynesian agenda is different to that of market liberalism. While market liberals see trade unions and employers organisations as distorting the workings of the market place, often working against the interests of the individual as a citizen, Keynesians see the world of functional groups as representing the world as it is. Keynesians would argue that functional interest groups can actually advance the interests of their members and also the wider community within the context of a civilised economy, since within the framework of consensus it is more likely that the public interest is advanced when compared with market liberalism and its concern with individual self interest.

In contrast market liberals would argue that the primary role of government is to enhance the rights of the individual where individuals are not treated as members of classes or by gender or race but as persons in their own right. Market liberals would suggest that the competitive market place is the least discriminatory as opposed to the political process which responds to those who have the time and the political knowledge. In this context market liberals argue that governments must provide a legislative framework which protects the individual from the narrow and vested interests of functional groups.

> Freedom for the common people is better ensured by economic democracy of the market of one man, one vote every day, than by the unpredictable political democracy of the ballot box franchise of one man, one vote every 1,000th day (more or less). On the other 999 days, political democracy serves politicians, bureaucrats and their clients in the organised interests of industry, the professions, the trade unions, the arts and the church.
>
> (Arthur Seldon, *Financial Times*, 26 September 1990)

Equally, market liberals would urge that government conduct economic policy-making with pre-established rules and procedures, and would therefore urge that the European Central Bank should be outside the control of government to pursue monetary policy independent from the political priorities of government. Market liberals see the politics of consent as developed within Keynesianism as reinforcing inequalities of access and opportunity since the central aim of vested interest groups is to protect the interests of their members. Keynesianism seems to legitimise the demands and the concessions which government have to make as part of their contract with strategic groups.

In contrast to the market liberal view that too much politics can put individual liberty at risk, authors who seek to provide an ethical approach to government have argued that politics is central in the process of securing justice and freedom. Hannah Arendt, while agreeing with the market liberal view that the individual should be seen as end and not a means to an end has also emphasised that

Freedom...is actually the reason that men live together in political organisation at all. Without politics life as such would be meaningless. The reason d'etre of politics is freedom, and its field of experience is action.

(Arendt 1961: 146)

The second part of the book seeks to explore the tensions between economic events and the political process. The central theme of these chapters is to show how government sought to explore the tensions of responding to economic events while at the same time seeking to give direction to economic policy. The argument to be presented here aims to show that UK governments in the post-war period have sought to deal with three problems of economic policy. First, there has been the problem of the balance of payments and the inability of the UK to enter the virtuous circle of export-led growth. The balance of payments constraint has usually resulted in sterling crises and 'go and stop' policies in economic management. The problem of the balance of payments has for most of the time been dealt with as a short-term problem, namely that of too much demand in the economy which had to be curbed either through public expenditure cuts, higher taxes, credit controls or high interest rates. While dealing with the issue as a demand management problem served the purpose of the electoral business cycle, the more fundamental question of how to improve Britain's export performance has usually been drowned by the political pressures of serving consumer demand. The study of economic policy would indicate that the only time the balance of payments was taken seriously was during the years of the 1945 Labour government when it was able, at least in the short term, to use the good will of the electorate to curb consumer demand and divert income from consumption to investment. However, Labour's austerity package, while it was successful in regaining export markets, was unsuccessful at a political level when Labour went on to lose the 1951 election and remained out of office until 1964.

The second major issue has been how to deal with the problem of inflation without deflating the economy. Again the common theme to emerge here has been the failure of UK governments to establish with the trade unions and employers a durable policy for wages and investment. While there were many forays in the world of incomes policy these initiatives tended to be short term to deal with the immediate pressures of sterling and inflation rather than with the longer term issues of generating employment and continued prosperity. While trade union leaders were often found to be willing to discuss incomes policy with the government and employers the nature of trade union organisations made incomes policy difficult to administer, especially as the informal system of collective bargaining tended to undermine the formal system. It was the informal system as conducted by shop steward committees in plant bargains which often led to problems of wage drift. The problem therefore was that very often trade unions were unable to maintain a coherent strategy as they came under pressure from their members to return to free collective bargaining. The reform of industrial relations were therefore always likely to become political in that the trade unions looked to the Labour Party to protect their immunities while the Conservative Party was increasingly seen as wanting to undermine trade union organisations. The attempts to reform industrial relations by the Labour Government in 1968 and the Heath Government through the Trade Unions Act of 1972 in one way reflects the failure to reach a voluntary agreement with the trade unions on the issue of wage inflation.

The third major concern is related to the issue of economic growth and employment. While the UK economy was growing at 2.5 per cent per annum during the 1950s and 1960s, Britain's record when compared to other major industrial countries including France, West Germany and Japan seemed to indicate that the UK was underperforming rather than experiencing economic failure or economic decline. Equally, during the 1970s, faced with oil price increases, Britain seemed to be less able to deal with problems of recession than its competitors. UK inflation and unemployment were always higher than the average for the OECD countries and also higher when compared to other EC countries. The attempts to break out of the cycle of slow growth and 'stop go' policies either again seemed to be temporary measures as government were forced to deal with the short-term pressures of the balance of payments and sterling crisis.

Although the issues of employment, growth, inflation and the balance of payments could be seen as being interdependent and therefore requiring structural solutions, the problem for the UK economy has not been so much the lack of experimentation with the British economy but rather too much. Discontinuities in macroeconomic policy and continuous disagreements on incomes policies have all contributed to a process of inconsistency and a decline in the credibility of government in setting economic priorities. Initiatives on industrial policy, including indicative planning in the late 1950s, Harold Wilson's Ministry of Technology in the 1960s, Mr Heath's Industry Act of 1972 and Labour's National Enterprise Board in 1976 tended to be short lived and often failed attempts by UK governments to pick industrial winners.

In this sense the election of Mrs Thatcher's government in 1979 was no different to their predecessors. Previous governments also had visions for the British economy. While the Thatcher government might have argued that they were seeking to break with the post-war consensus, the study of economic policy in the post-war would suggest that there was minimum consensus and that in one sense many aspects of Mrs Thatcher's revolution had been tried before. The reform of industrial relations has been part of the political agenda since the mid 1950s as has been the concern with

incomes policy. While one central achievement to Mrs Thatcher's revolution has been the reform of trade unions it would seem that the reforms
have not addressed the problem of wage inflation. The steady decline in
inflation during the early 1980s was accompanied with a steep increase in
unemployment while as labour markets did become tighter in the late
1980s there has been a return to inflationary pressures and trade unions
actually using ballots to signal to employers the degree of their members
grievances. While Mrs Thatcher's government would have been able to
point out that they did not have to resort to incomes policy and therefore
make concessions to vested interest groups they have still maintained
subsidies such as mortgage tax relief, tax allowances on pensions and other
subsidies to groups which are identified as politically strategic. Furthermore, the Conservative government has had a continuous incomes policy
for the public sector employees. The question is whether these employees
will in the 1990s seek to catch up in their pay relativities with private sector
workers.

Some commentators would argue that the years of Mrs Thatcher's
government represented the abandonment of Keynesian economics and
the triumph of market liberalism in economic policy-making, a revolution
which the British government would now like to export to the rest of
Europe. While it can be verified that the government did break with some
aspects of Keynesian politics it must also be emphasised that the Keynesian
political agenda had never reached the same level of maturity as in West
Germany, France, Sweden, Austria or Japan. In all of these countries
Keynesian economics had not been confined to an economic model but
had become part of an institutional arrangement between government,
employers and trade unions. In Japan, despite their commitment to market
economics, the Ministry of International Trade and Industry (MITI) is seen
as central to Japan's continued economic success. Long-term investment in
research and education are not left to the market but remain central to the
government's economic strategy, while in West Germany the concept of
responsible social partnerships has meant that even with changes in government between SPD and Christian Democrat there has been continuity
in industrial relations policy, industrial and training policies. In contrast
the UK has experimented with Keynesian economics in terms of demand-
management policy but also at times linking the economics with issues such
as incomes policy. Mr Heath's Industry Act and his attempt to formulate a
partnership with trade unions and employers and also the Labour
government's Social Contract reflect the cultural gap between Britain and
Europe. While in Germany, France and Italy the concept of building social
partnerships is seen as an essential part in the democratic process, in the
UK employers and trade unions both interpret in their own way that such
arrangements represent excessive state interference. British trade unions
still see that the interests of their members are best served through a

voluntary system of industrial relations and free collective bargaining. In this sense the Thatcher government did not have too much of a Keynesian project to abandon. As to the triumph of market economics the Thatcher government still continued to adhere to the pressures of the electoral cycle rather than the moral political agenda of market liberalism.

This book therefore seeks to show the importance of politics to economists and urges economists to stop treating politics as the black box which should be left to the politicians. Equally, it seeks to put economics and economic issues on the map for the students of politics and the emphasis which is often put on the concept of autonomy of political choice and political judgement. Economic policy reflects the dual relationship between the autonomy of governments and the constraints of the economic context.

Writing this text reflects long discussions with friends, colleagues and students over the last five years. However, there is a need for a special mention for my friend and colleague, Harry Fineberg, who has continuously reminded me of the intricate relationships between politics and economics, and to acknowledge his contribution in writing with me the two chapters on the politics of markets and Keynes. Harry Fineberg has also read the whole of the text and has continuously shared with me his ideas. I also want to thank Adam Dawson who continues to help me in times of crisis with my knowledge in information technology and his expertise on the graphics within this text. I would also like to acknowledge my partner Jackie and my son John who gave me support and tolerance, and Alan Jarvis at Routledge for his advice and encouragement. As always the limits and omissions of this text remain my total responsibility.

Maurice Mullard
July 1991

involved in a continuous process of persuasion and construction of images of competence in economic management.

The following sections therefore attempt to provide a framework for understanding the likely relationships between economics and politics and their impact on economic policy-making. The first model has as its core the view that economics explains political responses, while the starting point of the second model has the political factor as the one which determines economic policy. According to this approach the aim is to emphasise the dual relationship between constraint and autonomy in economic policy. In the first case the economy is the context and therefore the constraining factor on government, while in the second case economic policy-making has to be located within the political context. However, within this dual relationship of autonomy and constraint it will be argued that models of economic policy-making contain both economic and political dimensions. It will be argued that the connection between politics and economics provides five contrasting models of economic policy – the rationalist model; the institutional model; the political business cycle model; the cycle of influence model and the discursive societies model. Each of these models produces a different balance between the economy and government, and between economic strategic interest groups and government. External factors such as the international economy, financial markets and government, the influence of the Treasury, political judgement, electoral considerations and the impact of economists and economic ideas all influence economic policy – the problem being that these factors influence the policy-makers in different ways and at different times. The use of the proposed models is not to enforce a choice between models which are exclusive but rather to use the models as devices which seek to make simple that which is not simple.

AUTONOMY AND CONSTRAINTS IN ECONOMIC POLICY

The suggestion of the two-model approach – one economic the other political – would imply that economics and politics are concerned with asking different questions. Economics is perceived as being concerned with dealing with the question of scarce resources and unlimited demand while politics is defined as being the attempt to explain the resolution of conflict with regard to the distribution of resources. In accordance with this framework, therefore, the two worlds of politics and economics are seen as separate: the economists offering advice on 'economic' problems while the politicians decide on whether to accept or reject the diagnosis offered by the economic adviser. In this context the 'economist' provides the analysis of the situation, while the politician is seen as having a wider mandate for it is he who makes the decision.

The difficulty with attempting to suggest that politics and economics are concerned with asking different questions would be to assume that issues such as unemployment or inflation can be defined as representing 'economic' problems and that it is the task of economists to provide the explanations for the causes and also the cures. Equally, it is assumed that politics represents the world of choice between conflicting interests where politicians make choices between policy alternatives according to their political preference, the ideology of their party or as part of a process of political bargaining with vested interests. The economic model suggests that economists 'advise' and politicians 'act'. It suggests that there are problems which can be deemed as pure economic problems and furthermore that there is a discipline called economics where economists are in agreement as to what constitutes their subject. Furthermore, it assumes that while economics seeks to explain the world as it is, politics represents the art of deciding between competing interests.

However, the thesis that economic advisers give objective economic advice while politicians make the final political decision is obviously not that simple as recent experience indicates. Indeed, if such a separation of tasks did exist the Chancellor of the Exchequer Nigel Lawson would not have resigned his post in November 1989 thereby precipitating a crisis for both the government and the financial markets. It would seem that, despite frequent assurances by the then Prime Minister Margaret Thatcher that the Chancellor's position was 'unassailable' and that his decision was final, the role of economic adviser Sir Alan Walters was more than that of adviser and that he was also involved in influencing political decisions. Furthermore, the Chancellor argued both in the House of Commons and in a series of interviews that it was the politician who was accountable to the elected parliament and who therefore was responsible for decision-making. It was an argument that precluded advisers from the decision-making process. What must have made it more intolerable for the Chancellor was the publicity which surrounded Sir Alan's return to 10 Downing Street since Sir Alan had already made it clear that his 'views' were closer to those of the Prime Minister. The decision made by the Prime Minister must have been seen by the Chancellor as a political choice. She was choosing an adviser whom she believed could be relied on, while the advice of the Chancellor was therefore judged as being less reliable and to be questioned by the Prime Minister on the advice of her adviser. The Chancellor's position was no longer unassailable – the economic adviser was not just the 'economic' adviser.

It is equally inaccurate to postulate that all decisions are political decisions and that therefore it is the political which prevails. The political approach assumes that governments have complete autonomy in choosing between policy alternatives; yet governments do not have complete autonomy for they are faced by external constraints such as the international economy, market forces, and international agreements such as the European Community (EC) and the General Agreement on Tariffs and Trade (GATT). They are further constrained by internal factors, including strategic pressure groups such as employers and trade unions. These are organisations which do have a direct impact on the economy and are relatively free from government influence. Other internal constraints include public institutions such as the Bank of England or the Treasury whose views on economic priorities might differ from those of the government.

In seeking to provide an understanding of the relationships between politics and economics it would seem at this stage that both these models at best only offer a partial explanation. On the one hand the 'economic' model implies that economists provide the factual analysis and the policy alternatives while the politicians choose on rationalist grounds from the options put before them. In accordance with this model the economic advisers offer expertise on economic issues, that is on issues which are the concern of economics. The economists provide the economic alternatives without themselves having political preferences and political visions in outlining their policy options. In contrast the 'political' model would seem to suggest that it is political choice which dominates. In accordance with this argument all issues present choices and choices depend on issues which are the exclusive concern of politics. Examples include access to power, the availability of resources to influence governments, the impact of strategic groups and vested interests. This approach seems to assume that there is complete autonomy in the policy-making process and that the selection of policy depends on political choice alone. However, institutional constraints represent limitations on the range of political choice and autonomy of government.

In seeking to construct explanations of the relationships between economics and politics and their impact on economic policy', it is necessary to move away from models which endeavour to keep politics and economics separate. In contrast the aim would be to construct explanations which take into consideration the contributions of perspectives derived from economics and politics and which provide opportunities to create models that take into account both the political and economic dimensions at the same time, rather than attempting to keep political and economic spheres separate. In producing models which attempt this certain questions need to be addressed. For instance, can similar assumptions be made about politics and economics? Does the theory of the rational consumer as applied to economics also apply to politics? Are there markets in politics as in economics? Can political parties be located in the position of suppliers of goods, while the consumers are the voters, and can these agents also meet in the political market place within the context of the democratic process?

Rationalist model

The rationalist model has been outlined mostly in the work of Anthony Downs's *An Economic Theory of Democracy* (1957) and in Buchanan and Tullock's *The Calculus of Consent* (1965). The model is founded on an economic explanation of politics and also has the concept of rational individualism at its centre. It assigns 'rationality' to both political parties and voters, each seeking to maximise their 'welfare'. The aim of the political party is to win the next election; the cost to the party is the gain or loss of votes according to policies adopted. Votes are won or lost according to benefits or costs incurred by the individual voter who is aware of the costs of choosing between the commitments made by political parties. In the context of the rationalist model governments would seek to supply more goods as a form of benefit at the least cost possible. Equally, electors are also rational to the extent that they also seek to maximise their welfare by voting for parties which aim to increase their benefits at the least cost.

Continuing the economic analogy voters are assumed to have perfect information in choosing between the commitments made by political parties. Electoral manifestos can be equated to politicians advertising within the market place. The context of democracy represents a competitive market place with no barriers of entry for new parties to enter the market place. Equally there are no barriers to entry for the voters, the franchise gives one vote to each member of the electorate. Individual voters cannot therefore influence demand which means that the political parties have to compete for votes. Since voters are rational they move freely between parties in making electoral choices.

According to the rationalist model, government is judged on the ability to maintain, improve and protect existing living standards. Because of freedom of information, electors are informed as to the policy choices faced by government. The rationalist policy-making cycle involves three distinct phases:

1 Defining the problem. Governments are expected to gather accurate information on factors such as unemployment and inflation which means that they need to be well informed. It is assumed that defining a problem such as unemployment would not be problematic – namely, that those claiming benefits and registering as unemployed would represent the extent of the problem. However, even in seeking to outline the extent of the problem there seem to be 'choices' involved. For example, should participants on training and re-training schemes be considered as unemployed. Equally should women who are not entitled to benefits be calculated as part of the problem.

2 Having identified the problem it is assumed that government will look at various policies which are seen as the most relevant. Continuing with the theme of unemployment the rationalist government would then look

at various policy options directed at reducing unemployment. The government might look to micro labour market policies including those dealing with skills training to increase labour supply, regional policy, and labour mobility policies. It is assumed that the government would then cost each of the options to try and choose the most effective policy, namely the policy which costs the least but which is likely to create the largest number of jobs.

3 During the third stage the government adopts the most effective policy and then seeks to evaluate the effectiveness of the policy – in this case had they effectively reduced the level of unemployment by their actions. If the policy is seen not to be working – unemployment continuing to rise or fall more slowly than anticipated – then the government should return to processes identified at phase 2 to look at the policy choices again and identify the next suitable policy. This stage is known as the feedback loop. The government state the purpose of the policy and then evaluate the effectiveness of that policy.

The expectation that governments would aim to improve the public welfare and that elections had provided the opportunity for voters to appraise governments suggested that there was a direct relationship between government and voters. It was in the self-interest of the incumbent government, then, to make a success of economic policies to ensure winning the next election. There was therefore reciprocity between governments and electors – each pursuing self-interest. Economic policies directed to reduce unemployment were desirable because lower unemployment meant more output, higher living standards and a lower personal tax burden. Economic growth policies also increased living standards, produced higher tax yields, more public services and more individual consumption.

Constraints on the rationalist model

One major criticism of the Downs model is that this approach produces a simple and direct relationship between the individual voter, the government, and the electoral process, without theorising the impact of interests groups and other strategic interests which combine together. The question 'what impact do collectivities have on the relationship between the individual citizen voter and the elected government?' suggests that rationalist models need to include some understanding of groups and how they are likely to influence economic policy. Do pressure groups distort the democratic process or do they enhance the location of the individual in relation to government?

Some writers including Breton (1974) and Borcherding (1977) have argued that pressure groups are also involved in pursuing self-interest by combining the interest of their group members. Pressure groups are therefore also described as rationalist when they can be seen to be looking at the benefits and losses a specific course of action might bring to their members. Hirschman (1970) in *Exit, Voice and Loyalty* has suggested that pressure groups can deploy three separate forms of strategies. First, pressure groups can use the strategy of 'voice' which means the process of campaigning, gathering signatures, making petitions, hiring professional lobbyists, and utilising the media and other resources available to make their 'voice' heard. Second, groups can also use the process of 'exit' such as the use of the withdrawal of labour, exiting from processes of negotiation and dialogue, thus depriving governments of information. Third, pressure groups are also involved in the maintenance of individual 'loyalty' to the group. This ensures that group members 'identify' with the group's aims, thus maintaining its coherence and solidarity.

Accordingly, pressure groups are involved in rationalist strategies choosing between voice, exit or loyalty as the best form of strategy applicable in a specific context. This means that during periods of tight labour markets, trade unions might be more willing to utilise the strategy of 'exit' while during periods of recession when unemployment becomes a threat to member cohesion they will find that loyalty would be the more appropriate tactic. In this sense groups are rational because they seek to 'read' the environment and then look for the strategy that will most benefit the group.

Niskanen (1977) in *Bureaucracy and Representative Government* suggested that government including civil servants, health professionals and educationalists are 'rationalist' in seeking to maximise the budgets of their departments. Heclo and Wildavsky (1982) in *The Private Government of Public Money* likened the relationships between senior civil servants to that of a village community where members of the community behave according to certain ethics and other shared values. In contrast to the image of the public sector providing a public service, rationalist theory would suggest that these professional groups are also involved as producers of services and that they have specific skills and knowledge which put them in the position of strategic interest groups. Spending departments, therefore, pursue self-interest by continuously submitting new policy proposals which involve new public expenditures. Because of their monopoly of knowledge, public sector producer groups have the potential to use their strategic position in bargaining with governments.

Friedman and Friedman (1985) argue that even when governments are elected with the commitment to reduce the influence of these budget maximising groups, they usually fail because these interests create an iron triangle of beneficiaries, politicians and bureaucracy whose interest becomes the *status quo*. However, this tyranny of the *status quo* benefits privileged groups wanting to protect their insider positions, often at the cost of the 'outsider' individual voter:

Every special interest that was threatened proceeded to mount a campaign to prevent its particular government sinecure from being eliminated.

(Friedman and Friedman 1985: 10)

The inclusion of institutions within a rationalist model carries the major implication that the direct relationship between voters and parties and the electoral process becomes distorted. In between elections governments come under the pressure of institutions which act as a constraint on their autonomy and therefore are likely to influence or change government policy because of their special status. This means that some groups are likely to become more special than others.

Once the premise of inequality of access is accepted, it would also seem feasible to construct an argument that economic policy is not formulated within a competitive environment where governments behave rationally in choosing between policy alternatives. Instead, the absence of a competitive context would suggest that economic policy-making is influenced by institutional factors. This perspective points to the limits and constraints confronted by governments in evaluating policy choices. The point should be made that policy choice does not depend on 'rational' criteria as to the effectiveness of policy but rather it should be seen as part of a process which accommodates existing vested interests.

An example to illustrate the discrepancy of a rationalist model when evaluating the impact of vested interests would be the tensions between mortgage tax relief and its impact on industrial investment, inflation and wages. According to the rationalist model, governments become concerned about an economic problem such as the balance of payments. One possible solution would be to increase domestic capacity, thereby attempting to stimulate investment in the industrial sector. Whether this happens or not will depend to some extent on the ratio of industrial investment to housing investment, both being in direct competition for savings. By increasing interest rates the government will let the markets decide how savings are to be channelled, while a continuing policy of mortgage tax relief might be encouraging housing consumption. So on the one hand the government will have a policy which subsidises the cost of housing but on the other a policy which encourages the market to decide the rate of savings and investment. However, the subsidy on housing might push up the rate of interest which in turn deters industrial investment. One reason why the government might not opt to phase out mortgage tax relief may be in its large vested interest to maintain the *status quo* in housing policy despite the implication for economic policy. In this case the perspective of rational choice between policy alternatives is replaced by a policy which accommodates and makes compromises with a politically strategic interest group of home owners.

The institutional model

The rationalist model seeks to explain the relationship between politics and economics from the perspective of the rational individual pursuing self-interest. The 'institutional' perspective emphasises the argument that groups are involved in the pursuance of 'vested and particularistic interests' which implies that the process of politics tends to reflect the availability of resources and how these are distributed between institutions. Resources can of course be of the material (including financial) or the access to knowledge type. The implication of the institutional perspective is that the relationship between politics and economics is perceived to be constructed through intermediary factors and economic policy reflecting compromises and bargains. Policy alternatives as presented by economists are refracted through the priorities of competing interests. It means that the attempt to evaluate or criticise economic policy-making involves the correct reading of spaces of constraint and autonomy for governments. Such an attempt therefore requires an understanding of the way certain institutions become a constraint on government and it involves the resources such groups might deploy to influence the choice of economic policy.

One way of constructing an institutional model of economic policy-making will be to disaggregate the associations between governments and other institutions under three headings:

Internal constraints: the process of government

Government is made up of departments; some, such as the Treasury or the Bank of England, will carry more 'weight' in influencing the course of economic policy than others. In the expenditure cycle spending departments seek to live within a global figure for government expenditure as directed by the Treasury. Although spending ministers are involved in bargains with the Treasury ministers it is taken for granted that if a dispute emerges between spending ministers and the Chancellor that the Chancellor's (and therefore the Treasury) view would be supported by the Prime Minister. Confidence in the government depends on the ability of the Prime Minister to maintain the support of Cabinet ministers. Because the civil service is a village community the relationship between secretaries of spending departments and finance officers at the Treasury is more intimate. Therefore, the Treasury tends to be well informed as to the spending plans of departments.

The dominance of a Treasury view in economic policy-making implies that conflicts might arise between the government's longer-term economic objectives and the short-term policies which tend to be the more immediate concerns of the Treasury. Fluctuations in the value of sterling seem to require immediate responses from the Treasury. The Chancellor has to signal the markets as to what his policies are if the currency markets are to continue to show confidence in existing policies.

Studies of the Treasury and its impact on economic policy have provided competing interpretations of the relationship between politics and economics. Sydney Pollard (1982) in *The Wastage of the British Economy* has suggested that the preoccupation of the Treasury with short-term responses in economic policy has been harmful to the longer-term prospects of the economy. Pollard argues that the balance of payments constraint requires a strategic policy of shifting income from personal consumption to savings and investment – in particular investment which is directed to manufacturing industries. Pollard contrasts this 'considered' policy with the short-term *ad hoc* policy of interest rates which have often come into conflict with long-term objectives. Balance of payments problems are reflected as problems of sterling. Attempts by the Treasury to use a policy of interest rates to maintain confidence in sterling only deals with the symptoms of the underlying economic problem of improving exports. Pollard believes that the short-term policy of interest rates has actually contributed to the decline in manufacturing capacity.

The Pollard argument can be criticised for its failure to address the issue of political realities where governments are buffeted by markets and cannot construct long-term policy in isolation from the world economy. This has been argued, for example by Joel Barnett (1982) who was Secretary to the Treasury during the years of the Labour government between 1974 and 1979. Barnett in his book *Inside the Treasury* argues that Treasury ministers have had no choice but to respond to the external pressures of markets. Foreign investors and holders of sterling do not judge the British economy in terms of long-term prospects but rather obey market sentiment by continuously comparing investment in Britain with other countries. Barnett says that because governments are concerned with protecting the living standards of their population they will always have a policy for the exchange rate even if it means that exchange rate policy has to supplant other economic objectives.

The presence of a Treasury view leads to a third implication. Accepting that the Treasury view exists then the question might be asked as to what that view is. For example, does the Treasury view reflect a specific body of ideas? Is the Treasury view likely to be captured by Keynesian or market economists? Asking these questions is important because while it is feasible to argue that the Treasury must respond to changes in the exchange rate it might also be argued that the response of the Treasury reflects a paradigm, a set of beliefs as to how the economy works. This means that the Treasury view depends on which economic ideas are in ascendancy within the Treasury. The Treasury, it might be argued, operates within the boundaries of a conventional wisdom. In this sense there is a competition between economists to influence the Treasury view. For those who want to influence economic policy, the battle over economic ideas is crucial. For those who want to understand economic policy-making, the understanding of economic ideas allows them to judge the context of economic policy.

It is because governments recognise that the Treasury view reflects a specific conventional wisdom that they have embarked upon the practice of importing their own economic advisers into the Treasury in the hope that their advisers would create at a minimum a pluralist tension between the conventional wisdom of the Treasury and the ideas of economists which are in sympathy with the government. The choice of economic advisers to the Treasury, such as Nicholas Kaldor by the Labour government in 1964 or Sir Terry Burns by the Conservative government in 1979, gives some indication as to the economic ideas these governments wanted to prevail within the Treasury at the time.

The study of the process of government seems to provide two competing interpretations as to the impact of public institutions on economic policy-making. First there is the interpretation provided by Pollard which implies that conflicts arise between the long-term economic objectives of the government and the problem of responding to short-term crisis management. Pollard seems to suggest that the Treasury view dominates the thinking of the government. This argument has for example been reinforced by Barbara Castle (1980) in her diaries on the 1974 Labour government, where she argued that she and other Cabinet ministers felt incompetent to argue against the Treasury proposals to reduce public expenditure as part of the IMF agreement in 1976:

> none of us are equipped with the sort of economic advice that enables us to stand up to the dubious expertise of the Treasury. A sense of hopelessness engulfs me.
>
> (Castle 1980: 454)

According to this interpretation, therefore, the Treasury is perceived to have the better information and the better argument so that when the Treasury advice is submitted to the Cabinet it is most likely that the Treasury will get its way. This makes the Treasury central in economic policy-making. Furthermore understanding which economic conventional wisdom occupies the Treasury is crucial since the Treasury advice will always be founded on economic ideas.

Introducing the language of markets makes a number of points more apparent: the need of politicians to comprehend the meaning of markets, that market sentiment is beyond the control of government, and that therefore there are times when governments find themselves responding to market forces.

The need to study the impact of the Treasury on economic policy-making does not of course imply that the Treasury dominates economic policy-making. There are too many instances which show that the Treasury view did not prevail in Cabinet meetings and that politics has proved to be ultimately the more decisive factor. Yet it would be equally misleading to assume that it is always the 'politics' which dominates.

External constraints: the impact of interest groups

Constraints on the autonomy of government can be described as being 'internal' constraints and therefore include those influences which exist within the machinery of government. Constraints can also come from outside the government. External constraints are different from internal processes since the former refer to those who seek to influence government but are outside the process of policy-making. By contrast internal constraints are part of the decision-making process.

The analysis of the rationalist model pointed to the possibility of individual voters joining with others to form pressure groups on issues which called for collective action rather than individual action. The presence of interest groups outside and independent of the government corrects some of the imbalance of resources that are available to the government. However, the presence of interest groups is a double-edged sword; pressure groups are good for those who can join but can act against the interests of those who are at the periphery. It might be good for doctors to join together in attempting to improve their pay and conditions. It might not be that good for the patient if the new pay award is likely to come from existing resources and therefore at the cost of patient care.

One way of understanding the relationships between pressure groups and government would be to see certain pressure groups emerging as a direct consequence of government policy. These groups can be categorised as client pressure groups. Government can create deliberate client groups by offering specific groups certain subsidies. One such large client group would include owner-occupiers dependent on the continuity of mortgage tax relief. Other client groups include those who are dependent on some form of social security payment from the state including pensions, family credit, income support or housing benefit. The Child Poverty Action Group (CPAG) estimates that there some 14 million people dependent on state benefits in Britain. Another client pressure group includes those who are in direct employment of the government. The access to knowledge of some of these groups puts them into a special position when dealing with the government. These interest groups are likely to influence government economic policy in many different ways.

The client pressure groups

One of the more direct consequences of government intervention has been to create 'client' groups whose interests are directly dependent on government policy. The expansion of social security creates dependent client groups who in turn are represented by pressure groups who have become experts in evaluating changes in social security policy and seek to influence government. Among such expert pressure groups are included the Child Poverty Action Group (CPAG) Age Concern, and The Low Pay Unit. All these groups aim to highlight problems associated with poverty – for example, concern with unemployment, low pay, and part-time employment. The common strategy available to groups representing dependent client groups has been to provide Members of Parliament with information on the effects of economic policy. Members of Parliament are often found utilising this 'social' information to mount criticisms of government policy.

A second type of 'client' pressure group created by government becomes dependent on some form of government subsidy. A subsidy represents a policy which 'protects' specific individuals from market prices. Individuals who are already benefiting from existing subsidies would obviously prefer policies that protect their interests even if these subsidies are shown to be a hindrance to government autonomy. The largest subsidised group in Britain obviously consists of those owner-occupiers who are dependent on mortgage tax relief. Because this grouping now includes 75 per cent of the British population there is no need for official pressure groups to be formed as the pressure of the majority is always present. Thus it is difficult if not impossible for government to alter the cost of mortgage tax relief. Mortgage tax relief is therefore good 'for those who benefit but it harms the homeless'. This latter group continues to be at the margin of housing policy.

Mortgage tax relief implies a loss of revenue to the Exchequer yet that extra revenue could be channelled into health expenditure or expenditures which alleviate poverty more directly. Mortgage tax relief reduces the price of housing, encouraging over-consumption and conflicts with policies which seek to protect the environment. Equally, as subsidies reduce price and increase demand that new demand is likely to result in increased house prices which might overspill into wage demands. Investment in housing might also lead to lower investment elsewhere in the economy.

The third example of 'client' pressure groups are those who are employed directly by the government. Some of these groups represent a knowledge estate – their source of influence is their knowledge which governments cannot purchase in the market place. These groups would include the military, the police, educationalists and doctors. The nature of their service to the government puts these groups in a monopoly position in the sense that they are protected from market forces when compared with employees in the private sector. Workers in the private sector can price themselves out of the labour market if their wage claims have an adverse effect on the firm's ability to sell its product. Public sector employees are not faced with the same market discipline. If the cost of education increases there is no sudden change in demand by consumers.

Functional pressure groups

While some pressure groups exert pressure because of their clientele position in relation to the government other groups have the potential to influence policy-making because of their functional role within the economy. Increased division of labour and specialisation produces interdependence within the economy. So for example the Labour government of 1966 was judged to be vulnerable to the problem of the balance of payments. A threatened strike by dockers was seen as being a major threat to the government since dockers were key workers who had a major influence on the balance of payments. A strike by dockers would have led to a further deterioration in this area which would in turn have made sterling even more vulnerable to devaluation. In response to this militancy Prime Minister Harold Wilson, together with his Secretary of State for Employment Barbara Castle, issued immediate guidelines in a document *In Place of Strife* to seek a cooling off period and a ballot before a strike. Other strategic groups were the miners during the Heath years and skilled workers in the car industry who spearheaded events in Labour's Winter of Discontent in 1979.

British trade unions do have a major influence on economic policy. Trade union organisation in the UK is still the densest in Western Europe with membership reaching a peak during 1975 when it topped 50 per cent of the total working population. Throughout the last decade it has continued to decline from 12 million members to just over 9 million in 1990, yet this still represents over 43 per cent of the labour force. In contrast trade union membership in France is still about 25 per cent, in Germany only 30 per cent, and in the USA 20 per cent.

The main reason for the decline in trade union influence during the early 1980s was the threat effect of unemployment, which during this period did not fall below 3 million. However, since 1987 trade union influence in wage bargaining has re-emerged due to the continuous fall in unemployment and a gathering confidence among strategic workers. This has to be considered in the context of four major reforms in trade union law since 1980. Secondary picketing is now prohibited as an activity in the furtherance of a dispute, trade unions now have to ballot their members before a strike, trade union leaders are also to be elected by secret ballot, and trade union members have to 'contract in' to set up a political fund.

Trade unions do have a major influence on wage setting in the private sector and therefore play a key role in domestic economic performance. At a minimum, trade unions create a form of wage resistance by seeking to protect members' 'real' wages and also maintain a form of wages league. It is in the interest of trade unions seeking to maintain or increase their membership to show that they can secure improved wages for their members and maintain differentials between their members and those in rival unions.

The question for governments in Britain, however, has been what influence should trade unions have on economic policy. Although trade union influence is implicitly present, governments have sought ways to accommodate this influence either directly by constructing arrangements to make trade unions one of the partners in economic policy or by attempts to minimise trade union influence through the legislative process.

In dealing with trade unions governments in Britain have tended to adopt one of two strategies. One strategy has been to 'incorporate' trade unions into the decision-making process either through voluntary discussions or through public institutions. However, when compared with the corporatism of Austria, West Germany, and Sweden where trade unions have become 'legal' social partners, the British system can be seen to be voluntary in that trade unions, employers, and the government have not been obliged by law to maintain a durable partnership. At best, therefore, Britain has created tripartite structures rather than authentic corporatist arrangements.

Some governments have been unhappy with sharing their autonomy with 'functional' groups and have questioned the legitimacy of consulting with privileged groups. Instead these governments have often started off by arguing that they have been elected to pursue a mandate which serves the national interest rather than the vested interests of strategic groups. Governments which have therefore been committed to giving leadership have at times eschewed these tripartite arrangements.

Interest group politics

Interest groups, whether client or functional, can attempt to influence government policy-making either directly or indirectly. Client groups tend to adopt the indirect strategy of highlighting their interests but also protesting that their interests are also the public interest. Client groups such as teachers and doctors campaigning for more public resources need to persuade the public that they are campaigning for a public service. Their efforts therefore tend to be indirect since they are mostly seeking to mobilise the public first by making it more aware and then mobilising public interest to influence the government. Teachers seeking to secure a higher pay award have learnt for example that strike action tends to alienate public support if their crusade is perceived to be pursuing a narrow self-interest. However, when teachers seek higher pay by pointing to teacher shortages and/or lack of equipment in schools then their strategy becomes one of persuading and changing public perception.

In their strategy of persuasion then, client groups will use the 'bleeding stump' approach to give drama to their campaign: arguing the case for

Chapter 1

The politics of economic policy-making

INTRODUCTION

The principal concern of this text is to provide a framework for understanding the nature of economic policy-making. Economics and politics
provide the principles which underpin the continuing relationships between ideas, issues and policy. The argument to be adopted in this text is
that economic policy-making reflects a trade off between a process of
political judgement and at the same time the need to respond to economic
events, the continuing tensions between the constraints of economic
factors and the autonomy of government. This approach represents a
departure from those studies which seek to emphasise a clear division of
labour between the concerns of economics and politics. The approach
often adopted by economists has been to treat the political as the 'black
box'. This usually meant that while economists would make comments on
economic issues the choices made between competing policy options were
described as 'political' decisions to be left to government, implying that
economics was concerned with the provision of economic analysis while
the world of politics was to be left to the politicians. In contrast the study
of politics concerned itself with the understanding of political ideas and
the dynamics of political institutions, implying that while economists were
able to provide economic answers to economic questions they failed to deal
with political realities.

In an attempt to re-structure and blur the division of labour between
economics and politics this book suggests that economists need to understand the process of politics while politics needs to adopt some of the tools
of economics. It therefore asks what factors influence governments in
shaping economic policy? Are economic decisions qualitatively different
from other decisions which governments make? For example is the decision
to reduce personal taxation a social policy, economic policy or a political
decision? Rather than choosing whether a policy represents an 'economic'
policy or that it is 'political' or 'social' it would seem more feasible to suggest
that economic policy as made by government involves the making of both

social and political judgements. It is therefore difficult to judge what is economic policy. Decisions about unemployment, inflation, interest rates and sterling might at one level be perceived to be economic policies, but these policies cannot be evaluated in isolation and without reference to the social implications and political calculations.

One particular feature of the post-Second World War period has been the increased expectations of electors within Western democracies with regard to how their governments deal with issues of economic performance. For example, James Alt (1979) was able to argue that elections in Britain could be predicted by the impact governments had on economic policy. Alt argues that the continuous oscillation between Labour and Conservative governments since 1964 could be explained as a syndrome of 'kicking out the rascals'; the rascals being the incumbent governments and their failure to improve or maintain living standards. However, while it would seem safe to assume that modern governments cannot afford to ignore economic policy, it would be difficult to sustain the thesis that because economic issues are central, economists and their ideas have a major impact on government or that they dominate government and politics. Indeed, it would be preferable to argue that governments pilot a process of 'selective perception' in accepting economic prescriptions – this selective perception being shaped by the proximity between the political ideology of the government, and their political priorities. It is therefore more likely that governments will make use of the economic analysis provided by economists who produce an adequate rationale for their policy – thus reinforcing the ideology and the standing of the government – rather than a process where economics is seen as steering the government in a purely technical sense.

The question whether it is governments which give political direction to the economy or whether they simply respond to economic factors which are beyond their sphere of influence seems to lead to competing interpretations of the relationship between politics and economics. First, it might be argued that since economic issues decide elections that the economic context is likely to make governments respond in a similar fashion to economic problems irrespective of party or political ideology. Despite the rhetoric of political differences, the reality of the economy means that on economic questions there will be minimal or no differences between the parties since the economic analysis would require governments to act in a uniform manner. The second interpretation would point to the view that governments could be perceived to be 'empty vessels' waiting to be filled by the analysis which the economists present. In addition, because governments are primarily concerned with winning elections this means that they respond to the concerns and priorities made by the electorate. However, a third intimation would suggest that governments possess a political vision so that rather than responding passively as empty political vessels they are shortages of resources in health care is best highlighted through ward closures or sending patients home rather than through a debate about expenditure levels. The closure of wards is highly visible, as such action tells the public that there are problems of funding, and is therefore likely to produce protests from the public by putting pressure on Members of Parliament.

The direct approach is more appropriate to those groups which have a functional relationship in the economy and whose actions have a direct and immediate impact on the economy. Functional groups have the potential to alter the course of economic policy and to make governments appear to lack control in a given situation. The number of strikes, frequency of strikes and duration of strikes might at one level help the government by indicating their determination to stand against vested interests. However, such disruption works against the government if the public starts to question their competence. Because direct forms of intervention can work for the benefit of and against the government, they have to take notice and respond to functional pressures.

Political economics model

A third approach to the relationship between economics and politics and economic policy-making takes into consideration the political calculations which are made by politicians in devising economic policy. This approach does not aim to suggest that economic policy is dominated by political choice but rather aims to construct a framework to explain some of the processes which constitute the political sphere rather than leaving politics as the black box.

Electoral business cycle

According to the concept of the electoral business cycle, economic policy is constructed in such a way as to give maximum political advantage to the incumbent government. Much has been written on the electoral business cycle but the common theme is to explain economic policy in relation to the electoral cycle. This argument suggests that governments seek to influence macroeconomic indicators in relation to the proximity of an election. Accordingly, during an election year governments are expected to produce highly visible policy, such as reducing personal taxation or increasing pensions to the elderly. Lower personal taxation is seen as being highly priced by the electorate. Tax reductions can be made visible very quickly. Such a policy might also have the desired effect of turning down the unemployment rate. The criticism of the electoral business cycle is not to question the moral criteria for this form of economic management but rather to question whether the economic policy prioritised during an election year is appropriate and how it is to be judged in relation to the longer-term needs of the economy.

The importance of the electoral business cycle in relation to this text is that it stresses the important argument that governments do keep a close watch on the electoral cycle and economic policy is one important aspect on which the performance of the government is assessed during an election. When governments seek to win the next election, there is a high incentive to manipulate economic policy for the short term if it is likely to gain political advantage.

There are two main criticisms which can be made of the electoral business cycle. First it seems to assume that the electorate is myopic in its memory, remembering only short-term gains. This is the argument which says that governments can only fool the electorate some of the time. The electoral business cycle seems to start from the position that governments manipulate fiscal policy in the short term. They argue that this form of fiscal policy tends to be either inflationary or is likely to result in deterring the balance of payments still further. In the longer term, maybe after the election, politicians have to readjust economic policy. This usually means clawing back the tax reductions through high interest rates or through fiscal drag thereby ensuring that any benefits enjoyed by the electorate only last a short time. If the electoral business cycle is likely to succeed at the following election this means that voters have to forget what happened at the previous election. In other words the electorate are assumed to be myopic.

The second criticism takes the form of a question: if governments can influence macroeconomic policy during an election year why do they not try to do so throughout their term of office? To respond only during an election year seems to produce a perspective of wicked government only willing to deal with issues which are to the government's advantage.

Party politics considerations

While the political business cycle points to the thesis that governments are likely to respond differently to economic problems according to which stage of the electoral cycle has been reached, the approach does not take into account the possibility that governments represent political parties. Political parties do not serve just the purpose of competing for people's votes, they also hold political ideologies, visions and beliefs as to the type of society they would like to construct once the party becomes the government. In this way political parties are a reflection of society, both in offering competing visions and in seeking to persuade electoral majorities of the correctness of their vision. However, parties act as a constraint in offering choices of ideologies because electors are likely to be faced with restricted choices between political parties. The recognition that political parties constitute competing ideologies implies that when a political party becomes the government it will have ideological priorities in economic policy.

Tufte (1978) and Hibbs (1977) have both argued that political parties represent constituents with different interests in economic policy, suggesting that parties associated with Left ideologies are more likely to give a higher priority to the reduction of unemployment as a macroeconomic policy. In contrast parties of the Right are seen as giving a higher priority to the reduction of inflation. Parties of the Left tend to represent constituents who are more vulnerable to the threat of unemployment. According to this thesis political parties cannot be assumed to be empty vessels which can be filled by exogenous factors. It is because governments represent visions and therefore make commitments to the electorate according to their visions that makes the understanding of politics essential in the evaluation of economic policy.

Accepting the thesis that political parties do make a difference in the formulation of economic policy, it would seem that a series of issues develops from this argument:

1 If political parties seek to promote a specific vision and then attempt to persuade voters, then it would seem that the rationalist argument of parties seeking to maximise their votes by increasing the supply of public goods needs to be questioned. Rather than assuming that parties seek to maximise their vote it would be feasible to suggest that parties seek to persuade the electors. This makes the relationship between voters and parties one of adjustment and negotiation. Political parties do of course re-define their ideology as the context changes. Equally, however, voters tend to have fixed perceptions as to the principles which constitute the political party they are associated with. The suggestion that voters are ready to switch parties according to which party is offering the better vision seems to eliminate the possibility of long-term party affiliation that exists between voters and parties.

2 It would also seem plausible to suggest that the success of institutions in influencing governments depends on the proximity between the ideas of the institution and the ideology of the party. The distance between the objectives of pressure groups and the ideology of the government needs to be considered when seeking to explore the influence of groups on economic policy. It is more likely that trade unions will succeed in influencing the economic policies of a Labour government because of the continuity of relationships that exist between the Labour Party and the trade unions. Trade unions in Britain sponsor Labour Party MPs. Some trade unions are affiliated to the Labour Party and therefore have an important input in the party's policy formulation process. The trade unions have been described as the paymasters of the Labour Party as

their contribution is some 80 per cent of its funding. Likewise business interests are involved with the Conservative Party, with some individuals becoming prominent members; in addition, firms make financial donations to the party.

3 The impact of client groups also depends on their relationship with government. Client groups aiming to expand their budgets are more likely to influence the government which gives priority to the public sector as the mechanism to reallocate resources. In contrast public sector client groups might be kept at a distance by a government which seeks to promote self-reliance and less government.

The cycle of influence model

The construction of this model depends on some of the ideas outlined in the previous model, but rather than attempting to choose which model best explains the process of economic policy-making the attempt is made to show that there is a model that provides a framework for analysis and evaluation rather than yet another interpretation.

The cycle of influence model suggests that the question of who and what influences economic policy might be the wrong question, and that it is more profitable to understand the context of economic policy. According to the cycle of influence approach, therefore, there is an attempt to take some of the following issues into consideration:

1 That the electoral cycle is an important factor. Incumbent governments do seek to win the next election, hence economic management is likely to be influenced by electoral considerations. It seems likely therefore that economic decisions are much more likely to be implemented in the early years.

2 Accepting that political parties reflect competing political ideologies which represent different vested interests it would seem feasible to suggest that parties are more likely to be 'partisan' during the early years of government while economic policy is more likely to address the public interest as the election approaches. This consideration is compatible with the electoral cycle thesis but it adds the dimension that political parties do have visions and seek to implement them. However, because their visions tend to benefit specific groups these policies have to be pursued during the early stages of government. For example the Conservative governments elected since 1979 have made pledges to reduce the burden of taxation on higher income groups. Each administration since 1979 has sought to implement this policy at the earliest possible moment because the nature of the policy has been to benefit certain groupings. However, the Thatcher government also used the process of

the electoral cycle to pursue economic policies which were less party partisan during election years.

3 The predominance of internal constraints including the Treasury and/or the Bank of England is also part of the cycle of influence. The Treasury view is more inclined to prevail during periods of economic crisis when the governments feel they have been blown off course by economic forces beyond their control, rather than during periods when economic indicators are moving in the government's direction. However, Treasury ministers are equally likely to lose their credibility inside Cabinet if other ministers perceive that the Treasury team is not delivering economic success and is therefore likely to lead the party into electoral defeat.

The cycle of influence approach allows the student to explore the process of changing relationships between the economic and the political. This perspective emphasises the need to explore influences as ebbing and flowing. For example, trade union influence on economic policy-making is not constant, as that influence depends on the economic context which includes changes in the level of unemployment, the rate of inflation, wage settlements and trade union proximity to the thinking of the government. Political calculation is also not constant. Governments do not have complete autonomy in the choice of economic policies and there are times when they have to respond to external market pressures, to internal pressures, and to the influence of functional groups.

The concern of this chapter has been to explore the relationship between economics and politics and their impact on economic policy. The argument presented has aimed to suggest that there are three possible intepretations and that these are not necessarily exclusive nor are they competing explanations. According to the rationalist model it was assumed that governments choose between alternative economic policies according to the effectiveness and relevance of policy. It was suggested that this is compatible with the view that governments aim to win elections and that they are judged according to economic performance. The institutional model seeks to correct the rationalist approach by suggesting that governments do not have complete autonomy in constructing policy. Instead, governments are influenced by constraining factors of the external economy and how public institutions including the Treasury seek to respond to international markets. Governments are equally constrained by pressure groups which have a vested interest in the maintenance of the *status quo*. These include client groups who are served by subsidies through government policy. The political economics model emphasises the need to take political ideology into consideration since governments do not take office as empty vessels but come to office with their own ideas and visions. Economic policy also reflects the government's political priorities. The cycles of influence model combines elements from these approaches to seek to explain the constraints and spaces of autonomy that are available to government.

The influence of discursive societies

The challenge presented in this book is to utilise the theme of the cycle of influence to show why, how and what influenced economic policy in the UK since 1945. The crucial concern will be to maintain the continuous tensions between the influences of economics, the trade offs between economics and the politics of the government, and then the politics of governments and the political calculations which governments make to ensure that they can thread together electoral majorities.

The choice of economic policy depends on how individuals, institutions, governments and markets interpret the economic context. Interpretations of what needs to be done in turn depends on the paradigms or views of how the economy works. There are, of course, competing views at any one stage and these represent discrete discourses which belong to discursive societies. Economic policy is constructed in the context of a specific discourse. The question as to which paradigm is in the ascendant depends partly on specific economic outcomes which might challenge both the intellectual and practical foundations of an existing paradigm and which are likely to bring forward a paradigm shift. A paradigm shift comprises a different way of looking at the world.

The following chapters seek to fuse the relationships between economic discourses and political discourses. The argument is that since 1945 two forms of discursive societies have shaped economic policy-making. It will be argued that market and Keynesian discursive societies each represent a model of how the economy works, each provides a series of policy alternatives, and that both discourses represent different approaches to politics. Discursive societies therefore operate at three levels. They offer the analysis of the economic context, policy implications and a succession of government strategies.

However, the analysis of discursive societies is not designed to construct a theory of watersheds in economic ideas or to trace a break with some past in the influence of economic ideas. To argue that governments operated within a Keynesian paradigm which was challenged and replaced by a monetarist paradigm assumes that governments respond to new economic ideas. The theme of this chapter has been to construct approaches which emphasise continuity of relationships between economics and politics. The concept of discursive societies refutes the view that there is some fundamental explanation of how economics influences economic policy or that changes in economic ideas are, for example, the most influential in determining the outcome of economic policy. This was certainly the thesis presented by Keynes (1936) the ideas of economists and political philosophers, both when they are right and when they are wrong, are more powerful than is commonly understood. Practical men, who believe themselves to be quite exempt from any intellectual influences are usually slaves of some defunct economist. I am sure that the power of vested interest is vastly exaggerated compared with the gradual encroachment of ideas... sooner or later it is ideas not vested interests which are dangerous for good or evil.

(Keynes 1936: 383–4)

The view that economic policy is constructed by economist advisers who become the invisible decision-makers is based on implicit assumptions which need to be made explicit. The first assumption is based on the view that governments do not have their own political priorities, and that ideas as presented by economists are not political. The second and equally misleading argument is that the thesis portrays government as having complete autonomy. This argument implies that there are no external economic factors to which governments have to respond. It assumes that governments are not restricted by functional and strategic groups. Third it provides a view that governments are free to carry out their political priorities if only they have the political will to do so.

Governments are not likely to be captured by any one economic doctrine. Indeed governments often resort to using all economic levers available to them without necessarily asking whether a lever is a market or a Keynesian lever. Governments are involved in what Henderson (1986) calls 'do it yourself economics', where members of the government are not impressed by ideas which come from the trained economist because they themselves are economists who have to make practical decisions. According to Henderson there are two systems of economics. One is what he calls orthodox economics which has its roots in systematic economic training and which seeks to suggest that governments should not pretend that they can influence economic factors; the other system is the 'do it yourself economics' (DIYE) which represents the attempts by government to construct a view that they are in charge. Henderson suggests that

DIYE is bipartisan. Its influence extends as it generally has in past history right across the conventional political spectrum...those who are influenced by orthodox economic ideas have no pre-assigned place on the spectrum.

(Henderson 1986: 96)

In accordance with Henderson, therefore, the making of economic policy represents a tension between the economists who produce economic alternatives on the one hand, and on the other those who represent vested interests and government who offer 'do it yourself' alternatives in economics. Sir Alec Cairncross has also pointed to this tension as being between the theorists who seek to trap the inner secrets of the economy in their models and the practitioners who live in a world of action where time is precious, understanding is limited, nothing is certain and noneconomic considerations are always important and often decisive.

(Cairncross 1985a)

The making of economic policy cannot be explained in a causal model. The classical Keynesian view that economic ideas are the major influence in determining economic policy does not take into account the political priorities of government but dismisses the influence of vested interest on policy. It is not a matter of whether the government is the dependent variable with economic ideas as the independent variable (a model which explains economic policy through the influence of economists), nor the alternative of economics being the dependent variable and government the independent variable (which would suggest a model of government using economics to justify policy). The question of who is using who is therefore too restrictive. It is not a question of which economic ideas and economists are in the ascendancy, but rather the clustering of beliefs and perceptions which seem to gain ascendancy – views which are not just the property of economists but of politicians and other opinion formers.

Chapter 2

Liberal individualism and market economics

INTRODUCTION

In the global contest of economic systems between market liberals and the Marxist–Leninist doctrine, it would seem that the principles of individual self-interest, competitive markets, and prices have been shown to be more effective in producing economic prosperity than the decisions of planners and bureaucracies. The recent uprisings have confirmed the failures of the Soviet command economies to deliver essential goods and services and also personal freedom of choice. The new governments in Poland, Hungary, Czechoslovakia, and other Soviet states have proceeded to declare their commitment to Western-style democracies and also to move towards a market-orientated economy. The demise of Soviet centralised planning has therefore confirmed the limitation of governments and bureaucracy to prioritise and plan what goods to produce, how to produce them, and for whom. This disillusionment has reinforced the classical tenet of market liberal economists: namely, that it is always preferable to allow individuals to pursue their self-interest and to make their own decisions as to what goods and services are to be produced in the context of a market economy. The price mechanism is still seen as the preferred indicator to rationing imposed by politicians, since it registers the freedom of choice of consumers to buy services and also the willingness of suppliers to supply them according to a price mechanism signalled through the market place.

In contrast, the debate on the future role of government in economic policy within the economies of Western Europe, the USA and Japan, has been influenced by two distinct interpretations. On the one hand there is what can be called the constitutionalist view of economic policy which mainly embraces the influences of market liberal thinkers who tend to suggest that governments should seek to establish an ultra-minimalist framework enabling both markets and public welfare to flourish within a context that ensures the freedom of the individual. The concern of the constitutionalist is that governments should seek to depoliticise economic policy by setting rules and procedures so that economic policy would obey a set of established rules that enshrine the concepts of the enterprise of the individual but at the same time accepts that governments have a limited role in dealing with problems of market failure. According to this framework, economic policy is conducted with the primary objective of ensuring that restrictions are removed and for the spirit of the market place and competition to be used as the forces of economic and social change.

In contrast, the second approach suggests that governments should reject holistic visions, whether they derive from the ideas of market liberals or Marxism, and instead adopt a pragmatic and pluralist approach to policy-making. According to this approach the question of whether the government should intervene and how they should intervene in their domestic economy depends on whether such policies are directed at enhancing both the public and the individual interest. This interpretation has the government becoming the agent of change thus ensuring that issues are dealt with according to their individual merit, a contrast to the adoption of universal principles. Pragmatists, adopting a different argument to that of the constitutionalists, say that the governments which tended to succeed (such as West Germany, France, and Japan) had always left their options open and therefore had a greater choice between policy alternatives. According to the pragmatists, problems of income inequality, the environment, public goods, employment and inflation might best be dealt with as issues which are not necessarily connected. The argue, therefore, that it is the duty of government to be an open minded and 'moral' one rather than one which seeks to make issues fit within some predetermined set of principles.

One of the stated and consistently held aims of the Conservative government elected in Britain in 1979 has been to turn the UK economy into an enterprise economy and to generate employment and prosperity by constructing the framework where UK labour markets are made more flexible and competitive. For example the 1983 Conservative manifesto pledged:

> we shall go on reducing the barriers which discourage employers from recruiting more staff, even when they want to. And we shall help to make the job market more flexible and efficient.... That is why we have amended the Employment Protection Act and why we shall continue to minimise the legal restrictions which discourage the creation of jobs.
>
> (Conservative Central Office, May 1983: 14)

In the Green Paper presented to Parliament in January 1990 under the heading 'Removing the Barriers' (HMSO 1990), the government proposed further trade union reform. The proposals included the abolition of the pre-entry closed shop and the removing of immunities from trade unions engaged in secondary action. The government sees this as the final phase in their step-by-step approach to trade union reform which started in 1979. The 1987 Conservative manifesto declared:

Conservative reforms have redressed the balance between the individual and his union preventing coercion of the majority by activists and militants.... The result has been a transformation of shop-floor relations allowing management and work force to co-operate to improve working practices and introduce new technology to mutual gain.

(Conservative Central Office 1987: 23)

Furthermore, in responding to the Draft Social Charter, opposition to the Charter was echoed by Mrs Thatcher's government because the Charter was seen as a shift towards government intervention and therefore likely to result in the loss of jobs. The Charter, which proposed to introduce rights to a minimum wage, training pensions and holidays, was criticised by the UK government because it re-introduced new rigidities in the labour market. Britain it was argued had been able to create more employment than other European Community members because it had embraced policies directed at creating more flexible labour markets. On the eve of the twelve member states meeting in Brussels Norman Fowler, then Secretary of State for Employment, remarked that the Charter:

would take us in the opposite direction reducing the flow of new jobs and destroying many of the jobs we already have. The Charter would have one inescapable effect to add to labour costs of industry and put jobs at risk.... The Charter inhibits flexibility and harms competition...

(Norman Fowler *Financial Times*, 30 October 1989)

Some commentators including Keegan (1983), Jenkins (1987) and Young (1989) have argued that economic policy in the UK since 1979 has been influenced by the holistic visions of market liberals. During the last decade the government is seen as having adopted an evangelical approach, embarking on a package of measures which have been justified as addressing the problems of decline. These measures have included the lowering of national insurance costs to employers and reducing personal taxation which the government sees as improving the 'supply' side of the economy. The government has also embraced a programme of de-nationalising public utilities, ending exchange controls and compelling local authorities to move towards competitive tendering for public services. All these measures are described as being consistent with market liberal principles.

According to market theory, unemployment can be explained in terms of the presence of obstacles which prevent the labour markets from working effectively. These impediments to the market are also the result of government policy. Individuals seeking to maintain advantage in the labour market by protecting their skills or knowledge aim to produce a labour market for an insider group and thus attempt to prevent outsiders from influencing the level of supply or price. They thus creat dual labour markets of highly paid 'core' workers and outsiders working at the 'periphery' employed in low skills, part-time employment and in low pay. The government maintain that the system of social security payments influences the time people stay between jobs. Government can also impede the labour market by enforcing a minimum wage legislation. The presence of trade unions also affects the labour market because the strategy of trade unions is to influence the supply of labour. Sex and race discriminatory practices are also likely to influence labour supply by putting restrictions on the numbers entering the labour market. All these factors, according to market economists, are likely to increase the level of unemployment. They also represent attempts by privileged groups and government to 'buck the market' and protect existing vested interests.

Market economists would point out that through their government societies have a choice either to 'live' with the level of unemployment or make unemployment an economic priority which means questioning and reforming certain social practices. Through their government, societies have a choice between setting the level of social security according to some principles of equity or according to economic principles of efficiency. The market economist would suggest a policy that did not harm the workings of the market might mean setting the level of benefits below the social benefit level. This, market economists argue, gives government a policy choice between economic and social criteria. Likewise, market economists would suggest that setting a minimum wage might be a social goal which has to be costed against the level of unemployment. In addition, market economists would point to the economic costs for governments to accommodate strong trade unions. In each case they would suggest that governments have to make choices between policy alternatives, but would contend that the policy choice must be carefully costed and the costs properly publicised so that individual voters can make rational choices since policy is always likely to carry an opportunity cost.

The following sections seek to thread together the 'home' domain' of core assumptions which are seen as essential to the model of market economics. The central principle is the view of the individual who has the capacity to pursue self-interest. Furthermore, because the individual is perceived to be rational there can be no ordering as to what preferences are to be prioritised. The individual is therefore to be seen as an end rather than a means to an end. Each individual carries a different vision of the good society; each is to be given equal status without anyone having the right to impose their vision on others.

THE CONCEPT OF THE INDIVIDUAL

In dealing with the concept of the individual there are two conflated issues which need to be made clear since each issue carries a different set of assumptions and implications. The first issue deals with the question of whether individualism represents something abstract, that the term 'the individual' (like 'social structure', or 'class') represents yet another social science concept which is used to facilitate forms of thinking. In accordance with this thinking the individual, like social structure, does not exist as a concrete object. Individualism is a social construct.

The second layer of argument takes the individual as given, suggesting that the individual exists as a reality, exists separately from society and is neither a product nor a part of society. Individuals should be recognised in their own right as knowledgeable and able to make decisions which do not depend on others. The rights and freedom of the individual are described as being inalienable and not negotiable. Individuals' rights are described as natural rights not dependent on others.

Recognising this duality is important because each aspect raises different questions. In establishing the new political economy the advocates of classical market economists, starting with Adam Smith, wanted to promote the theme of the natural rights of the individual. Seeking to explain the changes in agriculture during the 1760s Smith argued that it was not government direction which had been promoting the new technology but rather the process of autonomous individual self-interest. The consequence of Smith's argument was that it was individual self-interest which was the real essence of humanity. The state, the monarchy, and feudal society had all acted as constraints on the freedom of the individual and were prime targets of classical liberal reformers.

The Adam Smith tradition of market liberalism takes as given the argument that individuals left to themselves would always choose to live within the context of the market place. Smith also pointed out that some individuals might combine together in order to subvert the climate of competition and thus act against the interest of individual consumers. He therefore accepted from the start the need for government to regulate the tendency towards mergers and monopolies which might act against the public interest.

The modern market liberalism of Hayek, Friedman and Brittan does not take for granted that the individual exists in nature, but rather that individualism has to be created and protected. According to this argument the individual is not perceived as having existed in some previous golden age but rather that the individual needs to be created. Smith's 'invisible hand' becomes a new voyage of discovery where it is the duty of governments to promote the climate of market liberalism.

Market liberalism advocates that government should be conducted through a process of law which ensures equality of treatment of all individuals. Individual liberty can only be guaranteed if government conducts itself in the context of rules, including a written constitution, that ensure the separation of powers within government and that majorities do not vote in such a way as to erode or put into question individual rights. According to market liberals, economic policy should be guided through a series of rules and principles which are publicised so that the individual is made aware of the conduct of government:

> the great aim of the struggle for liberty has been equality before the law. This equality under the rules which the state enforces maybe supplanted by a similar equality of the rules that men voluntarily obey in their relations with one another.
>
> (Hayek 1984: 80)

In contrast to the market liberal moral perspective of markets; the utilitarian perspective takes a pragmatic approach to individualism. While utilitarians are also concerned with the welfare of the individual their approach is to draw a balance sheet of costs and benefits to society. Utilitarians seek to promote the happiness of the greatest number even if this is at the cost of the individual. Markets represent one strategy available to promote individual well-being, while if the market fails then it is the duty of government to promote general welfare.

According to the utilitarian perspective, therefore, individuals exist but they do not necessarily represent a moral organising principle of society. Instead, the happiness of the greatest number is the moral principle. The utilitarian model argues that there is no reason in principle why the greater gains of some should not compensate for the losses of others, or (more importantly) why the violation of the liberty of a few might not be made right by the greater good shared by the many. While it is rational for the individual to pursue self-interest, it is right for society to set the net balance of satisfaction by considering all of its members.

It is important not to conflate these two sets of issues which sometimes become interchangeable in evaluating the theory of the individual. Making judgements about individualism seems to depend on our conception of the individual. Market liberalism suggests that the individual is separate from society, that the rights, preferences and needs of individuals should not be 'ordered' according to a society's preferences. Individuals should have inalienable and non-negotiable rights. In contrast, utilitarians might also argue that the individual is central but that society has to order welfare according to the benefit of majorities.

Market liberals recognise that markets might fail and would argue for measures to make markets work better or to construct markets to make the individual a reality. Utilitarians seek efficiency in the context of the market place but also through institutions outside the market place – even to the extent where the individual stops being an end and becomes a means to an end.

> The moral side constraints upon what we may do, I claim, reflect the fact of our separate existences. They reflect the fact that no moral balancing

act can take place among us; there is no moral outweighing of one of
our lives by others so as to lead to a greater overall social good.

(Nozick 1984: 105)

Market liberals take the argument that the individual always knows best
seriously in the sense that individuals always know better what their needs
are. The individual will always be more sensitive to personal needs and to
the likelihood that needs change. In contrast, replacing the individual by
bureaucracy or professionals and allowing them to define what is needed
and to prioritise the needs of society, is likely to lead to less flexibility but
also to a more homogeneous approach to a situation when individuals need
to be treated differently.

Individuals are therefore defined as rational agents because they know
best, and since they know best no one else has the right to announce on
behalf of the individual what real need is or to put order on preferences or
to moralise on behalf of the individual. The role of government should be
to provide a context based on rules which protect the right of self-interest.
Government does not encourage a selfish morality by legitimising self-interest, but rather a process which ensures the freedom of the individual
against the more arbitrary morality of others.

The individual is described as rational because that individual has both
natural competence and technical competence. Natural competence de-
notes the ability to maximise individual well-being. It means the ability to
be strategic in making choices, since alternatives carry costs. Natural competence, then, must be the ability to maximise personal well-being at the
least possible cost. The individual naturally seeks pleasure and naturally
seeks to avoids pain. Pleasure represents the purpose of increasing individual welfare. Natural competence represents purposive rationality with the
individual evaluating the costs and benefits in choosing between different
forms of welfare. In making accurate choices the individual is therefore also
described as being technically competent which means that self-interest
also involves the ability to search for information. Technical competence
means to be informed, to facilitate better decision-making. Individuals are
therefore involved in search and in evaluating the information gained.

To construct a theory of the individual it is necessary to assume that
decisions which individuals make are founded on information they have
available and that therefore such decisions could be different if different
information was available. It is because 'rational' decisions are contingent
that liberalism associates individualism with the market place. Only the
market is sufficiently flexible to respond to changes in decisions which
themselves depend on the state of knowledge at a certain point.

THE INDIVIDUAL AND THE MARKET

Markets are also contingent as they represent the revealed preferences at a specific place and at a specific time. It is because the market place is contingent that the nature of towns and cities change, that heavy industry is replaced by retailing and micro electronics. According to Hayek it is the spontaneous decisions of individuals which change the nature of the market place.

Markets are not a social abstraction, they exist in reality. Individuals produce goods because they have a theory that other individuals want to buy what they are producing. Market liberal feminists criticise discriminatory practices because they argue that they are primarily defined as women with specific social roles rather than as individuals in their own right who also have marketable abilities. Equally, individuals who are non-white experience discrimination because they are not treated as individuals in their own right but put in the category of members of an ethnic grouping and are therefore subject to stereotyping.

The competitive market place is therefore described as being the context which guarantees consumer sovereignty. It is because there are a large number of buyers and sellers with no barriers to entry that markets are non-discriminatory. The market place is best described as a process where buyers and sellers meet and make prices. The price set represents the willingness to buy by the consumer and also the willingness to sell by the supplier – a price which is of mutual benefit.

The theory of demand

Utilising the concept of rationality, the individual as consumer is described as rational because the quantity he demands is likely to change with the price of the good. The demand curve for a specific product is therefore constructed as being inversely related to price. According to this model of demand the quantity demanded changes in relation to price. This is described in economics as a normal good with a normal demand curve. However, the shape of the demand curve changes according to the level of elasticity or according to change in price. While some goods such as fruit are highly price sensitive other goods, including petrol, are less price sensitive. Therefore the demand for petrol can be described as being 'inelastic' because demand will not shift in relation to price, at least in the short term because the individual might not find a ready substitute for petrol. At the other extreme the demand for some goods can be highly elastic so that any change in price is likely to lead to individuals switching to another good which is a close substitute.

Demand is also influenced by changes in income, changes in taste or a change in the price of a complementary good. A change in personal income is likely to lead to an increase in demand thus shifting the demand curve outwards and to the right. Conversely a fall in income is likely to lead to a fall in demand. A change in taste can also influence demand in the same way as a change in income. One good example of a change in taste is the case of the individual becoming better informed on the relationship between the use of pesticides and the effect on the environment. The rational individual concerned about the environment changes demand for products which are now organically grown and encouraging a shift away from intensive agriculture. The change in taste means that the demand for organically grown products would shift outwards while the demand for other products will fall, forcing the demand curve to shift inwards.

The theory of demand suggests that:

1 Demand changes according to price for normal goods.
2 Some goods are not normal so that a change in price might not lead to a change in demand because the good is price-inelastic at least in the short term.
3 Demand is also influenced by 'external' factors such as a change in income, a change in taste, or a change in the price of other goods.

It is important to outline a theory of demand because it sets a chain of events in motion. Hence if the theory of demand is applied to the demand for labour, the tools of demand could be used to construct a theory of the labour market. The demand for labour depends on the price of labour – price in this case being the wage. If the price of labour is high, demand for labour will be low. Changes in technology are equivalent to a change in taste so that new technology might lead to a shift in the demand for labour.

The theory of supply

The theory of supply is also founded on the concept of rational individualism. As there are buyers registering demand through their willingness to pay a price for certain goods, equally there are those who are willing to supply goods and services for a price. The amount of goods 'supplied' is positively related to price so that at higher prices suppliers will be willing to supply more of a good; at lower price less goods will be supplied. The supply curve, like demand, will usually shift according to changes in variables such as technology. In terms of labour supply for example, changes in demography result in a shift in the supply curve. Increased child care facilities would enable more women to enter the labour market and thus lead to a shift in labour supply as would the removal of racial discrimination.

The dynamics of supply and demand

The theory of rational individuals both as suppliers and buyers of goods and services allows for these individuals to meet in the market place where the Walras auctioneer makes known the price and the quantity of goods the supplier are willing to provide and also allows for buyers to signal the price they are willing to pay. The price mechanism allows for all goods to be cleared. If suppliers signal a price which is too high then supply will outstrip demand, goods will be left on the shelves unsold signalling to the supplier a wrong price. Suppliers now have the choice to reduce the price to clear their shelves – the price mechanism therefore becomes the signal to buyers and sellers.

The consumer is described as sovereign in the context of market competition. Competitive markets reflect the preferences of consumers and these revealed preferences are reinforced by the price mechanism, the willingness to buy goods, and also the willingness of suppliers to produce that good. Consumer sovereignty means that the individual is the price-maker because under competitive markets consumers can choose between competitive prices. In this context the consumer influences the goods supplied and the price.

Market economists point to the argument that societies have to answer three crucial questions, one being a question of production – namely what to produce. How does a society decide whether it is going to produce washing machines or motor cars? The second question is how to produce that good; how are decisions to be made about the mix of resources between the amount of labour and capital inputs. The third, the 'for who' question, is concerned with the issue of distribution and redistribution of goods and services. The concern here is how are decisions to be made in order to determine who gets what. These three questions could be left to the politicians, the experts and the Civil Service to decide, assuming they possess the knowledge as to what to produce. Thus the few decide the preferences of others, ordering what they consider to be the real needs of the consumers. Equally, the few will be left to decide the amount of labour inputs and also how to distribute the product. In contrast the second approach is where all these questions are decided in the market place. Accordingly, the questions of whether to produce cars or washing machines or how to produce them, the use of robotics, the labour to capital trade off for example, and who is to get the product, are all best decided in the market place. Individuals make choices, revealing preferences through prices, and are therefore more likely to make better decisions on these questions of efficiency and equity than the few.

In contrast to the command economy where economic decisions are directed by the bureaucracy and where central planners make all decisions about production, resource allocation, distribution and prices, the market place represents a series of decentralised decisions where agreements are reached between consumers and suppliers in the context of prices.

The centrality of rational choice in market economics also contributes to the explanation of economic change. Since rationality represents decisions based on current knowledge then market economists would argue that as knowledge and information changes so will the decisions made by the rational individual. The Pearce Report (1989) *Blueprint for a Green Economy*, utilises the concepts of supply and demand and prices to provide the necessary solutions to the problems of the environment. Pearce argues that as the individual becomes more knowledgeable about environmental costs the environment will not be assumed to be a 'free' resource but that, like all other goods, it will carry a positive value and therefore a price. The pollution of a river by a firm might be seen as no cost to the firm but it is a cost to the community. Pearce suggests that governments should impose a carbon/pollution tax or make the polluter pay. This will in turn increase the price of goods, thus reflecting the environmental costs:

> the elementary theory of supply and demand tells us that if something is provided at a zero price more of it will be demanded. For example by treating the ozone layer as a resource with a zero price there was never an incentive to protect it.... The important principle is that resources and environments serve economic functions and have positive economic values.... This simple logic underlines the importance of valuing the environment correctly and integrating these correct values into economic policy.
>
> (Pearce 1989: 5, 7)

According to Pearce (1989), governments should now put a cost on the environment as part of economic policy. A policy of economic growth has to be costed in relation to the impact on the environment so that unlimited growth in future will not necessarily be taken to be a desirable objective. Rather, a 'sustainable' growth policy which takes into account the costs on the environment will be preferred. Equally, in future governments will have to make decisions on transport policy by deciding on the costs and benefits of providing subsidies for public transport as against the environmental costs of expanding private transport. On all these issues therefore the environment enters the equation as a price for both the consumers and suppliers.

The theory of rationality urges that all resources must carry a price. This includes not only material commodities but also 'time' which carries a cost. The theory of rationality embodies the concept of opportunity costs – the decision to produce one product means switching resources from producing another product as rational individualism implies an awareness of the costs in making economic decisions. The use of time also carries a price in terms of how that time could have been spent elsewhere. Rationality

Figure 2.1 The dynamics of the market model: rational agency, consumer/supply side

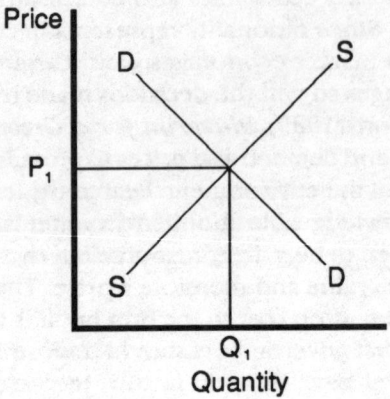

(a) Equilibrium model

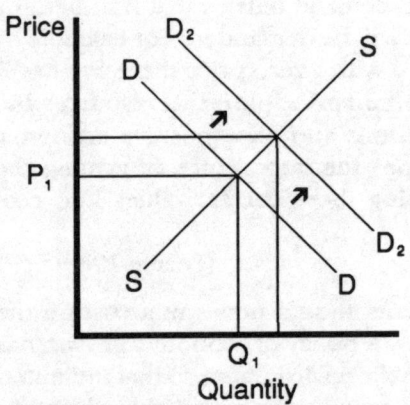

(b) Model with an increase in demand but unchanged supply. An increase in demand results in increases in both prices and quantity in the short term.

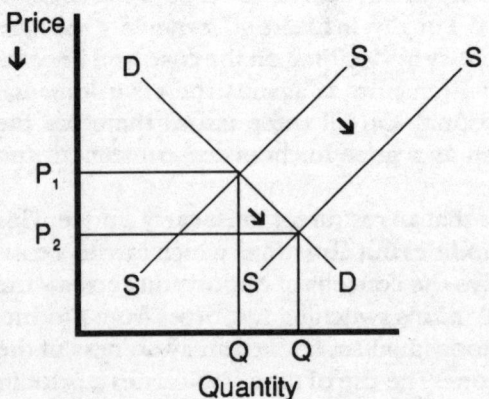

(c) Model with an increase in supply but unchanged demand. The increase in quantity will result in a fall in price.

therefore assumes a context where individuals make decisions in terms of the inputs of costs and outputs as benefits.

THE MODEL OF INTEGRATED MARKETS

The concept of the market and the principles of rational individualism of supply and demand and the price mechanism, are the tools which are applied to analyse all economic decisions. The decisions of what to produce, the question of how and for whom, are therefore decided in the market for goods and services, the market for labour, and the market for money. All these markets are described as being integrated markets, each market being the product of buyers and sellers and prices.

The goods market

This market resolves the question of what to produce. Decisions on production represent the outcomes of decisions – of suppliers making decisions on the quantity of goods and prices, and consumers registering their preferences according to their willingness to buy a quantity of goods for a certain price.

The labour market

The labour market is also a process of buyers and sellers where quantity becomes the level of employment and price the wage decided in the market place for a certain level of employment. The demand for labour however is decided in the goods market and is therefore derived from the willingness of consumers to pay a certain price for a quantity of goods. The supply of goods carries the cost of labour derived from the labour market, hence the argument that the level of employment depends on producing a good for a price which the consumer is willing to pay.

The market for savings and investment

According to market economists savings (leakages out of the economy) represent those who decide to forego present consumption for a price – that price being the rate of interest. Savers and investors also meet in the market place around the rate of interest and the level of investment. Investors represent the demand side of the equation with those wishing to invest representing those who borrow, the level of borrowing being decided by price (the rate of interest). Savers are therefore looking for higher interest rates to increase their savings; investors and borrowers are looking for lower interest rates to increase their borrowing. However the market for savings and investment clears in the market price around the rate of interest. Savings and investment are therefore assumed to be equal.

The market for money

The money market represents the quantity of money available and the cost of money. Market economists are not agreed as to what factors influence the demand for money. One view is that the demand for money is a derived demand, where the demand for money is decided in the goods market. The market for goods and services produces the level of total transaction in the economy. Total money demanded represents the amount of money in circulation to meet the number of transactions. According to this argument the demand for money is a stable demand (Friedman 1975). According to this argument the demand for money is interest rate insensitive. Individuals do not make decisions whether to hold money or to change their portfolio because of the rate of interest. The demand for money, therefore, does not respond to changes in the rate of interest – it is described as being an inelastic demand. Other market economists are not agreed on the shape of the demand curve for money. They would argue that demand for money changes according to the rate of interest, there is a cost attached to liquidity and that individuals therefore make decisions about the level of money demanded around the rate of interest. In this second case the demand for money curve is interest-rate sensitive and would therefore be a normal demand curve for money in contrast to the inelastic demand curve which suggests that the demand for money is stable.

The suppliers of money (that is, the financial authorities) include the banking system and the government. The issue of whether the government can influence the money supply directly or indirectly is an important one for economists but there is disagreement on the role of governments. The reason for the disagreement is crucial for those monetarist economists who want to argue that the government has complete control over the money supply since this links with the theme of demand for money. If monetary demand is said to be stable and interest inelastic, and also that government is totally responsible for the supply of money, then the argument presented by these 'monetarist' economists would hold (this being that it is government which increases the money supply and therefore is responsible for inflation). If, however, government is not in complete control of the money supply they may seek to control it indirectly, either by using interest rates or open market operations. Both these instruments influence the supply of money indirectly, either by increasing the cost through interest rates or by compelling banks to hold more money with the central bank. However, governments do not effect the creation of money, this being attributed to credit schemes created by the banking sector and financial institutions. According to this version government does not have control over the money supply and can only influence it indirectly; therefore the role of government in dealing with inflation is indirect – namely, by making explicit a policy that it will not 'accommodate' increases in the money supply generated by the banking sector.

THE CONCEPT OF MARKET FAILURE

While market economists would argue that it is the market economy which is the most effective in resolving the twin problems of economic efficiency and equity, nevertheless some market economists also recognise that the price mechanism and the market might not deal with questions which are also of importance to the individual. The recognition that markets might not address some issues are usually treated within the framework of market failure. The argument of market failure also has its starting point in the theory of markets founded on rational individualism but then seeks to question whether the rationality of the individual will always provide optimal solutions. The argument of market failure is, however, also a point of departure for those market liberals who wish to argue that the rationality of individuals and individual choice should represent the end state and be the ultimate objective of government. The choice of other objectives and other criteria is perceived to be a departure from the axiom that the individual should be treated as an end rather than as a means to an end. The concept of market failure implicitly starts to use the individual as a tool to achieve other end states and thus is criticised on a vision of the good society which might be arbitrary since not all individuals share that same vision. Using the levers of government to correct the failures of the market is therefore implicitly coercive. According to the ultra-minimalists the concept of market failure is inadmissible because the concept of market failure produces new and arbitrary judgements of the market. Those who recognise the possibility that markets are likely to fail would argue that their agenda for government does not undermine the principles of liberalism since ultimately the individual does not live as an atom but is part of a wider community, and that there are areas when the interests of the community can actually enhance individual liberty.

There are four areas of market failure, and this legitimises a role for government in a way that actually enlarges the freedom of the individual according to some market liberals. Brittan (1988) calls this agenda for government a moral political economy since it provides guidelines for intervention aimed at benefiting the individual as against benefiting vested interest groups. The four areas of failure come under the following headings:

1 The problem of externalities.
2 The problem of spillover effects.

3 Public goods.
4 Income distribution.

The problem of externalities

The problem of externality implies that the social costs are not properly internalised by the individual pursuing self-interest. The possibility that the right of the individual to self-interest might incur social costs and also the probability that individual self-interest might therefore not result in economic efficiency seems to present a dilemma for market economists. While ultra-minimalists would point out that the problem of externality is associated with ideas of using the state to redistribute resources between individuals, minimalist market economists argue that the process of not recognising externality problems might actually result in less freedom for the individual. Dealing with externality problems might therefore increase freedom for the individual.

The environment

There are two classical problems where conflict arises between self-interest and the social interest. The first externality problem is concerned with the environment. The concern for the environment is a communal concern and this asserts that such a problem cannot be left to individual self-interest. Even if, as the Pearce Report recommends, positive costs can be inputted on the environment, the question is whether the cost might not be sufficient to reduce the use of energy sources which seem to threaten the ozone layer. What rate of tax levy for example, will slow down the demand for cars and fuel and result in a switch to public transport? The car facilitates the autonomy of the individual to such an extent that no new levels of public transport or increases in the rate of the petrol tax levy would result in the individual surrendering that autonomy. In this context it seems that market pricing might not work and would even lead to conflicts between the social and the individual good, between the long-term protection of the environment, and individual self-interest.

Human capital investment

The second area of discord between individual self-interest and social cost arises in the context of education and training. The concept of self-interest addresses issues of education as a form of investment in the person; that is when education becomes a decision of investment in human capital. In accordance with market theory, investment decisions are based on the future level of demand, the price of the future commodity supplied, the future rate of interest, and the present cost of the investment. Investment decisions are therefore made on criteria on the cost of the investment and whether these can be recovered in the market place. Prior to embarking on new investments such as robotics in the car industry, feasibility studies are carried out as to the future of the car industry and what is likely to happen to the rate of interest.

Investment in human capital also involves making decisions about forgoing income now with the hope that investment in terms of time and fees in a college of education would bring higher future earnings to compensate for income lost while studying. Individuals pursuing self-interest must therefore make accurate forecasts as to the future and discount the cost of their investment in relation to future earnings. Market economics also assumes that the individual is technically competent which means that the individual would search for information before making decisions on any new investment decisions.

The issue of externality arises in education because individuals will underinvest in their human capital with the result that society as a whole ends up with underinvestment in education. Individuals making decisions about their personal investment costs will put a higher cost on investment whereas if society as a whole makes that investment decision the cost will be lower; thus more individuals will invest in their human capital at the lower cost. The question which arises is whether society recognises the underinvestment and is agreed on how to compensate individuals who make decisions to invest in their human capital which is seen as being of a benefit to the society and not just the individual. If society, through government, decides that individuals who invest in their human capital are already compensated in the types of jobs they find and in the money they earn, then investment in human capital remains an individual decision. If, however, a higher investment in human capital is proved to be highly correlated with higher living standards for the whole community thus affording better health care, more care for the elderly, and a better environment then that society would see investment in the individual human capital as an investment in the community also. Both the individual and society will therefore benefit from increased investment in human capital. The individual pursuing self-interest is also likely to benefit from an economy which is more prosperous. It is therefore in the self-interest of the individual to become involved in communal investment in human capital.

The presence of externalities in the context of market economies would suggest that there might be a conflict between individual self-interest and the interests of the wider community. Yet the presence of externality also reflects a departure from Smith's 'invisible hand' because it questions the assumption that it is the individual pursuing self-interest who in that process actually pursues the interest of the community. Instead the argument of externality provides an agenda for intervention by government but intervention which is guided by rules and principles which confirm that both the individual and the community benefit and show that the individual is not being used as a tool to achieve an arbitrary vision of the good society.

The problem of spillover effects

While individuals as 'suppliers' of skills and knowledge might overestimate the cost of investment in their human capital and thus would not invest in such a way that allows them to pursue their self-interest, there is the equally important problem that those who 'demand' skills and knowledge also underestimate the cost of these skills and therefore end up with lower levels of skills to produce a specific product. The question which arises is how do employers reward skills which are in high demand? Obviously one solution would be to let the market mechanism determine income levels between different skills and knowledge thus reflecting the differential between human capital investment. However, a problem arises when a shortage for certain skills appears. Although the market might signal a higher wage for those skill shortages an insufficient number of skilled individuals come forward to meet the market demand. Employers pursuing self-interest are reluctant to offer training opportunities since there is the likelihood that the newly trained employees would take the new investment with them to another employer able to pay higher wages without having to pay for the training. This is the process of spillover, with all employers following the same logic of not investing in training and therefore ending up with a less-skilled work-force overall. Because of this lack of skills and knowledge firms cannot develop new methods of production or produce new pro-ducts. The quality of their product might deteriorate and firms might be forced to close down because of a lack of demand for their products. During an upturn in trade such firms become less able to take advantage of fresh opportunities to meet the fresh demand, with the result that other firms with better quality products and a more skilled labour force are better equipped to take advantage of the new opportunities. The discrepancies between skills and vacancies become more apparent in an economic upturn. In this context unemployment will fall more slowly despite the growth in the number of job vacancies. Employers will now find it more difficult to find the new skills; 'bottlenecks' will appear in the economy with firms unable to meet the new demand; and job vacancies will rise while high levels of unemployment will persist among those with low or inappro-priate skills.

Because of the process of spillover and the reluctant attitude of employ-ers to invest in training, the role of providing a framework for training has to become the responsibility of government. With government providing training opportunities and all employers paying a levy towards a central pool then there is likely to be all-round benefit – more individuals will undertake training into the new skills and employers will not have to deal with the worry of their competitors 'poaching' key workers by offering higher pay. Equally, employers will not have to become involved in the process of labour hoarding by offering their key workers higher benefits. The practices of both poaching and hoarding actually harm the workings of the market. Employers do not have incentives to provide training for new skills, and actually become involved in making labour less mobile by offering incentives to specific workers.

Public goods

The logic of market economics would suggest that all activities have the property of being commodities for which there are likely to be suppliers and consumers. According to this view of society, the consumer registers a willingness to purchase a certain good; then, provided the price is right, suppliers would eventually emerge willing to supply the desired good. Consistent with this argument defence and law and order are commodities which consumers can purchase as individuals in the market place.

The concept of a public good suggests that there are certain public goods which do not easily transfer into commodities and prices. The nature of these goods suggests that it is society at large that benefits and that costs and advantages cannot be attributed to an individual. Examples of public goods would include the public provision of parks, gardens and public libraries. Society at large benefits from a good-quality public library. A library is there to provide information, and while the cost of information is now shared by the community it is individuals who become better informed. It is society which benefits from decisions which are made in the context of a better informed public. Leaving information to the market place means that it becomes a commodity which carries a price. Therefore there will be better informed individuals whose freedom will depend on less informed individuals who make decisions according to prejudice rather than rational argument founded on an informed public. It is thus in the interest of those who value their individual liberty to seek to live in a context of free information. In this context individual liberties are more likely to be secured when there is awareness. It is difficult to make individual liberties a commodity in a context where liberty has to be bought and maybe sold by the state. It is therefore not appropriate to levy a price for freedom on individuals although it is a price that society might be willing to pay.

Parks and gardens represent places of public access which, if left to individual self-interest to provide and enjoy for a price, would no longer be considered as spaces of public access but private properties. Since it is central to market liberals that individuals do not live like atoms but are individuals in the context of a society which respects the rights of the individual, areas of public access confirm the relationship between the society and the freedom of the individual. Again public places represent public goods because the benefits derived by the individual and society cannot be transferred into costs upon identifiable individuals.

It is equally crucial that expenditures on defence and law and order become the responsibility of society and not decisions that are left to the individual. Like public parks and libraries defence against external threat and the rights of public safety are aspects which guarantee the rights of the individual and yet it is society in general which benefits from these when threatened by invasion or war by external aggressors. The freedom of the individual depends on a society which is willing to pay as a whole to protect individual freedom.

Individual rights and liberties do not exist in a vacuum nor do individuals live as atoms separate from each other. The argument that individuals are part of the social context does not deny the rights of the individual or respect for individual rights. It is because individuals, through their society, create the environment where rights and liberties are protected that the individual can become a reality.

It is a misreading of liberalism to suggest that individual liberty depends on the axiom that individuals are seen as pursuing self-interest in competition with each other and therefore are unable to co-operate. Market liberals are of course aware of the inextricable relationships that exist between the individual and society but are also aware that if individual freedom is to be protected and individuals are not to be used as tools by others, their relationship to society has to be continuously reviewed and also be founded on a contract. The provision of public goods represents the confirmation that individuals are not atoms and that there is interdependence. This does not necessarily mean that the individual becomes an invisible part of society – that is a part of the whole who cannot be identified separate from the whole.

Income distribution

Some market liberals including Hayek (1988) in *The Fatal Conceit*, would argue that the rights of the individual are invariably linked to the rights of property. Hayek argues, for example, that only when the rights to property were established did the feudal monarchies stop treating others as 'subjects' to be used in the service of the monarch and the rights of property and individual rights emerged. Therefore, once it is recognised that individuals have a right to their property enshrined in law then others are compelled to observe the rights to property:

An important aspect of this freedom – the freedom on the part of different individuals to pursue distinct aims, guided by their differing knowledge and skills – was made possible not only by the separate control of various means of production but also by another practice, the recognition of approved methods of transferring this control.... The prerequisite for this existence of such property freedom and order from the time of the Greeks to the present is the same law in the sense of abstract rules enabling the individual to ascertain at any time who is entitled to dispose over any particular thing.

(Hayek 1988: 30)

The right to property and the protection of property is central in guaranteeing the freedom of the individual. Attempts by governments to use their arbitrary powers to redistribute property must therefore be seen as a form of coercion. This is the classical market liberal 'deontological' statement, meaning that the rights of the individual must always come before any claims of the general good. Any attempt therefore to redistribute property carries with it an implicit vision of the good society and is therefore teleological since it carries a vision of the good defined by someone on the behalf of others.

The right to private property therefore confirms the right of the individual to define self-interest. Private property also guarantees the autonomy of the individual against arbitrary decisions and reaffirms the Kantian assertion that the individual should be treated as an end rather than as a means to an end. According to Hayek the principle of taxation should be governed by rules of proportionality, so that each individual pays the same rate of taxation irrespective of income. Governments do not have the right to introduce progressive taxation since this form of taxation seeks to discriminate because of income. Such discrimination is arbitrary since governments can also decide to impose a differential tax on groups which may be defined as unpopular, maybe not because of their income but because of their beliefs or their race. In contrast, however, Nozick seems to be in favour of a tax which rectifies previous violations of justice. Hence, if the present distribution of property is judged to be founded on violation of individual liberty then the state has the right to redistribute property.

However, 'contractarian' market liberals including Rawls (1988) in *A Theory of Justice* and Brittan (1988) in *A Restatement of Economic Liberalism* have suggested that it is possible that the rights of the individual can be preserved in a context where the question of redistribution can also become the concern of a society where individual liberty is central. Rawls, for example, argues that it is possible to put the rights of the individual and questions concerning the distribution of resources in a lexical order, always putting the rights of the individual first as rights which are inalienable and non-negotiable, and also to construct a theory of justice which takes into consideration economic and social issues.

The first principle of equal liberty is the primary standard for the constitutional convention. Its main requirements are that the fundamental liberties of the person and liberty of conscience and freedom of thought be protected.... The second principle dictates that social and economic policies be aimed at maximising the long-term expectations of the least advantaged under conditions of fair equality of opportunity.

(Rawls 1988: 199)

Within a contractual framework Rawls argues that it is possible for individuals under a veil of ignorance to construct a constitution which ensures that all individuals are treated as equals, where there is freedom of conscience, freedom of thought and freedom of speech, but also under that veil of ignorance or original position these individuals will also construct a theory of just entitlement. Although agreement can be reached to construct the constitution which protects the rights of all individuals the question of entitlements will not lead to similar agreements.

The theory of just entitlement needs to deal with two separate issues. According to Rawls the first deals with the question of equal opportunity to ensure that all offices and careers are open to all individuals with each individual having equal access. The dimension of equal opportunity is therefore related to the 'principle of efficiency' and also to natural liberty. According to the principle of efficiency market liberals are concerned with the criteria of efficiency as they relate to production and resource allocation. If the distribution of income acts as a barrier to entry for certain individuals so that these individuals, because of lack of income, cannot fully explore their abilities then it can argued on efficiency criteria that resources are not being allocated efficiently. The problem of income concentration is therefore important for a market liberal concerned with the principle of economic efficiency. Lack of income acts as a barrier to entry into higher education and is associated with children from lower income groups leaving school at an early age. Income concentration is also a worry to market liberals since it is also likely to lead to monopoly: the monopoly of vested interest groups whose levels of income and property have the potential to influence government and therefore harm the rights of the individual. Market liberals must therefore be concerned with the question of the rights to property and also the rights of the individual. Hayek seems to assume that there is no tension between concentrations of property ownership and the rights of the individual. Indeed, Hayek argues against any attempt by government to discriminate in their taxation policy. Yet property can also be utilised as a resource by some against the rights of others.

Under the criterion of equal access to all offices the presence of income inequality is of concern to market liberals for two reasons. The first reason as argued above is when the presence of income inequality acts as a barrier to entry which means that the level of income determines which individuals are more able to utilise their potential. According to the principle of

efficiency all resources available must be used effectively. If human resources are not deployed effectively because of income then some market
liberals would argue that government must address the question of income
to improve efficiency. Income inequality is of concern to market liberals for
a second reason for it is also likely to deny natural liberty to some
individuals so that they will be less able than others to pursue what they
see as desirable and good. In other words, income inequality denies some
individuals the right to self-interest.

The second criterion for justifying income and social inequalities is
whether the market liberals can show that inequality is good for the
individual. According to Rawls, therefore, inequality can be justified if it can
be proved that inequality is likely to benefit those on low income. If high
income differentials do provide incentives for high income earners to
generate economic prosperity which benefits the poor then, Rawls argues,
income inequality can be justified according to the 'difference principle'.
This argument is similar to the 'trickle down theory' in housing economics
which suggests that as those on higher income move to more expensive
housing they generate new housing demand by making new housing
available to the next income groups.

Rawls is, also aware, however, that the question of 'everyone's advantage'
might also lead to individuals within the context of the veil of ignorance to replace the difference principle by the 'democratic principle'.
According to the latter principle individuals decide to redistribute income
according to egalitarian principles and, in contrast to justifying income
inequality as being to everyone's advantage suggests that creating the just
entitlement through less inequality is more likely to be to everyone's
advantage.

The contribution of Rawls on the issue of income inequality and why it
should concern market liberals is the ability of the author to show that there
will be no necessary agreement under the original position of what is likely
to constitute just entitlement. Rawls is able to disaggregate the question of
just entitlement under two criteria: the criteria of equal opportunity and
access. Market liberals utilising the principles of efficiency and natural
liberty would argue that if income acts as a barrier to entry to offices and
certain positions, then inequality is likely to generate inefficiency – not only
because of the monopoly power of income concentration but also because
income inequality is likely to deny natural liberty. On the second criterion,
that the distribution of income should be to everyone's benefit, Rawls
argues that individuals might decide on the difference principle and thus
justify income inequality as long as that rule benefits everyone. However,
there is also the likelihood that individuals might decide to agree on the
democratic principle which would involve a more egalitarian distribution
of income.

Market liberalism: principles for economic policy

The central core of market economics is the individual who is defined as rational in the sense that the individual is capable of deciding what is good and desirable. This assumption of rationality suggests that the individual knows best; that it is only the individual who has the right to order needs and that since each individual knows best no one else has the right to moralise or to attempt to order preferences which benefit society. The individual must be treated as an end in himself and not as a tool by others – that is, as a means to an end – to achieve the vision of the good society as defined by others. Furthermore, rationality is founded on the state of knowledge which means that as the individual acquires new knowledge and information that the process of self-interest will always change. It is because individuals are likely to change their preferences and choices that the market place becomes the most effective and flexible process which can reflect that change. Markets reflect a continuous process of decentralised decisions.

Market economics builds on the concept of rational individualism. It is because individuals make rational judgements both as consumers and suppliers that commodities are produced for exchange in the market place. The theories of supply and demand are derived from the concept of rational individuals.

The principles of markets not only explain how economies work but also prescribe a role for government in the process of economic policy-making. According to market liberalism, because the individual is central and it is the individual who knows best, the role of government should be that of constructing a framework for individuals to pursue self-interest. Obstacles to individual self-interest include those individuals who decide to combine together in ways that create barriers and harm individual self-interest. In this context the primary role of government is to make rules which prohibit the use of monopoly power. Governments should therefore make rules which ensure a competitive environment where individuals become equal.

Because of the coercive inclination of government, rules must also be constructed which ensure that its arbitrary nature can be controlled through various checks and balances. Market liberals would therefore favour a written constitution in which the separation of powers is made clear and where government is therefore conducted according to certain rules and principles. Checks and balances on government include decentralisation of powers and creating many centres of power as opposed to a centralised authority.

Government by rules and principles also includes the conduct of economic policy. Market liberals therefore favour an economic policy which is guided by fixed rules. For example, such rules include the separation of the central bank from the influence of government. In the United States the

Federal Reserve Bank is separated from government in accordance with the Constitution; the Bundesbank in Germany is also so separated. Market liberals favour this separation because it stops government from manipulating the banks to achieve political ends. The Gramm Rudman Amendment to the United States Constitution for example, also represents a liberal attempt to guide economic policy by rules and principles. The attempt involves the control of the US budget deficit by making fiscal policy a constitutional issue.

Constitutional economists argue that if governments do not conduct economic policy according to pre-set rules they will use arbitrary processes which are primarily politically beneficial to the government. The problem of pursuing electoral success in the conduct of economic policy is that government would seek policies which thread together majorities. Under these circumstances economic policy is conducted on behalf of groups which are influential in electoral terms. The government will also be tempted to provide benefits and subsidies for groups which can deliver electoral majorities. The conduct of economic policy according to this approach is driven purely by electoral concerns. Market liberals criticise this form of economic policy for the absence of moral judgement. Brittan, for example, argues that the conduct of economic policy according to rules represents a moral political economy because it protects the individual against the arbitrary nature of government and the influence of vested interests groups.

Market liberals would urge that the first principle in the conduct of economic policy is for government to formulate policy in the context of pre-set rules and principles. They would therefore favour constitutional government. Individual rights need to be set in a written constitution which clearly defines those rights which are inalienable and non-negotiable. The aim of constitutional government is to minimise the arbitrary nature of government and also to protect individual rights against vested interests. Economic policy is therefore a continuation of constitutional government where rules and principles are set for the conduct of monetary and fiscal policy, subsidies, competition policy and taxation. Constitutional government seeks to create agencies which are legally separate from the influence of government, with the central bank being able to conduct monetary policy independent of government intervention for example. Equally, government could set rules for competition policy to guarantee consumer sovereignty and to phase out subsidies which can be judged as discriminating between groups.

Within the parameters of constitutional government the rights of the individual are protected. Some market liberals such as Hayek and Nozick would want to confine the role of government to constructing a constitutional framework. Other market liberals such as Rawls and Brittan would argue that the agenda for government must be extended to deal with problems of market failure including the problem of externalities, spillover effects, public goods, and the issue of income distribution.

The agenda for government intervention in the context of constitutional government deals with the problems of market failure in a way that does not contravene individual liberty but deals with these problems according to criteria which extend the rights of the individual. Since individual rights are enshrined in the constitution, attempts to deal with market failure must be set in relation to the constitution where a series of checks and balances such as the Supreme Court in the USA can scrutinise government intervention. This, in effect, corresponds with Rawls's concept of reflective equilibrium where the rights of the individual and the social context are continuously reviewed.

As argued above government policy which seeks to deal with the environment, with investment in human capital, with the provision of quality parks and libraries, and to address problems of income inequality, can all extend the rights of the individual. No one individual living like an atom can buy private clean air if others are all busy polluting the environment. The individual cannot decide to opt out. Equally the presence of income inequality and the lack of investment in human capital can result in market inefficiency which can harm the potential for higher levels of prosperity. The self-interest of the individual can be combined with the self-interest of others voluntarily in such a way that ensures individual freedom to pursue self-interest within an improved social environment.

Chapter 3

Market economics
Labour markets, wages and employment

INTRODUCTION: MARKET PRINCIPLES

Whilst in the previous chapter the principal regard was to construct a general model of market economics, there was also the additional attempt to show how the model of markets could be applied to explain how economies work. Furthermore, it was also pointed out that while the market model seeks to describe and explain events, it is inexorably prescriptive since it endeavours to provide an agenda for government. This chapter seeks to take up principles constituted by market economists as a series of 'tools', and then to see how these tools contribute to explain certain economic problems such as unemployment and inflation. The concern here will be to use the tools of rational individualism, supply and demand and markets, and then to seek to explain the nature of UK unemployment and inflation and the economic policy alternatives that can be derived from market principles.

The market model is constructed according to three general assumptions of the nature of the individual and the relationship between the individual and the wider social context: First, that the individual is a rational agent continuously making decisions based on rational information; second, that the dynamics of the 'invisible hand' (namely, the right of individuals to pursue self-interest) remains the best way to increase the prosperity and welfare of the individual and of the community, and that the primary concern is always the rights of the individual to be able to make choices free from direction by a central authority; and third, that the individual is sovereign in the market place which means that there is freedom of choice and opportunities for individuals to realise their self-interest.

The concept of the rational individual suggests that the individual knows best which projects to pursue and also is aware of the costs and benefits involved in making certain decisions. Individuals are continuously involved in opportunity costs since all decisions tend to involve resources. Since decisions are also related to the state of knowledge which is available, it is therefore likely that with new or additional information the individual might change the order of needs and preferences. Market liberals suggest that the individual is not an atom living in a vacuum but that the individual is located within a specific social and historical context. However, the rational individual is capable of continuously questioning and renegotiating the priorities and preferences set by others.

The second assumption underpinned by the concept of the invisible hand, points to the argument that needs and preferences are best met through markets by individual consumers and suppliers making 'decentralised' decisions in contrast to direction coming from a centralist authority. The market represents the process of the invisible hand, invisible in that there is no overall direction on intervention by one authority to attempt to define what should be produced, how a product is produced and for whom.

The third assumption is that the market provides a context where people are likely to be treated as equal individuals. Because the market represents a process of many buyers and sellers without barriers to entry, the potential for discrimination between individual consumers is minimised since the spirit of competition ensures that individuals who feel discriminated against have the freedom of choice to move to new markets. It is therefore more likely that discrimination and the perpetuation of vested interests will be maintained in a context of monopoly.

MARKET PRINCIPLES: THE LABOUR MARKET

The concepts of the rational individual, the invisible hand, and consumer sovereignty represent the central tools of market economics. Dealing with the problem of unemployment therefore, market economics locates labour services as a commodity which is sold and bought by rational agents in the market. In a *Financial Times* article in 1982, Samuel Brittan (the economics editor) drew a comparison between labour and bananas as two similar commodities:

> If the price of bananas is kept too high in relation to the price required to balance supply and demand there will be a surplus of bananas. If the price of bananas is below the market clearing price there will be a shortage. The same applies to labour. If the price – i.e. the wage – is too high there will be a surplus of workers, i.e. unemployment. If it is kept too low there will be a shortage of workers.... Workers do sell their services just as banana producers sell bananas.
>
> (Brittan, *Financial Times*, 16 September 1982)

According to the concept of rational agents therefore, workers would adjust their wages in relation to the level of demand for their level of services. The rate of unemployment represents 'excess' labour supply at a certain wage level. Second, since the consumer is described as being sovereign, consumers have the right to choose in the goods market because there is competition between suppliers. Where price is the determining factor, the rational consumer will choose the product that offers the highest level of welfare at the lowest price. Furthermore, since the national economy is likely to be an open economy, this means that the consumer can choose between goods produced anywhere in the world. In the context of the 'open economy', the cost of the good produced in Britain has to reflect international competition which in turn means that British workers, when setting their wages levels are also faced by international competition.

The central thesis in market economics would suggest that in the climate of competition it is the consumers in the goods market who are choosing which goods to buy and thereby setting the price. The level of unemployment represents the failure of the market labour to clear at prices determined in the goods market and that therefore wages in the labour market have to adjust before labour markets clear at full employment. It is consumer sovereignty in the goods markets which determines prices. A high level of unemployment would indicate that the price of labour is too high and that wage levels would need to be adjusted downwards if labour markets are to clear. If the concept of rational agents is correct and prices are flexible, the question of why there is a lag between unemployment and wages arises. Why for example do wages continue to rise irrespective of the level of unemployment? Why in some sectors do the unemployed not seem to represent a threat to those at work? In some sectors of the economy the unemployed might as well be in Australia because they do not influence wage demands. The long-term unemployed, those who have been registering as unemployed for 18 months or more, tend to have low skills and are not geographically mobile. They are less able to move to parts of the country where there is a high demand for labour.

THE LABOUR MARKET OR LABOUR MARKETS

The problem for market economists is the question of whether the labour market can be studied as a homogeneous single market, whether there is a 'lump' of labour where all workers are in the one labour market and would therefore respond in a similar fashion. While labour market economists adhere to the concept of rational agents, an alternative theory can be derived which shows that workers inhabit different labour markets and therefore behave rationally in negotiating differential wage demands, especially if they feel insulated from unemployment. Although unemployment might represent excess labour supply this might not apply for the economy as a whole, so that while there might be excess labour and low demands for manual labour, the labour market for highly skilled technicians might be tight.

Although market economists are therefore agreed on the shared concepts of rational individuals' markets and consumer choice, the application of these concepts does not necessarily lead to common explanations. Using similar starting points market economists have proceeded to different interpretations as to how labour markets work. Although these interpretations are not necessarily mutually exclusive it is important to outline some of the differences and the nature of the argument.

The central argument is between macroeconomists and micro- or labour market economists. There are market economists who are interested in the macroeconomics of labour markets, who seek to provide links between macro levels of unemployment and wages levels in contrast to market economists who tend to look at micro labour markets, unemployment and wages. Macroeconomists seek to emphasise the context of general labour markets while microeconomists aim to explain how rational agents in the context of disaggregated labour markets produce different responses to changes in the levels of unemployment and wages. According to the microeconomists some workers are located in sectors which are less vulnerable to competitive markets, at least in the short term, because of their skills and knowledge differences. This applies equally to public sector workers, including teachers or doctors who do not sell a product directly to the public.

In dealing with the problem of unemployment, therefore, market macroeconomists and microeconomists tend to look at different variables. Microeconomists are concerned with the strategies available to different workers in aiming to influence the labour market and therefore tend to emphasise the process of disaggregated labour markets. Macroeconomists are interested in the process of wage determination, and in explaining how other macro variables including the rate of inflation, interest rates, and changes in the currency are likely to influence wage demands and therefore the rate of unemployment.

The rest of this chapter is arranged to provide an outline of the debate between macro- and microeconomists about the nature of UK unemployment. The following sections, then, will consider the various explanations of both macro- and microeconomists for unemployment and the implications for policy alternatives.

THE NATURE OF UK UNEMPLOYMENT

Throughout the period 1951 to 1964, UK unemployment averaged 2.5 per cent of the working population; that meant an unemployment average of 250,000. Unemployment reached 0.5 million in 1969 and in 1972 it had broken through the psychological barrier of 1 million. At the time it was felt that no government would survive that level of unemployment. Between 1974 and 1979, unemployment stayed above the 1 million level and throughout the 1980s it never fell below the 2 million mark. Unemployment actually peaked in the years 1982/3 at over 3.2 million which was equivalent to 14 per cent of the working population. In contrast to the 2.5 per cent in the 1960s therefore, unemployment rates of 13 per cent in the 1980s and even 10 per cent in the early 1990s would seem to suggest that unemployment in Britain has fossilised at a very high level compared to the period of the 1950s and early 1960s.

In explaining these changes in unemployment, the micro labour economists would argue that approaching the problem of unemployment through aggregated stylised facts acts as more of a veil in understanding the nature of unemployment and would therefore urge that the problem of unemployment needs to be disaggregated. The starting point for the microeconomists is therefore to treat employment and unemployment in the context of segregated labour markets, the argument being that there are different variables influencing labour supply and demand.

Regional differences

Labour market economists would point to factors such as regional variations in the incidence of unemployment. So although the UK average of unemployment might be 10 per cent within that average there are some wide variations with unemployment rates of 12 per cent in Yorkshire and Humberside, 14 per cent in Northern Ireland, and in contrast 5 per cent in East Anglia and the South-east. So while the economies of East Anglia and the South-east are experiencing tight labour markets, meanwhile the unemployment rates of the North of England remain comparatively high. Furthermore, even regional differences represent aggregates of unemployment levels. It is not the whole of Yorkshire and Humberside which is experiencing an even level of unemployment; the incidence of regional unemployment seems to be concentrated in specific areas in the cities of Bradford or Leeds and Sheffield. Travel-to-work studies show high correlations between the level of unemployment, the concentrations of ethnic minorities, low skills, and the occurrence of closures of major plants in the area. The decision to close down a textile factory with the loss of 450 jobs might at a macro level seem to be a marginal problem. To a local community which depends on that specific firm such a closure might mean the demise of a local economy with further closures of shops and other infrastructure facilities. The restructuring of a local economy has a longer time lag. To attract new investment there might be a need for a long-term policy of re-training the local labour force into new skills.

Race and discrimination

There are also problems of race and gender in employment opportunities and access to some labour markets. The regime of apartheid in South Africa is criticised by market economists because this form of discrimination represents the influence of a vested interest group – namely, a minority white community – in seeking to maintain and protect artificial privileges. Market economists would argue that apartheid represents an obstacle to market forces and the spirit of competition. By replacing apartheid with a policy of competition, labour supply in all markets would increase in South Africa thus widening the potential for black participants in the labour market. The presence of race and sexual discrimination represents attempts by vested interest groups to maintain privileges by using artificial barriers to certain labour markets.

Workers from the ethnic minorities who came to Britain in the early 1950s, for example, found easier access to labour markets which had been deserted as undesirable by local workers especially during periods of economic growth. Access to labour markets for black workers in Britain has therefore tended to depend on those labour markets in which there was no direct competition with white workers and where black workers were therefore a form of replacement labour to do work during unsocial hours. In addition there was better access to those labour markets which tended to be low paid and without trade union organisation. It would seem that in bargaining with employers, trade unions have also tended to bargain on 'the acceptability to the lads of black workers'.

Youth unemployment

An additional problem in labour markets is the issue of access of young people to employment. Youth unemployment tends to be higher than that for the whole population. Employers seems reluctant to employ young workers, especially when training is involved since this is likely to incur new costs on employers. However, young people from ethnic minorities are also more likely to be unemployed than their white counterparts even when similar qualifications are taken into consideration. According to the UK Labour Force Survey of 1985, 16 per cent of white youth between the ages of 16 to 24 are likely to unemployed; this has to be contrasted with the 33 per cent for young people from ethnic minorities.

Gender discrimination

Women who join the labour market are more likely to find easier access to part-time employment and low pay. Images created of women as not being the primary earners within families has resulted in discrimination towards women in employment opportunities. Jobs which are part-time and flexible are perceived to be more suitable for women because such forms of employment are seen as being in harmony with women's family lives and likely to bring 'additional' income to the family. Women are therefore discriminated against in access to labour markets which tend to require investment in training by employers because women's careers are seen to be characterised by a series of interruptions in their work histories in contrast to the more continuous careers of men. Women tend to leave work to have children and look after families. This means that they are not present in great numbers in certain employment areas. For instance, there are not many women who 'head' companies in Britain, there are not many women consultants in health care, and not many women barristers. There is therefore less investment in women's human capital.

Women have also been seen as a threat by men in specific skill areas so that attempts have been made by men to exclude women from certain types of employment. Women have been seen as a threat to skills, 'diluting' certain skills and making themselves available for employment at lower rates of pay. Men, through their trade unions, have therefore sought to restrict the number of new trainees entering their trade which has often meant discrimination against women.

Sex Discrimination Acts and policies on race relations are favoured by market economists since such measures do increase individual freedom. However, despite the Equal Pay Act of 1975 the gap between men's and women's pay has remained relatively static in Britain, the ratio of women's to men's hourly earnings remaining at around 73 per cent. This trend is also present in countries which also have similar legislation to that of the UK. Recent court judgments have found that even where women were doing work of equal value to that of men, there still was sexual discrimination in pay determination despite the legislative framework.

Figure 3.1   Market explanations of UK unemployment: effects of removing race/gender discrimination

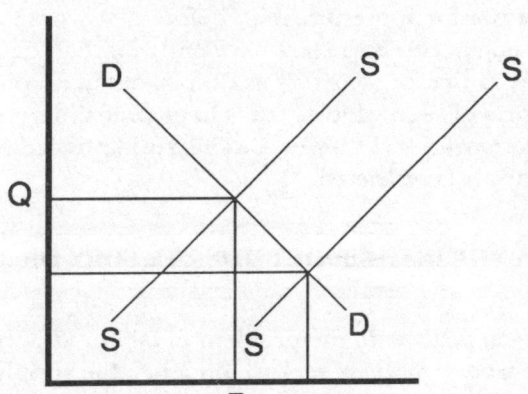

Removing discrimination: effects on the supply side. There is an increase in labour supply as more women and black people gain access to the market. This leads to a fall in wages and increases in employment.

LABOUR MARKET ECONOMICS: THE DUAL LABOUR MARKET

To explain the problems of race and gender discrimination in labour markets, models of dual labour markets have been developed. According to the dual labour market model the suggestion is that there is a need to move away from the notion of a lump of labour supply which can be treated as a homogeneous factor. Instead of there being one labour market represented by the notion of the total working population, in practice several quite separate labour markets exist (for men, women, white workers, black workers), and each can be described as being tightly segregated with little cross influence between them. Male workers from ethnic minorities tend to have more access to manual occupations which require little training, occupations which tend to be low paid and highly seasonal. Male black workers tend to be more vulnerable to the experience of unemployment than their white counterparts. There is no direct competition between black male workers and white workers. Male white workers tend to be insulated in highly skilled occupations. Workers from ethnic minorities tend to be geographically concentrated.

There are segmented labour markets for women also. While white women tend to enter occupations which are part-time and low paid, they also have more access to professional occupations in the public sector (including the teaching and the medical professions) than do black women workers who tend to be confined to a more narrow labour market which is part-time, low-paid employment.

There is a core of male white workers who are highly skilled or have access to specialist knowledge who belong to trade unions and professional associations and who seek to protect their income differentials from other workers through pre-entry closed shops and other exclusive strategies. Therefore, workers who enjoy access to specialist skills would seek (as rational agents) to combine together to protect their skills and also to exclude others with barriers to entry into these skills. Engineering workers, for example, set specific durations for apprenticeships before new workers can be classified as qualified engineers. Barristers have ensured that their profession is kept separate from that of solicitors as do consultants from doctors in health care. This form of segregation results in income differentials between groups of workers who feel they have skills and knowledge to sell in the market where supply is restricted.

LABOUR MARKET THEORY: THE INSIDER/OUTSIDER THEORY OF LABOUR MARKETS

While the dual market approach deals with the problem of labour supply and how workers in separate labour markets seek to influence the supply side through restrictive practices, the insider/outsider theory approach seeks to combine both the supply and demand side of labour markets to explain how labour cannot be treated as a homogeneous lump. The theory suggests that the rate of unemployment does not affect wages since the unemployed do not underbid the wages of those in work. The insider/outsider group interpretation suggests that workers are either 'core' workers and in employment or they are at the periphery of the labour market. Core workers tend to be at the heart of the firm and are workers who have specialist skills and knowledge on which the organisation depends. This core group tends to have easier access to management decisions. Managers are aware of the cost of losing key workers, and of the cost of replacement in terms of time and investment in skills. As core workers offer stability and continuity of production firms are aware that the demand for them is high and that poaching through higher wage incentives by other firms can make certain firms vulnerable and at risk. Core workers will therefore enter into bargains with their employers which ensure their retention, so that even during periods of economic slowdown when demand falls employers are likely to 'hoard' these core workers as they await an economic upturn.

In contrast, workers on the periphery of the organisation tend to be treated as the outsiders and they continue to stay on the outside of the organisation. Firms do not attempt to invest in the human capital of workers who are at the margin of the organisation or attempt to integrate them into the organisation. Outsiders are seen as easily replaceable and are therefore often made redundant during economic slowdown. Thus there is no attempt to hoard periphery workers as new ones can be trained at short notice in an economic upturn. The wages of the outsider group reflect their outsider status, namely that if they do not like their rates of pay they can look elsewhere as employers can always find new workers to replace them.

The insider/outsider theory questions the widely held assumption that there is a link between those in work and those out of work – namely, that those out of work can influence wage levels by underbidding the price of those who are employed. The reason why the insiders (the employed) are not directly threatened by the outsiders (the unemployed) is because of the cost incurred by employers in accepting the process of underbidding by outsiders. Firms are likely to lose on their productivity if they are involved in high labour turnover. Irrespective of the skills of the labour force, the insiders always have more knowledge of the productive process than the outsiders. High labour turnover is associated with low labour morale and adversely affects productivity.

MARKET ECONOMICS: THE MACROECONOMIC APPROACH TO UNEMPLOYMENT

While microeconomists are concerned with explaining regional variations in employment access for skilled workers, women, black workers and young workers, some market economists would still argue that there is a general market for labour and that general statements about the levels of unemployment and wages rates are still the main link in explaining unemployment. For example, in McCallum (1986) *Unemployment in the OECD Countries* suggests that employment is very responsive to changes in wage demands. The study concludes that an increase of 1 per cent in real wages was associated with a 1 per cent fall in employment.

Wage demands are not just a reflection of the labour market. In bargaining for wages, workers bargain on the basis on their wider costs of living. This means that if there is an increase in the cost of living due to high interest, a fall in the value of the currency, or a rise in the price of raw materials, employees will seek to maintain their standard of living by asking for higher wages. An attempt by government to increase personal taxation is also likely to lead to wage pressures as employees try to protect their take-home pay. Macro market economists are therefore concerned with the context of the macroeconomy and how it is likely to influence wage demands and unemployment. Inflation is a macroeconomic concern and as the rise in inflation erodes take-home pay it is therefore likely to lead to pressures for higher wage demands. A regime of higher interest rates also leads to high costs of living by increasing the costs of mortgages. Workers again will try to protect take-home pay and seek to bid up their wages.

Pressures for higher wages are therefore likely to be the outcome of the wider economic context and workers bargain as a homogeneous group in the wider economic context. It is because workers seek to protect their take-home pay without considering their location in the labour market that they are likely to price themselves out of the market. The ability of workers to adjust their wage demands so that labour markets clear, depends on rigidities within the labour market – rigidities created either through government policy or institutional rigidities created by workers to protect their privileged positions.

Macroeconomists would argue that pressures for wage demands are the result of factors which are independent of the labour market. Government macroeconomic policy therefore, can indirectly affect the labour market. Market economists would then seek to argue that the rise in unemployment shows that aspects of government policy either harm the labour market, or that government intervention in the labour market only works in the short term, and that problems of unemployment are resolved in the market place.

MARKET ECONOMICS: THE THEORY OF LABOUR MARKETS

Labour markets

Utilising the ideas of supply and demand in the context of labour markets it is important to revisit some of the assumptions which underpin the model. Taking the question 'what variables influence demand?' market economists have tended to construct models which show that demand is influenced by:

1 Changes in price reflect changes in demand, so that if the price rises demand will fall and if the price falls demand will increase. This applies to normal goods. There are therefore substitute goods and no barriers to entry.

2 Changes in disposable income influences the level of demand – increases in demand will fall for inferior goods with increases in income.

3 Demand is influenced by the price movements of other goods, so that if the price of a complementary good rises so would all other prices which means that demand might fall. Petrol is a complementary good to the motor car. High oil prices are likely to lead to a fall in demand for petrol and a fall in demand for cars with high petrol consumption.

The demand for labour

Substituting these general variables for demand for labour, it is therefore assumed that changes in the demand for labour are influenced by the price of labour with the provision that there is a direct substitute available. First, according to labour market theory there is no direct substitute for high skilled labour in the short term which means that skills and knowledge become a barrier to entry for new workers. Second direct substitute effects are more likely to be present in those labour markets which tend to be part-time employment requiring little investment in human capital. However, even when there are direct substitutes available there might still be high costs associated with high labour turnover.

Demand for labour is influenced by changes in disposable income so that for any change in income there will be a shift in the demand curve for labour. A shift in the demand curve is also the result of changes in the mix between labour and capital inputs so that a change in the cost of labour might lead to labour replacement by new technology. Also, changes in the cost of technology might lower the cost of new investment so that such investment becomes more widespread.

Changes in the demand for labour are also due to changes in complementary factors. The cost of national insurance represents an additional cost of labour so that changes in the cost of national insurance are likely to influence demand for labour. Legislation on pensions, rights against dismissal and cost of redundancy are also seen as increasing the cost of labour and therefore likely to influence demand.

Figure 3.2 Market explanations of UK unemployment: effects of reducing personal taxation and national insurance contributions

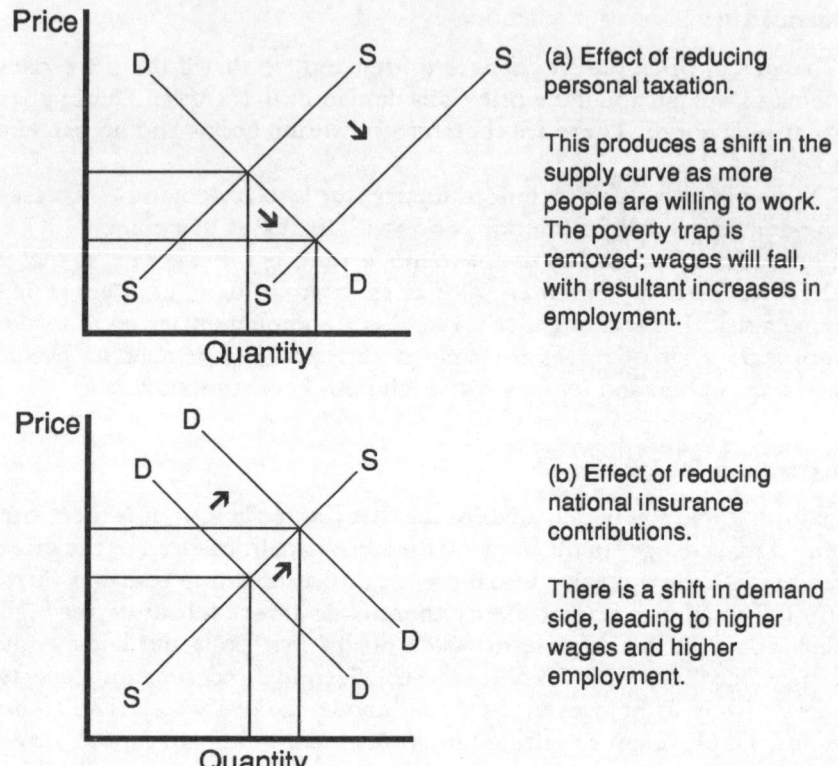

(a) Effect of reducing personal taxation.

This produces a shift in the supply curve as more people are willing to work. The poverty trap is removed; wages will fall, with resultant increases in employment.

(b) Effect of reducing national insurance contributions.

There is a shift in demand side, leading to higher wages and higher employment.

The supply side

Changes in the supply side are also influenced by changes in price. At a low price less workers make themselves available for work while the number available increases with an increase in price. In this context it might be argued that because of social security and the poverty trap created by changes in marginal tax, less workers would make themselves available to work at the lower wage and that changes in social security will influence the labour supply curve.

Demographic changes also influence labour supply. The level of pensions influence changes in labour supply so that high pensions may act as an incentive for workers to leave the labour market. The presence of race and gender discrimination also influence labour supply. Race relations laws and laws which seek to remove gender discrimination will therefore increase labour supply.

According to the process of Walras's tâtonnement, suppliers and employers of labour meet in the market place. The auctioneer signals the price employers are willing to pay, a number of suppliers of labour 'signal' their willingness to work for that wage. If the wage signal is correct employers will get the number of suppliers they require. If the price is too low then there will be a discrepancy between the demand for labour and labour supply. The process of auction however ensures that labour markets clear and that an equilibrium is reached between the quantity of labour supplied and the wage level.

The above model implies that labour markets are flexible and that supply and demand do respond to changes in price. Flexible labour markets also rest on the assumption that labour supply is perfectly mobile. Changes in wage levels are to reflect local labour markets so that labour can move freely to where there is demand.

EXPLAINING UNEMPLOYMENT

If asked why there is unemployment, the market economist would suggest that all unemployment is voluntary. The answer is not an attempt to moralise that the unemployed are feckless or lazy and would rather live on social security, but that unemployment is voluntary in the sense that within the context of a democratic society individuals as rational agents make certain choices. In that sense therefore individuals seek to trade off unemployment for other benefits such as a social security system, pensions, minimum wages, protective legislation on employment, and other forms of social considerations which are outside the influence of the market place.

The term 'voluntary unemployment' however needs to be expanded to show how certain influences represent voluntary choices in the labour market. These voluntary choices can be put into three different categories. The first series of voluntary choices come under 'institutional' influences. Within the category of institutional explanations the suggestion is that governments construct legislative frameworks and public institutions which seek to bring changes within the labour market. While institutions influence the context of labour markets, social concerns can also influence the supply and the demand sides of the labour market. Changes in social security are likely to influence the duration of job search, while changes in pensions will influence the number of elderly who seek to leave the labour market. So the second series of voluntary explanations can be categorised as 'social influences'. The third factor which also contributes to explain voluntary unemployment is the influence of 'collective action'. Trade union rights reflect a process of negotiation between elected governments, the rights of workers to be represented by trade unions and the rights of employers and workers to make contracts of labour. Although workers have rights to belong to trade unions, governments have to strike a balance in industrial relations to protect the rights of trade union members, the rights of individual workers and the rights of employers. The process of collective action represents the attempt by workers as individuals to combine together and through collective strength seek to influence the supply side of labour by restricting the numbers of workers entering the labour market, in that way protecting their wage levels. The influence of collective actors on the labour market leads to voluntary unemployment in the sense that in a democratic country voters reflect the balance between the rights of individuals to seek employment unimpeded by undue restrictions, but also to protect the rights of workers who wish to belong to trade unions. The institutional framework might include rights of appeals against dismissals, rights to sick pay and redundancy payments. Governments also create institutions to deal with employment counselling and also with payments of unemployment benefits. All these institutional influences are voluntary since governments are elected through a democratic process and therefore make commitments at election time. Voters have a choice on the nature of the legislature, whether they choose a government which seeks to intervene in the labour market and make it less impersonal or a government which might seek to remove what could be described as obstacles to the effective workings of markets.

Institutional influences

Governments can directly influence the labour market by constructing a legislative process which enshrines a series of rules and procedures. The legislative framework will therefore have a direct impact on the process of supply and demand when the price signalled by the auctioneer which decides the equilibrium level is also influenced by government directives. Employers have therefore to take into account, for example, the cost of compensation for dismissal. They are thus deterred from extending demand for new employees if the legislation is likely to involve new 'institutional' cost. So extending rights at work through employment protection legislation incurs an additional cost, with the overall effect being a fall in demand for labour and therefore higher unemployment.

Social considerations

In the previous chapter it was suggested that income distribution is a concern for market economists because a lack of income might act as a barrier to entry for individuals to take full advantage of education or health facilities. Although market economists are agreed that the issue of income inequality needs to be addressed, they are also concerned with the spillover effects which income distribution problems might have in the labour market. Market economists are agreed that taxation on personal income

Figure 3.3   Market explanations of UK unemployment: effect of social security on labour markets

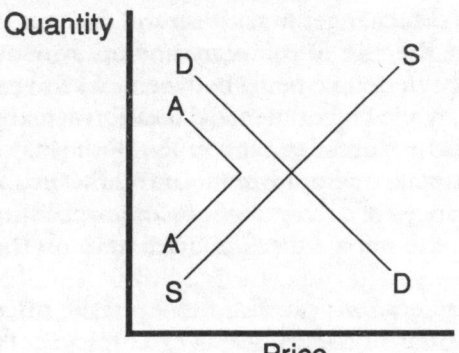

(a) High levels of social security mean that the curve AA shifts to the left with the result that numbers in between jobs and the duration between jobs both increase.

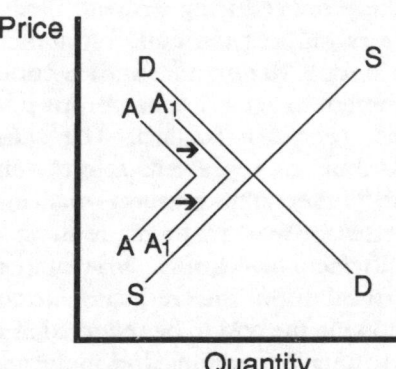

(b) Reducing social security shifts curve AA to the right. As a result, numbers in between jobs fall, with unemployment also falling.

should be progressive, even though it might create disincentives to those in work who feel that their marginal tax is higher than their marginal revenue and that there are therefore no incentives to extend labour supply. An increase in taxation is therefore seen as reducing the price of labour for those who supply labour, and that as the price falls so will labour supply. Conflicts arise between social objectives and economic efficiency. Increasing pensions and social security payments might all be desirable social objectives. Economists will, however, point out that changes in personal taxation to fund these equity objectives would harm the labour supply aspect of the labour market.

In addition to being a cost on labour changes social security also affects the duration of job search for those in between jobs. Higher levels of social security therefore mean that workers as individual rational agents can spend longer in between jobs searching for a more suitable occupation.

Likewise, a reduction in social security will shorten the duration of job search.

Market economists would argue that changes in taxation and changes in social security are likely to increase the rate of voluntary unemployment. Higher rates of social security results in people being between jobs longer with more time spent in job search, while higher personal taxation actually reduces the price of labour and also reduces labour supply. Both sets of policies therefore contribute to voluntary unemployment and market economists would predict the consequences of such policy outcomes utilising the concept of rational agents and the impact these policies have on the supply side of the labour market.

On the demand side, social considerations can also influence the price of labour. Increases in national insurance contributions by employers to finance new pensions increase the cost of labour for the employer, thus increasing the price of labour and therefore reducing demand. Reducing national insurance costs on employers reduces the costs of labour and therefore increases the demand for labour. National insurance contributions represent an attempt by government to act as an insurer for periods when workers become unemployed, retire, or fall sick. The actuarial principle of national insurance contributions represents a joint venture between governments, employers and workers. The question which market liberals ask is whether it would be better for workers to insure themselves as rational individuals against unemployment or sickness. This would mean phasing out the national insurance contributions thus reducing the cost to the employer but at the same time allowing the cost to be reflected in wage increases and then allowing workers to decide for themselves in the market place, the level at which they would wish to insure themselves.

Another method of balancing social concern with the labour market is the minimum wage. At a social level government can be concerned about workers who are not unionised and are in a weak position in bargaining with employers. The argument is that in some labour markets involving youth and part-time workers, employers of labour and suppliers of labour do not meet as equals. The argument is that government should intervene in these labour markets to rectify this imbalance by imposing a limit on the number worked and also minimum wages. There is a history of government 'patronising' women and children in imposing on them limits to employment opportunities. Women have been excluded from working in the mining industries since the 1830s in Britain. Women have therefore been perceived to be less able to decide for themselves where to work. Market liberals would judge this form of state intervention as arbitrary and as sexual discrimination, denying certain labour markets to women and the right of women to choose as rational agents equal to men. In addition there are in Britain today, about 3 million workers involved in part-time work in the retail industry whose wages are decided through wage councils. Imposing

Figure 3.4   Market explanations of UK unemployment: the effect of a minimum wage

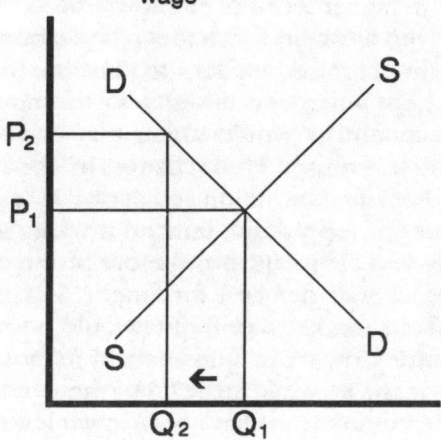

Without a minimum wage, wages will level at P_1 and employment at Q_1; with a minimum wage at P_2 employment will level at Q_2. Thus a minimum wage will lead to an increase in unemployment.

limits on the number of hours people work and setting a minimum wage actually increases the cost of labour which will therefore reduce demand and hence result in high levels of unemployment within those categories of work the government is actually seeking to help. Minimum wages are therefore likely to result in more hardship through unemployment than would occur by allowing wages to be determined in the market place. Market economists would argue that the better way to help the low paid would be by reducing the rate of personal taxation.

Collective action

Workers as rational agents seek to influence the supply side of the labour market. Workers can only influence wage rates by joining together and making rules which restrict labour supply and restrict access to those who are seen as a threat and likely to drive down wage rates. By influencing labour supply, the supply side will not reflect change in price. Workers join trade unions as rational agents because trade unions are organisations which directly benefit the members they serve. Workers in trade unions therefore influence the labour market because the trade union sector is likely to produce an inelastic labour supply curve so that at any wage rate the same amount of labour will be made available. With an inelastic labour supply curve and a rise in the demand side, this change will be reflected purely in higher wages without any increase in the number employed. In contrast, the non-unionised sector labour supply is seen as being responsive to changes in price. With a similar increase in demand in the non-unionised sector the increase in demand will be reflected in both higher wages and higher levels of employment. In the unionised sector a higher demand will not be reflected in higher levels of employment.

Market economists tend to work with a two-sector model of the labour market – a unionised model and a non-unionised model – to illustrate the impact of trade unions on employment when contrasted with the non-unionised sector. Labour market economists would argue that in the unionised sector wages are higher and less responsive to changes in labour supply and demand. Furthermore, because the unionised sector is less responsive to changes in the dynamics of supply and demand workers in the unionised sector tend to become less competitive and more prone to long-term unemployment when the overall demand for labour falls in contrast to the unionised sector. Labour market economists would point to comparative studies between countries, the trade union density in those countries, and the levels of unemployment. So while in the USA, where only 20 per cent of workers belong to trade unions, there have been lower levels of unemployment over the last decade and more people joining the labour market this has to be contrasted to Europe which is described as having a less flexible labour market because of a much stronger trade union sector. Unemployment in Europe has been higher than in the USA over the last ten years, and Europe (including Britain) has also been slower at creating employment in comparison to the USA.

The trade union sector is less responsive to change because there are barriers to entry on the supply side, which means that the trade unions actually create monopolies for their members. Members through their trade unions, can decide who becomes an engineer or a doctor and how many are to be admitted to the trade each year without influencing labour supply.

Market economists would argue that the trade union sector contributes to increases in the levels of unemployment because trade unions have an influence on labour supply – they restrict access to the supply side and it is because they are able to restrict access that prices and wages in the unionised sector do not reflect changes in demand or changes in labour supply. Workers in the unionised sector are more resistant to changes in their job specification and are therefore more likely to be involved in demarcation disputes in attempts to protect their skills. Highly unionised plants are less flexible to changes in demand in the goods market and are more vulnerable to job losses.

The unionised sector is also seen as the wage setter for the whole economy, setting wage norms for other workers so that the ethics of collective bargaining come to depend more on comparisons between different workers rather than reflecting market forces. Workers in the unionised sector are more concerned with keeping up with the wages leagues. It is in the interest of trade unions to show their members that trade unions are successful in securing the wages positions of their members. Trade unions are in competition for members with other trade unions

Figure 3.5   Market explanations of UK unemployment: how a reform of trade
unions will affect the supply side

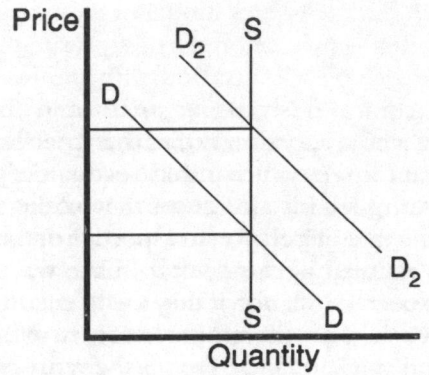

(a) Trade union effect:
inelastic supply.

An increase in demand when
the labour supply is inelastic
results in higher wages with
no increases in employment.

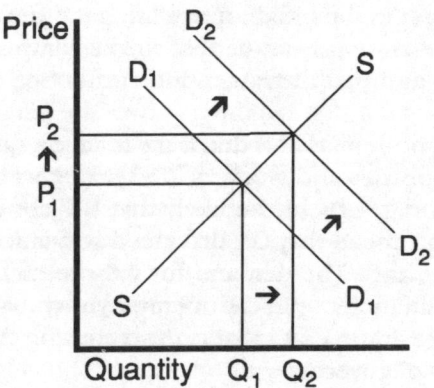

(b) Reform of trade unions:
normal labour supply.

With trade union reform there
is an increase in demand.
This results in higher wages
and higher levels of
employment.

who are seen as winning higher wage concessions likely to attract more
members. Although the British TUC has set up procedures under the
Bridlington Rules to minimise inter-union rivalry, trade unions still continue to fear the loss of members to other unions.

MARKET ECONOMICS: MACRO APPROACH

While the micro labour market economists are concerned with evaluating
the influence of institutional factors, social policies, and collective actions
and their effects on wages and employment in the context of the labour
market, the macro market economists would ask what exogenous factors
(those independent of the labour market) are likely to influence wages
demand and therefore employment. So rather than starting from the
analysis of the labour market as the determining explanation, macroeconomists are concerned with explaining the wider economic context and the

likely impact of changes in the wider context in relation to the labour market.

Inflation

Inflation is defined as a climate of continuously rising prices and its presence therefore tends to refer to the whole economy rather than specific sectors. The research group Income Data Survey which publishes quarterly reports on changes in wage trends have argued for a long time that workers tend to set wages in accordance with the rate of inflation irrespective of the levels of unemployment. Workers as rational agents seek to make wage settlements on the basis of future or expected inflation if they are to ensure that take-home pay stays unchanged. Workers are therefore concerned with protecting their real take-home pay and since inflation erodes the value of this workers tend to negotiate settlements in periods of inflation which reflect the inflation rate. Since changes in the inflation rate are not directly related to the labour market, macroeconomists argue that workers import other factors in settling wage claims and that the rate of inflation is one of those external factors.

The problem of inflation for the labour market is that if the inflation rate in Britain is higher than in other countries and workers are seeking wage settlements which reflect UK inflation it is therefore likely that UK labour unit costs would be rising faster. This mean that UK produced goods will cost more which in turn affects demand. The demand for UK-produced goods will fall which in turn means an increase in UK unemployment. For this reason market economists would argue that inflation and curbing the rate of inflation must be the priority of government.

The exchange rate

Associated with the problems of inflation is the policy directed at managing the currency. Market economists would argue that the demand for the currency represents the willingness of foreign investors to hold UK currency at the cost of holding other currencies. The reason why investors would want to purchase UK currency depends on the the strength of the real sector of the economy, namely that the UK is producing goods for export which consumers want. If the inflation rate is rising and UK unit labour costs are rising faster than those of competitors it is likely that demand will fall, with exports falling as a result along with the demand for the currency. The value of sterling will fall making imports more expensive which in turn puts further pressures on inflation. UK households buying imported goods will find themselves paying more which means that living standards are threatened and workers will again seek to negotiate wage settlements to reflect changes in the costs of imports. Under these circumstances governments cannot ignore changes in the currency since steep devaluations are likely to increase the pressure on inflation and wage settlements. The only weapon available to government to influence changes in the currency is interest rates. The problem is that high interest rates policy has perverse effects elsewhere in the economy and eventually on the labour market.

Housing and mortgage tax relief

Mortgage tax relief policy reduces the market price of housing since mortgage payers are not paying the real rate of interest. Since mortgage tax relief reduces the price of housing, demand will increase leading to over-consumption in housing but also putting pressures on house prices. Increases in house prices also have an affect on wage settlements. If house prices are rising fast and households want to buy new houses at the higher prices they will seek to negotiate higher wage settlements to offset the increases in house prices. Changes in the level of mortgage tax relief therefore have the effect of increasing the demand for housing increasing prices and putting pressures on wages.

Increases in the rate of interest to deal with problems of the currency also affect house prices since any increase in interest rates increases the cost of housing for existing households which again puts pressures on wage settlements.

Macroeconomists would argue that policies on inflation, the exchange rate, and housing are all likely to have implications for wage settlements and the labour market.

Structural unemployment

Macroeconomists would therefore seek to make connections between the macroeconomic environment, wages and employment. The presence of structural unemployment represents a mismatch between the number of vacancies and skills available as registered by the unemployed. Macroeconomists point to continuous changes in the national economy, the process of change in Europe from heavy industry, coal mining, engineering and textiles to service industries in banking finance, insurance, and information technology. All these changes are brought about in a competitive world economy. Lags in the adjustment from manufacturing to service economies mean that there are likely to be problems of structural unemployment of workers with skills in textiles or coal mining, whose skills (at least in the short run) are likely to be made redundant. Macroeconomists would argue that such changes cannot be left to the labour market, but rather that government should have a general policy on training and investment in human capital. As bottlenecks appear for certain skills, including computing and information technology, courses to develop these skills will lag behind the market. In this context governments are seen as having a key role to play in providing funding for the development of new courses.

Labour mobility

Differential increases in house prices between different regions make labour mobility more difficult. Mortgage tax relief affects the labour market since workers who become unemployed in one part of the country find it increasingly difficult to sell their homes and move to parts of the country where there might be vacancies. Differential house prices between the north and south of England make it increasingly difficult for workers from the north to move south.

CONCLUSIONS

Market liberalism: agendas for government

The argument presented in this and the previous chapter was that the central focus is the concept of the rational individual able to make strategic choices. Market liberals are aware that there are three major factors which mitigate against the individual. First there is the arbitrary nature of government. Government in a market liberal society must therefore act within a framework of rules and procedures which govern the conduct of the state. A written constitution sets out clearly the rights of the individual and predicates the parameters for government. A second factor which hinders the rights of the individual citizen is the collective actions of vested interest groups which in combining together would deny access to the individual. The group interest is therefore in conflict with the interests of the individual. The third factor is the context of public policy: whether it is aimed at creating a better society by using the individual as the means to an end. In contrast market liberals would seek a policy process which is deontological, that is a policy which does not order the preferences of society but a set of public policies which enhance the rights of the individual in the wider social context.

In the previous chapter it was suggested that the process of markets reflects the process of rational individuals making choices as consumers and suppliers and meeting in the market place as equal and rational agents. However, it was also argued that the market could not be left to itself because of four major areas of market failure. Markets failed to address problems of externalities; the conflict between individual and societal interests in dealing with problems of the environment, pollution and global warming – can these be left to the market?; can market values be correctly imputed on the environment? Second, it was argued that spillovers between markets create situations where employers underinvest in the human capital of their labour force because labour is mobile and there is always the threat of poaching by other firms. The spillover factor therefore suggests that there will be underinvestment in training. Third, it was argued that there are areas which represent pure public goods such as parks and libraries where costs and benefits cannot be ascribed to an individual. Finally, it was suggested that market liberals are also concerned about income inequality because income might act as a barrier to entry denying individuals the right to promote their self-interest, to explore their abilities and talents, and to achieve their potential contribution to society. Income inequality therefore may result in economic inefficiency.

Utilising the concepts of rational individualism, supply and demand, and markets it was argued in this chapter that a theory of labour markets can be outlined to seek to explain the process of wage determination, employment and unemployment. The aim of this chapter was therefore to show that the tools and principles of market liberalism could be used to address specific economic problems. However, it was also pointed out that although market liberals are agreed on these general key concepts their analysis and interpretations tend to lead to two different forms of explanations of wage determination and employment. The micro and labour market economists have argued that wages and employment are determined in the market place, that government intervention, social concerns and collective action all influence the workings of the labour market. In contrast, the macro market economist is concerned with macroeconomic processes such as inflation, the exchange rate, the balance of payments, housing policy, and how these have a direct relationship on wages and employment; and that although inflation is an external variable, workers take the inflation process into account in making wage claims which are then based on separate arguments from those which might be applicable to the labour market.

The labour market economist would argue, therefore, that unemployment is voluntary in that society chooses between different priorities – that is between employment and social concern, between employment and the right to belong to trade unions, and between employment or employment protection. All these institutional, social and collective factors represent dilemmas for a society. Market liberals would therefore argue that if society seeks to make employment the priority then other considerations need to become less important.

An agenda for a liberal government drawn up by microeconomists would include the following:

Collective actions

Society has to choose between the rights and immunities of trade unions and the rights of access to the labour by the individual. The trade unions sector affects labour supply by making the labour supply wage inelastic –

trade union reforms would therefore make the unionised sector more responsive to price in the longer term. Government should reform trade unions to address the problem of labour markets and wages. The 1982 Trade Union Act and the 1984 and 1986 Acts, together with the final stages proposed in 1990, could be judged to be attempts by the Conservative government elected in 1979 to address the problem of collective action imposed by privileged interest groups on the labour market and to bring about a balance in industrial relations between the vested interests of trade union members, the rights of the individual and the rights of employers and government. Trade union membership in the UK has declined from a peak of 12 million members in 1975 to 9 million in 1990, which meant that over 50 per cent of the labour force were represented in collective agreements in the 1970s in contrast to under 40 per cent in the 1980s. Trade unions in the 1980s were increasingly involved in bargains which sought to provide long-term stability in industrial relations with secure production, pay related to productivity, no strike clauses and single union agreements. The period of the 1980s is sometimes described as the era of the new realism for trade unions, a period when they recognised that the prosperity of their members, stable employment, and wages increasingly depended on their members ensuring that they did not price themselves out of the market place.

Supply side economics

The labour market economists are also concerned with those aspects of public policy which would improve the supply side of the labour market. As has already been pointed out high levels of taxation influence the supply side because taxation actually reduces take-home pay and therefore reduces the price of labour. At higher levels of taxation less workers make themselves available to work. The aim to improve the supply side of the equation implies a policy which increases incentives to work where more people make themselves available and join the labour market. The rate of taxation and losses of benefits for families with children means that the poverty trap actually acts as a deterrent to employment. People who join the labour market are threatened by losses of many benefits such as free school meals, school clothing allowances and housing benefits. All these benefits are reduced sharply at the stage of people joining the labour market and the losses in benefits sometimes are not made up by earnings. Market economists would therefore argue that reducing the personal tax burden actually reduced the incidence of the poverty trap. Furthermore, market economists also favour a system of income support of families on low earnings – a form of income support which can only be claimed by those in work. To reduce the duration of job search and the rate of frictional unemployment market economists would favour the reduction of the rates of social security payments.

Reducing the rate of taxation therefore increases the price of labour without increasing the cost to the employer. Workers will therefore be getting a higher price for their labour which means that more workers would join the labour market. Workers who are on the margin of poverty are also helped by lower levels of personal taxation. In addition, reducing the burden on labour actually increases real wages so that workers feel more prosperous thereby easing wage pressures on employers and keeping unit wage costs competitive. Annual budgets in the UK since 1980 have been continuously used as the vehicle for reducing the levels of personal taxation from 33 per cent in 1979 to 25 per cent in 1988 with new targets of 20 per cent being set for the 1990s. The Conservative governments have argued that the reduction in unemployment in the 1980s can be attributed to their supply side policies. Higher rates of taxation have also been reduced from 83 per cent to 40 per cent.

According to labour market economists, therefore, government can reform the labour market in four critical ways:

1 reducing the duration of job search by reducing the rates of social security payments;
2 increasing labour supply by reducing personal taxation rates which would increase labour supply;
3 by reforming trade union immunities so that the supply side of the trade unions becomes more responsive to changes in price;
4 by removing wage councils and minimum wage legislation since these are likely to increase the price of labour on the employer thus resulting in an actual fall in the demand for labour.

The agenda for government by the macroeconomist is also an agenda for a market liberal government, but rather than putting the emphasis of liberalism on the labour market macroeconomists point to those aspects of government which represent political calculation and social considerations rather than the moral political economy of liberalism. So macro liberals are concerned with the impact mortgage tax relief has on employment and wages arguing that mortgage tax relief represents a subsidy on housing, encouraging overconsumption in housing and increasing demand and prices. Increased house prices actually fuel wage demands.

Macro market liberals would also want an economic policy which is directed by rules and procedures – a constitutional economic policy which removes the ability of government to conduct economic policy in the short term for political benefits. Liberal economists would therefore favour a central bank which is independent of the government able to conduct monetary policy according to strict rules by direct changes in the money supply, the rates of interest, and inflation. This role already exists with the German Bundesbank and the Federal Reserve Banks in the USA. Monetary policy should therefore be conducted according to rules rather than by the arbitrary decisions of government.

Equally, in dealing with exchange rate policy and interest rates governments should have a currency policy which is directed at inflation rather than a policy influenced by the special pleadings of exporters or importers. Governments should make clear what their exchange rate policy is directed at, providing a policy which is coherent with domestic inflation policy. Changes in the rate of interest as directed by an independent central bank represents a response to changes in the money supply. An anti-inflation policy directed by the central bank should therefore provide a coherent policy between domestic concern and exchange rate policies.

In the context of conducting macro policy according to explicit rules and procedures, workers and employers are treated as rational agents in the labour market. Rational expectations theorists suggest that if the government conducts a clear monetary policy workers would negotiate wage claims taking into consideration the government's commitments on inflation. A consistent monetary policy therefore means that governments would not accommodate wage increases by allowing for a lax monetary policy. Instead a tight monetary policy signals to employers and workers the government's commitments on inflation. Equally governments would not accommodate increases in wage demands by using interest rates to devalue the currency to protect exports. Instead the exchange rate policy is directed according to changes in the money supply.

The macro liberal economists put their emphasis on minimising the arbitrary nature of government in the conduct of economic policy. The nature of economic policy in a liberal environment should be conducted according to constitutional rules which means that government makes explicit their intentions on economic policy. This means that government expenditure should be financed through taxation rather than relying on borrowing so that voters receive a clear message of their opportunity costs between increased public services and less personal consumption. Therefore, in using their autonomy to increase the level of borrowing the government is seen as not conducting a clear macroeconomic policy but instead giving priority to social and political calculations.

The conduct of economic policy in the context of explicit rules provides a stable environment for the conduct of wage bargaining. The priority of government must be an explicit anti-inflation policy not accommodating to pressures on the money supply. A policy commitment on inflation should therefore be the context for rational agents to submit wage claims knowing that take-home pay is safeguarded without having to guess the expected rate of inflation.

   Although this chapter has sought to outline two market liberal interpretations of labour markets, wages and employment it was also argued that market liberals are agreed on the central axioms of rational individualism, supply and demand factors, and markets. It would seem that while market liberals are arguing that the levels of employment and wages are determined in the market place, macroeconomists are suggesting that governments must conduct a macroeconomic policy according to pre-set rules on government expenditure, government borrowing and monetary policy to minimise the influences of exogenous factors being imported into wage settlements and therefore employment. The main objective of policy should therefore be to create competitive labour markets where there is equal access with no barriers to entry. Employees as rational agents would attempt to forecast the rate of inflation and negotiate wages on these predictions, which means that wages would not reflect supply and demand factors and would therefore result in workers pricing themselves out of the market. According to the market macroeconomist, therefore, the government should conduct macro policy according to predictable rules.

   In contrast microeconomists are concerned with the presence of rigidities in the labour market. These obstacles include institutional factors, social considerations, and the effect of collective action on the labour market. Microeconomists would argue that each of these sets of factors are likely to influence the supply or demand side of the labour market. The flexibility of the labour market depends on the movement in prices to reflect changes in the demand and supply of labour. Intervention by government on rights against dismissal, national insurance, personal taxation, and minimum wages are all likely to increase the cost of labour which means that either employers would demand less labour because of the higher costs or that fewer workers would make themselves available for work because of the low price. The conduct of government should therefore be to create competitive labour markets where there is equal access for suppliers and consumers.

   In conclusion, it might be pointed out that the common theme for the micro and the macro market economists is their concern for the individual. Market liberals are therefore concerned about the nature of government and the position of vested interests in relation to the individual. At both the macro and the labour market levels governments and vested interests need to be brought into an environment of constitutionalism which guarantees the rights of the individual.

Chapter 4

The political implications of market liberalism

Harry Fineberg and Maurice Mullard

INTRODUCTION

Certain clear implications seem to arise for any government or any political party which bases its policy agenda on a market philosophy. As we have seen in the previous two chapters, a market model makes certain assumptions about human nature: the way individuals make decisions, the relationships between individual self-interest and the public interest. Market liberalism seems to prioritise certain preferences and desires as the fundamental motives for human action. These are concerned primarily with providing the self with pleasure and the avoidance of pain. It therefore implies that each individual is able to define preferences and interests autonomously. This approach builds upon the Lockian axiom of individual self-ownership and each individual is therefore an end rather than a means to an end. People, it is concluded,

> understand their own business and their own interest better, and care for them more, than the government does, or can be expected to do.
>
> (Mill, in Arblaster 1984: 30)

As we can see in this approach the individual's declaration of preferences is sovereign. The nature of liberal individualism is to question the role of institutions, and in particular political institutions, since these institutions are seen as assuming the role of identifying choices on behalf of individuals. Where political institutions make such assumptions from a market liberal perspective they are guilty of assuming a despotic authority over individual choices.

The twin concepts of individual rationality and the individual's right to choose imply that the priority of government must be to adopt a minimalist role, which means that liberal government should always adopt a policy of minimum taxation since any form of taxation is associated with coercion and replaces the right to choose from the individual to the state. High taxes will always be associated with the loss of individual freedom of choice, since the state is now assuming the role that it knows best – how income should be spent and on what preferences. Within the context of this approach the process of political intervention becomes problematic.

PROBLEMS OF THE POLITICAL MARKET

From the viewpoint of the market liberals the political process too easily becomes the mechanism for the conveying of excessive expectations, high taxes, bureaucratic decision-making and political parties seeking to outbid each other at election times (Brittan 1977). The process of democracy may therefore become part of the problem for authentic freedom of choice. Where politicians have to trade in votes in order to ensure election or re-election, promises are made in order to satisfy voters' interests through the political process. In other words, politics becomes an alternative method of satisfying the preferences of some at the expense of others. In this sense the political market place is different from the economic market because the former is likely to surrender to the pressures of powerful functional groups and majorities, often against the interests of the individual. The political market is therefore discriminatory as it reflects vested interests while the economic market has to respond to the individual consumer. The interests most likely to be responded to by government are those having the political knowledge, the time to organise, and the ability to exert the greater pressure. In contrast those interests not able to exercise sufficient strategic influence only experience costs as the result of this process and receive hardly any benefits. Those who lose out are seen as excluded from the rewards of the political market.

Among the losers identified by market liberals we can identify the individual consumer, the self-employed, the disorganised poor or low paid, and those who pay high taxes for little perceived benefit. The common element for the losers is that they do not readily belong to vested interests or strategically influential groups. Their relationship with government is as individuals, as citizens and as voters at election times. Their ability to influence the political process is therefore low in contrast to the influence of organised groups.

The democratic political process is seen as the location of conflicts over who gets what in terms of welfare programmes or public ownership. The contentious issue of the fair distribution of wealth becomes the focal point of the political process. Irresolvable arguments about the criteria of fairness and equity are used and manipulated in the battle between interest groups. The competition for votes among political parties will lead in effect to a process of bribing the voter or interest group.

When voters and interest groups enter the political process they lose any sense of what can be afforded by government and, furthermore, there is little concern as to who pays and who is likely to lose. There are no 'budget constraints' in operation since those who are exerting pressure are themselves not involved in costs. There are only two likely outcomes; the maintenance of existing privileges or the extension of those privileges.

Costs are disguised when political parties compete with each other for votes. Voters and interest groups are made to believe that government can do virtually everything to satisfy voters' preferences. False expectations are thus generated by the political process leading eventually to higher levels of taxation which adversely affect the productivity and efficiency of the economy.

In addition political parties will take good care to cater for the interests of their most reliable supporters as well as seeking to carve out new constituencies of support by making new promises to new groups. This process is what Krieger (1986) calls the process of threading together arithmetic majorities. There is no morality in this form of politics, since policy is not driven by ideas of individual well-being but by pure political arithmetic where the criterion is ensuring that sufficient majorities benefit from policies to deliver the next electoral victory.

Governments are tempted to synchronise their economic policies with the proximity of the next election. The process of the electoral business cycle suggests that governments will use certain economic levers to deliver favourable outcomes as the election approaches. Typical examples of the electoral business cycle would involve the reduction of personal taxation before an election or increases in pensions to the elderly or a fall in the rate of interest to alleviate the problems of mortgagors.

The problems with the electoral business cycle strategy is that the attempt to manipulate economic indicators in the short term might be actually harmful to economic management in the longer term. For example, market liberals took exception to the welfare politics epitomised in the American New Deal after 1933. The strategy of 'tax, spend, vote' was criticised by market liberals on the grounds that it would lead to a crippling burden of taxation on the individual and also on the wealth-creating private sector. Thomas Dewey stood against Roosevelt in the Presidential elections of 1936 on the basis of this criticism. The Roosevelt era became increasingly associated with welfare, public works and big government. Contemporary market liberals would argue that the levels of inflation experienced since the 1970s reflect the attempts by government to maintain high levels of public expenditure without increasing taxation. The outcome was for governments to increase deficits and therefore the money supply and inflation.

Market liberals are therefore suspicious of the form of government which seeks to reward organised interests, which is seen as a form of bribery targeted at specific constituents, and which manipulates the electoral cycle for short-term political gain. This form of politics distorts the idea of the individual right to choose; the right of the individual to be treated as end rather than as a means to an end. It is also a form of politics which harms the running of the economy by attracting excessive expectations which in turn result in big government, high levels of taxation, and inexorable rates of growth in public expenditure.

THE CLASSICAL MODEL OF THE MINIMAL STATE

By considering the role of the state and politics in the classical age of market liberalism (1780–1850) we can reconstruct an ideal model of what a market-orientated politics should look like.

The first point to be made is that such a state should be minimal in its actions and should be absent from a wide range of activity. One classical liberal expressed the position in the following way, 'Government should interfere as little as possible...to remove prohibitions and protections' (Hume, in Greenleaf 1983: 30).

Statements are made by nineteenth-century liberals concerning

> the need to allow capital to find its most lucrative course, commodities their fair price, industry and intelligence their natural rewards...by maintaining peace, by defending property, by diminishing the price of law and by observing strict economy in every department of the state.
>
> (Macaulay, in Greenleaf 1983: 31)

To suggest that it is the responsibility of government to provide employment for those able to work is 'a most dangerous doctrine to advance'. Similarly, any attempt to control wages and prices by law would create artificial scarcity and 'state despotism'. While there might be a moral case for protecting young children from the excesses of factory life, the state had no right to interfere with the freedom of adult labour. Nor should government be directly involved in producing goods it needs, for it would only reveal its incompetence in such matters and increase unnecessary expenditure (Greenleaf 1983).

There was also opposition to political interference with the length of the working day, the setting up of a Public Board of Health, and to state involvement in education (Greenleaf 1983). All these developments were seen as undermining personal responsibility, individual free choice and the entire principle of self-ownership. There was a danger, it was thought of the individual becoming a client dependent on the state as a child depends on the parent.

THE MINIMALIST STATE AND THE IMPLICATIONS FOR PUBLIC POLICY

While there is general agreement among market liberals about the absolute need for the state to stay outside of economic activity, there is some disagreement as to whether the same principle of absence would apply to social issues such as education, public health, transport and housing. The position taken seems to depend on whether these areas are regarded as commodities which could therefore be subject to market forces or whether they should be regarded as public goods.

Adam Smith for example, believed that the state had a responsibility to maintain certain public works and institutions which are necessary but whose costs exceed any profit the private individual may gain from making such provision. These public works included roads, bridges, canals, and harbours. They are all necessary for the carrying on of trade but when left to private persons are often inadequately administered and maintained. Most interestingly, Smith insists that education should be regarded as a public institution provided by general taxation, for such education would guarantee public order and social peace (Smith 1988: Bk 5). We shall return to the difficult issue of social order in relation to market individualism in a later section.

In contrast to the flexible individualism as presented by Adam Smith there is the ultra-minimalist individualism of Herbert Spencer where we find an insistence that the state has no responsibility to provide a public sewerage system, to control rabies, vaccinate the population against infectious disease, provide an education system, run the postal service, make the coinage of the realm, or prevent cruelty to children. According to Spencer therefore, the state as presented by Adam Smith is actually a redistributive and intrusive state.

Spencer's is an extreme formulation and most market liberals would draw the line at his totally absent state, accepting some modified version of Smith's position. The issue remains, however, of where market forces may operate in the social sphere and current debates about increasing consumer choice in education and health clearly indicate that market liberals are uneasy about state domination of social provision. Ideally there would be a significant move towards private provision in these areas, gradually reducing state involvement and expenditure. The same argument goes for the contentious area of income maintenance. At one extreme is Spencer's position of total abolition of all Poor laws on the grounds that they weakened the individual's capacity to compete and struggle according to the extent of their natural powers.

The 1834 Poor Law Amendment Act saw a methodical attempt by a market liberal state to remove restrictions in the development of a more flexible labour market and to cut the costs of poor relief. Contemporary market liberals including Minford (1983) have, for example, argued that the expansion of social security payments contributed to the rise in unemployment in the later 1970s and the 1980s. The improvements in benefits have allowed for individuals to spend a longer duration involved in job search. Minford has advocated a reduction of 10 to 20 per cent in the payments of benefits as a way of reducing unemployment. These contemporary ideas continue and expand the strategy of the 1834 Poor Law. The concern is still the individual pursuing self-interest, taking responsibilities and encouraging self-help. Any form of state intervention actually leads to forms of dependency. More recently, David Green (1990) has questioned whether governments should be concerned with the issue of equality and the attempt to redistribute income since this form of state intervention is likely to harm the freedom of the individual.

The culture of dependency represents a problem for market liberals at two levels. First, market liberals are concerned with a context in which the primary concern of government is catering for a series of vested interests through public provision. The continuing massive involvement of government in income maintenance sustains a political arena in which powerful interests seek to exert pressure on the political process to win ever greater provision for their client groups funded out of general taxation. From this perspective poverty lobbies and trades unions have a vested interest in expanding these arenas. Finding a way of significantly reducing government involvement in the area of income maintenance remains elusive for market liberals.

The second concern is the one echoed by Brittan (1977), Rose and Peters (1979), and others who have argued that one major consequence of democracy is the increase in expectations created by parties seeking to outbid each other at election times and then when becoming the government actually failing to deliver these expectations. The problem of increased expectations is that it adds pressures on government to resolve the problem and that the process of increased politicisation is seen as endangering the survival of liberal democracy.

On the question of where to set the limits for government intervention a relentless individualism such as that outlined by ultra-minimalists has the advantage of consistency. All interventionist legislation is perceived as being wrong, simply because it emanates from government. When Cobden supported some of this legislation but opposed the rest he was opening the door to other arguments for intervention. If exceptions are allowed to the general rule of non-intervention then market liberals must seek consistency about the grounds on which they allow such exceptions. Also the introduction of market choice into the arena of public goods funded out of general taxation is fraught with contradictions, and even long-standing market liberals have argued recently that the government's attempts to create an internal market in the national health service is simply not viable.

Whatever the difficulties implied by the public goods issue it is clear that market liberalism demands the withdrawal of government from a range of interventions. The politician is not to be trusted with using the taxes of private individuals to make decisions on behalf of those individuals. Market liberals would prefer the conduct of government through a series of rules and procedures. Constitutional government is a means for ensuring the rights of the individual against the arbitrary nature of government. The written Constitution guarantees the rights of the individual and limits the powers of government. All government actions are therefore conducted within the context of the law. The Constitution sets the boundary between the government and the individual and also sets the parameters for government intervention. Obviously the Constitution is not a static document since there are likely to be constant revisions to the boundaries between the rights of the individual and government, but at least that revision takes place in a public debate. The Constitution also ensures the separation of powers to avoid central direction and avoids putting too much discretion at the disposal of the centralist state. The separation of powers means that the government at the centre has to share powers with local government, regional authorities and also state authorities. The rights of the individual are therefore to be guaranteed by taking powers away from central government and for central government to be forced to share powers with local authorities.

Market liberals would also suggest that the conduct of economic policy should be set according to a series of rules and procedures. Market liberals such as Buchanan have argued, for example, that the trillion dollar expansion of the budget deficit in the USA in the 1980s represent an abuse of powers by President Reagan. Market liberals, while supporting the tax reforms of President Reagan as confirming his administrations commitment to the 'supply side' economics they had advocated also criticised the Reagan administration for their failure to reduce public expenditure by similar amounts. However, because the government was also trying to please the budget maximisers and the voters, the government as usual took the easy option of relying on the budget deficit – a burden to be faced by future generations. Market liberals have therefore argued that the level of the budget deficit should be written into the Constitution. The Gramm Rudman amendment to the Constitution in 1984 has set a series of targets for the government to reduce their deficits through the mechanisms of the Constitution.

INDIVIDUALISM AND THE END OF THE ARISTOCRATIC CONSTITUTION

The language of individualism is not simply concerned with issues of economic efficiency or freedom of economic choice. It emerged from the struggles against traditional monopolies of power and wealth largely expressed through aristocratic high church and military values. Cobden as a classical free trade liberal thus referred to the English aristocratic constitution as a thing of monopolies and church-craft and sinecures armorial hocus-pocus, primogeniture and Pageantry!

(Greenleaf 1983: 39)

Cobden here sums up the targets for nineteenth-century liberalism – in particular the social and political dominance of the aristocracy and the Anglican Church and the privileges which attached to them. Their control of government and education was seen as a major obstacle to peace and progress. The campaign against the Corn Laws and the campaign for the secularisation of education were seen by free market liberals as a way of challenging the aristocratic constitution. In the words of one historian,

Prime targets were the universities, the public schools, the professions, the armed forces, colonial administration, the civil establishments patronage machine, the corporations, the old poor law and the criminal law.... Above all Whig and Radical attack focussed on the Church.

(Clark 1985: 412)

Liberal reformers were aiming at the destruction of what has been called a 'unitary society, a confessional State' (Clark 1985), held together by the political culture of the monarchy and aristocracy in Parliament and cemented by exclusive allegiance to the Anglican confession. Ideally, this wider reform programme should have resulted in the disestablishment of the Church of England, the abolition of the House of Lords and the monarchy, and the ending of discrimination on religious and other grounds, the creation of a secular educational system and of a free market in land.

The universal adoption of free trade was seen as the best guarantee of international peace for it would create a common interest between countries

thrusting aside the antagonism of race, and creed, and language, and uniting us in the bonds of eternal peace.

(Cobden, in Greenleaf 1983: 37)

Consequently, free trade liberals of the classical period draw on an Enlightenment tradition totally opposed to colonial and imperial adventures and glory seeking. Empires were regarded as distortions of free trade relations and were also morally indefensible. The imperialist mentality as the product of the corrupt aristocratic ethos was being challenged at home. Irrational passions such as the pursuit of national and imperial glory were to be replaced by a global economic interdependence making war the most irrational of actions. The spread of *laissez-faire* and free trade practice would lead to the replacement of these irrationalities by peace based upon a mutual recognition of rational interests.

THE POLITICAL AGENDA FOR A MARKET LIBERAL STATE

Market liberalism and the economy

Proposal 1 There should be no intervention by the government in the economy – the central role of government is the control of inflation since government is the main source for the control of the money supply. Government should conduct economic policy according to 'announced' rules, rules on the money supply and interest rates, rules on the government deficit, rules on the separation of the central bank from government economic policy.

Proposal 2 Government should not seek to influence the level of employment since this is determined in the market for goods and services. It is the willingness of consumers to purchase goods that will decide the level of employment and wages. Government should limit its role to removing obstacles in the labour market such as the impact of trade unions on access to the labour market and the presence of racial and sexual discrimination. Governments should take responsibility towards investing in human capital.

Proposal 3 Government should not seek to direct investment or to pick what might be perceived to be essential industries or winners in the economy. Levels of investment should be influenced by market forces according to decentralised decisions by firms rather than bureaucratic direction.

Proposal 4 The central purpose of a market liberal government is to reduce the scope of government and the rates of taxation which are seen as a form of coercion. Since the individual knows best, the level of taxation should be set at a minimum, thus allowing the individual to decide how to prioritise choices and preferences. The concern with the distribution of income and poverty should be limited to government redirecting income to these groups rather than government providing the service. The aim is always to give the individual choice – either through negative income tax, vouchers to buy education, vouchers to purchase training and loans for higher education courses.

Proposal 5 A market liberal must always be against any form of subsidy since this is likely to distort the real market price and also reinforce a preference to a special interest. Such subsidies include mortgage tax relief which is seen as having distorted the housing market, encouraging over-consumption in housing and overinvestment in housing at the cost of investment in industry; it is also a source of inflation. Subsidies to key industries such as coal also distort the market for energy with consumers using too much coal at the cost of the environment. Subsidies therefore result in the misuse and misallocation of resources because consumers and suppliers are not indicating the real costs. Subsidies also create league tables of groups which are dependent on the subsidy and therefore have a vested interest in the maintenance of the *status quo*.

Proposal 6   A market liberal must be concerned with the enforcement of contracts. The right of individuals to pursue self-interest means that individuals must have the right to enter contracts as equals and be treated as equals. This means that any imbalance between consumers and suppliers has to be regulated. A market liberal government must therefore perform a regulatory role ensuring that consumers rights are protected. The government acts as a regulator rather than the provider in a market liberal society. Government as regulator ensures that contracts are held as legally binding between equals. The privatisation of electricity, gas, water and telecommunications in Britain during the 1980s shifted these major industries from being public to private monopolies. In each of these industries the government has created a regulatory agency including OFGAS, OFTEL, the Regulator of the Water Industry and Electricity. All these regulators have a brief to ensure that contracts between individual consumers and the monopoly suppliers are delivered.

Markets and the problem of order

For the market liberal the problem of social order is not a cause of great concern. A society will become orderly and peaceful with the growth of economic interdependence. As individuals realise that their interests are best served through the myriad processes of market exchange, it will simply not make rational sense to allow disorderly irrational passions to dominate their behaviour. Internal strife, like war, destroys trade. As individuals come to realise that their prospects depend upon trade and market exchange, they will subordinate these irrational and destructive passions to the peaceful process of individual calculation of their interests. In Smith's words,

> Give me that which I want, and you shall have this which you want...and it is in this manner that we obtain from one another the far greater part of those good offices which we stand in need of. It is not from the benevolence of the butcher, the brewer, or the baker that we expect our dinner, but from their regard to their own interest.

> (Smith 1935)

Smith in this famous extract, summaries the optimistic expectations held by classical market liberals of the pacifying potential of market exchange and the calculation of interest. Others took the view that a commercially minded society would need only minimal supervision of individual behaviour. It would be a tolerant society as regards the variety of opinion and would be characterised by voluntary co-operation. For Smith, who elsewhere regretted the passing of aristocratic values, remarked on how

> commerce and manufactures gradually introduced order and good government, and with them, the liberty and security of individuals among the inhabitants of the country, who had before lived almost in a continual state of war with their neighbours and servile dependency upon their superiors.

> (Smith 1935)

A market economy based on calculation of interest will also constrain despotic government for no politician has the capacity to comprehend and successfully manipulate such a delicate and complex mechanism. All that is required is the legal protection of private property and enforcement of contractual obligations. The rest can be left to the market.

As has already been suggested, market liberals are concerned about the arbitrary powers of government and other vested interest groups. To redress the relationship between the government and the individual, market liberals see the written constitution with a bill of rights and decentralised forms of decision-making as the best way of protecting the rights of the individual, while also providing the framework for individuals to pursue self-interest. In dealing with the problems of those who seek to combine together into groups which mitigate against and exclude others, market economists would argue that it is the commitment of government to competition policy, the regulation of monopoly groups and interests which are likely to end these discriminatory practices. It is the competitive market place which ensures access to individuals as equals.

There is, however, a different and equally influential group of arguments which question the optimism of the market liberals in relation to the question of order. This group of thinkers, although committed to ideas of individualism in the economic market place will not necessarily accept that such principles can be transferred to the questions of order and government. The conservative sees the destruction of traditional forms of authority and belief as the central problem. There is little faith in the general pacifying qualities of the market. Conservatives and market liberals will find a strategic common ground in their contemporary hostility to the collectivist state but for different reasons. For the market liberal such a state threatens to remove individual liberty and freedoms of all kinds. For the Conservative however, such a state – in allowing the public conflict of interest and the making of open ended claims upon the state – will lead to a weakened and internally divided nation and reduction in the authority of government.

Hobbes and social order

In some respects the conservative position can usefully be described as Hobbesian in so far as the problem of order is seen as more important than the problem of personal freedom. For Hobbes civil strife and disorder are the results of uncontrolled passionately held beliefs which are allowed to intrude into the conduct of public affairs. Extreme and inflexible positions are taken and reasonable solutions become impossible. Only by prioritising cautious self-interest and subordinating irrational beliefs can this threat to social peace be avoided. In taking this view Hobbes seems closer to classical market liberals than to the conservative view. However, whereas the market liberal believes the psychology of self-interest will transform society spontaneously as markets and trade develop, Hobbes has no such faith in human nature. Individuals have to be persuaded to be cautious in their actions. It is the state's task to create and sustain order. People must be taught the priority of self-preservation and the need to calculate and benefit from each action. Human nature left to itself in Hobbes's view will be irrational. In Hobbesian terms rationality needs to be taught. Rational self-interest therefore is something inculcated by the state. It is this process which leads individuals to accept the necessity of a strong sovereign who guarantees peace and stability. The resulting individual would be fearful, cautious and disinclined to actions involving high risks. A society made up of such individuals will then not be inclined to form irrational factions. Thus, if people may be persuaded that property interests are more important than the pursuit of irrational beliefs, then a more careful, peaceful society will emerge. People must be encouraged to put their energies into their private interests and lives and to leave public affairs to the sovereign. The emphasis is therefore placed upon the creation of the obedient subject. The state is entitled to exercise sanctions against those who insist upon promoting public dispute. It will also guarantee social peace in exchange for obedience in public life.

Hobbes and modern conservatism

There are differences between Hobbes and the conservative view. The latter does not trust self-interest alone to secure order. On the contrary, the expression of interests may produce a new form of social disorder, unless they are kept in the private sphere. This may necessitate the imposition of restraint on democracy which often acts to represent conflicting interests in the public sphere. Conservatism will therefore put greater emphasis upon certain forms of identity through which the individual is reconciled and attached to the prevailing social order. A particularly important role is to be played by traditional institutions which are seen as providing identity, moral guidance and leadership. The individual is not seen as some autonomous calculating machine, motivated purely by pleasure and pain, but a person whose being is expressed through those institutions which have proved themselves viable in history. Parents must use their power and authority for the good of their children who by definition feel helpless in the family context:

> And it is a similar recognition of constraint, helplessness and subjection to external will that heralds the citizen's realisation of his membership of society; in this recognition love of one's country is born.
>
> (Scruton 1984: 32)

The implication here is that order can only be guaranteed through childlike submission to historically legitimate authority and through the recognition of binding moral ties. The relationship between the individual and the state is similar to that of the family – it is born out of love, of the individual for the state. This has to be contrasted to the market liberal and Hobbesian views of contractual relationships between the state and individual self-interest. The question which arises is not what does the state do for me, an instrumental calculation; but rather what I can do for the state, a state which continuously gives me identity and a sense of belonging.

Moral and emotional attachments are associated with a particular culture, country, history or way of life. Each national culture has its own way of doing things which, however incomprehensible to outsiders, has meaning and significance for those born into it and it is the primary duty of its members to preserve its uniqueness. There are no objective universal truths or standards by which each national culture can be evaluated. Family, church, nation, tradition, national history; these are the institutions which give meaning, identity and psychological integration to persons. The notion of the autonomous individual is regarded as unsatisfying and historically unreal. The conservative implicitly asks the market liberal, 'Of what use is individual freedom if you do not know where you belong?'.

The conservative is particularly concerned that the key institutions of society should perform their roles effectively. Where, therefore, the traditional family is being increasingly eroded by social and cultural change, this is a legitimate matter of concern and basis for policy intervention. One-parent families for example undermine traditional notions of authority. In particular they dispense with the role of the father. While market liberals are concerned with gender discrimination in the labour market and argue that all persons should be treated as equal individuals, this seems to conflict with conservative views of the family and the location of women in the family.

Where the established church is failing to give the correct moral lead in areas of personal conduct, this too is a matter for government intervention. Changes in the cultural identity of the population may be seen as weakening the cohesion and uniqueness of the national culture and again government must concern itself with resolving this problem. In dealing with the question of emigration and immigration, market liberals are concerned with the impact of such movements of people on labour supply and the labour market. The problem for a conservative becomes a crisis of national identity, a crisis of who belongs to the national community and who therefore is a citizen, and who, by definition, is to be excluded from the rights conferred on the citizen.

From a conservative viewpoint private property has to be protected not because, as for the market liberal, it is an essential pre-condition for individual freedom and wealth creation but because it provides security, stability and a private familiar world of order and meaning. It is thus closely linked to the conservative emphasis on the family. The more widely private property is spread the more secure and stable that society will be. It is therefore a priority for a conservative to widen the ramparts of property ownership.

A sharp contrast exists between market liberals and conservatives on the issue of property and the franchise. Market liberals would argue that democracy leads to increased expectation of government and therefore seek to restrict the role of government by suggesting that the protection of property is central to the protection of individual freedom In contrast the conservative unease about democracy stems from the fear that the new democracy would create social disorder. The legitimacy of government does not depend on the electoral process but on the ability of government to guarantee the desired objectives of order and stability.

CONCLUSIONS

The state in conservative thinking as in that of Hobbes, must not allow its authority to be questioned and undermined by being drawn into the world of competing vested interests. For one conservative at least that has been a major mistake of the modern collectivist state,

> The state has the authority, the responsibility and the despotism of parenthood. If it loses these ties then it must perish, and society along with it. The state must therefore withdraw from every economic arrangement which puts it at the absolute mercy of individual citizens.... Through the vast and rampant civil service, through local government, through nationalised industry, through all the advisory bodies and meddlesome councils that surround it, the government disperses its power among ignorant multitudes.
>
> (Scruton 1987: 111)

Here again is the peculiarity of the Hobbesian order discourse finding common policy grounds with the market liberal freedom discourse but for very different and opposite reasons. For the order discourse the state must withdraw from large areas of economic and social management so that it may avoid the dilution of its own authority and status. For the market liberal however, the state must depart because it will use its power to limit and erode individual freedom. How much for example, the Conservative Governments of the 1980s are market liberal or 'Hobbesian' in their hostility to state economic management, how much their concerns are to do with freedom or order, are matters to be taken up in Chapter 11. We can say that the conservative is primarily concerned with the strength and authority of the state rather than with individual freedom or economic efficiency. In the conservative discourse there is no place for utopias of international peace based on the interdependence of trade and markets. Politics and statecraft are essential to the expression and preservation of the national identity. This may even lead in certain situations to the deliberate use of war as a fundamental arm of national policy.

While the Hobbesian conservative wishes to see the state not making itself vulnerable in the role of economic management it is clear there is an interventionist role to play on matters relating to the maintenance of order – for example the enforcement of law and policing, moral leadership on family life, the security of the state and the cultural or racial definition of the national community in which minorities must give way to the cultural majority. All these areas of intervention are unacceptable to the consistent market liberal who would regard them as gross interferences with the rights of individuals and of how they should live. It is unclear therefore to what extent the discourses of individual freedom and national order can be reconciled either in theory or political practice.

Chapter 5

The economics of Keynes and Keynesianism

INTRODUCTION: THE MEANING OF KEYNESIANISM

In 1984, reflecting on both the fiftieth anniversary of the publication of Keynes's *General Theory of Employment* and the impact that the economics of Keynes had on the thinking of other economists and also of government, Lord Kaldor suggested that,

> Nearly 50 years after its [*General Theory*] appearance controversy still rages around its basic ideas and prescriptions, and I do not think that any major economist in the West would regard the issues raised by Keynes as finally settled.
>
> (Lord Kaldor 1984: 1)

The significance of Keynes needs to be judged at two levels. First, there is a need to evaluate Keynes at the intellectual level – the relevance of Keynes and the impact of his ideas on the subject of economics; and second, the influence that his prescriptions had on the policy-makers. Lord Kaldor has come to the conclusion that Keynes and the issues he raises are still controversial today. It is that ability of Keynes to raise questions which still create debate and argument, together with the attempt to influence the direction of policy, which makes his contribution a watershed both at the intellectual and practical levels.

In seeking to outline what can be described as a Keynesian model of the economy and the likely implications for economic policy-making, this and the succeeding two chapters do not make any claim for settling either some or any of the issues which Kaldor acknowledges. These chapters, therefore, do not aim to be a definitive interpretation of what Keynes said or what he meant to say. The task here is much more limited in scale and ambition. The aim is confined to an attempt at exploring what can be described as a Keynesian model which in itself is no easy exercise. Not all those who declare themselves to be Keynesians are necessarily agreed as to what central principles constitute a Keynesian model. The purpose of the three chapters is, then, to adopt the same approach as that adopted in the sections which dealt with the market model – that is, to thread together themes that can be identified to be the home domain of a Keynesian perspective and to apply the principles of Keynes to the specific economic issues of unemployment and inflation and finally to outline both the political and policy implications that derive from a Keynesian perspective.

The approach will be: first to provide an outline of a Keynesian model; second, to apply the model to specific economic issues; and third to derive the political implications of the model. This chapter is therefore concerned with exploring what might be defined as the core assumptions associated with a Keynesian model, then utilising these core assumptions as tools to explain how economies are supposed to work and the implications of the Keynesian model for policy-making. Chapter 6 then concentrates on the specific economic issues of labour markets, wages and employment – problems which were dealt with from a market perspective in the previous chapters – and to ask what contributions Keynesians made to explain these issues, and then to explain how and why a Keynesian perspective differs and challenges the views of market liberalism. Finally, Chapter 7 deals with the political implications of a Keynesian model.

The problem in constructing a Keynesian model is that such an exercise will always either ignore or attempt to homogenise some major and very important differences and areas of disagreements between economists who see themselves as Keynesian or post-Keynesians (Arestis and Skouras 1985). The problem in outlining a model as a vehicle for learning and discovery is, however, likely to emphasise the departures from market economics. Therefore, two points need to be made at the outset. First, that the construction of a general model as developed in these chapters is likely to be partial and also likely to emphasise differences from other Keynesian models. The problem is that there may be as many Keynesian models as they are Keynesians. As Harcourt has suggested,

> I certainly do not think that the approaches that come under this heading though they provide important and substantial insights, have yet reached a coherent steady-state ... the people who come under this umbrella (Keynesians) are a heterogeneous lot, sometimes only combined by a dislike of orthodox or neoclassical economics.
>
> (Harcourt 1985: 125)

The second point is that the Keynesian model as defined here does not aim to ascertain whether Keynesian economics represents a continuation of market economics. In dealing with the economics of Keynes the aim is to evaluate what contribution, if any, Keynes makes to market economics or the extent Keynes represents a major departure. Furthermore, there is no attempt to construct a synthesis between market and Keynesian economics. Instead the aim is to explore those aspects of Keynesian economics which seem to represent both a watershed and a departure in the world of economics and also politics. In this sense the following chapters tend to follow more in the traditions of Keynes himself. Keynes wanted to claim that his work sought to demonstrate major flaws in the assumptions associated with classical (market) economics and that his major ambition was to replace classical economics with a superior alternative:

> I shall argue that the postulates of classical theory are applicable to a special case only and not to the general case, the situation which it assumes being a limiting point of the possible positions of equilibrium. Moreover the characteristics of the special case assumed by the classical theory happens not to be those of the economic society in which we actually live.
>
> (Keynes 1971: 3)

According to Keynes, therefore, his theory could not accommodate the postulates of market economics because these did not even actually exist in reality. Instead his major aim was to show that his theory was closer to reality and had therefore to replace a body of knowledge which did not address the observed world. Keynesian economics was to be presented as a paradigm which competed with the existing market liberal ways of seeing and interpreting the world. Market liberal and Keynesian discourses were therefore incommensurate because they interpreted the world in different ways and because they were incommensurate it was not possible to accommodate both theories – in the Kuhnian sense these paradigms represented different languages. Keynesianism represented a challenge to the existing paradigm of market liberalism. A paradigm shift represented a break with one way of thinking and one way of seeing the world, and replaced these ways of seeing and interpreting the world according to the Keynesian paradigm.

In emphasising the areas of controversy and disagreement, the Keynesian model can be constructed as a separate and alternative way of seeing the world. Keynesianism represents a discursive society with a different series of beliefs which seek to challenge and replace the conventional wisdom of market economics. Keynesian discourse is associated with the argument that markets cannot be left to themselves, that markets do not clear and that prices do not adjust according to supply and demand.

Keynesianism represents more than simply agreement with the writings of Keynes, it reflects the political alliance of those who seek an interventionist role for government in the conduct of economic policy. Keynesianism represents an agenda for government against the centrality of individualism, the constitutional perspective of rules and procedures and the dominance of competitive markets associated with market liberals. A Keynesian discourse equivalent to market liberalism can be interpreted as the attempt to embark on a revolution which is both at the intellectual and practical levels as important as all other revolutions. Keynesians aim to persuade and mobilise the economics world in order to shift the thinking of departments of economics away from market economics and towards the research programme of Keynesian economics. However, if Keynesians are to be successful they, like the market liberals, have to persuade the political practioners and senior civil servants involved in the policy-making process. The Keynesian revolution represents a challenge and an attempt to displace the thinking of market economists both in the world of economics and politics. Like the market liberals, Keynesians offer an intellectual and a political agenda for government. Keynesians are also in the business of winning hearts and minds for their vision of the world and to make their novel paradigm the conventional wisdom.

THE CHALLENGE OF KEYNES

At the general level the essence of Keynesian economics is to explain the problems of disequilibrium and to justify intervention by government in economic policy. The main argument presented by Keynes in the *General Theory* was that the theory of equilibrium which is central to market economics only represented one possibility in economic outcomes and that this position of equilibrium did not necessarily mean that the economy was operating at full capacity employing all resources effectively. Furthermore, the theory of markets did not apply to all aspects of the economy.

Skidelsky in his *The End of a Keynesian Era* wrote,

> He [Keynes] had, seemingly, bequeathed to politicians the economic equivalent of the Philosophers Stone – the ability to turn slumps into booms and so create general and permanent abundance for the first time in history...and his name deserves to be given to an era which created at any rate the 'possibility of civilisation' for the people of the West.
>
> (Skidelsky 1977: 1)

Skidelsky suggests that Keynes not only offered governments the context for intervention in national economies but also a form of international Keynesianism for them to intervene strategically to ensure that the prosperity and welfare of societies were guaranteed. Rather than accepting a limited role for government as suggested by the market economists, Keynesians argued that the role of government needed to be extended. The idea of leaving markets to themselves, of not being able to influence the external pressures of the market place, needed to be replaced by the idea that the market place could be influenced so that government could offer hope rather than resignation:

> the period from the early 1950s to 1973 must be rated the greatest and most stable boom in world history. That period covered the flowering

of the post war international economic order of which Keynes was a principal architect.

(Williamson 1984: 87)

Keynesians argued that the markets could be reformed. Markets did not produce optimal outcomes, yet governments were always in a better position to analyse these outcomes and embark on policies which produced better results. The market liberal argument – that in the long-term markets would find their own equilibrium – was not a solution to people's daily lives:

> But this long run is a misleading guide to current affairs. In the long run we are all dead. Economists set themselves too easy, too useless a task if in the tempestuous season they can only tell us that when the storm is long past the ocean is flat again.

(Keynes 1971: IV, 65)

The argument that at the end of the day markets would adjust at some level did not offer any objective criteria for evaluating the conduct of economic policy. According to Joan Robinson there has always been a discrepancy between history and the theory of equilibrium. The observed rates of unemployment in the 1920s and early 1930s, wild fluctuations in unemployment in the 1890s and 1900s and the levels of unemployment in the 1980s all represent different histories of unemployment, yet within each of those periods the levels of unemployment and duration of unemployment were different. The unemployment of the 1920s was concentrated in certain industries, especially those industries directed at export markets. During the decade of the 1920s the number registered as unemployed was always above the 1 million mark, some 18 per cent of the total labour force. Unemployment reached its peak of 3 million in 1929. The argument that the markets would adjust in the long run was not of much use to those who were out of work; neither was such a prediction helpful to the government and the country. The country had lost out with output being lower while capacity had been left idle. Furthermore, the government had lost revenue from personal taxation contributions and national insurance which meant that public services including education services were actually curtailed during this period. The market solution to the problems of unemployment in the 1980s also seems to be in the long run. Unemployment rose steeply from 1.3 million in 1979 to a peak of 3.2 million in 1982. Unemployment remained at over 3 million until 1987 – a much longer duration this time than in the 1920s – and in 1990 unemployment is again on the increase. So for over a decade in the 1980s registered unemployment has not fallen below 2 million. It is in this context that Keynesians question the discrepancy of history and the theory of equilibrium. The theory of markets and the flexible price mechanism do not offer indicators as to when and how markets will clear.

According to the rational expectations view, rational agents have perfect information and are able to predict the relationships between supply and demand. Keynesians argue that the rational expectations school 'fail' to explain the lag between unemployment duration and the time it takes for labour markets to clear. Why are rational agents not responding with the same level of flexibility as is forecast by the theory? Keynesians have therefore criticised market liberals at the level of assumptions about the rational individual – that economy theory founded on the concept of rational agents responding to flexible prices in perfect competitive markets was crucially flawed. Markets do not clear perfectly in the short run and government intervention can therefore make a significant contribution for quite a while.

In contrast, Keynesians have constructed their economic analysis on theories of groups or class interests, on the presence of monopoly and price mark-ups, and on the concept of rigid wages and price stickiness as opposed to individual interests, markets and flexible prices. In this context Keynesians do not see their economics as a branch of market economics but an economics which represents a departure and which is qualitatively different. The challenge of Keynes to market liberalism includes:

1 A challenge to market liberal assumptions.
2 A rejection of the economics of scarcity.
3 A role for government in economic management.

A challenge to market liberal assumptions

The Keynesian challenge to market liberal principles occurs at two levels. First, Keynesians want to criticise the notion of rational individualism by arguing that decisions are fraught with continuous problems of uncertainty and risk factors. While market economists would argue that these problems are minimised through the process of having better informed individuals, Keynesians suggest that risk and uncertainty have direct repercussions on the assumptions for the ability of the market to clear. Second, Keynesians also want to argue that markets do not clear because of the presence of price mark-ups in the goods market, wage stickiness in the labour market, and the discrepancies between the intentions of savers and borrowers in the money market.

A rejection of the economics of scarcity

This is the argument that economics represents a series of resources constraints and opportunity costs and that market economics representing the accommodation of unlimited demand and limited resources should be challenged. Keynesian economics explores the possibility of changing the levels of 'effective demand' as the way of breaking out of the scarce resources syndrome associated with market economics. Market economists are accused of not offering a strategy for growth and prosperity. Market economics is concerned with explaining what *is*.

A role for government in economic management

The discovery of effective demand points to problems of equilibrium between levels of effective demand and potential economic capacity. Keynesians explore the possibility that economic capacity can outstrip effective demand which in Keynesians economics represents a deflationary gap – a context of unused resources. Equally, there is the possibility that effective demand would outstrip economic capacity which means that the levels of demand would create an inflationary gap. Both in the contexts of a deflationary or inflationary gap government could conduct an economic policy which influenced the levels of effective demand.

KEYNESIANS: THE CHALLENGE TO MARKET PRINCIPLES

The market model in general

Market economists argue that because we are rational agents we continuously make decisions as consumers, as suppliers of goods and services, and as investors and savers. As rational individuals we meet in the goods market, the labour market, and markets for investment and savings. Each market works according to the processes of supply and demand; each market obeys the price mechanism; and each market adjusts around an equilibrium price and quantity. The goods market determines the price and quantity of goods to be produced which in turn determines the levels of employment and wages. The demand for money is described as being stable because it represents the number of transactions in the good markets. Savers and investors meet around the rate of interest. Savings are influenced by the rate of interest, savers increasing savings if interest rates are high in contrast to investors whose investment decisions are inversely in relation to the rate of interest.

The problems of risk and uncertainty

The first challenge that Keynesians make against the market model is related to the twin issues of risk and uncertainty. Market economists are accused of relying on a narrow concept of rational agents making careful calculations from the past and correctly forecasting the future. Keynesians argue that because the future is so uncertain decisions about the future tend to be based on 'impulse' and 'sentiment' which means that decisions are more likely to represent a series of wild fluctuations between excess optimism and unwarranted pessimism. Decisions tend to follow more of the herd instinct of rushing forward in large numbers and also retreating, which means that economies would fluctuate between unsustainable booms and slumps. Because these wild fluctuations depend on sentiment rather than rational reasoning it is therefore not likely that levels of investment in the economy will match savings or that economic capacity will meet the levels of effective demand.

Risk and uncertainty in the goods markets

Within the framework of Walras equilibrium prices are the signal for both suppliers and consumers to adjust their expectations, so that if the price increase was too high goods would be left on the shelf. Suppliers seeing the unsold goods would reduce the price to meet the new demand. Keynesians argued that reducing the price was only one among other decisions available to suppliers. In contrast to reducing the price suppliers could reduce the level of output – the number of goods reaching the shelves would slow down as would supply. With unchanged demand and a falling supply, suppliers would be able to clear their shelves without reducing their prices. According to Keynes, therefore, a fall in demand was not necessarily addressed through flexible prices but through a fall in output. Suppliers could therefore make choices between their levels of output and the level of demand for their product. Even if demand fell suppliers could still aim to maintain the level of profitability.

According to a Keynesian model the likely outcome was that markets would eventually adjust at a higher price and a lower level of output. The decision to reduce output to meet the levels of effective demand for a given price was therefore likely to result in higher levels of unemployment – unemployment which according to the Keynesian model was involuntary since those in work could not directly influence the levels of effective demand or the decisions by suppliers to reduce output. In contrast, market economists saw unemployment as voluntary, while Keynesians argued that unemployment was beyond the influence of the individual.

Risk and uncertainty in investment and savings

Relating the themes of risk and uncertainty to the markets for savings and investment, Keynesians would argue that future investment was likely to remain unpredictable and uncertain because decisions about the future were hazardous and a gamble. Investment decisions were therefore likely to be swayed by current news and emotions about the present state of the market rather than rational forecasts. Once the premise of uncertainty and risk were included into the markets for investment and savings then it was likely that there would be discrepancies between the levels of savings and investment. Savers and investors represented different people taking different risks and faced with different uncertainties. It was therefore not necessarily true that investment and savings would be cleared around the rate of interest.

Because it was probable for gaps to occur between the levels of investment and savings it was imperative for government to shorten the lags between investment and savings. Asking the question 'why do savers save and why do investors invest?' Keynesians wanted to argue that these decisions were not just determined by the rate of interest as market economists had suggested. Dealing with the question 'why do savers save?', Keynesians suggested that savings were very much related to people's level of income. People consumed a ratio of their income and saved the rest, so that low income was likely to be associated with a high propensity to consume and a low savings ratio, while high income was associated with high savings. People therefore saved in relation to their income levels. However, people were likely to hold speculative balances which they used to purchase bonds and this speculative balance was related to the rate of interest. If the speculators sentiment was that interest rates had reached a peak and were likely to fall in the future they would move into bonds at the high interest rates and then sell these bonds as interest rates fell thus making profits on the price of their bonds.

Dealing with the question 'why do investors invest?', it was not just the rate of interest which was the determining factor but also sentiment about the future of the economy and future levels of demand. Decisions in the car industry to invest in robotics, for example, do not just depend on interest rates but also on forecasts about future trends in car ownership, costs of materials, costs of petrol, and decisions by government to build new roads. The rate of interest is one factor which influences investors about future investment decisions, but the forecast of future economic trends and the stability of demand are sometimes more crucial.

It is therefore because savers save according to their levels of income and investors invest because of sentiment about the stability of demand that there could be no guarantee of equilibrium. Keynesians would argue that savings were only equal to investment as an identity in that investment had to come from savings and that without savings there was not likely to be any investment but this did not mean that these were in equilibrium. The relationship between savings and investment was related to changes in the rate of interest but also the level of income. Income influenced the level of savings and income was also an indicator as to the level of aggregate demand.

The problems of non-flexible prices

While Keynesians pointed to the flawed assumptions of rational individualism and argued instead that the presence of risk and uncertainty were likely to produce non-equilibrium results, they also developed an economic analysis which questioned the validity of rational individualism and replaced this with theories of group or functional interests. The real actions of interest groups, were closer to economic reality than the abstractions of rational agents and rational expectations. It is because we do not relate to markets as individual suppliers and consumers seeking to promote our individual welfare that the impact of groups, classes, and vested interests are more likely to have a major influence on the economy.

The recognition of groups has major implications for economic theory and economic policy. Although market liberals recognise that some sectors of the economy cannot be described as competitive markets with large numbers of buyers and suppliers with no barriers to entry, the analysis of non-competitive markets is restrictive. Ultimately, within market theory there are no real monopolies which can totally dominate the market place which means that eventually even the non-competitive sectors have to obey the longer-term influences of the market place. The presence of price mark-ups and the implications for the working of the economy do not enter the analysis of macro liberal economists. The problems of monopoly are therefore a specific case for the microeconomists. Furthermore, as far as the microeconomist is concerned the aim is to regulate the non-competitive sector in order to remove those obstacles and rigidities which are seen as preventing markets from working effectively. As far as the market economist is concerned, therefore, the solutions to rigidities, inflexible prices or wage stickiness lie in the reform of those institutions which seek to influence the market place. Because Keynesians do not share this faith in markets their attempt to deal with price mark-ups has not been a strategy of creating markets. If price mark-ups reflect the absence of the discipline of markets, Keynesians seem to 'accept' that such institutional factors do influence prices and wages, but rather than aiming to 'reform' these institutions Keynesians would see them as part of society and would therefore construct economic theory and economic policies which reflected those realities as opposed to market liberal theory which seeks to create what does not exist.

Flex price and non-flex price markets

Keynesian economists including Kalecki (Sawyer 1985), Robinson, and Kaldor have all pointed to the problems of monopolies in different sectors of the economy. According to Kalecki, for example, it was more likely that the competitive markets were present in areas of the economy concerned with primary commodities such as agriculture, coffee growing, coal mining and other raw materials. In contrast, in the world of manufacturing and added value, Kalecki suggests that these industries are characterised by a system of administered costs. These industries do not calculate the value of the marginal costs of their labour or their marginal revenue but the mark-up price of their product by inputting the cost of materials, the cost of labour and capital, and adding an administered rate of profit. According to the world of administered prices therefore, firms do not adjust their output according to prices but rather start off with their administered price as given and then allow output to meet changes in demand at the mark-up price.

According to the theory of administered prices a fall in demand is not met by a change in price but by changing the levels of output. Firms can shut off parts of their productive capacity and also shed labour. For this reason Keynes, in 1929, opposed the market liberal argument which was to reduce wage rates as a way of reducing the level of unemployment. Keynes argued that wages could not be separated out from aggregate demand. If wages were allowed to fall, aggregate demand was likely to fall and firms would be left with unsold goods on their shelves. Their response, because of administered prices, was to reduce output which increased unemployment further. The new unemployed also depressed the level of aggregate demand because there was now less income in the economy. This meant that government would call for further wage reductions which in turn would depress demand further and again leave firms with more goods unsold, leading to further falls in output and further increases in unemployment.

A fall in price therefore responds sluggishly to changes in demand and output. It is only in the long run, as output falls further accompanied by additional increases in unemployment, that prices actually start to fall. In a modern economy, therefore, it was not the price which was the indicator to changes in supply and demand. A fall in demand was more likely to result in firms de-stocking and reducing their inventories and their labour forces in order to retain profits at a lower level of output:

> In a modern industrial economy with the manufacturing industries dominating production, the immediate signals of whether there is excess demand or excess supply are sent out not by changes in the level of prices but by changes in the level of inventories.
>
> (Bhaduri 1986: 74)

The important lesson to be emphasised by Keynesians from these observations was that the problem of unemployment was always to be associated with a lack of demand and underutilised economic resources. Since industries are likely to de-stock as demand falls this means that on the supply side of the economy there was always likely to be underutilised capacity. The supply side was therefore always likely to be more elastic and respond that much faster in contrast to changes in demand. This view completely challenged the thesis put forward by Marshall and other market liberal economists who have tended to argue that, in the short term at least, supply was likely to be inelastic since firms could not change their production process or their levels of output in the short term. Keynes suggested that completely the reverse was true.

The main repercussion of this Keynesian analysis was to show that if the level of demand was actually increased then that new demand would be met within the existing level of supply capacity. With a highly elastic supply curve increases in demand would only result in increased output and increased employment. In contrast market liberals argue that because the supply side is 'inelastic' then increases in the demand side would only result in higher prices.

From the economics of scarce resources to the economics of prosperity

The central concern of market economics is to resolve the problem of how to allocate limited resources in the context of unlimited demand. Market economists argued that the market was the best method to allocate resources. Markets were always more efficient and more flexible than any central authority. Furthermore, the market place was less likely to be discriminatory in deciding who gets what. The way to growth and continuous prosperity was for government to create a framework in which enterprise could flourish, enterprise being the ability to take risks, to see opportunities and take advantage of them. Enterprise could only flourish in the spirit of free markets. Governments had therefore to create an enterprise culture where people could be encouraged to take risks and have the incentives to take those risks.

> Since the endowment of resources available to a 'community' was supposed to be determined exogenously the welfare of the community could be maximised (or its misery minimised) only by the free play of market forces under an enterprise system with the minimum of government interference and regulation. Keynes asserted the contrary. His main proposition was that in normal circumstances production in general was limited by effective demand which determined how much of potential resources were effectively utilised. Here therefore was a scope for securing greater material welfare through the purposeful direction of the economy.
>
> (Kaldor 1984: 2)

The main criticism directed by Keynesians against the market liberal approach to economic growth and prosperity was that it depended too much on the enterprise of the individual. Within market economics the possibility of government being able to influence the level of aggregate demand was not entertained since demand was stable. Government, according to market economists, could only influence demand through increases in the supply of money as in Friedman's helicopter thesis of the money supply. However, such an increase was only a short-term solution. Increases in the money supply would in the short run lead to price increases which are higher than wage increases; this increase in price would lead to expansion in output and employment. However, in the long run workers would match increases in prices with increases in wages which would cancel out the price advantage and also the increases in output. Unemployment would in the long run return to the natural level. Market economists see government as having at best a neutral effect in influencing output, growth and employment. Furthermore, any such government interference was more likely to lead to higher prices and inflation.

In contrast, Keynesians argued that the level of aggregate demand could be changed by government either seeking to influence the level of individual demand and by government itself changing the level of their own demand on resources. Personal consumption can be changed by governments altering the rates of taxation and improving personal disposable income. Also, governments could influence aggregate demand through changes in public expenditure by either deciding to build roads or hospitals, or by employing more teachers or doctors. Such changes will have a multiplier effect on the economy so that an increase in government expenditure would lead to a larger increase in national income than the initial injection by the government. Government expenditure was more likely to change the levels of effective demand. Government tends to consume all resources while tax changes are likely to lead to both consumption and savings. Changes in aggregate demand depend on the ability of government to target consumption on groups with a high marginal propensity to consume which includes those on low incomes. It is for this reason that Keynesians see policies which seek to redistribute income through fiscal measures as not being purely social policies but also as policies which have a direct impact on the economy.

Demand is not taken as given but as an economic aggregate which can be changed and which is likely to influence output and employment. While market economists see demand as being indirectly influenced by changes in the money supply and being effective only in the short term, Keynesians argue that fiscal policies – including changes in public expenditure and changes in taxation – have a direct impact on aggregate demand and this will influence long-term employment and output.

To return to the theme of investment. As an essential element in decisions relating to investment Keynesians argue that the rates of investment depend on stable demand. By being able to show that the government are able to influence demand and guarantee demand, this in turn was likely to lead to an increase in investment and therefore output and employment.

The attempt to influence aggregate demand meant that government had a key role to play in the redistribution of resources. In his pamphlet *How to Pay for the War* Keynes showed that government, without resorting to deficit financing, could rechannel existing taxation and public expenditure to fund armaments (Harrod 1951). Keynes argued that government had a high propensity to consume and that by increasing the level of taxation and reducing personal consumption, the new taxation was to be spent on defence which in turn produced the equipment required but also employed people who in turn spent their income in the commercial sector, thus generating through the multiplier effect new income and taxation. Keynes argued that this form of redistributing income could influence aggregate demand within a balanced budget.

However, Keynesians also advocated that deficit financing could be used as a fiscal stabiliser arguing that when savings were outstripping investment because of 'sentiment' about investment decisions government could 'mop' up the unused savings and re-input these otherwise idle resources back into the economy as government investment which was likely to influence demand and private sector investment. The increased demand and higher levels of investment would result in increased levels of sustainable employment.

The influence of government and the international economic order

While Keynes rejected the assumptions that markets would clear at full employment equilibrium and also opposed the market economist reliance on the entrepreneur to generate growth and prosperity, he also provided a context for the intervention of government. It is within this context that most Keynesians disagree as to what role government should have in economic management. Although most Keynesians agree with the major flaws of the market model, they are not so readily agreed as to how and what should replace the central role of the market. For example, in his 1929 pamphlet *Can Lloyd George Do It?* Keynes did not seem to have a problem in advocating that government could direct investment into export industries, implying that it was not against the notion of individual freedom for government to direct savings and investment (Harrod 1951). Furthermore, Keynes was also sufficiently political to recognise that a policy of cheap money was likely to produce conflicts of interest between the financial and the manufacturing sectors of the economy. A cheap money policy implied that government should conduct a policy which would lower the rate of interest for the manufacturing sector which was more important than protecting high interest rates which benefited the banking sector. The interests of banking, therefore, had to be subordinated to manufacturing.

In the immediate post-war period Britain needed to expand its manufacturing capacity to produce more goods and reduce dependence on imports. It was only this form of policy which was likely to strengthen the value of sterling. Keynes, therefore, argued that it was essential for the manufacturing sector to be able to borrow money at a cheap rate.

The attempt by one country to pursue a cheap money policy, however, was likely to fail in the international context. If one country did decide to go it alone and reduce interest rates than this action was likely to lead to an exodus of foreign holders as they searched for higher interest rates. The priority was, therefore, for countries to come together and co-ordinate their monetary policies which meant that each country was not competing with another on interest rates. A co-ordinated approach to currency and interest rates meant that governments could deal with financial interest rates together. The alternative policy of restricting imports and extending protection by individual governments was likely to lead to a beggar-my-neighbour policy with each government seeking to export their national unemployment to another nation. Protectionist policies were likely to lead to a contraction of world trade and a decline in prosperity.

Keynes is therefore associated with an international economic order. His advocacy has continued to be the co-ordination of policy by governments in contrast to the market liberal argument that governments cannot buck the market. Instead of government living with the market, Keynes argued that at an international level government could co-ordinate their monetary policies to ensure international economic stability. The establishment of the Bretton Woods agreement is seen as the confirmation at the international level of the influence of Keynesian thinking.

> Keynes was not just an economist writing a memo on whether we should have a crawling peg or not, he was somebody who believed passionately in a new, decent, liberal and effective international order which was based on conditions which allow prosperity and expansion to be.
>
> (Meade 1984: 130)

The possibility and willingness of governments to construct supranational institutions which could influence national economic policies meant that by surrendering some of their national interest into the international context governments were actually contributing to international stability and also to the prosperity of people they sought to represent. Governments could no longer ignore the fact that economies were becoming more interdependent and that national economic policies have to be made in an international context.

Keynesians would argue that the push towards interdependence of the world economy has continued to accelerate in the 1980s and would continue to do so in the 1990s. The breakdown of the Bretton Woods accord in the 1970s meant that national governments reverted to economic policies which indicated national priorities. Instead of international co-or-dination, the 1970s and early 1980s were characterised by policies which were designed to be remedies for national economies. Bretton Woods was replaced by a regime of floating exchange rates, of countries competing with each other in their concern to maintain the strength of their currencies. That meant that governments have had to compete by relying on the level of interest rates as a policy to stabilise the exchange rate. The policy of high interest rates has, therefore, slowed down the rate of new investment which in turn has led to lower levels of employment and also resulted in the recession of the early 1980s. Keynesians would argue that the establishment of the Group of Seven as an attempt to re-establish policy co-ordination in the late 1980s has again vindicated Keynesian thinking. The decision to reduce interest rates after the Stock Exchange crash of 1987 has encouraged Keynesians to argue that a new form of Bretton Woods now actually exists where governments no longer rely on interest rates to conduct domestic exchange rate policies, although there is no explicit Bretton Woods level of exchange rates. Unemployment has continued to fall in the leading Western economies in the late 1980s. Unemployment in Europe, for example, has fallen from 14 million to 9 million while in Britain it has fallen from a peak of 3.2 million in 1983 to 1.6 million by April 1990.

In the meantime, since October 1989, the attempt by the UK government under the then Chancellor John Major to reduce the pressures of inflation through interest rates seems to have reversed the opportunities for expansion created by the former Chancellor Nigel Lawson. Since June 1990 unemployment had again started to rise and there are signs that the UK economy is entering a new cycle of inflation and rising unemployment.

KEYNESIAN ECONOMICS: GOVERNMENT, DEMAND MANAGEMENT, AND THE INTERNATIONAL CONTEXT

In addition to the preference of co-ordination of exchange rate policies, Keynesian economists have also tried to show how governments can influence the level of demand both at the level of the domestic economy and also in the international context. As has already been argued above, Keynes had pointed out that one of the major flaws of market economics was the failure to realise that while economies would in the long term gravitate towards a new equilibrium level which meets the level of effective demand, that equilibrium would not necessarily coincide with the economy fully utilising the supply side. This meant that at an equilibrium level the economy was not operating at full capacity. In this context Keynes argued that governments could influence the level of effective demand through fiscal policies – including changes in personal taxation and government expenditure – and that because of the multiplier effect the national economy would actually grow at a faster rate than the initial fiscal stimulus.

Taking the concept of effective demand further, Keynesians would also argue that unemployment is associated with unused capacity and that, therefore, a fiscal stimulus would first of all absorb the level of unemployment before prices start to rise. However, Keynesians have also recognised the possibility that the economy could be operating at full capacity alongside the presence of unemployment because of de-stocking and a fall in the level of inventories. In this situation any increase in demand was not likely to be met within the domestic economy but through an increased rate of imports. Keynesians would argue that in this case governments have to be selective in their fiscal stimulus, which means that instead of increasing demand through individual consumption, government expenditure should be used in a way less likely to lead to a rise in imports. Furthermore, Keynesians could argue that government could actually 'target' an increase in personal consumption to those groups whose propensity to consume was less likely to increase imports. This targeted consumption would, for example, include increases in pensions thus encouraging the elderly to demand more energy and food in the winter, and also be directed to parents with low incomes who would use the increase in their disposable income to purchase clothing and food for their children. Such a fiscal stimulus was, therefore, less likely to lead to an increase in imports.

At an international level Keynesians have argued for a recycling of international income from those countries with a low propensity to consume to countries with a high level of propensity. Keynesians have pointed out that the oil price increases in 1973 and 1974 and in 1980 and 1981 had been deflationary to the international economy because this process had actually directed income to the oil producers who have not been able to consume the new income, this resulting in a leakage of resources. Keynesians have, therefore, urged policies of income recycling from the oil producers to prevent stagnation of the world economy.

The Brandt Report on the North–South divide has also pointed to the problems of discrepancies of income levels between the rich northern countries and those countries in Africa and Asia. The Brandt Commission has suggested that it is in the self-interest of the North to attempt to redistribute income to the South and to increase the consumption levels of the South as a form of international demand management policy. This policy would in turn benefit the North since people in the poorer nations would be consuming goods coming from the North thus reducing the level of unemployment in the North.

A KEYNESIAN MODEL OF THE ECONOMY

A Keynesian model of how the economy works needs to take on board the three principles derived above, namely:

1   that markets left to themselves cannot guarantee a state of full employment equilibrium;
2   that the economics of scarce resources and unlimited resources leaves too much to the spirit of enterprise to generate improved prosperity; and
3   that government have a central role to play in economic management both at the domestic and the international level.

The following sections, therefore, explore the themes of the IS/LM model as developed by Hicks and Hansen and outlined in economic texts including Begg, Dornbusch, and Fisher's (1987) *Economics*. The aim is to develop the model as being central to the economics of Keynes but furthermore the concepts of IS/LM also represent a model of the global economy.

The IS/LM model represents the economy in two sectors: the real sector as represented by the investment/savings curve (IS) and the relationship of IS to changes in income and the rate of interest. The monetary sector of the economy represents changes in the total demand for money in relation to changes in income and changes in the rate of interest (LM).

Changes in savings and investment (the IS curve)

The relationships of savings and investment to changes in income and changes in the rate of interest include the following Keynesian principles:

1   Savings are positively related to changes in income – people save according to the level of income so that national savings are related to national income.
2   Savings are equal to investment; as there can be no investment without savings so the level of investment must be the level of savings. This is not to say that savings and investment are at an equilibrium as decided by the rate of interest. In the Keynesian sense the relationship between savings and investment is an identity.
3   Investment is inversely related to the rate of interest – at low interest rates investment is likely to be high, at high interest rates investment is likely to be low.
4   Combining investment and savings to income and rate of interest, low savings are associated with low income, low income is associated with low investment and low investment is associated with high interest rates.

According to the IS aspect of the model, therefore, there is a correlation between a low national income, low savings, low investment and high interest rates. Economies which tend to be associated with low national income, therefore, will also have low savings which means that investment will be low and to attract savings there has to be high interest rates which in turn means that high interest rates are likely to deter investment.

Figure 5.1 The Keynesian economic model: relationships between savings and investment

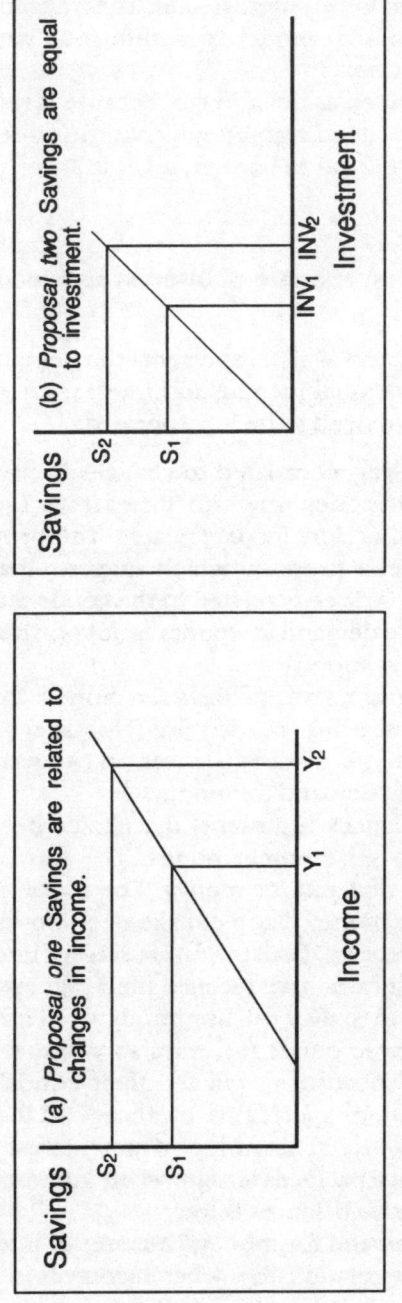

(a) *Proposal one* Savings are related to changes in income.

(b) *Proposal two* Savings are equal to investment.

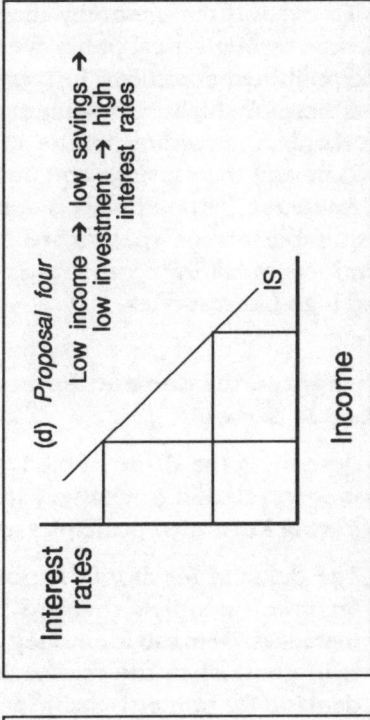

(c) *Proposal three* Investment is influenced by changes in the rate of interest — high interest rates result in low investment rates; low interest rates result in high investment rates.

(d) *Proposal four*
Low income → low savings → low investment → high interest rates

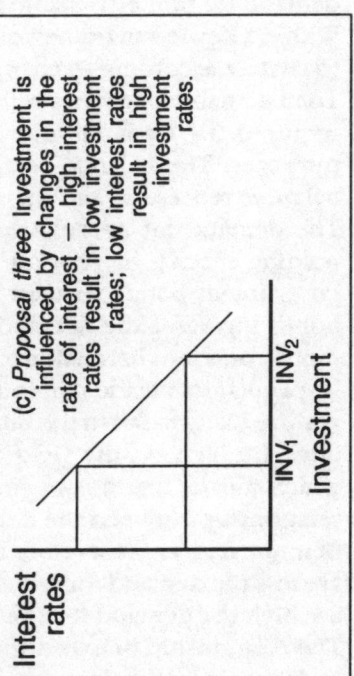

To expand the economy there first has to be an increase in national income through fiscal policy which includes changes in personal taxation and public expenditure. The increase in income will result in higher savings and therefore higher investment and lower interest rates. The transmission mechanism according to the Keynesian model is to influence national income and then savings and investment.

An increase in oil prices is described as deflationary because it reduces disposable income – people are now spending money income on oil-related products. A fall in income results in a fall in savings, a fall in investment, and high interest rates.

Changes in the demand for money, the rate of interest and income (the LM curve)

In describing the shape of the LM curve which represents the demand for money in relation to changes in national income and interest rates, the following Keynesian principles again need to be incorporated:

1 The demand for money is positively correlated to changes in national income – people's demand for money tends to increase as income increases. Demand for money is therefore income related. This proposal is in contrast to the market liberal proposal which suggests that the demand for money is stable and is directly related to the goods market. Within a Keynesian framework the demand for money is not passive only to change according to changes in supply.

2 Total demand for money represents a trade off between money which is required for transaction purposes and money used for speculative purposes. The balance between speculative balances and transaction balances represents the aggregate demand for money.

3 The demand for speculative balances represents the choice between holding money or moving into government bonds. The move into government bonds reduces the demand for money. The move out of bonds increases the demand for money. People make decisions about money or bonds in relation to forecasts about the future rates of interest. If speculators decide that interest rates have reached their highest level and are likely to fall in the future then they will buy bonds when interest rates are high. As the yield of these bonds increases so will the price which means that at this point speculators will sell their bonds. The relationship between the demand for speculative balances and the rate of interest rates is therefore a positive relationship. When interest rates are low the demand for speculative balances is high, when interest rates are high the demand for speculative balances is low.

4 The relationship between the demand for money, the rates of interest, and income is therefore a positive relationship. When income is low the

Figure 5.2 The Keynesian economic model: relationships between income, money supply, and interest rates

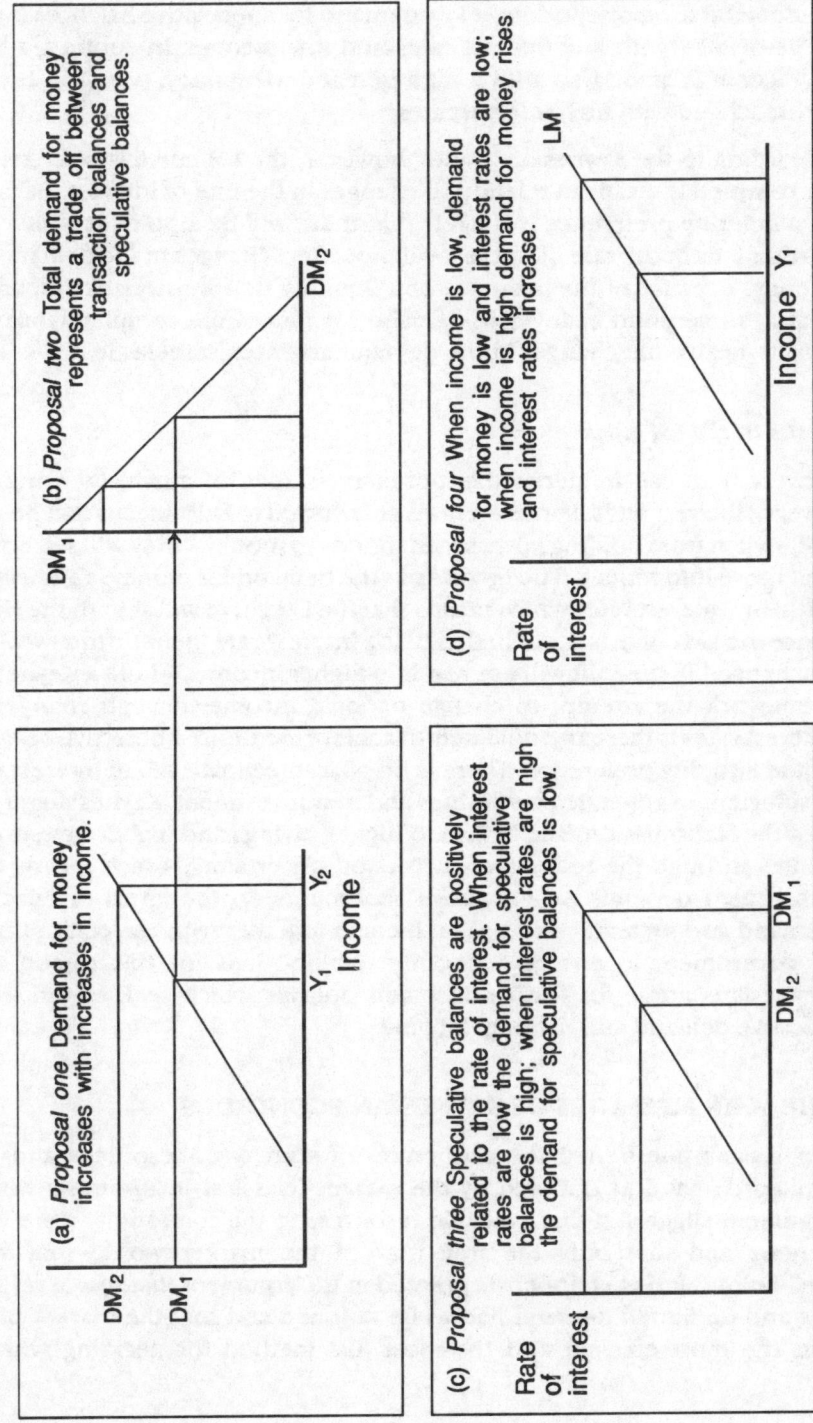

(a) *Proposal one* Demand for money increases with increases in income.

(b) *Proposal two* Total demand for money represents a trade off between transaction balances and speculative balances.

(c) *Proposal three* Speculative balances are positively related to the rate of interest. When interest rates are low the demand for speculative balances is high; when interest rates are high the demand for speculative balances is low.

(d) *Proposal four* When income is low, demand for money is low and interest rates are low; when income is high demand for money rises and interest rates increase.

demand for money is low; a low demand for speculative balances is also associated with low interest rates and low income. In contrast a high income is associated with a high demand for money, which in turn is associated with high interest rates.

According to the Keynesian model, however, the LM curve is not likely to be completely elastic in relation to changes in the rate of interest. Because of a liquidity preference it is likely that there will be a point at which any further falls in the rate of interest will not effect changes in the demand for money. Because of the presence of a liquidity trap Keynesians will argue that at some point changes in demand for money are completely elastic, which means that changes in the demand are interest inelastic.

Shifts in the LM curve

Government can influence the monetary sector (LM curve) by using the lever of interest rates. If interest rates are allowed to fall it means that people will switch from holding government bonds to money – they will sell bonds and move into money. The increase in the demand for money is associated with low interest rates which means that the LM curve will shift to the right. Since the LM curve is described as being interest-rate inelastic then with an unchanged IS the shift will not result in higher income. Within a Keynesian framework the attempt to change national income through changes in interest rates is therefore not likely to achieve the desired objective because of the liquidity preference. There is no guarantee that a fall in interest rate is sufficient to generate new savings and new investment. Keynesians argue that the transmission mechanism to higher savings and higher investment comes through the reduction of risk and uncertainty, which means that investment depends on long-term sentiments on the levels of effective demand and increases in national income together with the commitment of government to ensure economic stability. It is for this reason that Keynesians argue for fiscal policy and policies which seek to influence effective demand and national income.

THE MAIN MESSAGES OF KEYNESIAN ECONOMICS

Keynesians questioned the economics of scarcity of resources and unlimited demand as outlined by the market (classical) economists whose argument suggested that available resources to the community were exogenous and that only the free play of the market would maximise well-being. Market economists pointed to the argument that scarce resources and unlimited demand had to be rationed and that the market place was the most efficient and the most just method for deciding what is produced, how goods are produced and for whom. The price mechanism represents the signals of consumers and suppliers.

Keynes asserted the contrary. He argued that production was limited by *effective demand* which determined the quantity of resources utilised. The scope of a community to increase welfare and prosperity depended on the capacity to increase the levels of effective demand. Market economists depended too much on the spirit of the enterprising individual and of government creating the right climate for enterprise to flourish. Keynes wanted to show that government can make a contribution to welfare and prosperity by seeking to influence the levels of effective demand, meaning that they could use taxation and public expenditure as a way of influencing consumption.

Keynesian economics are also associated with an international economic order. Keynes urged governments to replace mercantilist policies of seeking to improve exports and the exchange through export-led growth and protectionist policies with a policy founded on international co-ordination. Keynesians want to point to the increased international dependence of the world economy where the beggar-my-neighbour policy of exporting unemployment actually harms world trade. Keynesians want to expand world trade through a process of governments agreeing on a system of fixed exchange rates and stable interest rates which subordinate the priorities of financial interests to the interest of industry. Growth and prosperity, according to a Keynesian framework depends on increased savings and investment which means that governments have to ensure that cheap money is made available to industry to invest in new technologies.

Keynesian economics undermine two central themes associated with market economics. First, the economics associated with Say's law which states that all economic activity consists of the exchange of goods and services between different agents with the view that supply generates an equivalent level of demand. The shift from a barter to an enterprise economy means that the existence of money does not guarantee equilibrium. Money can be saved and can therefore act as a leakage out of the economy, so demand generated by supply may not be enough to generate the employment of all resources. Because the recipients may not spend all their income, firms will mark-up their prices for a certain level of goods to generate a stable level of profits. This view challenges the whole notion that firms would maximise output to maximise profits. Instead firms might opt for a stable level of profits and lower levels of demand.

The second is the challenge to the Walras law of flexible prices. Keynesians have argued that it is not price which is flexible, but that changes in prices are the end process of a change in output. Because suppliers mark-up prices, a fall in demand is not matched by a fall in price but by a fall in output. It is the fall in output which eventually might result in a fall in price. Price change therefore is not the signal, but the result, of change to price resistance. In this context the level of unemployment is associated with underutilised or underused capacity. An increase in demand is therefore likely to be met with idle resources. While market economists asserted that markets result in full employment equilibrium and that unemployment represents rigidities which act as obstacles to the market. Keynesians recognised that the assumption of perfect competition did not hold and that perfect competition represented an artificial world which market economists seek to create. Keynesians want to live with reality as it exists, where the world is therefore made up of unequal competitors with unequal access and is therefore dominated by a series of price mark-ups and wage stickiness.

Keynesian economics are therefore associated with a revolutionary paradigm shift in that they represent a challenge to the market liberal paradigm. The classical paradigm rested on two assumptions: (a) Walras equilibrium of rational agents which leads to market equilibrium solutions, this means that there would be no unemployment, no problems of interest rates and investment, and that the consumer would be sovereign in the goods markets; (b) Say's law, that supply would generate its own demand and therefore the need to look to supply-side factors and micro foundations to macro analysis.

The Keynesian challenge is: (a) that markets would not necessarily result in equilibrium solutions – that there could be demand deficiency problems in the economy; (b) that equilibrium could mean a stationary economy where unemployment is associated with price marks, insufficient investment, demand deficiency risk and uncertainty; and (c) an argument that a theory of rational expectations would lead to unstable markets. Rather than the market being self-clearing Keynesian economics provided an approach which justified an active role for government, where government could contribute to growth in the economy and iron out business cycles.

CONCLUSIONS

The challenge of Keynesianism is not just a challenge in the sphere of economics. Keynesianism cannot be confined to the controversy with classical and market liberal economists. Keynesianism, like market liberalism, represents a discursive society which reflects a form of thinking that embraces the economic, the social, and the political. While market economics associates individualism with consumer choice in the economic market place, rational choice in the political sphere and the freedom of the individual in social issues, Keynesianism is inherently associated with collectivist ideas in social policy, a positive role for government in economics, and the politics of interests and groups.

One major concern of Keynesian economics is the concept of effective demand, which inevitably locates Keynesian economics with social issues of income distribution. Keynesians argue that the level of effective demand can be influenced in the context of a balanced budget by governments redistributing disposable income to groups with a higher level of personal consumption. It is therefore Keynesian to use personal taxation to influence the levels of demand of people in low income so that income redistribution to reduce individual poverty is no longer a concern of social policy but in a Keynesian sense also becomes an economic policy issue. Equally, Keynesians are concerned with effective demand as a global issue, so that income disparities between Europe, Africa and Asia are seen as influencing demand and prosperity. It is therefore Keynesian to utilise the tools of effective demand and to show that recycling of income between countries would actually benefit world trade and benefit global prosperity.

Keynesians therefore blur concerns which are social and economic. In contrast, market economists separate economics and social issues; they equate economics with questions of efficiency while social issues such as income distribution, externalities, spillovers, and public goods are treated as areas of market failure and therefore justify intervention by governments where the market fails. In contrast, because Keynesians do not hold the market as central, the social, the economic and the political become increasingly blurred. Keynesians, for example, recognise that full employment requires a political arrangement which allows government to maintain a commitment of full employment without the threat of inflation. Inflation and unemployment in a Keynesian sense are therefore political in that governments can create institutions and arrangements to deal with the trade off of employment and inflation. Keynesians are thus associated with tripartite and corporatist politics as deliberate arrangements to resolve economic problems in a political context. The involvement of trade unions in economic policy-making, of seeking to construct arrangements which bring together government, employers, and trade unions is associated with a Keynesian perspective. Equally a large public sector, public investment in capital goods, public services including health and education, are also associated with the influence of Keynesian thinking.

Finally, Keynes was also explicitly political in giving more priority to the interests of manufacturers and the real sector of the economy as opposed to financial interests. He was always aware that the major limitation to increased prosperity was a balance of payments constraint. Countries with an adverse balance of trade could not sustain a policy of economic growth through demand management since the latter was likely to result in an increase in imports, a further devaluation of the currency, worsening balance of payments, and inflation. Keynes was against a policy designed to increase exports through the setting up of tariff barriers to protect the domestic economy. He argued that this form of beggar-my-neighbour policy would actually restrict world trade and lead to a global economic decline. Instead, Keynes argued for a policy of currency co-ordination between governments so that they were not competing with each other on interest rates policy. Instead the pegging of exchange rates and interest rates would produce economic stability and new investment. Keynes was therefore against the interest of the *rentier* class, which included the interests of banking and finance. Keynes felt that governments had to break free from the continuous threat of financiers who were continuously looking for new speculative opportunities. Rather, governments had to show more concern for the interest of manufacturing and industry through a policy of cheap money, thus clamping down on financial interests. Keynes also argued that if the private sector did not utilise the opportunity of cheap money to invest in new technology then it was the responsibility of government to become involved in socialised investment.

In conclusion, it would seem that Keynesianism is implicitly a political agenda. The nature of the challenge to classical economists is the rejection of the idea that governments have a neutral effect in economic policy. Instead, Keynesians want to show that all economic policies involve political choices. Governments have the political choice as to whether or not they commit themselves to maintain full employment. Employment therefore involves political choices. Equally, inflation is political in that governments again have the choice of how to deal with the problem; they can either restrict demand and allow unemployment to increase to dampen down inflationary pressures or they can construct institutions to moderate wage pressures as a trade off with policies of full employment. The main contribution of Keynesian economics is therefore to continuously reinforce the idea that a society has sufficient autonomy to make economic choices, that it is not inevitable that people have to live with the outcomes of market forces. There are always other options and choices available and it is these ideas of Keynes's which are still unsettled fifty years after he wrote his *General Theory of Employment*.

Chapter 6

Keynesian economics

Wages, the labour market and employment

INTRODUCTION: THE KEYNESIAN CHALLENGE TO MARKET LIBERALISM

In the previous chapter, it was suggested that a strong argument can be made to show that Keynesian economics represented not just a 'special case' but indeed a fundamental challenge to (classical) market liberal economics. Keynesian thinking challenges market economics at three levels. First, Keynesian economics confronts market liberalism at the level of assumptions which are 'implicit' to the market model – namely, the principles of rational individuals, the concept of competitive markets, and flexible prices. At a second level, Keynesian economics challenges market economics because the latter presents economic decisions as a series of inevitable outcomes – the interaction of market forces. In contrast, Keynesian economics provides a series of policy options and choices which are continuously available to governments. Third, Keynesian economics aims to show that individual self-interest is not a sufficient ethic to guide economic policy. The ethics of civic virtue, social justice, and the principles of democracy are issues which are inextricably related to the wider concerns of creating a civilised economy founded on principles of entitlements and obligations.

THE CHALLENGES TO MARKET PRINCIPLES

The concept of individualism

Keynesians challenge the central concept of rational individualism and the assumptions of market clearing prices as implied by both the Walras law of flexible prices and Say's law of market equilibrium between the level of output and demand. In contrast, Keynesians have argued that the presence of price mark-ups in the goods market, wage rigidities in the labour market, and the liquidity preference challenge the central theme of flexible price. Prices were not as flexible as market economists had suggested. Instead

Keynesians have attempted to construct their economics in the context of a series of 'administered prices' where the concern becomes price stability rather than profit maximisation. Within the context of non-flexible prices Keynes argued that in the short term a fall in demand would be matched by a fall in output rather than a fall in prices and that it was these deflationary processes which were likely to lead to an eventual fall in prices.

The challenge is also directed at Say's law and the argument that supply creates its own demand. Instead Keynesians have shown that in a monetary economy there is no guarantee that the level of savings will be matched by the level of investment. Consumers will not necessarily consume all their income, therefore supply could outstrip the level of demand. Because the aggregate marginal propensity to consume (MPC) was less than unity, an increase in supply as suggested by Say's law was, in itself, not likely to bring forward an equal increase in demand. The consumption function measured in terms of disposable income shows a positive relationship with income which means that people would consume more with increases in income. However, the rate of increase in the level of consumption would not be the same as the rate of increase in income:

> The fundamental psychological law, upon which we are entitled with great confidence...is that men are disposed as a rule and on the average, to increase their consumption as their income increases, but not by as much as the increase in their income.... These reasons will lead, as a rule, to a greater proportion of income being saved as real income increases.
>
> (Keynes 1936: 96–7)

The challenge to Say's law is central to Keynesian economics not only because it challenges the assumption of equilibrium between supply and demand in the goods market but also because of the assumption of equilibrium between savings and investment. According to a Keynesian approach people save in relation to their income while investors are influenced by future market sentiment and also interest rates. According to this analysis therefore, it is likely that savings will exceed the level of investment, with the implication that not all available resources will be fully utilised unless the government does intervene to alter market sentiments or to utilise the unused savings. Government has a marginal propensity to consume of unity which means that they will consume all resources made available to the public sector.

The economics of scarce resources

Second, Keynesian economics questions the economics of scarce resources and unlimited demand. The classical argument that available resources to the community were exogenous, where only the free play of the market would maximise well-being, was challenged by Keynesians who argued that the economy was not an external factor but represented a series of choices for the community. Keynes asserted that production was limited by the level of 'effective demand' which in turn determined how much resources were utilised. Since the levels of effective demand could actually be altered then, Keynesians argued, the limits to the economy could be changed by altering demand. The scope of the community was therefore to increase effective demand.

Individual self-interest

The third challenge relates to the competing visions of economics and politics derived from market liberal and Keynesian perceptions. While market liberals locate individualism and self-interest as central themes to explain human motivation, by contrast Keynesianism is associated with arguments for civic virtue and the civilised economy. While Keynesians are also concerned with the preservation of the right of individuals to pursue self-interest, this concept of individual interest is seen as not being sufficient to construct other desirable ethics of entitlements and obligation. The concern of Keynesian economics is therefore to combine individualism and self-interest with civic virtue and to show that decisions on employment and inflation require a political willingness to construct enduring contracts which are of mutual benefit.

In addition to the vision of human motivations of civic virtue and contracts Keynesian economics is best located in the context of a democratic society where agents reach agreement by consensus rather than through imposition. The difference between Keynesians and market liberals is that Keynesians seek to live with the world as it is; recognising the influence and legitimacy of interest groups and therefore seeking ways to make these institutions reach agreement to produce long-term economic policies. Market liberals start either with the assumption that such institutions do not exist or urge their reform, arguing that such institutions represent major obstacles to the working of the markets. For example, while market economists argue that trade unions contribute to unemployment and therefore advocate the reform of trade unions, in contrast Keynesians would argue that the way to reduce unemployment is to show trade unions the benefits of full employment and then to try and reach agreement on trade union behaviour in making wage claims in the context of full employment. The context of a civilised economy becomes possible when unemployment is not used as a tool to discipline the labour force but rather to utilise the process of dialogue as the means to reach civilised agreements on employment and inflation.

The arguments presented in the following sections will be to show that any discussion of Keynesian economics needs to take into consideration the duality of a civilised economy and democratic society, and that in dealing with economic issues including labour markets, employment, wages and inflation these economic issues cannot be separated out from the wider context of civic virtue in a democratic society.

KEYNESIAN ECONOMICS AND THE CIVILISED ECONOMY

In the previous chapter, it was suggested that one major contribution that could be attributed to Keynesian economics was that, within a Keynesian paradigm, people did not have to live with the outcomes of the market place, but that it was essential for humanity and civilised societies to change the nature of the circumstances in which they found themselves. The perception of having to live with the market and not being able to influence market forces because they represent immutable laws implied that people and their governments had little or no autonomy in the conduct of economic policy but had to live with the constraints of the market place. Market liberalism implies an acceptance of the *status quo* since what *is* represents the outcome of market forces.

In contrast, Keynesian economics suggested that the aim of any community was to discover ways of improving welfare and general prosperity. Societies were therefore continuously faced with choices in responding to economic issues, so that although the economy appeared to be a series of exogenous factors, it was always within the sphere of political choice as to which policies were to be selected or prioritised. Economic policy alternatives always represented political choices.

Keynes's (1936) *General Theory of Employment, Interest and Money* is still described as a most important contribution to economics in the twentieth century. The reason why Keynes remains so central to economics is that his analysis was able to challenge the concept of rational individualism and therefore the series of economic assumptions which were constructed around the idea of individuals pursuing self-interest. Keynes did not seek to challenge the rights of the individual. Indeed he had argued that the rights of the individual, the right to pursue self-fulfilment, and diversity were essential to human freedom:

> [Self-interest] is the best safeguard of personal liberty in the sense that compared with any other system it greatly widens the field of personal choice...it is the most powerful instrument to the future.
>
> (Keynes 1936: 27)

While Keynes accepted that it was essential for individuals to pursue self-interest, he was also aware that the concept of self-interest was too limiting and certainly not sufficient to explain motivation and humanity. Therefore, his main preoccupation was to show that markets did not actually work as market economists had suggested. Markets might have indicated an equilibrium but such an equilibrium did not necessarily coincide with the full employment of all resources. This meant that even at an equilibrium, societies and their governments were not using all resources efficiently.

What Keynesian economists have contributed is the prospect and vision that in dealing with economic problems it is not sufficient to rely on the tools of individual self-interest but also to include the theme of civic virtue. Making civic virtue an integral part of Keynesian economics implies that Keynesians take a wider view of human nature. In addition to the individual being a rational agent pursuing self-interest, Keynesians also borrow from the Greek perception of the 'polis', of a human nature involved in politics, continuously debating and therefore making choices. Here the individual is an integral part of the community, deriving dignity and well-being because of being a member who participates as part of the wider community. The individual does not pursue self-interest in a vacuum but does so where self-interest represents a series of motivations which are part of the community interests. Civic virtues therefore reflect a context which preserves individual freedoms but also an environment which encourages the recognition of both rights and obligations. Civic virtue means the rights and expectations of individuals to be treated as equals – not just as consumers in the market place but also within the political sphere. However, besides the right to be treated as equals there are areas of mutual benefit for society and the individual including the obligation of society to provide a context where individual excellence is allowed to flourish. At the same time there are obligations on the individual to make a contribution to ensure that the context of rights and obligations is sustained. There is a need, therefore, to establish a continuous contract of entitlements and obligations.

It is important to recognise that an essential element in Keynesian economics is the assumption that individuals are capable of carrying out wider social contracts which are founded on mutual respect and the recognition of interdependence rather than instrumental contracts based on self-interest. Keynesian economics can therefore be seen as being founded on assumptions of mutuality, of the ability and willingness of individuals to relegate their self-interest to the wider social interest, and that a form of continuous contract can be constructed between the state and other key agencies in society.

Although the concept of civic virtue might appear remote and abstract, it might equally be argued that the concept of civic virtue is, in a way, no more abstract than the concept of rational individualism. The concept of rationality provides the foundations for the market liberal approach to economics. To include the concept of civic virtue in Keynesian economics, therefore, is to show the implicit assumptions that equally underpin Keynesian economics and politics. Keynesians have always been aware that once governments 'commit' themselves to a policy of full employment they remove the discipline of the market place to deal with the problem of wage inflation. Once workers are no longer threatened by unemployment, since government indirectly underwrites their wage demands through fiscal policy, then it is obvious that a policy of full employment requires mutuality between governments, employers, and workers. Governments cannot guarantee full employment without also having a policy to deal with wage and price inflation. Employment and inflation in a Keynesian framework therefore represent political choices. They also represent the context for the emergence of civic virtue with workers recognising the benefits of stable demand, secure employment and improved living standards, but also recognising the obligation to moderate wage demands. Incomes policy is central to a Keynesian economic strategy; it represents the way to a civilised economy of constructing contracts between governments, industry, and workers. Within the context of an incomes policy all three agents make certain commitments to achieve an enduring contract. The government guarantees a level of stable demand and employment; workers, governments, and employers then decide on investment levels, wage levels and public expenditure. The growth in the economy is therefore redistributed into investment goods, wages, and the social wage within the context of incomes policy. Such an arrangement replaces the ethics of self-interest, of competition between trade unions to achieve the best settlement for their members. The wider interest of all workers displaces sectional interests since full employment, stable demand, and the social wage are seen as the better way to higher levels of prosperity than the pursuance of narrow self-interest. Workers recognise the benefits of the social wage such as increased expenditures on education, health, and pensions and are willing to trade off increases in their social wage for increases in their wages from employment:

> An incomes policy is not just a device for limiting the wage gains of organised workers. Rather, it represents a means of determining the annual, non-inflationary rise in all the different types of incomes that accrue to households.... Moreover, in a democratic society an incomes policy cannot be imposed. It must gain acceptance among the different economic interest groups as the fairest and most equitable basis for distributing the fruits of technological progress.
>
> (Eichner 1979: 175)

The Keynesian argument concerning unemployment reinforces the view that unemployment is 'involuntary' and that rational individuals do not choose to be unemployed but that unemployment implies unused resources, lost output and lost opportunities for greater prosperity. The presence of wage rigidities and price mark-up means the individual cannot influence the going wage even if that individual is willing to work for a lower wage. It is because workers tend to negotiate around money wages that markets for labour are not sufficiently flexible to respond to changes in demand and that therefore unemployment is likely to be involuntary. Societies which make individual self-interest the central ethic therefore offer no foundations in which individual self-interest can be replaced by a civic virtue based on rights and obligations.

In dealing with the problem of unemployment market economists seem to suggest that communities, through their government, are faced with a series of policy choices. These policy choices would include, for example, the levels of social security payments which prevent hardship and the unemployment consequences of job search. A second policy choice is between the rights of individuals to belong to trade unions which again seems to imply that people either have to live with the outcomes of market forces or to accept to live with unemployment but rights to join trade unions. Keynesian economics, because it seeks to integrate ideas of civic virtue with political democracy, would suggest that societies can have trade unions, social security, and full employment with low inflation provided they are willing to recognise the equation of entitlements and obligations. This means a willingness to recognise that entitlements to social security benefits, trade union rights, and stable employment also require a series of obligations including the obligation to moderate wage demands – in other words to trade off wage demands for other benefits such as social security and pensions. It is the recognition of entitlements and obligations which provides the opportunity for a civilised economy.

Keynesian economics is therefore seen as belonging to the tradition of collectivism where individual self-interest has been rejected as the main motivating force in society. Instead the encouragement of self-interest has been associated with encouraging greed and a fractured society where the material prosperity of some and the experiences of deprivation of others are seen as divisive, offering no opportunity for constructing contracts which could actually improve general welfare:

> personal liberty without the full employment of all our national resources is still uncivilised. Less-than-full employment of resources is not wasteful but it also strikes at the heart of community values and the spirit of excellence. Jobs provide people with the basis for the practice of excellence in a very important sphere of their lives. For our society and others, occupations also play a part in creating individual roles and developing personal dignity...for it is barbaric to require that certain people in society be denied employment.... A nation which thrives on the hardships of its members cannot be called civilised.
>
> (Davidson and Davidson 1988: 20)

KEYNESIAN ECONOMICS AND THE DEMOCRATIC PROCESS

The concept of civic virtue, however, also needs to be located in relation to a specific political context – civic virtue like the rational individual cannot exist outside the social context. Civic virtue is therefore a description of human relations rather than a set of principles which are attached to the individual. The issue is not whether human nature is concerned with self-interest or whether true humanity is concerned with civic virtue, but rather how self-interest and civic virtue are actually translated in the real world. Keynes criticised market liberals for not taking note of the real world. Keynesian economics are therefore related to the context of a democratic society, where no agency has the power to impose its wishes on society and where government has to rule by seeking a wider legitimacy – in other words, that the ethics of civic virtue cannot be imposed but have to be created by mutual consent.

The democratic process seems to impose different limitations for economic policy-making between market liberals and Keynesians. Market liberals seek to put constraints on the arbitrary nature of government and of other vested interest groups and therefore emphasise the needs for a democratic process based on written rules and procedures. On the other hand, Keynesian economics is founded on the view that government is already restricted by the presence of functional groups and that it is the presence of a plurality of interests which ensures the continuity of the democratic process. Accordingly it is the presence of various countervailing forces which guarantees that different interests are continuously articulated. It is therefore not the individual restricted by the state which is central, but the idea that the individual is likely to belong to competing interest groups and that it is the presence of such interest groups which puts a constraint on the arbitrary nature of government. Furthermore, with a Keynesian framework the role of government within the economy is not purely confined to controlling public finance and inflation; government has a more positive role to play in guaranteeing economic stability and prosperity. Keynesians have a more positive vision of government.

Keynesian economics need to be located in the context of a form of politics by consent which is also seen as essential to securing a civilised economy. The legitimacy of government depends on the abilities of government to secure a wider public interest rather than responding to specific and particular interests. In this sense Keynesians challenge market liberals as offering a veil for justifying the *status quo*. The idea of individual self-interest disguises the degree of unequal shares in resources in society and also the inequality of access to resources. Market liberalism is therefore seen as a political agenda which sustains the specific and the particular interests of those who have resources and access to those resources, and which denies others the opportunities of access on the basis that market liberals are concerned primarily with securing individual rights and freedom from the state.

KEYNESIAN ECONOMICS AND THE LABOUR MARKET

While market economists argue that there are dual and segmented labour markets, the theory of labour supply is still influenced by the relationship between wages and the quantity of labour. In the unionised sector labour supply is described as being inelastic to show that irrespective of change in wages, the level of labour supply will remain static. An increase in the demand for labour in the unionised sector will therefore lead to increased wages without any compensatory increases in the levels of employment. In the non-unionised sector the labour supply curve responds to changes in wages so that at a higher wage more labour will be available. In the context of this sector any increase in the demand for labour with unchanged supply will lead to higher wages and higher levels of employment.

According to the market model, therefore, the labour market determines the real wage level and the level of employment. The real wage is also known as the product real wage because it combines the marginal product of each worker and the marginal revenue derived from each marginal product. Real wages therefore reflect the contribution of output by each worker.

Within the context of market liberalism wages are therefore determined in the market place according to the supply and demand for labour and the levels of productivity. Differential wages are justified according to market criteria which are determined by consumers in the goods market, their willingness to purchase the goods supplied, and the price at which the goods are supplied.

The Keynesian challenges to labour markets and wages are threefold. First, there is the argument about the shape of the labour supply curve. Keynesians would argue that even in the non-unionised sector wages are not completely flexible. 'Social' arrangements such as social security ensure that wages are likely to be 'sticky' downwards. This means that wages will not fall below a certain level and that workers will not be willing to work at a wage rate which is below the levels of social security benefits. Second, wage bargains are struck around the 'going rate' at which labour supply changes without any change in wages. Third, only at a certain level of employment does labour supply start to respond to increase in wages. This means that at the going wage rate there is likely to be an increase in labour supply without increase in wages and only as the labour market tightens is labour supply influenced by changes in wages.

According to a Keynesian model, wage setting cannot be explained in terms of the product real wage as determined in the labour market. Workers also bargain around the consumption real wage (Sapsford and Tzannatos 1990). The ability to incorporate wider social pressures in wage bargaining helps explains the presence of wage rigidities from a Keynesian perspective. Keynesians would argue that wage pressures are created outside the labour market. Workers do not bargain in relation to their productivity but are mainly concerned with the levels of their take-home pay. This in turn means that in wage bargaining workers are influenced by the general prices level, the impact of mortgage repayments on their living standards, changes in the exchange rate, the impact of import prices on living standards and also the level of taxation. Therefore, in dealing with wage determination Keynesians also take into consideration the wider social context which influences wage setting. Keynesians would argue that wages are influenced by the following factors.

The context of employment and unemployment

The rates and levels of unemployment do represent a threat to those in work. Unemployment does act as a form of discipline in wage setting, a point recognised by Kalecki in 1943. Kalecki was aware that a commitment by governments to embrace a policy of full employment represented a political choice because,

> 'the sack' would cease to play its role as a disciplinary measure. The social position of the boss would be undermined and the self-assurance and class consciousness of the working-class would grow. Strikes for wage increases and improvements in conditions of work would create political tensions.
>
> (Sawyer 1985: 151)

Keynes was also totally aware of the repercussions of full employment and the lack of agreement between government and trade unions on wages, and he equally accepted that this was a political rather than economic problem:

> Of course I do not want to see money-wages soaring upwards.... It is one of the chief tasks ahead of our statesmanship to find a way to prevent this. But we must solve it in our domestic way, feeling that we are free men, free to be wise or foolish.
>
> (Keynes 1944: 429)

Keynes had argued that his concern was with economic problems – unemployment was an economic issue. Whether full employment was compatible with holding down wage inflation represented a different problem:

> I do not doubt that a serious problem will arise as to how wages are to be restrained when we have a combination of collective bargaining and full employment. But I am not sure how much light the kind of analytic method you apply can throw on this essentially political problem.
>
> (Keynes, in Lord Kahn 1974: 371)

Figure 6.1   The Keynesian labour market model

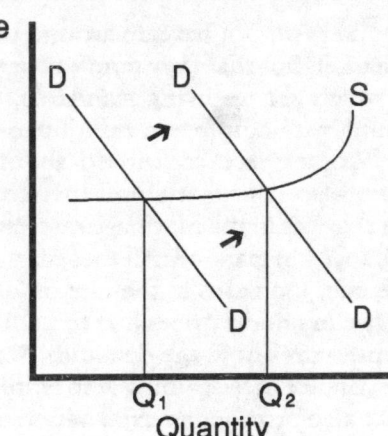

Here, the labour supply is an inflexible constant – wages rigidities and institutional factors meaning that changes do not influence it.
This contrasts with the market model where an increase in demand will mean higher employment without any effect on wages – while there is spare capacity there will be no increases in wages or prices.

The repercussions of full employment for wages was also noted in the Employment White Paper of 1944. Rising unemployment has always been recognised by Keynesians as being a major influence in wage determination. Layard and Nickell (1987) and Layard (1989) have also been able to show that the rise in unemployment during the early 1980s did act as a dampening factor in wage settlements but have also argued that the rise in unemployment was not an enduring factor for it only acted as a short-term break on wage pressures. According to the work of these authors it is the rate at which long-term unemployment is rising which acts as a threatening factor in wage bargaining. The labour market insiders are not threatened by the long-term unemployed. Employers are less likely to employ the long-term unemployed and the long-term unemployed are also less likely to be involved in job search. During the 1980s the rise in unemployment is highly correlated with the rise in long-term unemployment and it is for this reason that unemployment has had only a temporary effect on wage pressures.

The level of unemployment, therefore, does not necessarily dampen wage pressures. The relationship between the number of vacancies and the number unemployed is not even. There are now widening disparities in the degree of tightness of labour markets between the North-west of England, where unemployment in 1990 continues to persist at above 9 per cent – in contrast to a national average of 7 per cent – and the South-east of England where unemployment is around 3 per cent. Because of the tight labour markets in the South and South-east of England, together with the inability of workers from the North to move south, wage inflation has again emerged as a major problem for the 1990s despite the recent high levels of unemployment.

Wage bargaining and the social context

Keynesians have also argued that workers do not bargain around the real wage as determined in the labour market, but that they tend to bargain in money wages. It is money wages which secure living standards, which means that workers in their bargaining with employers are influenced by other price rises in the economy. Workers are concerned about their consumption real wage. Workers are also consumers and therefore are aware of consumer prices, including changes in the mortgage rate, changes in the cost of food or energy, and changes in taxation. All these factors do have an influence on disposable income. Increases in the rate of interest, higher mortgage repayments, and a rise in import prices due to a fall in the exchange rate are likely to increase pressures on wage demands. Workers are therefore involved in real wage resistance in bargaining with employers.

The concept of real wage resistance also provides an explanation of how workers, in seeking to protect their take-home pay, are also likely to respond to changes in taxation. According to the Treasury model (Artis 1989) workers in the UK do transfer changes in taxation into wage pressures. Therefore, increases in direct and indirect taxation to fund public expenditure are likely to meet with worker wage resistance since the latter will seek to compensate for these reductions in take-home pay by instigating wage bargaining.

Wages and trade union influence

The third factor that needs to be considered is the influence of trade unions on the labour market and wages. The market economists' view of trade unions is restricted because it relies on the twin concepts of supply and demand in the labour market and the influence of trade unions on labour supply. According to the market liberal approach trade unions can only influence wages labour supply. According to this model, therefore, competitive labour markets will reflect differences in demand and supply of labour and also help to explain wage differences.

Keynesians have argued that the influence of trade unions on wages requires a wider understanding of how trade unions as organisations respond in the workplace, and therefore a much more complex model was needed to that produced by market economists. Keynesian economists have for example, tried to show that trade union density (the number of workers in trade unions in relation to the total labour force), trade union militancy, and the willingness of workers to withdraw their labour, have all been important factors in wage determination in Britain. Work by Bain (1984), and Bain and Elsheikh (1976) has shown that the growth of trade unions can be attributed to economic factors including unemployment and wages. Bain and Elsheikh have for example argued that individuals are likely to join trade unions during periods of economic prosperity because trade unions are associated with the ability to secure higher living standards for their members. In contrast, unemployment represents a threat effect to trade unions because the unions are seen as unable to protect jobs or the unemployed – the unemployed have no incentive to continue with their membership of trade unions for the benefits which are obtained are directed to those in work. These studies of trade unions are important because they explore the relationships between trade unions, individuals, and the economy as a complex set of interactions which are not purely concerns of labour supply and the labour market.

Trade unions are therefore concerned with issues of comparability between workers; they tend to bargain around a wages league ensuring that their members either retain their position in the wages league table or even aim to go to the top of the league. One thing that trade unions cannot afford to do is to allow their members to fall down in the wages league since this is likely to mean a reduction in union membership as workers drift to the more efficient unions. The study by Phelps Brown (1977) has, for example, shown that the stability of the wages league in Britain seems to suggest that wages are more likely to be determined by questions of relativities.

Keynesians have also outlined approaches to industrial relations to show the impact of centralised and shop floor bargaining on wages. Decentralised bargaining in the context of tight labour markets has been associated with wage drift and leapfrogging as groups of workers compete with each other for higher wage claims. In contrast, the formal system of industrial relations brings together employers' organisations and trade union leaders who make bargains for the whole industry with the hope that the settlement reached will be adhered to by both sides of industry. This form of collective bargaining provides for stable industrial relations because it minimises the number of wildcat strikes.

KEYNESIAN ECONOMICS AND THE PROBLEM OF INFLATION: TRADE UNIONS AND WAGE INFLATION

The differences in perceptions between market liberals and Keynesian economics are not just related to the issue of wage determination and employment but also have implications to explanations of inflation and policies related to the problem of inflation. While monetarist and market economists seek to blame the monetary authorities for increasing the money supply and therefore inflation, in contrast Keynesian economists have wanted to argue that because of price mark-ups and wage rigidities, inflation was not purely a money matter but was caused by cost-push factors. While market economists assume a model where the trade union effect on inflation is neutral and trade unions are therefore seen as a thermometer reflecting inflation, in contrast Keynesian economists see trade unions as having a 'furnace effect' rather than a 'thermometer effect'. According to the furnace approach trade unions are seen as being the cause rather than the consequence of inflation.

Monetarism, inflation and trade unions

Since market economists are concerned with the analysis of trade unions in relation to the labour market and labour supply they tend to neglect the role of trade unions and the possible links between trade unions and inflation. According to the market economic model inflation is always a monetary problem – that is, an excess in the money supply in relation to the amount of goods available in the economy. In Chapter 3 it was argued that studies by market economists, including Friedman, had all shown strong relationships between changes in the money supply and inflation. According to these studies the direction of causation had confirmed that it was the money supply which was the cause of inflation. The demand for money is described as stable since it reflects the number of goods in the economy and represents the velocity of money in relation to transactions of goods and services. Because the demand for money is stable and the number of transactions are determined in the goods market, any changes in the money supply will always result in an increase in prices and, therefore, an increase in the rate of inflation.

Within the context of a monetarist theory of inflation, therefore, trade unions are not a cause of inflation but a consequence. It is government and the monetary authorities which are responsible for the money supply. The attempt by government to influence 'demand' through fiscal and monetary policy is only made possible through an increase in the money supply. Some monetarists would argue that such a policy would only work in the short term. Government in the short term increases the money supply and this will lead to an increase in output. Because workers adapt their wage demands in relation to inflation in the short term there will be a gap between price increases and wage increases, with workers suffering from money illusion in the short term. As prices are rising faster than wages in the short term, firms seeking to maximise profits will increase output and hence employment. Unemployment, according to an adaptive monetarist approach, will only fall in the short term. In the longer term, however, workers will adapt more quickly to changes in prices and output brought about by government. Because governments can fool people some of the time but not all of the time in the long term any attempt by government to increase the money supply will be met by demand for wage increases to compensate for the increase in prices. In the long term, therefore, prices and wages will rise together with firms reducing output and also employment. In the long term, any gains in employment will be lost as unemployment returns to its natural rate.

In contrast to the adaptive monetarists, the rational expectations school would suggest that since individuals are rational agents with perfect information, that even in the short term there will be no monetary illusion. Thus any attempt by government to increase the money supply and prices will be immediately matched by wage increases. According to the rational expectations school the role of government in influencing output and employment is neutral.

Within the context of market economics trade unions do not cause inflation, they purely reflect changes in prices in their wage demands. Workers cannot alter the laws of supply and demand. The problems of employment and inflation are not related. Unemployment is a labour market problem where trade unions seek to influence labour supply and access to labour markets. In contrast inflation is a monetary problem caused by the central authorities increasing the money supply.

Therefore, within this model trade unions act as a thermometer reflecting the temperature of inflation within the economy. Trade unions adapt their wage demands in relation to changes in prices. To break with the expectations of inflation government needs to make explicit rules on how they seek to control the money supply. By making explicit rules on the money supply and issuing targets for it, the government make explicit their commitment to the control of inflation. If the increase in money supply exceeds the announced monetary targets then interest rates are used to control the demand for money. The government does not accommodate any changes in the demand for money; the money supply has to be consistent with the rate of inflation. Once government indicate their commitment to the control of inflation then workers will break with wage bargains which seek to adapt to future inflation.

Keynesian economics and inflation

While a market liberal approach to inflation would fit within the category of 'demand-pull' explanations, Keynesian approaches to inflation need to be separated out between 'demand-pull' and 'cost-push' explanations. Although Keynesians also have demand-pull models of inflation, the Keynesian transmission mechanism is very different from the market liberal approach to demand-pull. As was suggested, the market liberal approach to inflation is through the money supply, using Friedman's helicopter syndrome of government 'printing' money thereby increasing the level of demand without a corresponding increase in output. The increase in the money supply therefore increases demand in excess of output thus pushing up prices and inflation.

The Keynesian approach to inflation falls into the two categories of demand-pull and cost-push theories. The demand-pull theory is underpinned by the Phillips curve thesis which suggests that there is a strong relationship between the rate of inflation and the levels of unemployment. This argument hypothesises that inflation represents a process of overheating of the economy when the level of demand exceeds economic capacity. The level of demand is represented by the unemployment rate. Inflation in this context represents a condition when all resources available within the economy are being fully utilised and not meeting the level of effective demand. According to the demand-pull theory governments are faced with a menu of policy choices between employment and inflation. Inflation is caused by tight labour markets which increase the competition for labour and wages. In the context of full employment and rising inflation governments have to make political choices between the rate of inflation and the politically accepted level of unemployment. If, on the other hand, the government decide to reduce the level of demand to curb inflationary pressures then the fall in demand is likely to lead to a fall in output and an increase in unemployment. In contrast, if the government decide to live with rising inflation but maintain a commitment to a policy of full employment then they will have to look for policies which deal with wage inflation.

According to the cost-push model inflation rises independently of demand-pull factors or the level of unemployment. The ability to influence prices arises because both industry and workers can mark-up their prices irrespective of the level of demand. Within the context of administered prices, therefore, changes in prices do not reflect the dynamics of the market place but rather the continuing process of concentration of firms and their ability to mark-up prices as well as the ability of workers to initiate wage claims and earn wage settlements which are independent of the process of supply and demand in the labour market. This argument, therefore, hypothesises that cost-push inflation is the result of concentration, mergers, and the rationalisation process of firms which increasingly make the economy less competitive. On the other hand workers are able to negotiate higher wage claims by combining together into trade unions.

Demand-pull inflation and the Phillips curve

The pioneering work by Phillips (1958) established for the first time the connection between the level of unemployment and the rate of wage changes. Phillips argued that when unemployment was low, wages would rise fast due to the competition for labour while when unemployment was high wages would fall but would fall less rapidly because of worker wage resistance. The relationship between wages and unemployment was an inverse Phillips curve. The Phillips study included the period 1861 to 1957 in which Phillips argued that he had established a robust equation between unemployment and inflation. The significance of the Phillips curve cannot be sufficiently emphasised because what this model offered both to Keynesian economists and government was a menu of policy choices.

Phillips seemed to be saying to government that if they chose a policy of low inflation then the policy cost of low inflation was high unemployment. Equally, if government adopted policies to reduce unemployment then they had to live with rising inflation. In this sense Keynesians were able to establish a trade off between unemployment and inflation, this being in contrast to the market liberal view that unemployment was a problem of market rigidities and inflation a problem of government. However, the perception of a stable trade off and a stable Phillips curve was directly undermined by the work of Friedman (1968) whose contribution led to the concept of an 'expectations-augmented' Phillips curve. Friedman argued that the Phillips trade off was based on the assumption that workers only bargained around nominal wages. Friedman returned to the argument that workers might suffer from money illusion only in the short term and that in the long term would therefore bargain for real wages. Because agents bargained on real wages, then bargains were likely to be struck around the expected rate of inflation and the expected real wage. The higher the expected rate of inflation the higher the level of nominal wage inflation consistent with a given expected real wage and level of employment. The trade off between unemployment and inflation was not stable and because of the presence of inflation and workers trying to compensate for future inflation it was more accurate to argue for an augmented Phillips curve which showed an unstable and increasing trade off between the unemployment rate and inflation.

Cost push inflation: the trade union factor

One of the major differences between market economics and Keynesianism is the role assigned to trade unions and inflation in respect of the two models. While market economists construct a model which separates explanations of inflation from those of unemployment, in contrast Keynesian economists going back to Keynes himself have always argued that there were policy trade offs between the levels of unemployment and wage inflation. For market economists the possibility of cost-push inflation does not exist because although some organisations might be able to influence some prices, they cannot distort the market because the market is always bigger than any one organisation. Market economists therefore reject the concept of administered prices because there are no organisations big enough to monopolise the market – either in the domestic or the global economy. Where organisations do start to dominate any sector other organisation are likely to enter and compete for market share. There are therefore no monopolies and no administered prices. Only governments and the central bank can influence inflation by increasing the level of the money supply.

Within the context of price mark-up and non-flexible prices, Keynesians see the process of inflation reflecting a series of relationships between firms which can mark-up prices, with the impact of trade unions on wages, inflation and government being an important factor. These can be described as

1 the wage–wage spiral which reflects a context of competing wage claims within different sectors of the economy, the impact of decentralised bargaining and wage drift;
2 the wage–price spiral where the rate in wage rises squeezes out the profit margins which in turn leads to firms marking up their prices;
3 the price–wage spiral which occurs through shock increases in prices such as the oil price increases in 1973 and 1974 which resulted in workers attempting to increase their wages to protect their take-home pay.

Wage–wage spiral

Keynesian economists have pointed to problems of wage drift in collective bargaining especially in industrial relations systems governed by informal arrangements between local shop stewards and management. Studies by Mulvey (1976) and Pencavel (1974) indicate that in the UK the impact of unions upon wages stems from the strength of local bargaining agents. The problem with decentralised bargains is that local managers might find themselves too weak to deal with organised trade unions and would therefore prefer to deal with trade unions through national arrangements. Local bargains tend to be of short duration with shop stewards often reflecting or giving leadership to local militancy. Decentralised bargaining has therefore been associated with wage drift and the wage–wage spiral.

Wage–price spiral

While market economists have tended to argue that trade unions are not the cause of inflation. Keynesian economists have produced studies to show (a) that the level of unionisation does have an impact on wage inflation, and (b) that trade union militancy is also a major contributory factor to wage inflation, wage inflation acting as a furnace for a general price increase. The work by Purdy and Zis (1974) has shown that trade union militancy and the willingness of trade unions to embark on action does have a strong influence on wage inflation. Firms faced with disruption in production have to decide between the costs of lost production and the longer-term wage claims. Firms not wishing to lose key workers or market share are under pressure to give in to trade union militancy. Hines has also argued that the degree of unionisation, both at a national level and at the local level, is also a major determinant in explaining wage inflation. Firms faced with lower profits because of higher wage settlements are likely to pass the wage increase on to the consumer as a price mark-up which eventually leads to other workers demanding higher wage settlements to compensate for the price increases.

Price–wage spiral

Keynesian economists describe the oil price increases in 1973 and 1980 as having both an inflationary and deflationary effect on the British economy. Market economists, by contrast, argue that while the oil price increase did lead to higher prices in the oil goods sector, the price of other products was likely to fall with no inflationary effect. The market liberal thesis is based on the assumption of flexible prices. The oil price increases force consumers to pay more for oil because in the short term at least demand for oil products is inelastic. Since consumers are spending more of their disposable income in the oil goods sector, they have less income available for other goods. This means that demand for other goods will fall and as demand for other goods falls so will the price in the other goods sector, thus countering the increase in prices in the oil goods sector with no net increases in the rate of inflation.

In contrast, Keynesians argued that the total effect of the oil price increase was likely to be inflationary because of non-flexible prices. The oil price rise increased the price of the oil goods sector. Furthermore, since the prices of other goods were not flexible, the increase in the price of oil was not to be matched by the fall in the price of other goods. The oil price increase was therefore likely to be inflationary because of non flexible prices which in turn was also likely to increase wage pressures as workers sought to compensate their losses in disposable income.

In addition to being inflationary an external price shock can also be deflationary within a Keynesian framework. Utilising the twin concepts of IS/LM Keynesians would argue that an overall increase in prices is likely to influence the level of effective demand. An increase in price results in a fall in disposable income and consumption which means that as national income falls, so will the level of savings. As savings fall so will investment, the net result being that the IS curve shifts to the left. With an unchanged LM curve, interest rates will fall but so will national income. The fall in national income will result in an increase in the level of unemployment.

Within a Keynesian model of non-flexible prices it is therefore possible to have both inflation and unemployment. Because prices are not flexible the increase in prices in one sector is not likely to be matched by a fall in prices in other sectors of the economy, which in turn leads to an overall price increase. If prices outstrip wages then this is similar to a cut in wages, which means a fall in disposable income and a fall in demand which leads to a fall in national income and an increase in unemployment. To remedy

Figure 6.2   The dynamics of a Keynesian model: the effect of oil price
increases on the UK and international economies

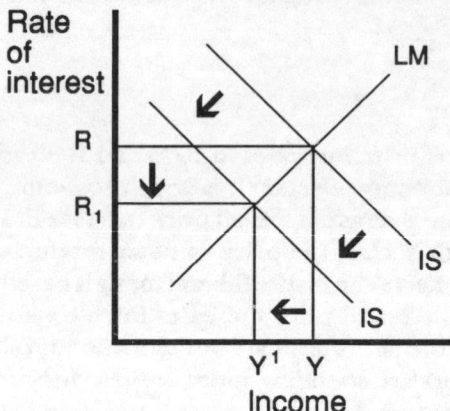

(a) Oil price increases mean a fall in national incomes, which means a fall in savings with a resultant fall in investment; the IS curve shifts to the left leading to a fall in income and low interest rates, with increases in unemployment as income falls.

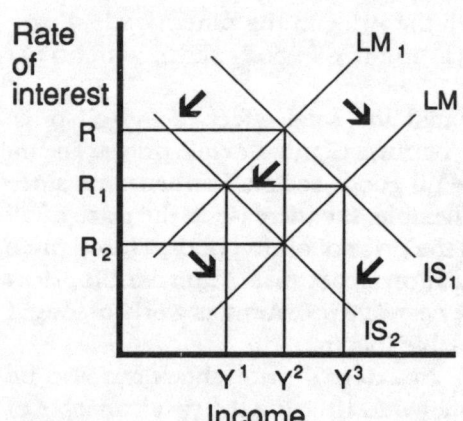

(b) The Keynesian remedy is to increase public expenditure and reduce taxes. This shifts the IS curve and also reduces interest rates; the LM curve shifts to the right.

the deflationary effect of an external price shock Keynesians would urge a relaxation of LM by reducing interest rates further which will result in an increase in investment, in national income, and employment.

In contrast market economists will see the fall in interest rates as a signal for an increase in the money supply and as a danger leading to inflation. Despite the deflationary effects of the oil price shock, market economists would seek to tighten interest rates to their original position which means that rather than shifting LM to the right this will shift LM to the left increasing interest rates and worsening national income and also unemployment.

Figure 6.3   A monetarist response to the effects of an oil price increase

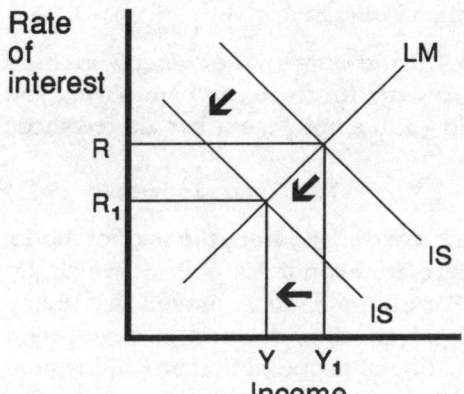

An increase in oil price is deflationary, shifting IS to the left. The fall in the rate of interest is seen as leading to an increase in the money supply and inflation.

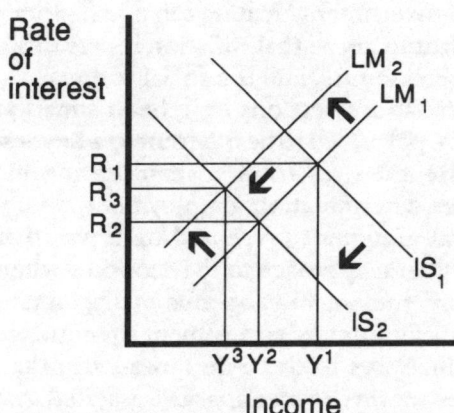

The monetarist response is to increase interest rates, thus shifting LM to the left also. Keynesians see this as being more deflationary for it reduces income from Y_1 to Y_2 to Y_3 with higher levels of unemployment resulting.

KEYNESIAN ECONOMICS AND ECONOMIC POLICIES

Keynesian economists have emphasised that dealing with problems of unemployment and inflation represents a series of political choices. Once governments accept that through the process of demand management, fiscal and monetary levers can be used to influence the level of demand and employment, then they have also to find ways of dealing with the problem of inflation if unemployment is not going to be used as the instrument to achieve wage moderation. The 1944 Employment White Paper represented an undertaking by the British government 'to the maintenance of a high and stable level of employment'. Other countries such as the USA and

Sweden made similar commitments to those of Britain in 1946. In all these countries the commitment to full employment became a political choice. This choice was stated quite clearly in a *Times* editorial:

> Such a commitment means the loss of authority for the owner who could always say – if you do not want to work for the wage I am paying you there are plenty more who would – full employment has altered those relationships.
>
> (*The Times*, 23 January 1943)

As there are economic policies which are derived from the market model of how the economy works, so there are economics policies which are based on Keynesian prescriptions. For example, the argument that unemployment always represents a lack of effective demand is obviously a Keynesian statement as is the market liberal proposal that unemployment represents a labour market problem. This applies to the explanation of, and cures for, inflation, with market liberals arguing that the problem of inflation is a monetary problem – of government creating too much money to fund its borrowing. Keynesians would argue that inflation represents a series of tensions between politics, economics, and the social context.

The arguments constructed in the above sections have been aimed at outlining certain principles which are perceived to be inherent to a Keynesian economic model, and to utilise these as tools to explain specific economic problems including wages determination, employment, unemployment and inflation. The central argument presented here was that Keynesians depart from the market liberal approach to the economy when it comes to the potential role of government in economic management. While market liberals argued that any attempt by government to influence markets was a misguided policy which was likely to do more harm than good to the future prospects of the economy, Keynesians have asserted that the argument that markets would find an equilibrium at the end of the day was not a good enough policy criteria when individual aspirations and life chances were at stake.

According to Keynesians, the economy cannot be left to itself because the equilibrium could not guarantee the full employment of all economic resources. Market liberals, Keynesians argue, had underestimated the problems involved with the presence of risk and uncertainty. These factors were likely to lead to markets being driven by sentiment rather than rational calculation, which by nature was likely to result in oscillations between optimism and pessimism. The inability to predict future trends was therefore likely to lead to a mismatch between savings and investment, since savings were related to the level of income while investment tended to depend on the stability of demand. In this context Keynesians argue that government have a role to play in economic management in smoothing out these fluctuations and guaranteeing a level of stable demand.

However, one important aspect of demand management which seems to be missing from some Keynesian models is the need to institutionalise such a policy. Demand management is not purely an economic technique, a lever to be manipulated according to the business cycle. Demand management needs to be integrated within the context of civic virtue and democratic society. The need to establish demand management as an institution includes the establishing of public institutions and arenas where the prospects of demand management can be discussed between government and key economic agents. Countries such as Sweden, West Germany, and Austria can be cited as examples of institutionalised demand management. By contrast, both in Britain and the USA Keynesian demand management remained an economic technique only. Institutionalising demand management in these countries has involved the establishing of permanent forums where members of the government, industry, and trade unions are able to discuss the prospects for the economy. The forum acts as a vehicle for the setting up of contracts between these agencies. While the government on its part makes commitments to stable demand management, the other agents also make commitments on the levels of investment and wages. According to this approach the government seeks to underpin growth and prosperity in the economy while business makes commitments on investment in relation to the planned growth; trade unions on their part trade off wage demands against future investment policy, the employment of their members and also commitments by governments to social concerns such as training, pensions, health care and education. It is this process of dialogue which is central to a Keynesian framework – the ability of economic agents to discuss, debate and make agreements.

Goran Therborn (1986), in his book *Why Some People Are More Unemployed Than Others*, has argued the case that the central reason why some countries were more able than others to cope with the recession and unemployment of the 1980s was the differences in institutional arrangements in these countries to manage economic policy. The author was able to point out that in those countries which had established and mature institutionalised agreements, unemployment was less severe than in those countries which had relied on market forces.

Underlying the variations there seem to be two common important patterns, which are certainly inter-related. One is the remarkable national unity around a set of concrete policy priorities.... Second, largely because of this consensus, there appear to be strong expectation by all important actors in the successful countries that there will be a fairly long-term continuity in basic government policy orientation.

(Therborn 1986: 132)

Therborn goes on to argue that in countries which had established a national consensus, that faced with the consequences of recession government was able to persuade trade unions to behave as responsible agents and reduce wage demands to maintain their competitive edge while employers were also persuaded to invest despite the context of recession. In these countries, therefore, workers reduced their costs in a co-ordinated way which ensured continuity in employment while government and employers increased private and public investment. These countries were in a better position to increase their share of world trade and as exports increased economic prosperity, West Germany, Sweden, and Japan were also able to maintain stable exchange rates and interest rate policies while countries such as the UK and the USA experienced wide fluctuations in interest rates and in the exchange rate. High interest rates together with a high exchange rate in the UK during the period 1980 and 1981, for example, have been blamed for the steep rise in unemployment during this period – from 1.5 million in 1979 to over 3 million in 1982 (Keegan 1983).

The context of institutionalised demand management provided a mechanism in some countries which enabled strategic economic agents to be brought together to make policy choices in the context of a global market economy. Rather than accepting the economic context as immutable and non-negotiable, governments in these countries facilitated conditions in which policy choices could be addressed. Japan and West Germany, which in contrast to Britain were completely dependent on oil imports were aware of the oil price increases and the impact on their domestic economies. Rather than allowing economic agents to drive up wages to compensate for their losses in take-home pay governments in these countries were able to reach agreements with the trade unions and employers about the necessity of wage moderation, reducing unit labour costs and increasing exports to compensate for the increase in import costs. In contrast the response in

Figure 6.4   UK unemployment, 1979–90 (in millions)

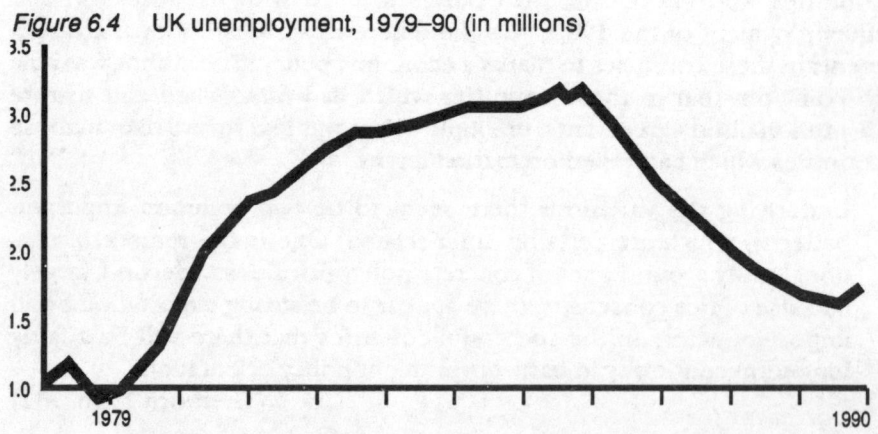

Source: Datastream, December 1990

Britain was that the government after 1979 actually abolished incomes policy, arguing instead that wages should be determined in the market place. Furthermore, they downgraded the importance of the National Economic Development Council (NEDC) which was the only forum available in the UK for employers to meet with government and trade unions. Although NEDC does not have any statutory powers, it still provides a potential for the conduct of debate about economic policy choices. It would seem that in the early 1980s while Sweden, West Germany and other countries were strengthening their institutional arrangements, Britain was moving further towards market solutions.

Two other studies need to be mentioned here to illustrate the impact of Keynesian thinking on economic policy in the 1980s. Both studies, similar to the work of Therborn, have argued that the rise of unemployment in the 1980s can be attributed to the abandoning of Keynesian economics. First, there is the work by Layard and Nickell (1986, 1987) where the authors concentrate on UK unemployment in the 1980s. These have attempted to combine Keynesian and market liberal explanations of unemployment into an econometric model of unemployment and have grouped their explanatory variables as:

1 The demand management variable – a Keynesian variable to show the impact of fiscal and monetary policy on the economy and its impact on demand and employment.
2 The national insurance variable – a market economic variable associated with increased costs of labour to the employers and therefore likely to reduce the demand for labour.
3 The institutional variable including the closed shop, rights of dismissal, and other legislation likely to influence labour markets.
4 The labour mismatch between skills and vacancies.
5 The benefit system and the impact of social security on search and unemployment duration.

The authors argue that between 1979 and 1985 unemployment had risen by 11 per cent – the Keynesian variable of demand management explains over 60 per cent of the increase in unemployment. The authors postulate that the reductions in public expenditure, increases in taxation, and higher and higher interest rates all had a major impact on demand and employment. In contrast, when evaluating the market liberal variables and their impact on unemployment only the increased costs of national insurance could be considered as a significant variable.

The second study includes the work of McCallum (1986) in an article on 'Unemployment in the OECD Countries in the 1980s'. In a way McCallum reinforces the results produced by Therborn (1986) and Layard and Nickell, but while Therborn looked at the institutional factors McCallum attempts to look at the differences between fiscal and monetary and wages policies within the sixteen major industrial countries of the Western economies. McCallum concentrates on the 'tightness' of fiscal and monetary policies and asks why, after 1984, unemployment started to fall in the USA in contrast to the European Community countries. His results seek to contradict the market liberal argument that European countries suffer from 'Eurosclerosis' (an inflexible labour market) because of the influence of trade unions. He contrasts this to the USA where a low trade union density implies a more flexible labour market. Market economists will therefore argue that the USA will always have a greater capacity to create more jobs. Comparing the fiscal policy and wage rigidities as the competing explanatory variables, McCallum suggests that:

> The basic conclusion is that differences [in unemployment] have been due largely to fiscal and monetary policy with the real wage variable playing a minor role.... These results shed light on the issue of why unemployment has increased by so much more in Europe than in the United States.... The results indicate that over the period 1979–84 differences in fiscal and monetary policy account for about 100 per cent of the 3.3 percentage point increase in the gap between unemployment in Europe and the United States.
>
> (McCallum 1986: 942)

According to McCallum, therefore, it was the willingness of the Reagan administration to use classical Keynesian fiscal policies which actually reduced unemployment in the USA. The US government reduced personal taxation and increased the budget deficit to finance expenditures on defence during the period 1983 to 1985.

What is common to these three studies is the application of Keynesian techniques to explain the economic context of the 1980s. The argument has been that Keynesian economics was on the retreat both intellectually and practically because Keynesian theory was not equipped to explain both the unemployment and the inflation that dominated the period. Keynesian economics has tended to be downgraded as belonging to the era of slump and recession of the inter-war period. However, it has been argued in these two chapters that because Keynesianism embraces economic, social, and political arguments, Keynesians have been quite well equipped theoretically to explain the causes and cures for the inflation and the unemployment. But as Keynes himself was aware governments always have choices between policy alternatives, and the alternatives are judged according to political choices. The studies by Therborn, McCallum, and Layard and Nickell all reinforce the argument that Keynesians have been able to provide explanations and, furthermore, that some governments have continued to embrace Keynesian principles while others have decided to abandon these principles. However, because some governments have decided to embrace market principles, this does not imply that Keynesian economics are in retreat like the ebbing tide. If Keynesianism has been in retreat it was because some governments made the deliberate political choice to shelve Keynesian options. However, there is also a need to emphasise that while some governments might have abandoned Keynesian economics at the level of rhetoric and embraced supply side economics, there was always a discrepancy between the policy rhetoric and reality – the US government might have put forward supply side arguments but still used Keynesian tools to reduce unemployment. Equally, the decision by the Group of Seven to reduce interest rates in October 1987 to counter the deflationary effects because of the fall in share prices, could also be seen as a return to international Keynesianism. The Group of Seven meetings have produced a new forum for co-ordinating exchange rate policies, replacing the early 1980s monetarist proposal of countries not being able to buck the market and thus advocating free exchange rate policies. The Group of Seven seem to be signalling a return to a fixed exchange rate although this time, unlike the Bretton Woods agreements, the level for the exchange rate will not be announced but remain implicit in government policy. The decision of the UK to join the EMS in October 1990 also confirms the movement towards a fixed exchange rate within the European Community.

CONCLUSIONS

The election of the Thatcher government in Britain in 1979 and that of President Reagan in the USA in 1980 seemed to confirm, for some commentators at least, the end of Keynesian thinking and the influence of Keynes on economic policy-making. Both these governments were often seen as reflecting the new mood of the market liberal counter revolution of the 1980s against the Keynesian corporatism of the 1960s and the 1970s. In contrast the 1980s are associated with the rights of the individual as against the vested interests which dominated the Keynesian era. The Thatcher decade and the impact of Mrs Thatcher's brand of market liberalism was assessed as follows in November 1989 in a *Financial Times* editorial:

> She believes in self-reliance, enterprise, thrift, law and order and a limited state. She abhors trade unions, spongers and left wing intellectuals. The triumph of these attitudes was no accident. It reflected the failure of socialist corporatism to deliver acceptable economic performance or social harmony. Her government is criticised for over centralisation of power... Only a powerful state Mrs Thatcher believes can protect the people from the barons of corporatism. Within society more is now in the hands of the individual: but within government more is in the hands of the Prime Minister.
>
> (*Financial Times*, 21 November 1989)

The above quote is striking because it captures the market liberal sentiment as to what went wrong in the 1970s and also seeks to make links between the issues and the intellectual environment. The market liberal critique of what is seen as the Keynesian era is twofold: first, there is the argument that Keynesian perceptions of government and politics are naïve and also incorrect; second that economic policy founded on politic choices fails to deliver on both economic performance and social harmony.

Market liberals would argue that Keynesian economics legitimised the importance of functional groups in the making of economic policy. Because the commitment to full employment requires economic agents to make certain concessions the process of government becomes a series of bargains between groups and the government. Thus in seeking to get trade unions to moderate their wage demands, market liberals would argue that the government had to pay a high price in obtaining such a concession. Governments therefore became increasingly dependent on vested interests, often at the cost of those individuals whose interests were not represented by the strategic groups involved in the policy process; the individual as consumer, as tax payer or pensioner was at the margins since Keynesian corporatism was dominated by groups involved in production.

While Keynesians would argue that the public forum is essential for creating a civilised economy as against the dominance of self-interest, market liberals would argue that such forums actually produce the new barons of corporatism who decide behind closed doors who should get what, when, and how. Market liberals would also point out that such decisions are likely to be more arbitrary and unjust than the market place and that it was always better to leave decisions to the market and individual self-interest since these are invariably more likely to be just than those produced under Keynesian corporatism.

In the above sections it was suggested that Keynesian economics represented a Kuhnian revolution, a paradigm shift from the neo-classical paradigm. Keynesian economics challenged the ethics of rational agents, market equilibrium, and flexible prices, and replaced these with ideas of civic virtue, government, and intervention as the ethics which should influence economic policy-making. Keynes argued that living with the argument that markets would at the end of the day adjust at equilibrium prices was not a criteria for a society concerned with well-being and prosperity. Rather than seeking to create a vision of competitive markets, Keynesians have sought to produce a pragmatic politics of living with reality as it is.

The market liberal argument that Keynesian economics produces new vested interests often acting against the well-being of the individual needs to be countered by the question of whether a market liberal vision actually replaces one set of vested interests with new interests. While it might be argued that one of the central achievements of the Thatcher government has been the reform of trade unions, the question arises as to what economic policies are available to the government to deal with the inflation of the 1990s. While Keynesians recognised the problem of wage inflation in the context of tight labour markets, market liberals continue to ignore the problem of wages pressures as a major cause of inflation. Keynesians would argue for the relevance of a political forum to decide on wages, employment, and investment as the way to economic prosperity. In contrast, market liberals ignore the problem of wage inflation, while their approach continues to be limited to the use of monetary policy and interest rates to control demand. Yet as demand is brought under control the only weapon for government continues to be unemployment (and the threat of unemployment) as the way to control wage inflation.

The experience of the 1980s, however, has also changed Keynesian thinking. For example, only a few unreconstructed Keynesians would still argue that unemployment always represents a problem of effective demands without thinking about the supply side of the economy. Few Keynesian economists would argue today that an overall increase in public expenditure would continue to reduce the level of unemployment without thinking that the problem is not just of demand but also a problem of training in human capital. New Keynesians are therefore aware of the need to 'target' public expenditure – not by increasing overall disposable income, but by using public expenditure to deal with human capital to produce a better trained labour force which can produce new goods and is able to meet demand. Equally, Keynesians are aware of regional variations in unemployment and also the problems of unemployment in the inner cities – unemployment associated with youth ethnicity and the long-term unemployed. All these problems require different solutions. Increasing demand in a classical Keynesian fashion will not deal with the problem of unemployment for ethnic minorities. Again this requires a form of Keynesian targeting of policies directed at urban regeneration and training opportunities. Also, there are problems for women wanting to enter the labour market where the obstacle remains the lack of child-care facilities.

All these issues would require an 'interventionist' approach and such a policy could be equally justified both within a market liberal context and a Keynesian framework. Market liberals concerned with issues of market failure, of spillover problems, investment in human capital, and ending discriminatory practices, would justify an agenda for government intervention. Keynesians, on the other hand, would suggest that the market liberal acceptance that markets do fail is central to Keynesian thinking and that this justifies a more interventionist role by government. Where Keynesians would depart from market liberals is that rather than perceiving these policies as dealing with the micro concerns of the labour market they would see them as macro problems, arguing that the issue of investment in human capital and training is not purely an issue of labour markets but a macro concern. Human capital investment is connected with the balance of payments, with increasing exports and macroeconomic performance. Keynesians would argue that investment in human capital and training needs ought to be part of the national forum where strategic economic agents, together with governments, make training a macroeconomic priority.

For both market liberals and Keynesians, therefore, the economic context presents a series of pressures and policy options on government. Issues concerned with the environment or pollution, training and investment in human capital, and redistribution of income are as much part of the market liberal moral political economy as the agenda to create a more civilised economy is for the Keynesians. The problem is that governments do not make policy choices purely in relation to economic ideas. There are the added concerns of political calculation and social considerations. Such issues do have the potential of overriding purely economic criteria.

Chapter 7

The politics of Keynesianism

Harry Fineberg and Maurice Mullard

INTRODUCTION: ECONOMIC DECLINE AND POLITICAL CHANGE

The alternative to classical market liberalism advanced by Keynes in the *General Theory* did not emanate in a vacuum. The proposition of this chapter will be that in order to make sense of the political implications of the economic theory it is necessary to locate Keynes and Keynesianism in a number of historical and political contexts.

First, it is legitimate to speak of a crisis juncture of both *laissez-faire* capitalism as a form of economic organisation and of market liberalism as a theory of political and economic behaviour. This dual crisis represented a challenge at both the intellectual and practical levels. This predicament is seen as beginning gradually in the 1870s, intensifying in the 1920s and coming to a climax in the great slump of the 1930s. The confidence in mid-Victorian politics and economics was first shaken by the series of economic recessions between 1870 and 1914. During this period Britain's economic growth and leadership began to slacken from its mid-Victorian high point as serious challenges emerged from Germany and the United States. As Britain was overtaken by its main rivals in critical areas of economic performance, the faith in free trade and *laissez-faire* began to falter and advocates of a system of imperial tariffs to protect British trading interests began to emerge. This issue of free trade versus fair trade, as it was called – together with other issues such as Home Rule for Ireland and the emergence of socialism – began a new stage in British politics and also launched a major conflict within the Liberal Party, which had been the dominant force in mid-Victorian Britain.

As the classical Cobdenite vision of global free trade and international peace seemed increasingly marginal in the new world of imperial rivalries and British economic decline, so positions were increasingly taken up in relation to the role of the state in economic and social problems. On one side of this process a sustained move of support can be identified from the Liberal Party to the Conservatives from the 1880s onwards by landowners, shareholders, and property owners generally. This move was caused not only by economic crisis but also by the emergence of a collectivist liberalism prepared to use the state to address these problems and by the emergence of an independent Labour and socialist politics which began to attract working class support from the 1890s (Perkin 1989: 40–6).

In opposition to these interventionist tendencies the Conservatives offered a grand alliance of property interests – incorporating aristocratic landowners, manufacturers, shopkeepers and suburban houseowners – against the higher rates and taxes made implicit in the interventionist programmes of both the Liberal and Labour Parties. At the same time the Liberals were losing skilled working class support to the idea of independent labour representation, a process stimulated by the founding of the Independent Labour Party in 1893 and accelerated by the trade unions both in their affiliations and in the eventual formation of the Labour Party in 1918.

The Liberal Party joined by Keynes in the 1920s, had been further divided by a leadership conflict in 1916 and was therefore a Party increasingly remote from political power. In a crucial sense however, this freed leading intellectuals to develop new ideas and new policy recommendations to deal with the economic crisis. It would seem feasible to argue that as the Liberal Party entered the political wilderness, it became a think-tank of leading thinkers, including Beveridge and Keynes who were now able to use the Liberal Party not only as the platform for their ideas but also as an attempt to influence both Conservative and Labour thinking.

LIBERAL COLLECTIVISM AND THE RE-EMERGENCE OF THE STATE

Intellectually the first sign of a crisis in Victorian *laissez-faire* can be found in the later work of J. S. Mill. He comes to accept that state intervention in areas such as education, gas, water and railways, provision of a subsistence minimum and public responsibility for a range of local services, are all legitimate practices on the grounds that private individuals may not be the best judges of needs or may refuse to perform certain essential actions. Mill held to the established view that the production of wealth depended upon on the laws of classical political economy and thus believed, unlike Keynes, that the state had no role to play in direct intervention in the productive process. But the question of the distribution of wealth was a matter of public policy for only through a more widespread and a more equal distribution of income could individual improvement take place. By implication this could not be achieved through the random operations of the market. There had to be some conscious direction of the distributive process and this had to involve the role of public policy and politics (Greenleaf 1983: 113–21).

Mills's later views were to be taken up and developed in the idea of positive freedom by collectivist liberals such as T. H. Green, and Hobhouse and Hobson. Here freedom was not merely concerned with the avoidance of pain and satisfaction of desires, but was an ethical state in which each individual can develop morally, aesthetically, ethically and intellectually. If individuals are totally free in the choices they make their own self-development may be frustrated through ignorance and the consequences of poverty. Green observes,

> Our modern legislation...with reference to labour, and education, and health, involving as it does manifold interference with freedom of contract is justified on the ground that it is the business of the state,... to maintain the conditions without which a free exercise of the human faculties is impossible.
>
> (Greenleaf 1983: 136)

In practical politics certain interventionist trends are discernible from the 1870s, beginning with Joseph Chamberlain's transformation of the role of local government in Birmingham – a theme to be taken up by the Progressives and the Fabian Society with their emphasis upon municipal control and ownership of gas, water, transport, education and health in London's local politics. One of the strongest arguments advanced by these local collectivists was that municipal control made possible the application of consistent and reliable standards of performance and safety throughout a city or town without the disadvantages of varying standards which had arisen from private sector provision. The local authority was also seen as an employer able to intervene in the local economy to reduce levels of unemployment. All of these measures were financed through rate increases rather than substantial central government spending.

Aspects of this local collectivism were to be translated to the level of national policy in the legislative record of the reforming Liberal government of 1906 to 1914 with the introducing of state pensions and insurance against unemployment for vulnerable workers such as building workers and farm labourers. The Liberal government also introduced the concept of free school meals and rights to secondary education. The social reforms of 1906 have been seen as creating the foundations for the British welfare state.

Furthermore, in the important area of industrial relations the Trade Union Act of 1906 established wider legal immunities for trade unions in the furtherance of industrial disputes without incurring crippling costs, thus recognising the rights of workers to take collective action – the aim being to bring an equal balance in the relationship between employers and the labour force. This legislation actually enshrined trade union rights until the Trade Union Acts of the 1980s.

Within the structures of government itself, particularly through the role of the Board of Trade between 1890 and 1914, there emerged a growing realisation that a stable system of industrial relations would be of economic and social benefit. Consensus and negotiation were, respectively, the ends and means favoured in the relation between capital and labour. Trade union recognition by employers was encouraged by the Board of Trade, as was collective bargaining. The terms on which the labour market was to operate were no longer those of individual contracts between the firm as an individual and the individual employee. The collective interests of both employers and workers were to be recognised as an unavoidable reality. The Board also developed its conciliation service to deal with difficult industrial disputes. This development was an explicit attempt to move away from the confrontational character of industrial relations and the hands off approach by government (Fox 1985). This general attempt to involve trade unions into what has been called a tripartite relationship with employers and government is sometimes seen as the first attempt to construct a corporatist politics in Britain.

Furthermore, during the 1920s, trade union officials were being recruited to conciliation boards and their unions were called upon to help administer the national insurance scheme. Within the political parties there seemed to be an increased willingness to search for a new consensus, so that leading influences – including Harold Macmillan in his book *The Middle Way*, Lloyd George, and others – took up the idea of the Industrial Parliament, of integrating trade union and employer organisations into the process of policy-making and expanding state intervention in an economy especially designed to reduce unemployment and improve industrial efficiency. By this time Keynes was beginning to make his own contribution to the debate.

THE POLITICAL CULTURE OF KEYNES

Strongly influenced by A. E. Marshall, his Cambridge teacher in economics, Keynes shared the former's view of the purpose of economics as a way, 'to open up all the material means of a refined and noble life' (Moggridge 1976: 30). Keynes as we have seen, took the view that modern industrial economies possessed the capacity to resolve the basic needs of each individual citizen without the threat of insecurity and unemployment. The purpose of a national economy was to increase the sum total of human welfare and development. He saw economics as a moral science concerned with values and priorities and rejected the implications of a fixed scarcity model of economic activity. Rather,

> Economics is a science of thinking in terms of models...which are relevant of the contemporary world.... The object of a model is to segregate the semi permanent or relatively constant factors from those which are transitory or fluctuating so as to develop a logical way of thinking about the latter.
>
> (Moggridge 1976: 28)

The emphasis placed by Keynes upon the importance of fluctuating factors implies an equivalent importance for the role of public policy and politics to deal with new problems. What was unthinkable in the mid-nineteenth century was no longer so and what was assumed to be the truth then, needed rethinking and radical revision in the 1920s. Intellectual flexibility was a major priority if new and appropriate forms of action were to be devised.

In parting company with the market liberal view of a scarcity model and in insisting that every citizen's capacity could be developed, Keynes accepted the positive idea of freedom in which judicious and appropriate state action helped to secure the realisation of human abilities. What he called moderate planning, however, would be successful only if a correct ethical outlook was upheld by those public officials who would implement the process. Keynes, therefore, fitted comfortably into the Liberal Collectivism discussed above. He signalled his sympathies well before the publication of the *General Theory* in his lecture on 'The End of *Laissez-Faire*' given in 1926. Here the broad philosophical assumptions of classical market liberalism are give short shrift:

> Let us clear from the ground the metaphysical or general principles upon which from time to time laissez faire has been founded. It is not true that individuals possess a prescriptive 'natural ability' in their economic activities.... The world is not governed from above that private and social interest always coincide. It is not so managed here below that in practice they coincide. It is not a correct deduction from the Principles of Economics that enlightened self interest always operates in the public interest. Nor is it true that self interest generally is enlightened; more often individuals acting separately to promote their own ends are too ignorant or too weak to attain even these.
>
> (Keynes, in Greenleaf 1983: 173–4)

Keynes was centrally involved together with other leading liberal collectivists in the creation of *Britain's Industrial Future*, popularly known as 'The Yellow Book' and published in 1928. It asserted in its general principles that the task of economic and industrial policy was to ensure that all citizens were able to live 'a full and free life'. More intervention could ensure greater freedom of the individual:

> There is much positive work that the state can do which is not merely consistent with liberty but essential to it.
>
> (The Yellow Book, in Greenleaf 1983: 176)

The Yellow Book sought to make the case out for a new industrial order in which government takes an interventionist role in relation to investment, the gathering of relevant economic data, compulsory arbitration in industrial relations, the pursuit of industrial co-operation through the establishment of trade boards and joint industrial councils, and lastly a large scale public works programme to reduce unemployment.

It is clear that Keynes and Keynesianism emerged from that attempt to rehabilitate the constructive view of state intervention which spread across the political spectrum from One Nation Conservatives to Fabian Socialists but which is particularly associated with the new liberal collectivism which sought to reconcile state intervention with individual freedom. Keynes's rebellion, in its rejection of mid-Victorian ideas of deferred gratification and the discipline of scarcity, was aesthetic as well as ethical. In this sense he belongs to what has been called 'the late Victorian revolt'. In terms of specific policy implications the Keynes of The Yellow Book is implicitly moving in the direction of the integration of strategically important institutions as a way of solving economic and social problems.

Two further contexts have to be taken into account, one because of its direct bearing on Keynes's own theoretical work and the other as a major *de facto* contributor to the rehabilitation of the state. The world slump and economic recession of the early 1930s was a major stimulus to Keynes's thinking. It not only presented the final case against traditional scarcity economics with its deflationary implications, when there was clearly – in Keynes's view – sufficient productive capacity to prevent such a crisis through appropriate government intervention, it also raised the central issue of political stability and the maintenance of liberal democracy in the face of the extreme anti-democratic alternatives of Fascism and Soviet Communism.

Keynes sought to put a range of strategies in the hands of Liberal Democratic governments which would enable them to avoid mass unemployment, economic collapse and the political destabilisation that threatened to follow. The question was to arise, however, as to how such governments could use Keynesian methods without the discipline of the market place and without undermining classical liberal concerns with the individual's right to choose. Market liberals in the United States, for example, confronted by the New Deal polices of President Roosevelt in the 1930s argued that these interventionist policies were only slightly less despotic than the totalitarian regimes in Europe.

The other contextual factor during this period was of course, the *de facto* massive increase in state intervention during the Second World War. The centralised direction of economic activity constituted government deciding what shall be produced; how much shall be produced and where; how it shall be distributed; the distribution and supply of labour power; the fixing of wages, prices, working conditions and hours; total control over food supply and transport, and a range of similar controls. With the exception of the Soviet Union, Britain had a greater level of co-ordinated state control of the economy during the war than any other major participant including Nazi Germany. Planning, for example, became a favoured concept and practice during these years when before 1939 it was regarded with suspicion. It could be said that institutions and practices in place by 1942 would have facilitated not just Keynesian demand management but a more fully planned command-style economy. It was in this environment that Keynes was able to successfully challenge the views of orthodox economists and sceptical politicians, including the Chancellor of the Exchequer Kingsley Wood who had argued in favour of traditional balanced budgets. The first Keynesian deficit budget appeared in 1941 as the war effort itself took on new and greatly extended dimensions. The move towards deficit spending therefore represented a major departure in British economic policy. The idea that government could borrow to finance public sector projects meant that in future governments did not have to rely on raising personal taxation in order to increase social spending.

It is an open question as to whether the rehabilitation of the state, which was crucial to the development of Keynesian intervention, should be seen as a permanent development in Britain. What was acceptable in wartime was very soon unacceptable in peace, and while demand management clearly does not need the same powers as a fully planned economy the re-emergence of an individualist free market culture suspicious of big government was to become a major problem for Keynesianism as well – particularly from the late 1960s onwards. Keynes's contribution to the rehabilitation of the state was to go beyond the need to provide public works to reduce unemployment for ethical and social reasons or to increase the purchasing power of the poor through welfare transfers for similar motives. The economics of Keynes provided, therefore, a theoretical justification for state intervention. He also provided the state with a number of instruments without needing to accept a command model economy. What is still left open to debate is the question of the strength of the roots of this development in British political culture.

THE POLITICAL IMPLICATIONS OF FULL EMPLOYMENT

The technical reasons why Keynesians see full employment as a necessary objective of government has been dealt with in the previous two chapters. Here we are concerned with the political problems that arise from such a commitment. If the political concern is to maintain the stability of liberal democracy certain problems have to be resolved or at least contained. The failure to achieve this containment may produce a 'crisis of ungovernability' as it has been called in recent literature – see for example, Rose and Peters (1979) *Can Governments Go Bankrupt?* and Samuel Brittan (1983) *The Role and Limits of Government*.

The most significant implication of the full employment strategy is the new bargaining power of trade unions in a context where the discipline of the market place and the threat of unemployment is therefore reduced.

Keynes was aware of this consequence but was not able to provide any clear guidance:

> One is also, because one knows no solution, inclined to turn a blind eye to the wages problem in the full employment economy.
>
> (Keynes, in Moggridge 1976: 137)

The problem of wage inflation as far as Keynes was concerned is a political problem and therefore is to be left to the politicians:

> The task of keeping efficiency-wages reasonably stable (I am sure that they will creep up steadily in spite of our best efforts) is a political rather than an economic problem.
>
> (Keynes, in Moggridge 1976: 137)

Not only does this gap in Keynesian strategy leave the door open to wage inflation as an economic problem, it also invites potential social and political conflict in which the more powerful sections of the trade union movement are perceived to be exploiting their bargaining strength in the labour market to gain higher wages while inflicting the possible inflationary consequences on groups less able to protect themselves. Here we have in mind consumers, people on fixed incomes including pensioners, the self-employed, small businesses, the low paid, and the unemployed. All of these groups may bear the costs of an inflationary process without the benefits of continuous wage increases.

What type of solution politicians were supposed to find is not clear in Keynes's thinking. There seems to be an implicit assumption in the Keynesian model that in the context of full employment powerful producer groups would exercise their bargaining power in a restrained and responsible fashion, always taking into account what governments have to say about the needs of the economy as a whole. Within this model, therefore, powerful producer groups would perceive their interests not just in terms of their particular group but act upon some ethic of public interest. Keynes restricted himself to discussing inflation as a problem of excess demand in the economy. He did not discuss the possibility of wage inflation, the problem of a wage–price spiral, and the consequences of increased prices for wages and employment. His agenda for governments was to use the budget to influence demand in relation to the economic cycle. The pressures of wage inflation indicated to politicians that overreliance on the budget as the only means to deal with inflation was not appropriate and that other means, including self-restraint on prices and incomes and statutory incomes policy, were to become economic policies to be considered by government.

It would seem that there are three possible agendas for a Keynesian government. First, there is the strategy which seeks to develop the machinery of industrial conciliation; second, to offer social benefits in exchange for wage restraint; and third, to impose sanctions such as a statutory wage freeze. The basic requirements of the first option include the appropriate kind of institutional culture, a high level of institutional cohesion and commitment to consensus, and the voluntary co-operation of producer groups.

The second option must be built upon a commitment to welfare expenditures which will be seen by producers as being part of their wage. The priority attached to the social wage as opposed to the monetary purchasing power of wages will be decisive in determining the ability of trade union leaderships to deliver their members for such an arrangement. Another problem may arise from the government's willingness to exchange welfare expenditure for wage constraint. The strategy may encourage the making of social claims by a wide range of lobbies and interests including the poverty lobby and what Samuel Beer (1982) identifies as the 'subsidies and benefits scrambles'. Keynes and Keynesianism have been accused of the failure to realise that policy-making is part of the political market place where the strongest vested interests flourish at the expense of the objective pursuit of the national interest carried out by socially responsible agents (Skidelsky 1977). Keynes clearly underestimated the problem of interests and overrated rational thinking as the determinant of policy,

> The power of vested interests is vastly exaggerated compared with the gradual encroachment of ideas.
>
> (Keynes, in Skidelsky 1977: 46)

A further implication of this strategy is that government itself will be drawn into an endless process of negotiation prioritising between different interests and seeking some kind of consensus in relation to the recognition of social claims.

The third option of a statutory wage freeze will always be a short-term strategy, since trade unions are likely to resist such an option and ensure a return to free collective bargaining once the policy is lifted, bringing new problems of re-entry and 'catching up' for those groups who feel that their wages have lagged behind an increase in prices.

KEYNESIANISM AND CITIZENSHIP

Keynesianism, through its commitment to full employment, implicitly favours a language of fundamental social rights compatible with ideas of social citizenship as developed in the Report on Social Insurance and Allied Services 1942 (Beveridge Report) and in the field of social administration. Lord Beveridge had been commissioned by the wartime coalition government to produce a report on social security as part of the agenda for post-war reconstruction. Beveridge identified five giants associated with poverty including squalor, idleness, want, disease, and ignorance. The

Beveridge plan to abolish poverty represented a 'holistic' approach to social policy, arguing that abolishing want required a high quality of health care, housing, and education, together with a plan for social security. However, in financing the welfare state the Beveridge plan seemed to depend on two aspects associated with Keynesian economics. First Beveridge assumed that government would commit themselves to a policy of full employment. In the context of full employment therefore, unemployment duration was only likely to be short-term. Unemployment insurance was therefore aimed at dealing with short-term unemployment. The second assumption was that Keynesian economics would produce growth and prosperity and therefore generate the necessary income to finance the welfare state.

The links can also be established between Keynesian politics and the United Nations Declaration of Human Rights of 1946 in which the right to work, to social security, education, and leisure irrespective of age, race, gender, religion, or social class is set out. Keynesian politics is thus a universalising discourse and practice seeking to define citizenship based on inclusion rather than exclusion. Unlike market liberalism which disaggregates into individual free choices and Hobbesian conservatism which emphasises duty and the obligations of the subject, Keynesian citizenship asserts the right to a fulfilled life for all citizens. They are not to be obedient children nor individual consumers concerned only with market choice and self-interest, but citizens of a public culture as well.

Far more than market liberalism or Hobbesian conservatism, Keynesian politics must depend on some element of consensus between interests which may be opposed to each other and therefore necessitates a political and institutional culture which can sustain such a consensus. To rely upon the power of reason and expertise as Keynes seemed to do is to leave the policy process to chance. Keynesian politics does not seek to silence social claims through the expansion of private choice or through hierarchical authority, but recognises these claims and integrates them as a fundamental and necessary part of a mature society. That makes the appropriate institutional arrangements and supportive political culture all the more vital for the success of the Keynesian project.

PLURALISM AND CORPORATISM

Because Keynesianism seeks to address changed circumstances and situations and to evolve a model which allows for such changes, it must also find a place for changing institutional practices and the accommodation of interest group politics. As we have seen however, there is an important gap in the model concerning the area of political analysis and strategy. The problem is not merely one of individual freedom against a more powerful state, but what to do about powerful factions in the making of policy. Market liberals and Hobbesian conservatives, for very different reasons, regarded the development of the political process and as a provider of negotiated benefits as opening the way to the unrepresentative dominance of powerful interests able to exert destabilising pressures on government and the individual.

Keynesian economics and pluralist politics

At one level, Keynesian economics departs from market liberal thinking in that there is implicitly a recognition of the unavoidable existence of interest groups and that it is the presence of such interest groups which explains the problems of wage stickiness and non-flexible prices. It is therefore central to the Keynesian model to explain the impact of functional groups on the economy and therefore the attempt by governments to mitigate the impact of these vested interests on economy policy-making. It would, then, seem feasible to argue that there is continuity between the theories of pluralism as developed in political science and the perspective of interest groups as developed in Keynesian economics.

In the classical pluralist model as developed by Dahl and Downs, each interest group is involved in bargaining and negotiating with government but there is little concern as to the impact of dominant interest groups. Indeed, according to the classical view there is no one single group which dominates since each group does get served at the end. Interest groups therefore represent competition between issues where some groups win on one issue but might equally lose on another:

> Since different groups have access to different kinds of resources, the influence of any particular group will generally vary from issue to issue.
> (Heald 1987: 189)

The market place of competing interest groups was seen as a defining characteristic of a stable liberal democracy. Ultimately the groups will balance each other out, as each interest group will give rise to a counter-vailing group. The classical pluralist theories did not share the unease of market liberals over the financial irresponsibility of powerful interest groups in which not only are benefits acquired from government but costs are allocated to others, especially those who are less organised and there-fore at the margins of the political process.

The implications of such a model would be a stable society in which all the claims of interest groups are satisfactorily negotiated and reconciled. That in turn assumes a set of institutional arrangements to make this outcome possible. Such a political culture would have to seek common ground and would have to operate through a rationality based on common values. It may well be that Keynes himself assumes such a normative pursuit of consensus:

The question is whether we are prepared to move out of the 19th Century laissez faire state into an era of liberal socialism by which I mean a system where we can act as an organised community for common purposes and to promote social and economic justice, whilst respecting and protecting the individual – his freedom of choice, his faith, his mind and its expression, his enterprise and his property.

(Keynes, in Moggridge 1976: 46–7)

These normative assumptions avoid the problem of a hierarchy of interest groups defined by unequal access to resources and in which the more powerful exert more influence over policy-making. In the Keynesian scenario interest groups have to act with some element of normative consensus seeking. They must be prepared to make concessions over group objectives in order to achieve political stability. However, the Keynesian strategy cannot survive for very long by making the pluralist assumption that interest groups will balance each other out. Nor can it assume that a normative consensus is bound to be present. This latter characteristic depends very much upon the prevailing historical, institutional and political culture.

Although later pluralist theory took up some of these criticisms (see Dahl 1965), this still leaves the problem of how to deal with a situation in which there is a hierarchy of interest groups and in which the more powerful are able to gain more from the policy process, which may in turn lead to problems of economic stagflation and political instability.

Keynesian economics and liberal corporatism

In modern Continental Europe the problem of powerful interest groups has been more directly confronted than in Britain, and the most common response has been called liberal corporatism. First of all it is useful to reflect upon the difference between corporatism and pluralism. For some analysts pluralism seeks to reconcile interests in a voluntary, competitive, non-hierarchical environment. Thus the insistence of British trade unions upon free collective bargaining assumes a pluralist model in which all wage earners are free to bargain on the same terms. In effect, the more powerful unions gain benefits which cannot be acquired by weaker unions or by those who do not belong to trade unions. Free collective bargaining is built upon an instrumental rationality which abandons any concern for consensus or stability. Because of the voluntary character of such bargaining, negotiators are free to withdraw or not to join in. They are not bound by any binding rules or norms. As a result the negotiating process is often volatile, unstable and unpredictable. In certain circumstances such a situation can lead to political instability or an extreme political reaction. Individual electors excluded from such bargaining processes, reject the cost of exclusion and political instability and will be inclined to vote for a political party committed to the taming of powerful interest groups.

As we have noted, the attempt in Continental Europe to resolve these problems has taken a liberal corporatist form. A standard definition of corporatism refers to,

> a system of interest intermediation in which the constituent units are organised into a limited number of singular, compulsory, non-competitive, hierarchically ordered, and functionally differentiated categories, recognised or licensed...by the state and granted a deliberate representational monopoly within their respective categories in exchange for observing certain controls on their selection of leaders and articulation of demands and supports.
>
> (Schmitter, in Schmitter and Lehmbruch 1979: 65)

The most important elements in this definition include the emphasis upon compulsion; the need for chosen interest groups to work within certain rules, norms and sanctions accepted by all parties; the guaranteeing of a monopoly status by the state; and the absence of competition. In the context of liberal corporatism there is no pluralist political market. To a considerable extent this entails the surrendering of bargaining autonomy. The interests and objectives of other groups have to be taken into consideration in formulating a bargaining position. Instrumental rationality is displaced by a normative rationality based upon some notion of the public interest. Within the context of liberal corporatism interest groups are ordered into a hierarchy of relative strengths but where the state seeks to subordinate powerful interests through a series of rules and constraints. While market liberals seek to resolve the problem of interest groups by expanding the sphere of the privatised individual and reducing public expectations of the state, liberal corporatists point to the essential and also unavoidable role politics has to play in achieving a reconciliation of interests. According to the liberal corporatist perspective the retreat to a world of private choice implies a Utopia which is wholly unrealistic about the viability of dissolving group interests and the role of public institutions. The real world is constituted of strategic groups able to pursue very narrow and particularised interests which can destabilise the state and harm the general interest. They cannot be wished away nor made to disappear through the legislative process. Furthermore, even if a world of privatised individualism was made possible, it would imply the abandonment of the public interest and the denial of society, and would therefore – according to liberal corporatists – result in increased economic insecurity and political instability. For the liberal corporatist, unlike the market liberal, politics represents the best possible method available for achieving a civilised economy and society.

Liberal corporatism also implies that the state has the ability to establish the order of the hierarchy since government and civil servants are involved in the process of identifying the social agents whom they see as crucial to the obtaining of the public interest. Potentially such an arrangement therefore does allow for an authoritarian state, coercing interests into co-operation on the terms as defined by the state while completely by-passing representative institutions such as the elected Parliament. Fascist Italy, for example, developed a variant of corporatism along these lines in the 1920s. How then is corporatism to be reconciled with individual freedom and therefore liberal representative government, given that Keynes wished to preserve such a politics and observed in an essay apparently supporting the role of interests in the making of policy that ultimately they must be,

> subject in the last resort to the sovereignty of democracy expressed through Parliament.
>
> (Keynes, in Schmitter and Lehmbruch 1979: 27)

Corporatist arrangements go beyond casual consultation between government and interest groups or the mediation of industrial crises. A summary of the Austrian social partnership process will give some idea of the type of institutional political culture which a Keynesian strategy requires if it is to flourish:

1 Large interest groups are organised into 'Chambers' which are statutory public corporations with compulsory membership. Examples of these Chambers are those of Business, Agriculture, and Labour. The Chamber of Labour is linked to the Austrian Confederation of Trade Unions (GOB). Member industrial unions have to seek the consent of the GOB before taking industrial action or even submitting wage demands.
2 Institutionalised co-operation between Chambers is constituted in bodies like the Parity Commission for Questions of Prices and Wage Regulation. The Commission consists of three Chambers plus the GOB and representatives of the government. Decisions on prices and wages are made by committees of experts. All wage bargains are directed through the Parity Commission which also controls about one-third of consumer prices.
3 The major interest groups are also represented in the national bank.
4 The Chambers are consulted about proposed government legislation before bills are presented to the Parliament. The agreement of the Chambers is required before a bill is presented. The legislation to establish worker participation in the management of companies was actually prepared by the Chambers before it was taken up by the Government.
5 Austrian public opinion strongly supports the notion of the social partnership. The Chambers are therefore aware that to withdraw from the partnership would incur strong public disapproval. The political

culture is prepared to accept a certain curtailment of competition and market forces (and the political control of wages and prices) because of the social and political stability the social partnership seems to generate.

Unions are prepared to accept a surrendering of bargaining autonomy to the Chamber of Labour for similar reasons. Within such an environment interest groups and government are able to create a less conflictual society. Legislation cannot be partial. If there are to be wage constraints there also has to be a ceiling on prices. Keynesian strategies can then operate securely within such a political culture, where the emphasis is constantly upon the reconciliation of interests. Government is not coercive but an equal partner in the process of giving political legitimacy to the consensus. Styles of management within enterprises become more consultative than authoritarian as a result of worker participation. Guiding rules and norms are accepted by all parties. Welfare expenditure proposals are subject to the same procedure and are assisted by a political culture which does not regard an increase in taxes to finance social expenditures as a threat to individual freedom. The positive definition of freedom is almost taken for granted in the Austrian case, as is the role of corporate bodies. The idea that the individual stands in opposition to these corporate interests has little resonance in the Austrian context. Much of what has been said about the Austrian case applies to West Germany, Scandinavia, Holland, and other Continental societies with allowance for local and national traditions.

According to market liberals, Britain's economic decline and adversarial industrial relations has been due to a failed Keynesian corporatism during the 1960s and 1970s. If the Austrian case comes as close as any to defining what a liberal corporatist politics looks like, we can use it in later chapters to evaluate whether Britain was ever meaningfully corporatist or not, and whether Britain's economic problems were caused by too much corporatism or by the failure to develop a genuinely liberal corporatist political culture at all.

A Keynesian economic strategy is likely to succeed more in a consensus-seeking political culture in which interest groups recognise their interdependence, seek representative coherence and convergence, are prepared to make concessions as regards their negotiating autonomy in exchange for mutual and secure benefits, set political limits to unconstrained competition, submit to rules and norms for negotiating procedures, relate wage and price movements to each other as a matter of institutional practice and integrate interest group negotiation with the broader political process.

Such a consensus would set the scene for consensus on economic, industrial and financial strategies at the macro level. The position of the currency and of the balance of payments may be more securely anticipated and subject to rational control without wages and monetary demand getting out of hand. Cultural attitudes towards how much capital should be absorbed into house ownership will also influence the effectiveness of industrial policy. Without such a context Keynesian economic policies are highly vulnerable to the pursuit of autonomous sectional interests and are therefore likely to collapse in a crisis of wage-led inflation, low investment, and balance of payments crisis.

Chapter 8

The Labour government and economic policy, 1945 to 1951

INTRODUCTION

There are implicit similarities to be drawn between the impact of the 1945 Labour government and the Thatcher governments on economic policy, in the sense that both are associated with influencing major departures in the expectations by people of their governments. The Labour government, it is argued, broke with the paradigm of the minimalist state of the 1920s and 1930s, urging instead a more interventionist and collectivist approach to government. Equally, much discussion on the nature of economic policy in the 1980s has been associated with the language of the Thatcher revolution (Jenkins 1987), or the Thatcher economic experiment (Keegan 1983). What is common in the study of the 1980s is that it seems to represent, a watershed, a break with the post-war settlement as constructed by the 1945 Labour government, and from the welfare state and full employment. The Thatcher revolution, it is argued, seeks to break with the corporatist and consensus politics of the post-war, and seeks to replace the principles of collectivism with the ethics of markets, enterprise, the individual, and the pushing back of the frontiers of government.

Sir Keith Joseph (1975) in his book *Stranded in the Middle Ground* has described the post-war period as representing a continuous upward ratchet of socialism, of waves of state intervention not being pushed back but actually consolidated during the years of Conservative governments. Joseph argues that the 1945 Labour government established the parameters for economic policy-making after 1945, which Conservative governments accepted as the conventional wisdom when they took office – that is until Mrs Thatcher became their leader in 1975. Instead of reversing the programme of nationalisation, the welfare state and central direction on incomes and prices, Conservative governments of the post-war period sought to manage Labour's socialism rather than replacing it with market liberal principles.

Because we Conservatives became identified with the shifting middle ground, we were inhibited from fighting a vigorous battle of ideas; we became identified with an unworkable status-quo; we therefore allowed the crisis of British Socialism to be presented as the crisis of capitalism by default.

(Sir Keith Joseph 1976: 25)

Much in the same vein, but for different reasons, Tony Benn has modelled the Labour government of 1945 as the carriers of the banner of socialism. The Benn argument points to the commitments of that Labour government on nationalisation and the National Health Service as setting the principles for socialism which other governments were forced to follow.

That Labour Government, coming out of the war-time coalition headed by Churchill, laid the foundations for a consensus which lasted until the IMF cuts in 1976 and can be seen as having ushered in, and later seen out, a new era in which there was general agreement that full employment and the welfare state were to be permanent features of British society.

(Benn 1988: xv)

THE FRAMEWORK FOR ECONOMIC POLICY-MAKING

In the previous chapters it was suggested that market liberalism and Keynesianism represented two distinct paradigms. However, the first point to be developed in this and subsequent chapters, will be that it is rather simplistic to associate government with the adherence to a coherent strategy attached to one set of economic ideas as against another. For example, the view that the Attlee and Thatcher governments reflected clear breaks between the Keynesianism ushered in with the Attlee government and the market liberalism of the Thatcher government would imply that governments readily surrender certain economic levers which are available to them because these are not consistent with the governing paradigm. Indeed, an essential part of the art of government is surely the ability of governments to use all the tools which are available to them without necessarily admitting that they are surrendering principles.

The second issue of concern in what follows is the argument that the study of economic policy cannot be judged in terms of the relative influences between competing economic ideas and government. The criteria for the study of economic policy involves a wider set of relationships than those between the ideas of economists and their impact on policy-makers. Economic policy-making represents a series of trade offs. As was suggested in Chapter 1, governments do not have complete autonomy in deciding economic priorities. Indeed, very often governments have to approach the economic context as a constraining factor. For example, as will be argued in this chapter, the central concern for the Labour government of 1945 was the exchange rate. The crisis of sterling reflected the weakness of the British economy in the aftermath of war. Britain had lost export markets and manufacturing industry was run-down. The Labour government therefore inherited an economic context which was not of their choosing, but at the same time had no choice other than to manage the economic context which they found. Britain is part of the global economy and changes in exchange rate have a direct effect on people's living standards. However, government do not have complete autonomy in managing the exchange rate.

The third argument is that while the economic context represents a constraint on government, at least in the short term, this does not mean that governments produce *ad hoc* policy responses. Governments are not just empty vessels, they come to office with their own political priorities. In dealing with the 'constraint' of the economy governments have a series of policy alternatives. The aim of government is to resolve the tensions between the political priorities set by the ideology of the party and to reconcile these political priorities with the economic context. While the Labour government was faced with a sterling crisis in 1947, the Chancellor Hugh Dalton resisted Treasury demands to reduce public expenditure as the means of reducing overall demand in the economy. Public expenditure on health, education and pensions were seen as being crucial to Labour's programme. It was against the background of protecting Labour's priorities that the government sought to deal with the problem of sterling, which in turn meant that the government had to opt for policies of increasing taxation and rationing as the means of curtailing demand. Both policies were equally unpopular options.

The making of economic policy can be best described as a triangle of forces – one part being the economy represented as a series of constraints on government; second, there is the government elected to fulfil a series of pledges and commitments; while third are the pressures of economic ideas, including perceptions on how the economy works and prescriptions for policy. Government is about making continuous decisions. Politicians need the analysis and the ideas of the economists to clarify the policy options but these options always imply social and political costs. The choice of policy alternatives is never innocent, policy choices always imply political calculation and that is why governments do not readily adhere to one doctrine. The electoral judgement does not depend on whether the government can show its adherence to a set of principles but whether it can succeed to deliver on economic performance and living standards.

THE OBJECTIVES OF ECONOMIC POLICY

Economic policy is directed at four major objectives. These include a policy to deal with unemployment; a policy that produces price stability; a policy that produces growth in the economy, increased prosperity and living standards; and a policy directed at an equilibrium in the balance of trade. Governments are aware, however, that this quadrilateral of policies is likely to produce tensions and incompatibility between different policy priorities. The desired policy objective of full employment is therefore likely to come into conflict with a policy directed at curbing inflation. Equally, a policy directed at growth through increased demand is likely to aggravate the balance of payments – especially in the UK which has a high propensity to import – so that increases in demand are likely to be met through imports which then are likely to lead to a balance of payments deficit and an attempt to curb demand to reduce imports and to regain market confidence in the exchange rate. These policies eventually lead to new problems of deflation and unemployment.

The concern of this chapter is therefore an attempt to analyse how the Labour government of 1945 sought to deal with the problems of unemployment, inflation, economic growth, and the balance of payments. The emphasis is not to produce a chronology of what the government did but rather to produce some understanding of the process of economic policy-making. The aim, therefore, is to show the relationships identified earlier – namely to construct an outline of the economic context, the responses of the governments (taking into consideration both the political priorities of the government and the attempt to reconcile economic pressures with political priorities), and the impact of economic ideas on the priorities of the government and on the conduct of economic policy.

THE 1945–1951 LABOUR GOVERNMENTS

Labour's economic strategy

The priorities of the Labour government elected in 1945 had been outlined in two major policy statements; first in *Labour's Immediate Programme* published in 1937 and second, in Labour's election manifesto of 1945 – *Let Us Face The Future* – which contained the electoral pledges and commitments for a future Labour government. The programme of nationalisation was central to Labour's programme, since the objective of public ownership had been a central aspiration of the Labour Party programme as set out in the Labour Party Constitution of 1918 and the famous Clause IV which declares that the Labour Party would seek

> to secure for the workers by hand or by brain the full fruits of their industry and the most equitable distribution that may be possible upon the basis of common ownership.
>
> (Labour Party Constitution, Clause IV (4))

The Labour Party had argued for common ownership to replace the ethics of individualism and the market place. Individualism was associated with income inequalities, poverty and economic inefficiency. Labour's analysis of the depression and the levels of unemployment of the inter-war years pointed to the need for a more interventionist state. The commitment to social ownership, therefore, satisfied Labour vision to create a more egalitarian Britain at four levels:

1 That common ownership would lay the foundations for a classless society.
2 That common ownership would eliminate the economic inefficiencies of the market place.
3 That nationalisation would facilitate economic planning.
4 That this would improve the position of workers In arguing the case for common ownership.

Hugh Gaitskell in 1937 wrote:

> So long as production is left to the uncontrolled decisions of private individuals, conducted, guided and inspired by the motive of profit, so long will Poverty, Insecurity and Injustice continue.
>
> (Gaitskell, in Williams 1982: 72)

At one level, therefore, Labour's economic objectives were to be founded on the theme of bringing industries within the control of the public sector in contrast to leaving the workings of the economy to be determined through individual decisions in the market place. The economic objectives of sustained growth, full employment, the balance of payments and inflation had to be viewed within the context of wider state intervention and of public ownership.

Labour's economic policy was also firmly tied with the wider social objectives of reducing social inequalities by creating more opportunities in education, removing income as the barrier to health care, provision of public sector housing, and improving pensions, social security and family allowances. Labour's social programme depended on Labour's successful management of the economy, and nationalisation was therefore a crucial aspect of economic policy where both the social and the economic were part of the same argument. Private ownership of industry produced inequalities and insecurity. The reliance on individualism and markets had failed to produce effective welfare provision to address problems of income inequalities. The barrier of income inequalities was depriving people of opportunities to education, housing, good health care or pensions. In contrast, public ownership was going to replace the impersonal forces of the market, remedy the failure of the market, and was therefore more likely to generate economic property to finance Labour's social programme.

In addition to the strategy of common ownership, Labour's economic thinking on the conduct of the process of economic policy had also been very much influenced by the economics of Keynes. Hugh Dalton, in his book *Practical Socialism for Britain* (1935), together with Douglas Jay's *The Socialist Case* (1937), provided the foundations for combining the concept of demand management as outlined by Keynes with Labour's socialist aspirations of full employment and income redistribution. Dalton had pointed out that demand management was not sufficient to generate full employment and that socialist planning needed to be added to the economics of Keynes. Labour's programme of nationalisation, together with commitments to economic planning, was therefore compatible with the Keynesian proposals on demand management. Dalton agreed with Keynes as to the need to establish a National Investment Bank to generate the necessary savings and investment. Hugh Dalton became Labour's Chancellor in 1945 while Douglas Jay was appointed financial secretary to the Treasury.

The third aspect of Labour's economic policy dealt with the relationship between the Labour Party and the trade unions. The emergence of the Labour Party as a separate political force after 1900 had depended on the trade unions changing their allegiances from the Liberal Party to the newly formed Labour Representative Committee in 1900 and later in forming the Labour Party in 1918. The relationship between the Labour Party and the trade unions has been described as more of a marriage of convenience rather than an alliance based on one shared socialist vision. Both the trade unions and the Labour Party recognised their interdependence, with the Labour party relying on trade union financial assistance and the trade unions recongising the need to have their interests represented in Parliament by a Labour government.

The Labour Party/trade union connection was an important issue to Labour's economic policies for two reasons. First, as suggested above, the Labour government could lay claim to their special relationship with the trade unions. The trade unions were an integral part of the Labour Party Conference and were therefore directly involved in policy formulation within the Labour Party. Labour's programme for the 1945 election represented the aspirations, pledges and commitments of the Party and the affiliated trade unions. Leading trade unionists including Ernest Bevin and George Isaacs were in the Labour Cabinet of 1945.

The trade unions had a direct interest in ensuring that Labour succeeded in office. Trade unions including the railworkers, miners and transport workers had all embraced the concept of common ownership in their constitutions. The trade unions had also argued that the government should commit themselves to a policy of full employment and had also campaigned for the Beveridge Report of 1942 to create a comprehensive welfare state.

For these reasons it was argued that a Labour government was more likely to reach an understanding with the trade unions on the issues of inflation, wage settlements, the welfare state and full employment. Labour's interventionist strategy was seen as being more conducive to create a forum for discussion of economic issues between governments, employers and trade unions. Labour's commitments on full employment, the welfare state, and nationalisation depended to some extent on the special relationship with the trade unions.

The following sections will seek to evaluate Labour's record at four levels, the first being to provide an outline of the economic context for the period 1945 to 1951. The questions which arise here for example, is whether the British economy was in a better condition when Labour left office in 1951. The second issue relates to constraints of the economy including the deterioration in the balance of payments, the crisis of sterling and devaluation and the influence such constraints had on Labour's political priorities including public expenditure on schools, housing and health. At a third level, there is the question of whether Labour's economic strategy of intervention did address Britain's economic problems, and lastly whether the tensions between political priorities and economic constraints actually proved too much for the Labour government. Labour had won an unparalleled landslide victory in 1945 bringing forward high aspirations to establish a social revolution in Britain, yet Labour's majority of 146 was reduced to 5 in the 1950 election and Labour went on to lose the election of 1951.

The economic context

At an overall level the British economy in 1951 was in a better shape to face the future than in the immediate aftermath of the war. The economy had improved in the sense that by 1951 Britain had recovered most of its export markets. Exports had risen from 50 per cent below the pre-level to nearly 55 per cent above and by 1951 were paying for 85 per cent of imports. By 1951, Britain had the best economic performance in Europe while output per person had increased faster than in the United States (Williams 1982). The years 1946 to 1951 was also a period of continuous full employment when living standards increased by about 10 per cent and the economy was growing at 3 per cent per annum, perhaps the longest period of sustainable growth in British economic history – a better record even than when Britain had claimed to be the workshop of the world.

Within this overall picture of achievement and economic recovery, it would be misleading however to assume that Britain's economic recovery represented the fulfilment and vindication of Labour's economic strategy. Indeed, instead of a smooth and continuous recovery the period was much more of a series of crises management; whether it was the coal crisis, the continued austerity and rationing, the shutdown of industries because of a lack in power supplies, the increase of 2 million on the unemployment register, the convertibility crisis of 1947 and devaluation in 1949. Indeed Cairncross argues that, the Labour government was ill prepared for the hectic years ahead. It was committed to programmes of nationalization without having given much thought to the way in which nationalized industries should operate. It wished to embark on highly expensive schemes of social welfare which it had never costed. It had little idea what to do about inflation. It could not even count on the whole hearted support of key groups of manual workers such as the miners.... On one economic issue after another they were slow to grasp the true options of policy and had great difficulty in reaching sensible conclusions.

(Cairncross 1985b: 20)

According to the Cairncross thesis the Labour government did not have a coherent economic strategy on taking office. There was no clear purpose behind the nationalisation programme and how this fitted within Labour overall economic strategy. Furthermore, there was no attempt to cost Labour social programmes and finally, there was no coherent policy on demand management, employment and inflation. This interpretation seems to be reinforced by some biographers of Labour leaders of the period including Pimlott's biography of Hugh Dalton and Phillip Williams's on Hugh Gaitskell. All these authors are agreed that rather than seeing the Labour government as giving leadership to economic policy by drawing on a predetermined economic strategy, it was much more of government engulfed by circumstances not of their making but seeking to respond in such a way that would do minimum damage to their electoral pledges and political priorities.

Cairncross argues that the major success in economic policy during the period was the ability of the government to hold down personal consumption. Cairncross divides the increase in national income into three categories – consumption, investment, and exports. His argument is that while for the whole period 1946 to 1952 the economy had expanded by 15.3 per cent, consumer expenditure had only increased by 5.9 per cent, with government consumption actually falling by 12 per cent. In contrast, fixed capital formation grows by 57 per cent and exports by 77 per cent. Imports in the meantime had grown by 14.5 per cent. Cairncross argues that during their period in office Labour had learned that prosperity depended on Britain improving its export performance and this meant holding down personal and public consumption.

At one level it seemed paradoxical that a government which had made commitments on justice, equality and efficiency was able to control the level of consumption to redirect income to exports and investment when consumption (especially the growth of public consumption) was central to Labour commitments on education, health and housing. However, it might also be pointed out that the change in strategy from consumption to investment and exports proved too costly for the Labour government.

Labour's attempt to hold down private consumption through rationing contributed to their unpopularity, despite the bonfire of controls in 1950. More damaging to the Labour government in 1951 were the resignations of Wilson, Bevan and Freeman over increased health charges which they saw as direct attacks on the fundamental principles of free health care.

Labour's austerity programme was consistent with the overall strategy for a planned economy founded on justice and equality. Sir Stafford Cripps, who replaced Hugh Dalton as Chancellor in 1947, had argued against the frivolities of the free market economy, pointing out that market economies were likely to produce an excess of luxury goods without providing for the real necessities of shelter, food, and clothing. Labour's programme of rationing, food subsidies and rent controls were therefore seen as the way of providing justice and avoiding profiteering by a few. The problem of austerity was that although by 1951 everyone was healthier, people in Britain – especially the older generations – were feeling increasingly restricted and deprived of choice:

> Although the nation as a whole was healthier by 1951 than it had ever been, due to the even distribution of basic foods, the average adult's resistance to infection was often like his spirits low.... The adult world continued to be one of queues and shortages.... It seemed sometimes as if no one could go anywhere or do anything without producing some kind of permit or coupon (or as Sir Stafford Cripps would have it, 'coupong').
>
> (Sissons and French 1964: 36)

Economic constraints

Throughout the period 1945 to 1951 the Labour governments were faced with what seems contradictory economic priorities. On the one hand the government was under pressure to respond to the short-term problems of sterling. These included the convertibility of sterling in 1947 and the sudden collapse in the values of sterling between May and August 1947, when the government decided to suspend convertibility. Equally, there was the decision to devalue sterling in 1949, which in turn brought problems of inflation, and the need to curb demand and public expenditure. On the other hand the underlying problems of the balance of payments, the decline in export markets, and the underinvestment in manufacturing industries required a longer-term strategy. There was a need to construct policies which shifted the axis from consumption to investment and exports. Such a strategy could not produce indicators of the successes at least in the short term and certainly not through improved personal consumption. New investment in manufacturing directed to export markets was only likely to succeed as a longer-term policy. In the meantime, therefore, the Labour government needed to make time and space from external pressures. The conditions set out by the US government to make sterling convertible against the dollar by 1947 were always likely to cause problems as long as British exports had not recovered sufficiently. Yet, because Britain was under pressure to rejoin the world economy, there were increased tensions between responding to short-term market pressures while seeking to construct a longer-term strategy.

The balance of payments deficit

During the years of war the British coalition government had been able to direct all economic resources to the war effort. The implicit agreement between Britain and the USA was that of a division of labour, with Britain directing all its human resources to the winning of the war and thus not worrying about producing goods for exports, while the USA – under the conditions of Lend-lease – allowed Britain to have food and raw materials. The problem for Britain was that within a few days of the Japanese surrender, the Americans ended Lend-lease leaving Britain in a very vulnerable position.

> Not only were there to be no new shipments but supplies in the pipeline would have to be paid for.... Thus what had provided the United Kingdom with roughly two-thirds of the funds needed to finance an external deficit of £10 bn over six years of war was withdrawn unilaterally and without prior negotiation.
>
> (Cairncross 1985b: 4)

Overnight therefore, the Labour government had inherited an external deficit of £1.2 billion a year which needed to be financed. Keynes who had joined the government as an adviser was immediately dispatched to the USA to negotiate a loan to give the government breathing space to recover some exports. According to O'Morgan (1984) and Cairncross (1985b) Labour leaders naïvely believed that their allies would make a loan available with no interest rate attached. Instead, the best that Keynes could negotiate was a £4.4 billion loan at 2 per cent interest but suspended for the first five years, and also a stipulation by the Americans for sterling to be made convertible against the dollar by 1947. Part of the Lend-lease Agreement had been the elimination of tariff barriers and preferential treatment in international commerce. The Americans were aware that Britain's imperial preference policy had guaranteed Britain access to markets in Australia, New Zealand and Canada which was to the disadvantage of the USA.

Although the Loans Agreement seemed risky, at a minimum it seemed to achieve the short-term purpose of buying time for the Labour government to implement their radical programme. The price was the convertibility crisis of 1947 but in the meantime the temporary easement was essential for Labour to implement their political priorities of increasing expenditure on housing, health and food subsidies. The Chancellor, Hugh Dalton, was quick to recognise the contribution of Keynes to these negotiations:

> Even those colleagues who least like some details of the Agreement are loud in praise of your skill, resource and patience.... And now come home and rest. I look forward very much to seeing you again and shaking your hand.
>
> (Hugh Dalton to Lord Keynes, 5 December 1945)

The years 1945 to 1947 were the high-water mark of the Labour government. It was during this period that Labour implemented most of the programme of nationalisation including the Bank of England, gas, electricity, railways and the coal industry. It was also during these years that Labour established the National Health Service and started to build high quality public sector housing. According to Andrew Shonfield reflecting on the period,

> The Labour Party's creative period of office was over by 1948. By then the major acts of nationalisation had take place, the state had acquired a commanding position in a crucial sector of industry and the post-war advance in social welfare has reached its climax.
>
> (Shonfield 1958: 160)

Despite the adverse external balance, the Labour government created sufficient space to implement most of their radical programme between 1945 and 1946. Dalton had called 1946 the *annus mirabilis* of the Labour government. It was the year when the Chancellor had reduced personal taxation for the low paid, introduced child allowances, a national insurance scheme and had phased out the Poor Law. It was also the year when the five giants of want, ignorance, idleness, ill-health, and squalor, identified by Beveridge, were, it was argued, at last under control.

However, for some critics, including Corelli Barnett (1986), the space gained by the Labour government in the loan agreement had been mishandled. Labour had channelled the new resources to achieve the New Jerusalem of the welfare state rather than directing them to confront Britain's balance of payments problems. The vision of the New Jerusalem excluded those arguments that Britain needed to regain overseas markets, new investment (especially in export led industries), and education and training to produce a more skilled labour force.

Economic advisers, including James Meade and Harold Robbins, agreed with Keynes that the problem of the external deficit reflected the excess of demand and suppressed inflation in the economy. This inflationary gap, argued Keynes, would only be attacked through the budget process by the government taking demand out of the economy through increased taxation, lower public expenditure and phasing out food subsidies. The

Chancellor, Hugh Dalton, supported by Cabinet colleagues, resisted this advice throughout the period 1945 to 1947. Labour's concern was to prevent the economy falling into recession as had happened after the First World War when the boom was followed by slump. Dalton felt that it was better for a Labour government to have a bit of inflation rather than deflation:

> Before the war we had deflation which was not suppressed, and which was not potential but actual, and if we must choose between a slight – and I emphasise the word slight – between a slight inflationary flush and a slight deflationary pallor, I prefer the slight inflationary flush.
> (Dalton, lecture to the Fabian Society, 13 November 1946)

The priority of the Labour government was the commitment to full employment. Any attempt to reduce demand through fiscal policy was therefore likely to be deflationary and a threat to employment. Labour's attitude to inflation was mainly guided by the view that inflation represented an increase in prices rather than excess demand, and that increases in prices required controls similar to those set up by the wartime government. For this reason, therefore, Labour's anti-inflation strategy up to 1947 was the control of prices through rationing, and public subsidies on food, fuel and rents.

The convertibility crisis of 1947

If 1946 was the *annus mirabilis* of the Labour government, then 1947 was the *annus horrendus* since it was the year when the space gained came to an end. In the harsh winter of 1947 the coal stocks ran out, industry closed down, and 2 million people lost their jobs. The criticism of the Labour government was that much harder since coal was now in the public sector and therefore a central part of Labour's planned economy. The industry had lost some 38,000 miners since 1938, capacity had fallen by 46 million tonnes, and productivity was 10 per cent lower than in 1938. In addition to the problems of declining capacity, the industry also had to cope with the increases in demand by individual consumers and industry.

The second major issue for the government in 1947 was the sterling convertibility crisis in May of that year. As part of the Loans Agreement, sterling joined the international currency markets but only to make more explicit the weakness of the currency. Within a few days Britain was experiencing a dollar drain with holders of sterling now freed to sell sterling. The total outflow of gold and dollars increased from $900 million dollars in 1946 to $4,100 million dollars in 1947. In the last week before suspension on 20 August 1947 it reached an equivalent outflow of $1 billion per month. This drain created immediate problems for the government, especially when Britain still depended on dollar-traded imports.

The convertibility crisis carried the strong message that the government had now to take the external deficit more seriously. The issue of excess demand and how to use the budgetary process to influence demand became the concern of Labour Chancellors after 1947. Dalton, in his last budget in November 1947, took the opportunity to increase indirect taxation on beer, spirits and purchase tax while putting a ceiling on food subsidies in his attempt to dampen demand. Dalton could now boast that his budget was in surplus and furthermore that it offered a 'defence against inflation', which in a sense represented a major shift in Labour thinking. Inflation was now seen as the problem of excess demand rather than a problem of rising prices. His budget, he argued, sought to cut purchasing power to reduce demand for imports and therefore allow for increases in exports. In the meantime, further austerity measures announced by Sir Stafford Cripps, the Minister of Economic Affairs, were greeted with little resistance within the Labour movement. Cripps had outlined a series of reductions in bread and petrol allowances to curb US imports.

The crisis of sterling and devaluation in 1949

While the crisis of sterling in 1947 was due to the over optimistic and misguided conditions imposed during the Loan Agreement of 1945, the pressure to devalue sterling in 1949 was due much more to what seemed to be a faltering US economy and a decline in the value of the dollar against sterling. The problem for the Labour government in 1949 was one of success, the holding down of consumption demand and shifting resources to exports had meant that by 1949 Britain had achieved its pre-war position in regaining export markets. The decline of the dollar against sterling meant that the value of sterling was rising, making exports less attractive.

The decision of the government to devalue sterling threatened new problems for the domestic economy. A devaluation of sterling increased the cost of imports and therefore threatened living standards, which meant new threats of inflation especially if the trade unions felt that the cost of imports was likely to evoke industrial unrest. The problem of an inflationary threat was likely to make it more difficult for the voluntary code on pay negotiations to hold and yet the government could not allow the rise in the value of sterling to result in further falls in exports.

The devaluation was a steep one from $4.03 to $2.80 and a major repercussion was the increase in the price of a loaf of bread from 4½d to 6d. Cripps tried to persuade the trade unions in the meantime that devaluation would not lead to more than a 4 per cent increase in the cost of living. The TUC agreed to sell a new pay freeze to their members. They managed to get the freeze accepted with a large majority in 1948, but that majority had narrowed with 4.3 million in favour and 3.6 million against by 1951 and after two-and-a-half years of incomes policy.

However, the decision to devalue sterling also carried other implications, both for Labour's social programmes and for unity in government. Gaitskell had argued in Cabinet that the decision to devalue brought new threats of inflation which in turn meant that if the government was to devalue then they also had to bite on the bullet of public expenditure cuts to reduce government demand. Hugh Gaitskell, now at the Treasury and substituting for Sir Stafford Cripps, 'insisted' in Cabinet for a £280 million package in expenditure cuts which included increases in prescription charges and cuts in the housing programme. The pressures on Hugh Gaitskell, and the division within the Cabinet on the issue of devaluation and the cuts in pubic expenditure, were recorded as follows by Hugh Dalton:

> He [Gaitskell] was now very frightened of 'inflationary pressures' and says that, if we don't deal with it, we shall have another dollar crisis in the spring. If this morning's clash came to a break he would be with S.C. [Stafford Cripps] against A.B. [Aneurin Bevan] and so, he thinks would the country and most of the Party. A.B. he thinks should have been moved by the P.M. before now from a Spending Dept. to say, the Ministry of Labour, where he would do very well...he finds A.B. very difficult.
>
> (Hugh Dalton, Diaries, 12 and 13 October 1949)

The clashes within the Cabinet between October 1949 and February 1950, illustrate the tensions between the government seeking to respond to economic problems while at the same time attempting to reconcile economic policy with political priorities. The decision to devalue sterling in 1949 was to create new problems on how to deal with the inflationary pressures of devaluation, public expenditure, and wage restraint. A weaker sterling meant higher costs of imports, including essential items such as food. Also, inflationary pressures were likely to be exacerbated by too much consumption demand in the economy, either through government consumption or private consumption.

On the private consumption side the government needed to persuade the trade unions through the TUC to hold down wage demands as a way of curbing demand, while the government also needed to hold down public consumption by holding down the costs of food subsidies. Public consumption, however, also represented Labour's social priorities and included expenditures on public housing and health services. Gaitskell argued that spending ministers, including Aneurin Bevan, had to live with the expenditure estimates agreed in Cabinet. In contrast Bevan felt that this represented a shift in priorities from those of the Treasury responding to needs to a position where spending departments had to live with the strictures as constructed by the Treasury.

The problem of incomes policy

Alan Flanders (1970), while asking the question 'What Are Trade Unions For?', suggested that the primary aim of trade unions was:

> They [trade unions] are interested in regulating wages as well as in raising them; and of course, in regulating a wide range of other issues appertaining to their members' jobs and working life.... Stated in the simplest possible terms these rules provide protection, and a shield for their members. And they protect not only their material standards of living but equally their security, status and self-respect – in short their dignity as human beings.
>
> (Flanders 1970: 41)

According to this perspective the role of trade unions must be to protect the interests of their members through collective bargaining in the workplace against the power and authority of employers, and to ensure that their members work in a safe environment where there is regulation on safety and insurance. According to Flanders, therefore, the collective bargaining process was not just limited to wages but also to furthering the dignity of members in the workplace. Equally, in accepting this role of regulation, Flanders also pointed out that trade unions should seek to replace the narrow ethic of 'the free for all' of collective bargaining for a regulative form of bargaining which sought to establish order and justice in wage settlements:

> Regulation is now needed on a national scale.... Some attempt must be made to tame this industrial jungle war. There is no prospect of bringing more order and justice into our national pay structure, or even to improve the position of low paid workers, unless we have some national rules or guide-lines to regulate the 'free for all'.
>
> (Flanders 1970: 46)

Flanders went on to advance the case for an incomes policy as a permanent institution not as a short-term option for governments and trade unions to cope with balance of payments problems. An agreement to create permanent institutions to facilitate such agreements similar to those of Sweden and West Germany was essential if government was to deal effectively with the dual problems of inflation and unemployment.

In contrast to Flanders, Hugh Clegg (1960) has described trade unions as the permanent opposition which cannot become the government. According to Clegg trade unions exist to protect their members' interests and to bargain with employers. Trade unions should therefore avoid becoming co-opted by employers or government. Trade unions had therefore to avoid the policing of joint agreements with employers as this was likely to lead to discontent and conflict between trade union officials and their rank and file members. The independence of trade unions and their ability to be an effective opposition was an essential element to a democratic society.

The perspectives outlined by both Flanders and Clegg reflected the continuing tensions and dilemmas facing both the trade unions and Labour governments on the trade off involved in reaching agreements on incomes and prices policies. According to the Flanders view, trade unions had to seek a wider definition of 'regulation' which meant taking into account other factors in addition to wages when making collective agreements with government and employers; the Clegg argument pointed to the tensions within trade unions as undermining their central role of opposition.

Labour's thinking on the problem of inflation was confined to prices and the commitment of a Labour government to continue to use wartime price controls as a means of achieving just prices. The word inflation was not even mentioned in the 1945 Election Manifesto, yet the Labour Party had committed themselves to 'full' employment rather than the objective of the White Paper in 1944 of 'high and stable employment'. Therefore, in 1945 Labour had not entertained the possibility that full employment, a high level of effective demand, and price stability were likely to create incompatible priorities in economic policy, yet over the whole period of the Labour government the attempt to establish a comprehensive incomes policy became more essential to economic policy.

As suggested earlier the question of the external balance was a major problem which Keynes had already addressed in 1945, having pointed out to ministers that the trade deficit represented a problem of excess demand and an inflationary gap. From the outset therefore the Labour government was made aware of the need to construct a policy to deal with the issue of inflation. The Working Party on Wages Policy had actually been set up in October 1945, authorised by Sir Edward Bridges, the permanent secretary to the Treasury. The government also reconstituted the wartime tripartite group, the National Joint Advisory Council (NJAC), in the spring of 1946. However, it would seem that between 1945 and 1948 the trade unions were reluctant to accept the strictures of any formal incomes policy while within the Cabinet both the Minister of Labour George Isaacs (an ex union official) and Ernest Bevin continued to resist any move towards a formal incomes policy. The government therefore had to rely on exhortations to the trade unions pointing out to them the needs to moderate wage demands, to increase exports, and to allow wages to reflect the market place. In this sense, therefore, the government had shown that they did not have any policy on manpower planning if that meant deploying workers to key sectors of the economy, nor had they the wish to use statutory incomes policy to deal with wage inflation. The government had argued instead that supply and demand would deal with the problems of labour shortages and price controls, and that rationing and food subsidies were the weapons to deal with inflation.

The convertibility crisis in August of 1947 forced the Cabinet to develop a more coherent strategy on inflation. Although some ministers had proposed a statutory pay freeze it would seem that when the final version of the White Paper did emerge, the government had retreated on the issue of a formal pay freeze and instead had agreed with the TUC that the pay freeze would be voluntary and under the control of the trade unions. In reaching this concordat, however, the government also agreed to extend price subsidies and also undertook to persuade the Federation of British Industry (FBI) to accept voluntary dividend limitation. The decision on devaluation in 1949 again put further pressures on the government and the trade unions to continue with the voluntary pay freeze for another twelve months. Although the TUC did manage to secure a majority in favour of the freeze in 1951, the majority was slender – 4.3 million had voted for the freeze and 3.6 million had voted to reject acceptance.

The voluntary pay freeze had the consequence of squeezing wage differentials. While skilled and semi-skilled workers observed the incomes policy, those workers classed as being on low pay either had their wages settled through the wages council or received awards in the form of a sliding scale to protect their living standards. Bevin warned the government that the narrowing of differentials by the 1948 pay guidelines had already caused unrest and that any further attempts to continue with the pay freeze was likely to meet with worker resistance. Furthermore, the attempt by the Chancellor Hugh Gaitskell in February 1951 to set up a new tripartite forum – the Wages Advisory Council – had to be abandoned because of TUC resistance, with the government also dropping plans to introduce a new White Paper on full employment.

The government's economic priorities had obviously changed by 1950; under conditions of full employment, inflation and wages were to become more pivotal issues. Both the proposed White Paper and the advisory council were seen as attempts to create a forum which established a context of permanent incomes policy outlining the responsibilities of government and obligations of employers and trade unions to maintain full employment. During the period 1945 to 1951 trade union membership had increased from 7.9 million to 9 million while their bargaining position had been strengthened through the Trade Union Act of 1945. During the years 1945 to 1951 – in the absence of a wages freeze – wages had been rising at 8 to 10 per cent per annum; in contrast, during the years of voluntary restraint pay had been rising at 3 per cent per annum. Real wages between 1948 and 1950 either remained stationary or had fallen. Attlee's voluntary wage restraint had therefore enjoyed a high degree of success both in moderating wage demands, curbing inflation and improving Britain's export performance.

The breakdown in 1951 highlights the tenuous relationship between a Labour government and the trade unions. On the one hand, the Labour government did develop a political programme which benefited trade union members – including the programme of nationalisation, the National Health Service, pensions, and family allowances. But on the other hand, in the context of rising prices and falling living standards, it became more difficult for senior trade union leaders such as Tewson (General Secretary of the TUC), Deakin (TGWU) and Lawther (NUM), who were all committed to the success of a Labour government, to continue to deliver better wages to their members.

The relationship had been put under strain during Hugh Dalton's budget in 1947, when despite the pressures on dollar prices he did not allow prices and subsidies to increase in line with the rise in prices. In effect, this meant an increase in prices while the trade unions were being asked to observe a voluntary wage freeze. The second area of tension developed during the devaluation package in 1949 when Chancellor Hugh Gaitskell pointed to the looming threat of inflation likely to be caused by devaluation, and actually pushed for a package of expenditure cuts which included an increase in prescriptions charges and further restrictions on price subsidies. By 1950 therefore, the balance in the initial contract established between the government and trade unions in 1945 had changed. While in 1945 the understanding embraced the commitment to full employment, the commitment to social expenditures, and the containment of prices through subsidies, this had been replaced in 1950 with an understanding founded on the much narrower agenda of wage controls. The FBI were unhappy about the trade union demands for a ceiling to be put on dividends and argued that such a ceiling was likely to have an adverse affect on new investment and therefore on the prospects for employment. Also, because the nature of the agreement was likely to be voluntary, the government could not compel business to limit dividends. Furthermore, the economic strictures of convertibility, devaluation, and the deficit on the balance of payments ensured that the government could no longer offer open-ended pledges on public expenditure and therefore all estimates on public expenditure were to be brought under closer Treasury control.

The decision by the government to abandon the idea of establishing a permanent forum under the Wages Advisory Council (where it was hoped the trade unions, employers' organisations, and government could discuss the economic context) confirmed the view that trade unions and employers were reluctant to enter into corporatist arrangements in Britain. In contrast, in countries such as Sweden, West Germany, and Austria the idea of concerted action was seen as essential to the successes of full employment and low inflation. In those countries, therefore, trade unions were willing to become social partners to seek to influence the direction of economic policy, while in Britain the agreement on incomes policy was always seen as a short-term measure to deal with the short crisis of the balance of payments. The trade unions argued that the best way for them to protect their members' interests was to return to free collective bargaining in a system of industrial relations based on 'voluntarism' which meant a system of collective bargaining free from state direction.

The history of British trade unions is one of suspicion of state intervention, since on so many occasions the state has intervened to question the *raison d'être* of trade unions. Because of this ambivalent relationship with the law, trade unions in Britain have always preferred the system of free collective bargaining:

> Traditionally the trade unions had been on the defensive, and took whatever they could obtain from collective bargaining. This was a habit that in the absence of structural, constitutional and philosophical re-evaluation, could only be suspended for a limited period. This lesson proved rather traumatic for the moderate trade union leaders and was a black warning for future governments, a warning that was too readily ignored or glossed over.
>
> (Jones 1987: 47)

In addition, although the TUC would generally seem to be giving a coherence to trade unions in Britain which is lacking in Europe it has little power to give direction to them. While trade unions agree to serve on the General Council of the TUC, their primary role is still to promote the independence of individual unions so that they may pursue their own interests free from both government or TUC interference.

The lesson of incomes policy for the Labour government was that while some trade union leaders saw the Labour government as their government, the attempt to secure a wages freeze which threatened both living standards and wage differentials was always likely to be a temporary solution. At the end of the day trade unions wanted to reinforce the economics of the labour market, of bargaining for their members according to the state of demand for their skills, this being dependant on the ability of the craft unions representing the skilled workers to control the level of labour supply without undermining wage rates or diluting the skills of their members.

Furthermore, while most trade union leaders argued for the need to save the Labour government, rank and file members seemed to reject the argument that wage demands had to be traded against the context of full employment, inflation, and the welfare state. Also, as skilled workers were not directly threatened by unemployment they felt sufficiently secure to push up their wage demands in line with the inflation rate. In addition, the idea of the social wage had not really entered the British political agenda. Policies directed at social concerns including pensions, health, housing and child allowances, were seen as separate from the wage bargain. While most trade unions were being educated into the idea of the social wage, the majority of trade unionists still felt that welfare was a political issue for governments to deal with and that the process of determining incomes had to be kept out of the political bargain.

CONCLUSIONS

During the election campaign of 1951, the Labour Party could claim that they had established the foundations of the welfare state. Furthermore, they could also point to some remarkable successes in Britain's economic performance. In the context of welfare, the government had established the principles of free health care according to need, family allowances, better pensions, a programme of public sector housing, and national insurance. The dreaded Poor Law and the workhouse had been finally abolished. As to economic performance they could point to the new investment in the infrastructure of the economy, in the nationalised industries including the coal industry, electricity, and gas. In addition, Britain had been reintegrated into the world economy in the aftermath of war and by 1951 had recovered most of its exports with an economy that was operating at full employment.

However, while the government could make these claims, critics have also pointed to their failures and have sought therefore to explain why the Labour Party lost the 1951 election despite these successes. Some of these critiques fall under the category of Labour's betrayal of the voters of 1945. These voters are seen as ushering in a social revolution by electing a Labour government; yet with Labour in power most of these expectations had been betrayed. Ralph Miliband (1975) in his *Parliamentary Socialism* for example, points to the history of Labour government as a series of betrayals by Labour leaders of the pledges and commitments that are expected of a Labour government. Miliband therefore points to Labour's failure to deal with the central problems of class inequalities in terms of power and income and criticises the limited ambitions of Labour's nationalisation programme. He argues that Labour had a mandate to nationalise the commanding heights of the economy yet this programme of nationalisation was brought to an end in 1948 at the first opportunity that Party leaders had to depart from the commitments to public ownership. Miliband points to the tensions in the Cabinet and at the Labour Conferences of 1949 and 1950 when the consolidators argued that Labour had gone far enough with its programme of socialism and that now was the time to consolidate their achievements. In contrast, trade unions and constituency parties were urging the Party to commit themselves to a continued radical programme. Miliband therefore points to the unwillingess of Labour leaders to embrace further radical commitments and to their failure to give the electorate a real vision of socialist principles as fundamental reasons for their fall from government.

The Miliband thesis seems to be founded on two assumptions, which although implicit to the analysis need to be made explicit in order to understand this perspective in relation to economic policy-making. First, if Labour leaders are perceived as having betrayed the programme of the Party, government must have complete autonomy in the conduct of economic policy provided they have the political will to carry out their political priorities. Some Labour leaders are seen as being less committed to the 'class' which has elected them and always ready to surrender their political priorities.

The second assumption is that the economy does not act as a constraint on the government. The Labour governments ended up managing the economy between 1945 and 1951 without seeking to alter the nature of a capitalist economy. So although the economy does appear as a series of constraints, the Labour governments had sufficient autonomy to alter its nature. To say that the balance of payments, inflation, employment, devaluation, and convertibility represented crises which government had to respond to would induce the reply from Miliband that such pressures narrowed the choices for the government but only because they did not show the political convictions to implement their own policy alternatives.

While Miliband directed his argument on members of the Cabinet, Panitch (1976) also points to Labour's failure with his argument concentrating on the relationship between the Labour government and the trade unions. As far as Panitch is concerned this failure is due to the adherence by trade union leaders to two-and-half years of wages policy without a ceiling being put on dividends. The government reduced food subsidies, which in turn led to price increases which culminated in the trade unions being used as the agents of the government to police an incomes policy which the government said was voluntary and which some trade union leaders accepted on behalf of their members. Panitch argues that this form of corporatism weakened the Labour movement because the Labour government and trade union leaders were being increasingly associated with reducing their members' living standards, this eventually resulting in conflicts with the rank and file. It was therefore not surprising that this form of restrictive incomes policy broke down in 1951 and the Labour government had to abandon any plans for establishing a permanent forum to deal with prices and pay. Panitch argues that incomes policy eventually lost Labour the election because the Labour government appeared to be holding down the living standards of those who had put so much store in the Labour government of 1945.

In contrast, the accounts by Cairncross (1985b), Kenneth O'Morgan (1984), and Henry Pelling (1985) tend to be more pragmatic in their assessments of the Labour government because each takes into account the triangle of forces involved in the process of economic policy-making. Each of these authors recognises that the economic context does represent a constraining factor on government. Each also recognises that governments have their own political priorities and also that choices of policy alternatives are influenced by ideas as to how the economy works; yet each of these authors puts a different weighting on these processes.

Within the Cairncross account the emphasis is put on the government's lack of strategy, of their lack of preparedness in costing social programmes, and in the constructing of a policy to deal with the problems of the balance of payments. According to Cairncross, therefore, the years of the Labour government are best seen as a process of ministers being buffeted by economic factors which most of the time seemed to be beyond their comprehension. In contrast to the betrayal thesis of Miliband and Panitch, Cairncross argues that the government devoted too much energy to their political priorities without developing a coherent economic policy to achieve their social objectives. The government should have therefore produced a more effective policy to deal with the problem of inflation rather than allowing the issue of incomes policy to drift between 1945 and 1948. Instead the government should have dealt with the inflationary gap at the outset by restricting demand through the budget process. Cairncross argues that the government's policy of curbing prices was not effective in deaing with the problem of excess demand. Further, he argues that the budget of November 1947 represented a watershed in Labour's economic strategy. Dalton's last budget embodied the needs to use the budget process to influence the level of effective demand. Both Sir Stafford Cripps and Hugh Gaitskell in their economic strategies continued to utilise the budget as their defence against the pressures of inflation.

While these perspectives provide both positive and negative assessments of the Labour government's record there were some economic issues which seemed to transcend the political priorities of the government and that any government which succeeded Labour had to confront. The first issue was the balance of payments constraint. In this it would seem that the Labour government did succeed in shifting resources from consumption to investment. The government did enjoy enough goodwill to continue with wartime rationing of essential goods in the short term, but in the longer term the balance of payments constraint had to be resolved both in an economy free of rationing and also in the context of free trade. The policy also succeeded as long as the trade unions were willing to adhere to the incomes policy, which again was seen as a short-term remedy. In the longer term, trade unions wanted to return to free collective bargaining.

The second issue was how to develop a longer-term anti-inflation strategy. While the Labour government used price controls the problems of inflation were only being artificially suppressed because of the absence of goods, rationing, and the cost of exchequer subsidies.

The third issue was the trade off between employment and inflation. Once governments had embraced the commitment to full employment policy, labour markets were likely to be tight. This necessitated the construction of permanent arrangements to deal with the problem of wage inflation, the rights and obligations of trade unions, governments, and employers in the context of full employment. The breakdown of incomes policy, despite the special relationship between the Labour government and the trade unions, showed the commitment of the unions to return to the system of collective bargaining which was free from government interference and also their unwillingess to trade off wage increases for the commitment of full employment or for social policies which increased public resources for education or health services. These social objectives, although desirable, were not seen as being part of the collective bargaining process. The commitment to full employment and the welfare state represented the government's contract with the electorate. In contrast, the need to protect wages and living standards represented the much narrower contract between the trade union organisations and their members.

The fourth area of concern was the financing of the newly founded welfare state. There were likely to be two major issues related to the impact of the new public sector on economic policy-making. The first concern had to do with the question of whether social programmes were going to determine the levels of public expenditure or whether it was expenditure which was going to decide social programmes. If the answer was going to be that social programmes decided expenditure then it was spending ministers who were going to decide the resources for the public sector, while the Chancellor and the Treasury had to decide how to finance the public sector through constraining private sector consumption or for the Treasury to make forecasts about the likely growth for the economy and channel resources to the public sector in accordance with the forecasted growth. The second option suggested that it was the Treasury which decided the resources which were available for private and public sector consumption and then for ministers to decide how those resources were to be prioritised.

The clashes within the Labour Cabinet between Aneurin Bevan and Hugh Gaitskell reflected this dilemma within the government. On the one hand, Bevan represented the view that it was the spending ministers who were responsible for their departments and therefore that it was the major responsibility of ministers to outline the demands for their departments. In contrast, Hugh Gaitskell firmly believed that the Chancellor of the Exchequer and the Treasury had the responsibility for the economy and that it was for the Treasury to decide the resources available and for spending ministers to live within those resource constraints. According to Gaitskell it was resources which directed spending, while Bevan argued it was spending which decided resources.

The establishing of the welfare state after 1945 meant that certain levels of expenditures were now committed to the public sector – including expenditure on education, health, and housing. All these expenditure programmes were expanding as spending ministers and civil servants were finding new demands and therefore new pressures for additional finance for their programmes. The concept of free health care, for example, did not result in a levelling of expenditure as Bevan had predicted but rather that expenditures on health need to expand to meet new demands and new expectations. The problem for the government was to reconcile these increasing expectations within the context of such economic constraints as the deteriorating balance of payments, sterling crisis, and inflation.

The enduring question of the public sector was how governments were going to achieve increases in both private and public consumption since the electorate were likely to favour lower taxation but at the same time high-quality public goods? In seeking to answer this question it would seem that during the first years of the Labour government, the Loan Agreement was actually used to finance the welfare state without the government having to make choices between private and public consumption. The convertibility crisis in 1947, however, showed that the government could no longer postpone making decisions between diverting resources to investment as against consumption. When the government did decide to rechannel resources into investment and exports, the problem with this policy objective was that it could only be achieved either by government reducing public sector consumption or by reducing private consumption through controls on incomes, rationing, and increased taxation. The package agreed within the Cabinet represented a series of measures which reduced both private and public consumption. However, as the Labour government soon discovered, such a decrease in consumption represented a direct threat to living standards and therefore such a policy was only likely to have short-term success.

These four areas of economic policy, including the balance of payments constraint, the problem of rising inflation, the maintenance of full employment, and public expenditure control were to become of central concern to all governments of the post-war period. However, the responses adopted could be put into one of two categories: either governments sought to adopt an *ad hoc* response or they adopted the strategic approach. This meant that policies evolved either as a series of responses directed at meeting economic issues separately and according to different priorities, or that economic issues were to be perceived to have linkages which required vision and a coherent strategy. So while the Labour government used rationing and import tariffs to deal with the balance of payments, incomes policy to deal with inflation, and public expenditure control as a short-term policy, they were criticised for the lack of a coherent strategy to link these different policies.

The advocates of the coherent strategy perspective argue that the overriding problem and the main priority for the British economy post-1945, was the loss of export markets and the balance of payments deficit. All policies, therefore, should have been directed at the problem of excess demand much earlier, which would have meant there should have been no attempt to increase expenditures on welfare programmes since these expenditures were likely to result in increased pressures on consumption. Furthermore, the government should have embarked on a pay policy earlier rather than relying on exhortation, and should have used the public sector to generate exports through investment in the infrastructure of the economy and investment in human capital. The objective of government was to make the UK labour market more competitive and to improve investment and productivity in Britain's leading industries by providing incentives for investment in these industries.

There are two major limitations to the coherent strategy perspective. First, there are as many coherent strategies as there are advocates of coherent strategies. While Miliband and Panitch are agreed with Cairncross's criticism that the government lacked an overall strategy, their visions of strategies would be very different. Miliband and Panitch, for example, criticise the Labour government for their failure to develop a coherent strategy of social ownership. By contrast, Cairncross criticises the programme of nationalisation as being misplaced and points out that it failed to address the problems of the trade deficit.

The second limitation is that those who urge coherence tend to forget that economic policy reflects a series of tensions between political will, economic necessity and political expediency. While governments might have the will, the short-term economic pressures might be difficult to reconcile with this will. Furthermore, and maybe the most important, is that governments are political in the sense that they need to secure electoral support for their programmes which sometimes means less political will and more political calculation, less strategy and more *ad hoc* responses.

Chapter 9

The economics of Butskellism and collectivism

Economic policy, 1951 to 1970

INTRODUCTION: THE BUTSKELLITE CONSENSUS

In the previous chapter an attempt was made to evaluate the argument that the Labour governments of 1945 to 1951 constructed the political agenda for economic policy-making in the post-war period. The argument that the post-war period represented a Butskellite and collectivist consensus rests on the thesis that economic policy-making in Britain after 1945 and until the election of the Thatcher government in 1979, was conducted within the context of the Post-War Settlement which included the commitments by all governments to the maintenance of full employment, improved living standards and the welfare state:

> In one sense, therefore, the new state represented the cost of social peace, full employment of resources, and an expanding domestic market. The government now took over directly the responsibility for formulating the 'national interest' in economic matters, and undertook to promote by its policies not merely full-employment, but stable prices, economic growth and a trade surplus.
>
> (Gamble 1974: 31)

The proponents of the existence of the Post-War Settlement have tried to show how economic policy-making became less political, that governments – irrespective of party – became less ideological in addressing economic problems and therefore tended to pursue common economic objectives. The aftermath of the Second World War, which in contrast to the First World War had been more of a people's war of common experiences meant that the political parties had to become alike in constructing programmes for the reconstruction of post-war Britain.

In addition, the election of the 1945 Labour government confirmed that people in Britain wished for better times, for an era which promised full employment, prosperity, and an expanded welfare state with free health care and improved pensions, education, and housing. In this context, therefore, the Conservative Party was under pressure to change its image, to break with the past and its association with the economics of *laissez-faire*, the slump, and the unemployment of the inter-war years. The 'progressives' within the Party were therefore in ascendance after the Labour victory of 1945, and it was they who were now in a position to guide Party policy towards the new consensus if the Party was to regain power. R. A. Butler, seen as the architect of the post-war Conservative agenda, warned the Party of:

> our need to convince a broad spectrum of the electorate, whose minds were scarred by inter-war memories and myths, that we had an alternative policy to Socialism which was viable, efficient and humane, which would release and reward enterprise and initiative but without abandoning social justice or reverting to mass unemployment.
>
> (Butler 1971: 132)

As far as Butler, Harold Macmillan and other 'new progressives' were concerned the Conservative Party had to retrieve the 'conservativism of one nation' – the tradition of Disraeli and Chamberlain – against the market liberal thinking which had gained ascendancy in the Party during the 1920s and 1930s. R. A. Butler therefore urged the Party to rethink its position on the role of trade unions in a new Britain. Trade unions had a role to play as responsible social agents if there was to be a commitment to full employment. The relationship between trade unions and the Conservative Party was still influenced by the repercussions of the General Strike in 1926 and the Trade Union Act of 1927. First, Butler wanted the Party to move towards a new politics based on voluntary consent, of a Conservative government being able and willing to consult with the employers and trade unions in the making of economic policy. Second, the new progressives had to persuade the Conservative Party and the nation that the public provision of welfare belonged to a Conservative tradition, that it was the Conservative Party which had first intervened with the Factory Acts, Public Health Acts and education reform as against the market liberal thinking of non-intervention. Third, the new progressives also argued that the commitment to high and stable employment had also to become a Conservative priority, which meant that the Party had to become more interventionist in seeking to influence investment and consumption.

While the Conservative Party was under pressure to change after the 1945 electoral defeat, the Labour Party came under similar pressure after their defeat in 1951 – increasingly so as they went on to lose three successive elections. The Labour Party, in turn, had to address the issue of social change. The argument in the Labour Party was between those within the Party who wanted to strengthen the politics of Labourism, and the Revisionists – so called because they were seen as wanting to revise the meaning of socialism. Revisionists criticised the doctrine of Labourism as seeking to represent the partial interests of those who were in work and members of trade unions. While Labourism sought to improve the quality of life of those who were involved in the productive process this was seen by the Revisonists as not representative of the new age of the consumer society. In contrast Revisionists wanted the Labour Party to move away from commitments to further nationalisation, to break some of the close ties with the trade unions, and instead to appeal to the emerging professionals, the new white collar workers, and to address themselves to the concerns of families and pensioners. Hugh Gaitskell and Tony Crosland, in their writings and speeches gave leadership to the Revisionist thinking within the Labour Party. They continued to urge Party members to rethink their definition of socialism in the context of the prosperity and affluence of the 1950s, arguing that the path to socialism was not necessarily through public ownership. Instead, they suggested that the path to a more equal society was more likely to be achieved through government using taxation and public expenditure as the mechanisms for the redistribution of income and resources:

> I am a Socialist and have been for some 30 years. I became a Socialist quite candidly not so much because I was a passionate advocate of public ownership but because at a very early age I came to hate and loathe social injustice.... I am a Socialist because I want to see fellowship.... These to me are the Socialist ideals. Nationalisation is the vital means but it is only one of the means by which we can achieve these objects.
>
> (Gaitskell, Labour Party Conference, October 1955)

After the third electoral defeat in 1959, Gaitskell determined that it was crucial for the Labour Party to abandon Clause IV from its Constitution since he considered that the Party no longer believed in 100 per cent public ownership of the economy but that public ownership will always be one of the means to the classless society:

> We should make two things clear...that we have no intention of abandoning public ownership...that we regard public ownership not as an end in itself but as a means...to certain ends.... While we certainly wish to extend social ownership...our goal is not 100 per cent State ownership. Our goal is a society in which Socialist goals are realised.... The pace at which we can go depends on how quickly we can persuade our fellow citizens to back us.
>
> (Gaitskell, Labour Party Conference, November 1959)

Under pressure of electoral defeat therefore the Labour Party, like the Conservative Party, had been engaged in the 1950s in rethinking the political priorities of socialism. During the years of Conservative administration, Harold Macmillan, Conservative Prime Minister was able to claim during the 1959 election campaign that Britain had 'never had it so good'. The Conservatives had managed to phase out all import restrictions, removed rationing and all feeling of austerity. People in Britain were encouraged to increase personal consumption as more cars, TV sets and washing machines became available. The Labour Party was therefore being forced to redefine the meaning of its socialism. The Socialist programme as outlined in the 1930s had addressed only the problems of production and the ownership of production as the path of socialism; the question for the 1960s was the attempt to remodel socialism towards a more individual consumer society. The aim of the Revisionists was to move the Labour Party from the politics of Labourism and to attempt to reconcile the priorities of the trade unions with the Labour Party to a situation where socialism sought to address a wider audience – the audience of the individual consumers of private and public goods, the aspirations therefore of people concerned with social justice, equal opportunities in education and high-quality public services. The Revisionists, including Roy Jenkins for example, wanted to question the relationship between the Party and the trade unions and asked whether such close ties were actually damaging to the Labour Party.

The thesis that the conduct of economic policy in Britain reflected the emergence of consensus politics for at least thirty years, has been underpinned by the argument that within both the Labour Party and the Conservative Party there were shifts towards the acceptance of Keynesian thinking. Keynesian economics had been adopted by the 'one nation group' of the Conservative Party. They had advocated a more interventionist role for a future Conservative government, the acceptance of the mixed economy without further nationalisation, and an economy which rewarded enterprise and recognised the benefits of the price mechanism without subordinating government to the forces of the market. Equally, Keynesian economics had already been integrated in the thinking of the Labour Party. Hugh Dalton and Hugh Gaitskell had resorted to the use of the budget mechanism to influence economic policy during the 1945 Labour government. The Revisionists within the Labour Party wanted to take Keynesian economics further by embracing them as the means to achieving a more equal society without having to resort to nationalisation. According to Crosland it was no longer who owned the means of production which mattered but rather how the proceeds of the economy were distributed. Keynesian economics showed governments how to use the budget to redistribute income to lower income groups, both as a means to create more social justice and also as the way to influence demand and economic management.

The term 'Butskellism' has been used to describe the nature of the political consensus during the post-war period. The term is the amalgam of the two Chancellors of the Exchequer: R. A. Butler who was the Conservative Chancellor during the 1951 government and Hugh Gaitskell who had been the Labour Chancellor between 1950 and 1951. The term is therefore used to indicate similarities in the thinking of the two Chancellors, who although they had represented different political priorities followed common economic objectives.

THE CONCEPT OF ADVERSARIAL POLITICS

While it might be correct to argue that after each electoral defeat there were attempts to shift the thinking within the major political parties, it would be rather misleading to carry forward the argument that these shifts also resulted in the end of ideology in the sense that both parties, when they became the government, accepted the economic agenda set by the previous administration. Indeed, in launching Labour's campaign during the 1964 General Election, Harold Wilson, the Labour leader, made clear the distinction between the priorities of the Labour Party in contrast to the Conservative government. Wilson described the Conservative record as follows:

> every four or five years a deliberately engineered consumption boom is generated which after a few months, calls forth spectacular increases in national production.... A rapidly expanding home market exerts a dangerous pull on exports; a disproportionate rise in imports is needed to feed our factories and shops. So the green light changes to amber, interest rates rise, social programmes are cut back and within a year the red light of economic crisis...bringing the economy grinding to a halt.
>
> (Wilson 1964: 23–41)

Labour's argument during the 1964 election was that the thirteen years of Conservative government between 1951 and 1964 had been more concerned with the manipulation of demand to influence short-term electoral gain rather than in addressing economic policy at long-term economic issues. In their argument, therefore, the Labour Party in 1964 urged the need to modernise the British economy to deal with the problems of new investment in science and technology to regenerate manufacturing industry after what they saw as thirteen years of Tory misrule. This was hardly an attempt at reconciliation between Labour and Conservative economic priorities.

As in 1945, the Labour Party argued that the problem was still the trade gap, high import penetration, and the inability of Britain to take advantage of increased world trade. Labour's election campaign in 1964 concentrated on 'the new Britain', on the 'white heat of technology' in using the nationalised industries and a new Ministry of Technology to support British industry. So although the Labour Party did not commit itself to new nationalisation in the 1964 programme, nevertheless their argument for intervention was directed towards utilising the state in selective aid to industry.

Labour also criticised the government's lack of strategy for dealing with the problem of inflation. Wilson pointed to the inability of the Conservative government to reach an agreement with the trade unions on incomes policy, and the need for a government which could establish a long-term relationship with trade unions and employers in order to deal with the planning of the economy, investment, and wages. The Conservative governments had embarked on a strategy of *laissez-faire*, a free for all in industrial relations and wage bargaining. A future Labour government, Wilson argued would make it a priority to establish a long-term understanding with the trade unions.

The Conservative Party had won the 1951 election on the pledge of removing control and rationing, for allowing more freedom to market forces, and in giving the consumer rights to choose. The Conservative attitude to the welfare state was also founded on selective benefits targeted at groups in need, this being in contrast to Labour's universalist ideas of welfare. Furthermore, while the Conservatives pledged to end the wages freeze and to reinstate the right to strike, they still argued that trade unions had a duty to moderate their wage demands. Finally, as far as the Conservative government was concerned the trade gap represented a short-term problem of excess demand in contrast to Labour's structural approach.

The central question of this chapter is to what extent can the thesis of a Butskellite consensus be sustained? while it might be pointed out that during the period 1951 to 1970 there were twelve sterling crises which forced both governments to respond in similar ways – namely, by curtailing the level of demand, using purchase tax, interest rates, and bank deposits as the major economic levers to regain market confidence – it might also be argued that when other policies are considered the theme of Butskellism becomes less convincing. The argument being that while both governments might have articulated different political priorities before achieving election success, once in power they had to face similar problems and produce similar policies. According to this perspective, therefore, the Butskellite consensus represented the convergence in economic policy.

While the concept of Butskellism points to consensus and continuity, the theme of adversarial politics embodies the view that in the conduct of economic policy, both governments had different political priorities which each sought to implement, and that rather than the period being one of consensus and continuity it represented increased discontinuity and disagreement. According to the adversarial thesis both governments had different perceptions as to what needed to be done despite the problems of the exchange rate and the balance of payments. While the Conservative governments sought to use demand management as the major lever to influence the levels of demand, in contrast the Labour government searched for strategic policies to improve Britain's export performance – by introducing new public institutions such as the Department of Economic

Affairs which was given the authority to introduce economic planning, a Ministry of Technology, and the Industrial Reorganisation Corporation.

Both Conservative and Labour governments also constructed different strategies to deal with the problem of inflation, with the Conservatives relying on influencing the level of demand and arguing that inflation was a demand-pull problem. In contrast the Labour Party had criticised the Conservatives for the 'stop–go' effects of their policies and argued that a Labour government would work towards the development of a new understanding with the trade unions to produce a more durable incomes policy to cope with wage inflation. While the Conservative governments were reluctant to reintroduce prices and wage controls the Labour government, in making claims for their special relationship with the trade unions, were again facing problems of strain in that special relationship after 1968 when once more the trade unions resisted attempts by the government to establish a permanent incomes policy. The trade unions, as in 1950, demanded a return to free collective bargaining, confirming in a way the Conservative argument that any attempts by government to limit wages, prices, and dividends represented excessive intervention which was only likely to succeed in the short term.

The evaluation of the performance of the British economy during the period 1951 to 1964 seems to produce different judgements. At one level, when compared to other countries, the performance could be judged a failure but in terms of Britain's economic history the period could be perceived as a success. Throughout the period UK economic growth averaged between 2.5 and 2.9 per cent per annum; in contrast the French economy was growing at an average rate of 7 per cent per annum and the West German at 5 per cent per annum. While other European countries were taking advantage of the expansion in world trade, Britain's inability to compete in overseas markets meant a lower share of world trade – it actually fell from 16 per cent in 1960 to 11 per cent by 1970. In addition Britain also seemed to be experiencing a higher inflation rate while the unemployment rate was higher than the average of other industrial countries.

However, in terms of Britain's economic history, the period represented an era of continuous growth which had produced increases in living standards, a high level of consumption, stable employment, and higher wages. Indeed, this was the decade associated with the new affluent society. According to the Brookings Institute, therefore, the problem of the UK was not so much of failure but of underperformance when compared to other industrial economies.

Britain's relative economic failure has been blamed on the Butskellite consensus and the *ad hoc* short-term 'stop–go' policies which were associated with the use of demand management policies. Equally, however, the sluggish economic growth and the high inflation rates have been blamed on adversarial politics and the inability of governments to create permanent structures to achieve consensus in the conduct of economic policy. Market liberals have criticised the emergence of Butskellism and the commitments to intervention and collectivism because they felt that government had caused more harm than good to the economy. In contrast, the critiques of adversarial politics point to the discontinuity in policy including disagreements on industrial policy, breakdown in incomes policy, and the failure to generate a coherent strategy towards the nationalised industries.

The following sections deal with economic policy during the period 1951 to 1970 and ask to what extent do the models of Butskellism and adversarial politics contribute to explain the influences which guided economic policy-making during this period. The assessment of economic policy under each government is located under the themes of the balance of payments and exchange rate policy, budgetary policy and policies directed at inflation and employment.

THE CONSERVATIVE GOVERNMENTS 1951 TO 1964

In the conclusion to the previous chapter it was argued that the problems of the trade gap, rising wage costs, and employment policies became increasingly related during the last years of the 1945 Labour government. The years of austerity, rationing, the curbing of domestic consumption and the wages freeze had all contributed to improving Britain's export performance and the balance of payments. However, the Conservatives had won office in 1951 on the commitment of ending rationing and subsidies and replacing state controls by market forces. The problem for the Conservative government, therefore, was how to maintain the commitment to full employment and wage stability, and how to sustain Britain's export performance without state controls. The Conservative government during the early 1950s sought to break with some of the Labour government's measures on wages, prices and subsidies, and had limited themselves to using the budgetary process to influence the balance of payments while the problem of wages was left to negotiation between trade unions and employers. However, after 1955, the arm's length approach to incomes policy was modified as the government became more interventionist on incomes and prices.

Economic policy: the overall strategy

During the 1951 election the Conservative Party had a difficult path to tread. As R. A. Butler had indicated, the Party had to persuade the electors that a Conservative government would not undo all of Labour's measures. They therefore had to make pledges on the health service and also public housing, promising that a Conservative government would build more houses than the Labour government. However, while committing the Party to an expanded welfare state, the Conservatives also had to show that they would depart from Labour's interventionist strategy in the economy, replacing government direction by market forces and allowing more room for individual enterprise and individual choice. In committing the government to a market strategy, the Conservatives also pledged themselves to the maintenance of full employment.

Economic policy: the balance of payments

While the Labour government had used rationing and price controls to curb personal and public sector consumption of goods and services to boost Britain's export performance and devaluation to address the problem of the balance of payments, the incoming Conservative government had also inherited a balance of payments deficit on taking office. The government could not use rationing or price controls since they had pledged themselves to phase out rationing and price subsidies. They therefore argued in 1951 that the problem of the trade deficit represented a short-term problem of excess demand which was leading to a high level of imports. Accordingly, during his first budget in 1951, the Chancellor increased the level of personal taxation and purchase tax as the way of restraining demand.

The Conservatives therefore differed in their strategy on the balance of payments from the 1945 Labour government. The Labour government had argued that Britain needed a structural strategy to improve on export performance, which meant the introduction of policies which reduced labour costs in relation to our competitors and methods of improving productivity. In contrast, the Conservative attitude towards the balance of payments was as that of a short-term economic problem which required a 'touch on the brake', either by increasing personal taxation or reducing public expenditure or increasing interest rates.

The government's *ad hoc* approach to the balance of payments did change after the crisis in sterling during 1960 when it became increasingly clear to Prime Minister Harold Macmillan that Britain needed to escape from the balance of payments constraint and the constant stop–go policies which were proving to be damaging to Britain's growth performance. During the 1960s, therefore, the Conservatives seemed to be moving towards a more interventionist economic policy, arguing for the needs of planning and also for securing an agreement with the trade unions on incomes policy.

On the issue of planning, Selwyn Lloyd in 1961 had taken the first steps to bring together employers, trade unions and the government within the forum of the newly established National Economic Development Council (NEDC). The primary objective for discussion within the new forum was the question of how to improve Britain's economic performance and agreement on setting an objective of a 4 per cent growth per annum. The NEDC also discussed ways to improve Britain's export performance which included arguments about the need of the government to sustain a stable level of demand to generate new investment and increased exports, and also the need to reduce labour costs.

In seeking to break out of the balance of payments constraint, in 1962 Harold Macmillan encouraged the new Chancellor Reginald Maudling to produce a 'go for growth' strategy which meant increasing demand in the economy despite the pressures on sterling and the trade deficit.

Employment, inflation and incomes policy

While the Conservatives were in opposition R. A. Butler and Walter Monckton had been given leave by the Conservative leader Winston Churchill to explore a new approach to the economy and industrial relations which would be implemented by the next Conservative government coming to power. The outcome was the Industrial Charter of 1947 in which the Conservatives pledged to recognise certain workers' rights, including the right to belong to a trade union and the right to strike. The Charter also suggested that a future Conservative government would not seek to denationalise any of the public utilities and also pledged the Conservatives to economic planning and expansion in social expenditure. The Charter was accepted by the Conservative Party Conference in May 1947 and was seen as a clear restatement of Conservative economic policy. Indeed, according to Anthony Eden, who was then deputy leader of the Party, the Charter confirmed the true tradition of Toryism:

> We are not a Party of unbridled brutal capitalism and never have been. Although we believe in personal responsibility and personal initiative in business we are not the political children of the laissez-faire school. We opposed them decade after decade. Where did the Tories stand when the greed and squalor of the industrial revolution were darkening our land? I am content with Keir Hardie's testimony: 'As a matter of hard dry fact, from which there can be no getting away, there is more labour legislation standing to the credit of the Conservative party on the Statute Book than there is to that of their opponents.'
> (Conservative Party Conference Report 1947: 42–3)

While the Conservative Party committed itself to the maintenance of full employment, growth in the economy, intervention, and the welfare state, the Party also had to emphasise its commitment to free enterprise, the rights of the individual, and the end of state direction on prices and rationing. Furthermore, on the issue of wages, the Conservative Party pledged to end the wage freeze and to allow trade unions the rights to strike and to free collective bargaining.

The claim for the special relationship between the trade unions and the Labour government seemed rather hollow in 1950 and 1951 as the trade unions through the TUC Conferences confirmed their inability to carry Labour's incomes policy further. At the 1950 TUC Conference, an ETU resolution which was highly critical of the Labour government was carried by Congress:

Congress is of the opinion that until such time as there is a reasonable limitation of profits, a positive planning of our British economy and prices are subject to such control as will maintain the purchasing power of wages at a level affording to every worker a reasonable standard of living there can be no basis for a restraint on wage applications.

(TUC Conference Report 1950: 467)

The lessons of the breakdown of the wages freeze as far as the Conservative Party was concerned meant that a Conservative government committed to a more market-orientated economy with less price controls and less subsidies was also less likely to succeed to reach an agreement with the trade unions on incomes policy. The reduction of subsidies and the phasing-out of price controls would increase pressures on prices and wages at least in the short term, and therefore if the government was to succeed in removing controls then it was better to allow for wages and prices to be determined in the market place without the government having to resort to direction.

The willingness of the trade unions to work with the newly elected Conservative government in 1951 was made clear in a statement issued by the TUC:

It is our long standing practice to work with whatever government is in power and through consultation jointly with Ministers and with the other side of industry to find practical solutions to the social and economic problems facing the country.

(Wigham 1976: 106)

After nearly three years of wage restraint, it was soon made apparent to the government that most trade unions were submitting wage claims to restore differentials. The strategy of the government up to 1955 was always to give way on wage claims under pressure, as long as major industrial disputes were being avoided. In the public sector it was the railway workers who were at the forefront of wage settlements, and in 1953 and 1954 when the rail unions rejected awards made by tribunals the government actually intervened to make a settlement to avoid threatened strike action. Equally, in the engineering industry which was at the forefront of the private sector wage bargaining, the willingness by the engineering employers to fight it out and resist a trade union claim was frustrated by the government when Ian Macleod, as Minister of Labour, forced both sides to accept the findings of a Court of Inquiry.

Between 1951 and 1955 the government did not seem to have a specific anti-inflation policy, nor did they attempt to establish any forum where wages and prices could be discussed. R. A. Butler's exhortation that increased wage claims had to be accompanied by increases in productivity had received little support within the trade unions since they felt it was his decisions on reducing price subsidies that had created the pressures on wages. The trade unions had passed a resolution at the TUC Annual Conference in 1956 supporting 'the rights of labour to bargain on equal terms with capital and to use its bargaining strength to protect workers'. Furthermore, new union leaders – including Frank Cousins of the TGWU – were less prepared than their predecessors to enter discussions with the government. Cousins pointed out that in the climate of a free for all trade unions were part of the 'all' and that while there was no attempt to control prices or profits then trade unions had to preserve their members' living standards through collective bargaining. In the meantime, in the White Paper *The Economic Implications of Full Employment* (HMSO 1956), the new Chancellor Harold Macmillan had pointed to the danger of free collective bargaining in the context of full employment:

> in order to maintain full employment the government must ensure that the level of demand for goods and services is high and rises steadily as productive capacity grows. This means a strong demand for labour and good opportunities to sell goods and services profitably. In these conditions, it is open to employees to insist on large wage increases, and it is possible for employers to grant them and pass the cost to the consumer.... This is the danger which confronts the country. If the prosperous economic conditions necessary to maintain full employment are exploited...price stability and full employment become incompatible.
>
> (HMSO 1956: 10–11)

According to the government the solutions to the maintenance of full employment and wage inflation lay with voluntary wage and price restraint. While the government provided the framework of full employment, workers were guaranteed employment and employers had stable markets. In this context the government argued that the absence of self-restraint would lead to higher wages and higher prices, making it more difficult to maintain levels of demand and therefore full employment.

The problem of industrial relations

In addition to the problem of collective bargaining and incomes policy, during this period there were two further developments which were also to have long-term effects on industrial relations. One development was the drift towards unofficial disputes and the loss of control by trade union officials to local shop steward committees. The move towards decentralised bargaining and the increase in the number of wildcat strikes also had a major influence on pay bargaining. The new shop steward committees did not enter into long-term binding agreements with their employers, which in turn destabilised industrial relations within the plant as trade unions sought to leap-frog each other in striking bargains with local employers. These two developments – including the drift towards an informal system of collective bargaining, the increase in the number of unofficial disputes, and the problem of wage drift – were to become major political issues for the next thirty years. The pressures for the reform of industrial relations became an issue for the Conservative governments in 1955, 1959, 1970 and 1979 and equally for the Labour governments in 1966 and 1974. In 1990, eleven years after the election of the Thatcher government, the Conservative government of Mr Major is still seeking to come to grips with the issue of trade union immunities, the problem of unofficial disputes, and wage drift.

The problem of wage drift, together with what seemed a series of retreats by government under the threat of industrial action, was brought into sharper focus as a new crisis of sterling emerged in 1957. In seeking to negotiate a short-term drawing right on the IMF, the government had to draw up a strategy to deal with the issue of wage inflation. It was in this context that Peter Thorneycroft agreed to set up the Council on Prices, Productivity and Incomes (CPPI) to introduce the concept of a guiding light on wage claims. Also known as The Cohen Council and The Three Wise Men, the CPPI was not intended, however, to act as an instrument of government to bring together government, employers, and trade unions or to make any judgements on wage claims; instead the aims were confined to making general statements on the economy. Between 1957 and 1959, the Council seemed to reinforce the government's argument against incomes policy and therefore tended to come out in support of the government's policy of dealing with inflation through the budgetary process. The Council also seemed to suggest that the problem of inflation was related to the issue of 'overemployment' in the economy and that price stability could be achieved by allowing unemployment to increase.

Peter Thorneycroft and his Treasury team, including Enoch Powell and Nigel Birch, had decided that the problem of inflation lay with excess demand and a lax monetary policy. Thorneycroft therefore preferred a policy of tighter monetary control and ended the cheap money policy of his predecessors. He increased the base rate from 2 to 7 per cent, making borrowing that much dearer, and thus arguably made employers more reluctant to give in on wage demands. Thorneycroft also produced a package of public expenditure reductions as part of his deflationary strategy. However, worried by the rise in unemployment the Cabinet approved a rise in public expenditure of £50 million in January 1958 which was supported by the Prime Minister against the advice of his Chancellor. Peter Thorneycroft and his Treasury team resigned *en masse* in January 1958.

By 1959, the Council's Third Report seemed to reflect major changes in government policy. The Report was now critical of the government's reliance on the budget to deal with inflation, arguing that the syndrome of stop–go and deflationary policies had done more damage to the economy:

> It is evident that the method of restraining demand had serious disadvantages: we believe that there would be a great gain in finding some other way of avoiding a continuous rise in pay, profits and prices.... But a better way of preventing this progressive rise has not so far been found.
> (HMSO 1961: para 116)

In its fourth and final report of 1961 the CPPI reflected on the substantial shift of policy that was taking place. The Report now argued that the problem of inflation was a cost-push problem and the syndrome of a wage–price spiral which could not be dealt with through demand restraint. The Report therefore seemed to reject the earlier alternative of using unemployment to deal with the problem of inflation and instead argued that inflation was an institutional problem which required governments to deal with organised interests involved in income determination. The Council therefore urged the government to commit themselves to incomes policy.

In July 1961, in the absence of reaching a voluntary agreement with the trade unions, the government imposed a pay freeze which was followed by a White Paper in February 1962 *Incomes Policy: The Next Step*, in which the government outlined proposals for keeping wage increases in line with increases in productivity and called for restraint on profits. The government also launched the National Incomes Commission (NIC) to investigate wage claims on criteria of growth in the economy, skill shortages, and the effects particular wage settlements might have on other employment. Although the NIC was being asked to play a more interventionist role in income determination, the lack of co-operation by the trade unions meant the NIC was again confined to making moral exhortatory statements that bargains between employers, and trade unions had now to be conceded in the context of the wider national interest, taking into account the problems of inflation and the need for self-restraint.

Like the Cohen Commission before it, the NIC proved to be an ineffective instrument in influencing pay and prices. While the NIC criticised the expansion in plant bargains and the problem of wage drift, it did not have statutory powers to establish rulings on wage claims or to define what was the national interest. It might be argued that the brief histories of the CPPI and the NIC confirmed the Conservative government's reluctance to expand the involvement of government in industrial relations or to seek to secure trade union support for an incomes policy. For a Party committed to the dismantling of controls, highly critical of rigidities and bureaucracy in the economy, the direct involvement of government, employers, and trade unions in economic policy was seen as being a major departure from a market approach. Too many risks were involved in a process which was seen as politicising industrial relations. Incomes policy meant replacing the principles of bargaining and markets by principles of comparability, justice and fairness – principles to be decided by governments and other strategic economic agents. In the end, therefore, while the Conservatives were agreed on the urgency to achieve an incomes policy, they also felt that the crossing of the boundary between a voluntary system of industrial relations and a corporatist system was too high a political cost which in the end they were not willing to pay.

The failure to secure an agreement with the trade unions on incomes policy, together with the growth of the informal system of industrial relations, led some leading Conservatives to urge the Party to break with the post-war consensus on the role of trade unions in politics and their impact on the economy. In a pamphlet entitled *A Giant's Strength*, published in 1958 by the Inns of Court Conservative and Unionist Society, the authors had pointed to the problem of trade union immunities and the new problems of wildcat strikes and secondary picketing. The Inns of Court suggested that strikes should be formalised through the official channels of trade unions, since at present trade union leaders were retreating from threats imposed by unofficial disputes. The Inns of Court therefore recommended that for strikes to be legal they had to be formalised, with trade unions setting up ballots before a strike, and also that a 'cooling off' period had to be established before a strike was called.

The impact of this pamphlet cannot be underestimated since most of its recommendations became the foundations for the Heath government's approach to industrial relations in 1972 and again in the 1980s during the years of the Thatcher governments. It might also be argued that some of the issues identified in the Inns of Court pamphlet were echoed in the report of the Donovan Commission on trade unions in 1968 and again in the Labour government's White Paper *In Place of Strife* published in 1968. It would seem that the problem of the informal system of collective bargaining, together with the problem of wage drift, was becoming central to government economic policy by the late 1950s, and that if Britain was going to improve on its economic performance then it was becoming increasingly clear that the issues of unit labour costs together with improved productivity, were closely related to the conduct of industrial relations.

Harold Macmillan, who had been Prime Minister since 1957 and had encouraged a policy of collaboration and consultation between a Conservative government and the trade unions rather than one of confrontation and strikes, had by the time of the sterling crisis in 1961 come to the conclusion that labour was both irresponsible and conservative in its approach to industrial relations. Macmillan felt that workers in the new industries, including the car industry, were now taking advantage of the context of full employment and stable demand and using their bargaining strength without considering the pressures their wage claims were having on the wider economy. In addition he felt that the unwillingness of the trade unions to co-operate within the CPPI, the NIC and NEDC confirmed the conservatism of trade unions. As far as the Conservative government were concerned therefore, the experience of the 1950s showed that trade union preference for free collective bargaining meant that they were not willing to influence the process of economic policy-making and instead preferred to pursue the narrow and particular interests of their members.

While the wages problem did take up a lot of the government's time between 1951 and 1964, it was relatively insignificant when compared to the 1970s. Inflation had only edged towards 5 per cent at its peak, with the exchange rate steady at $2.80 – the same as at the last devaluation in 1949. In addition, the level of unemployment only rose above half a million twice, compared to the increases to over 1 million in 1972 and 3 million in 1983. Furthermore, there was never any question during the 1950s that the government would eschew demand management policies, and that these levers would be replaced with an anti-inflation strategy irrespective of the likely effects on unemployment.

THE LABOUR GOVERNMENTS, 1964 TO 1970

Economic policy: the strategy to modernise the economy

As indicated in the introduction to this chapter, the Labour Party in opposition had been pressured to redefine their economic policies. The Revisionists led by the Party leader Hugh Gaitskell together with Tony Crosland, had won sufficient support within the Party Conference during the 1950s and early 1960s that for a consensus to be reached when Labour came to fight the 1964 election the issue of further nationalisation of the economy would no longer be central to the Party's economic strategy. Although the Party had still retained Clause IV in the Constitution, there was no mention in the 1964 Manifesto of the essential need to nationalise the commanding heights of the economy. Instead, under their new leader Harold Wilson, Labour entered the 1964 election arguing for the modern-isation of the British economy and criticising the Conservative government for failing to make commitments to new investment in the economy. Labour therefore argued that the Conservatives had been too dogmatic in their adherence to a free market strategy which had failed to generate investment in high technology industries, and that a Labour government would commit themselves to a National Plan under the direction of a new ministry, the

Department of Economic Affairs, but this time in consultation with the private sector of the economy and with the state sector being a part of the plan:

> Labour will set up a Ministry of Economic Affairs with the duty of formulating with both sides of industry, a national economic plan. This Ministry will frame the broad strategy for increasing investment, expand exports and replacing inessential imports.... Within the National Plan each industry will know both what is expected of it and what help it can expect in terms of exports, investment, production and employment. The public sector will make a vital contribution to the national plan.
>
> (Labour Party Manifesto 1964)

According to Labour's programme, outlined in the document *The New Britain: Labour's Plan* (1964), the central theme of Labour's strategy was for breaking out of the stop–go cycle in economic policy. Labour argued that the Conservatives had relied on the narrow and short-term influences of fiscal and monetary policies, pointing to the government's failure to secure a permanent incomes policy and its reluctance to intervene in the economy to generate exports and new investment. Labour's plan for the modernisation of the economy can be outlined under three categories.

Institutional reform

Labour had argued in opposition that economic policy had been dominated by the Treasury view which was essentially a short-term perspective aimed at maintaining market confidence in the exchange rate. The Labour Party were therefore committed to the view that the functions of the Treasury were to be split within two departments, each representing the different aspects of economic policy – one department to monitor the long-term economic strategy of the government, the other to supervise government finances. The Department of Economic Affairs (DEA) aimed to establish Labour's National Plan, setting out objectives for economic growth and resources available for private and public consumption, investment and wages. Labour had criticised the previous government's economic record pointing out that Britain's growth rates of 2.7 per cent per annum had been outpaced by our European competitors. Under the National Plan, George Brown, the new Secretary of State responsible for the DEA, suggested that Britain should plan for a growth rate of 4 per cent per annum.

Labour also pledged to reform other public institutions which had been dominated by a privileged class system which had harmed Britain's economic performance. Wilson therefore set up a Royal Commission on the Civil Service to look at the system of recruitment into the higher Civil Service. The Fulton Commission eventually reported in 1968 and seemed to confirm Wilson's criticism, namely that the top grades of the Civil Service were dominated by graduates from Oxford and Cambridge, who tended to be generalists and therefore amateurs in economic and other public policies. Fulton recommended that in the modern age Britain could no longer compete without specialist Civil Servants trained in economics and social sciences. The Civil Service had to become more professional if it was to manage a modern economy.

The white heat of technology

The second strand to Labour's strategy represented the commitment to new industries involved with research and development, new technology, and the drive towards export-led growth. The new Ministry of Technology aimed to bring together industrialists, trade unions, and the government to construct plans on productivity, unit labour costs, and competitiveness. The Industrial Reorganisation Corporation (IRC), established in 1965, sought to encourage the rationalisation of various industries in order to compete with European industries. The IRC produced reports on the rationalisation of the electronics industry and also on the motor industry.

Wages and inflation

The third strand was founded on Labour's claim on its special relationship with the trade unions. Wilson argued that a central aim of Labour strategy was the development of a permanent incomes policy with the trade unions to deal with the problem of reducing labour unit costs in Britain. Wilson argued that the Labour government would be able to achieve a voluntary incomes policy with the trade unions because of Labour's willingness to deal with the problems of prices in the nationalised industries and a willingness to make concessions on social expenditure – especially on pensions and prescription charges. Labour abolished the National Incomes Commission and replaced this with the National Board on Prices and Incomes (NBPI). The TUC Congress of 1964 had reiterated its opposition to an imposed incomes policy but had pointed out that an 'acceptable' incomes policy had to be based on ideas of social justice, which meant taking into account rents, interest rates, and profits. The TUC had therefore hinted that if Labour were willing to put a ceiling on profits and dividends and also increase social expenditures, then the TUC would support the need for an incomes policy. In accordance with this understanding with the trade unions the Labour Manifesto of 1964 pledged,

> To curb inflation we must have a planned growth of production. To achieve this a Labour Government will enter into urgent consultations with the Unions and the employers organisations concerned.... Labour's incomes policy will not be unfairly directed at lower paid workers and

public employees, instead it will apply in an expanding economy to all incomes, to profits, dividends and rents as well as to wages and salaries.

(Labour Party Manifesto 1964)

Labour had inherited a balance of payments deficit which on Treasury estimates seemed to be much larger than the outgoing Conservative administration had estimated. The Treasury suggested that this deficit would increase to about £800 million per annum, a sum likely to create new pressures on the exchange rate and a new crisis for sterling. While institutional reform was seen as being inextricably linked with Labour's economic strategy, the reforms were likely to have longer-term effects. In the meantime, the government had to develop a strategy to deal with the problem of the trade deficit and the problems of the exchange rate, in an effort to regain the confidence of the international markets at least in the short term.

The Labour government was therefore faced with the dilemma of producing short-term policies to deal with the exchange rate at the cost of their long-term strategy aimed to increase competitiveness and exports. The new government had also broken with the wage freeze of the outgoing government, but still had not secured an incomes policy with the trade unions during 1965. Furthermore, Labour had increased pensions, abolished prescription charges and committed themselves to growth in public expenditure. Treasury advisers and the Bank of England therefore argued that pressures on sterling would increase since the government did not seem to have a policy to deal with inflation and excess demand. Harold Wilson (1971) has suggested that he resisted Treasury advice to devalue sterling in 1965, pointing out that the previous Labour government had devalued in 1949. Wilson felt that a policy of devaluation at that time would have been disastrous for the Labour government since it would be seen as a policy always associated with the Party and therefore likely to increase the pressures on sterling,

The financial world at home and abroad was aware that the postwar decision to devalue in 1949 had been taken by a Labour government. There would have been many who would conclude that a Labour government facing difficulties always took the easy way out by devaluing the pound. Speculation would be aroused every time that Britain ran into minor economic difficulties or even without them.

(Wilson 1971: 6)

Therefore, despite the pressures on sterling, the Prime Minister and the Chancellor decided not to devalue during 1964 and to hold fast at $2.80. Wilson and Callaghan held to that commitment until 1967 when eventually the government did devalue to $2.40. The Governor of the Bank of England had advised the government during 1964 that devaluation was likely to result in higher prices, which in turn would make negotiations with the trade unions that much more difficult. Furthermore, devaluation had an impact on import prices and increased the rate of inflation. In the context of rising prices the government would then have been under additional pressures to reduce demand by reducing public expenditure.

The budgetary process, public expenditure cuts, and deflation

Labour's fiscal policy was aimed at both economic and social policy objectives. The social objective was to use fiscal policy to redistribute income. In 1964 the government therefore produced a budget which aimed to increase personal taxation and to introduce corporation tax and capital gains tax while increasing expenditure on transfer payments including pensions and social security. In the meantime the government was aware that there was pressure on resources caused by consumer expenditure, which in turn was putting further pressure on the balance of payments and sterling. A dilemma for the government in 1964, therefore, was how to protect their social programmes, reduce consumer demand and avoid devaluation.

These tensions in the budget process also need to be located in Labour's economic strategy. On coming to office, Labour had argued that the problem of the balance of payments could not be resolved by short-term fiscal and monetary policies and that a strategy was required to deal with the balance of payments as a longer-term structural problem. Labour's plan involved the modernisation of the British economy. Modernisation implied a strategy for the government to pick winners in industry and redirect resources to these sectors as the means of reducing imports and also increasing exports. The implication of this for the budget was that expenditures on public investment – including the nationalised industries, housing, roads, and research and development – were seen as essential to achieving the target of the National Plan, while expenditure cuts aimed to achieve the short-term objectives of reducing consumer demand and the budget deficit were seen as being incompatible with Labour's strategy.

During 1965, in addition to increasing taxation and reducing public expenditure, the government had also allowed for the bank rate to be increased from 5 per cent to 7 per cent. In the meantime the trade deficit had increased from £13 million a month in April 1965 to £49 million in May, bringing further pressures on sterling and new expenditure cuts on capital projects. The responses to three major crises in sterling in 1965, 1967, and 1968 now seemed to follow a similar pattern, reducing public expenditure with expenditure on investment projects taking the main brunt of the cuts, tightening hire purchase, and increasing the bank rate. The cuts of January 1968 were particularly significant because they did represent a watershed in public expenditure trends. While expenditure had increased to 4.5 per cent a year between 1964 and 1968, after 1968 it was planned to grow at 2.5 per cent. Furthermore, the 1968 budget was described as the most 'formidable deflationary budget' since the war, with increases in taxation of over £900 million The combined effects of expenditure cuts and tax increases were aimed at meeting the IMF's Letter of Intent of 1967 which was to reduce the public sector deficit to under £1,000 million. The actual outturn was that Labour ended with a budget surplus in 1969. At the end of 1968 there was a clear turning point in the balance of payments, the balance had actually moved into a £400 million surplus.

Labour's incomes policy

Labour's initial strategy on wages was to rely heavily on a voluntary incomes policy. The White Paper *Prices and Incomes* published in April 1965, established price controls and a pay norm of 3 to 3.5 per cent per annum. However, within eight months the government had moved towards a statutory pay freeze. The National Board for Prices and Incomes (NBPI) had been given statutory powers to investigate pay claims and to defer claims up to three months. The sterling crisis in the summer of 1966 forced the government to introduce additional legislation. The White Paper, *Prices and Incomes: An Early Warning System*, announced a statutory freeze on wages for the next six months to be followed by a further six months of restraint. The government did also extend controls on housing rents and also on distributed profits. Between 1966 and 1969, therefore, the Labour government had – like the previous government – to resort to a statutory wages policy.

Labour's incomes policy was initially conceived as permanent with permanent institutions including the DEA and the NBPI setting the framework for a policy aimed at sustained growth. The major problem for the Labour government throughout the period was the continuous resistance by key trade unions, including the Transport and General Workers Union (TGWU), and their continued opposition to incomes policy. The inability of the TUC to create a large enough majority among affiliates to make income policy durable meant that the government became increasingly dependent on the voluntary code set up by the TUC. At the September 1968 Congress the motion supporting the TUC voluntary incomes policy scraped home with a majority of only 34,000. Furthermore, by 1968 the government had also become disenchanted with attempts at voluntary incomes policy, arguing that trade union leaders could no longer deliver their membership, since the growth of unofficial disputes such as the damaging docks strike in 1966 and the shift of focus from national to local bargains meant that it was the informal system of bargaining which was setting targets for wages. This view was strengthened by the report from the Royal Commission on Trade Unions and Employers' Associations (HMSO 1968), which stressed that collective bargaining had become decentralised and that the formal system of industrial relations was being undermined by an informal system led by shop stewards.

Reform of industrial relations

By 1969, therefore, some members of the Labour government were coming to similar conclusions to those reached by their Conservative predecessors – namely, that it was essential to reform industrial relations and in particular to deal with the twin issues of unofficial strikes and the status of agreements reached between unions and employers. Some Labour ministers urged that trade unions ought to be 'returned' to their officials and to strengthen the formal system. This meant removing the autonomy of local shop stewards by making legal binding agreements between trade unions and employers of a minimum twelve-month duration, by introducing the right to ballots before strikes, and also by calling for a cooling off period of 28 days before strike action thus allowing trade union officials to be involved in negotiations. The proposals were contained in the White Paper *In Place of Strife* (HMSO 1969), which was presented to Parliament in April of that year. Wilson emphasised the importance of the reforms for the British economy, and also for the survival of the Labour government, at a meeting of the Parliamentary Labour Party prior to a vote on the Bill in the House of Commons,

> The Bill we are discussing tonight is an essential Bill. Essential to our economic recovery. Essential to the balance of payments. Essential to full employment. It is an essential component of ensuring the economic success of the Government. It is on that economic success that the recovery of the nation, led by the Labour Government depends. This is why I have to tell you that the passage of the Bill is essential to its continuance in office. There can be no going back on that.
>
> (Harold Wilson, Speech, 17 April 1969)

At their special Congress in June 1969 the TUC put forward a set of voluntary proposals in their 'Programme for Action'. Wilson rejected the proposals, arguing that they did not offer 'copper bottomed' guarantees on unofficial disputes. The opposition from the TUC, some Labour Members of Parliament – fifty-seven Labour MPs had already voted against the Bill in March 1969 – and leading members of the Cabinet including James Callaghan, forced the Prime Minister and the Secretary of State for Employment Barbara Castle to abandon the Bill in exchange for a 'solemn and binding undertaking' from the TUC, that trade unions themselves would deal with the problem of unofficial action. However, despite the personal efforts made by TUC General Secretary Vic Feather to make the voluntary code work, between July 1969 and June 1970 the number of strikes had increased to 3,982 compared to 2,733 in the previous twelve months; at the same time the number of working days lost had increased from 4.3 million to 10 million (Wigham 1976):

> it is apparent that the trade union movement made little attempt to carry out the undertaking entered on its behalf, and it does not appear that any disciplinary action was taken by the TUC against unions or by unions against members. As a means of reducing the number and cost of strikes the solemn and binding undertaking was a complete failure because it was not carried out.
>
> (Wigham 1976: 154)

Meanwhile, in their opposition to the White Paper, the trade unions had ignored those aspects of the Bill which seemed to give them new rights; these included workers' rights to industrial democracy, rights against unfair dismissal, and also rights to belong to a trade union. All these concessions were aimed to strengthen the position of trade unions by giving them more influence in the investment decisions of companies, in increasing membership, and in protecting members against dismissal.

The resistance by the trade union movement to surrender their rights to free collective bargaining, their reluctance to become involved like their European counterparts in 'liberal corporatist' agreements or long-term arrangements on incomes policies during the 1950s and 1960s, in a way reflected the strength of trade unions in Britain. Trade union confidence in the 'voluntary' system of industrial relations free from state intervention, indicated that unions were able to pursue their members' interests in the context of the market place.

During this period trade unions argued that it was not valid for governments to ask them to make concessions on wages as a trade off for full employment. Employment was a problem for government, governments could not use the weapon of unemployment to dampen wage demands without political risks. In the meantime, the growth of the informal system of industrial relations, accompanied by an increase in the number of unofficial disputes and wage drift, increased the pressures on both Conservative and Labour governments to rethink their attitudes towards industrial relations. Despite the attempts to create tripartite forums in the shape of the CPPI (1957), the NIC (1960), NEDC (1962) and the NBPI (1965), both governments seemed to have reached similar conclusions about the need to reform trade union law. By the late 1960s it seemed that the cause of Britain's failure to achieve similar growth rates to those of other industrialised countries was the inability of governments to secure an agreement with the trade unions on unit labour costs, and the failure to develop an agreed policy which restrained personal consumption and increased exports.

Between 1964 and 1969 the annual rise in average earnings had been 6.5 per cent. The period included a year of freeze and wage restraint. In contrast to the years 1962 to 1964, when wages were rising at 7.5 per cent per annum, there seemed, to be little improvement in controlling earnings between governments. However, the period was also characterised by devaluation, increased prices, and higher taxation, which meant that wages actually increased at a slower rate. Furthermore, taking the period 1969 to 1972 into account when wages were rising at 12 per cent per annum, it would seem that during the years of the Labour government trade unions had been willing to accept lower settlements.

CONCLUSIONS

The period between 1950 and 1970 represented a paradox in economic policy. At one level Britain seemed to experience stable employment, with unemployment throughout the period remaining at around 250,000 (less than 2.5 per cent of the working population). To be in stable employment represented a clear break with the experiences of the inter-war years. The economy throughout the period was growing at between 2.5 per cent and 3 per cent per annum with an inflation rate which peaked at 5 per cent and a bank rate of 7 per cent. Britain was experiencing a story of success in employment, and continuous growth and prosperity both within personal and public consumption. This was the period of 'treble affluence' when the growth in the economy meant increases in income, increases in individual consumption and also expansion in expenditures on welfare including health, education, and pensions. During the years of the Labour government expenditure on welfare had been growing at over 4 per cent a year.

However, the period is also associated with failure and disillusionment when compared with other industrialised countries including the USA and European competitors. The world economy grew and world trade expanded, but Britain seemed to be taking a lower share of trade. While Britain was growing at 3 per cent per annum, the French and West German economies were experiencing a growth of over 5 per cent per annum. Furthermore, it seemed that Britain was suffering from an intractable problem of a balance of payments constraint which was acting as an obstacle to more rapid growth. Britain was not taking advantage of the new opportunities and therefore was not producing the right goods for export to finance the cost of imports. Equally, by the end of the period it had become evident that there was a lack of a coherent approach towards trade unions and industrial relations. The inability of governments to secure permanent institutions to deal with incomes, prices, investment, and profits needs to be compared to the West German approach to 'concerted action' where employers, governments, and trade unions since 1945 have been able to reach agreements with the minimum of industrial disruption. Institutionalised bargaining had also been established in France, Sweden and Austria whereas in Britain trade union and employer resistance to any form of corporatist arrangements was seen as contributing to Britain's relative failures.

One recurring problem during the period had been the continuous pressures on the exchange rate which limited the autonomy of government. The crises of sterling in 1951, 1957, 1959, 1963 and 1967 were accompanied with a deterioration in the balance of payments. Both Conservative and Labour governments, irrespective of their policy intentions were forced to produce short-term responses to restore market confidence. The prevailing view of the Treasury seemed to be that the balance of payments represented a signal of excess demand which was leading to a high level of imports. The Treasury argument, therefore, was that the government had to curb demand through fiscal policies such as reducing public expenditure and increasing taxation, and also through monetary policies by increasing the bank rate and tightening the rules on hire purchase. Although these policy prescriptions did deal with the sterling crisis at least in the short term, the balance of payments still continued to be a major economic concern.

Furthermore, the Treasury view had failed to take into account the effects short-term responses were having on the economy. The short-term approach to fiscal and monetary policy was not producing a stable context for investment decisions, which in turn meant that Britain was not taking advantage of new technologies and improved productivity. Engineering, tool-making and textiles were coming under increased pressures from West Germany, Japan and the USA. In addition, the *ad hoc* approach to public expenditure meant that the brunt of the reductions was usually directed at capital investment, including the railways and telecommunications, which again seemed to reflect the absence of a coherent plan on infrastructure investment when compared to the indicative planning in France and the strategy of 'picking winners' in West Germany.

The attempt to secure an incomes policy remained an essential objective to both Conservative and Labour governments because incomes policy seemed to be the answer to the problem of inflation, and to the problems of the balance of payments and employment. However, the attainment of a voluntary policy which was likely to be permanent, but more important a policy which the trade unions could deliver, remained an elusive objective. Concessions on prices, employment, and welfare expenditures made at different times by both governments only seemed to gain trade union acquiescence in the short term, while the long-term trends indicated an increase in militancy, increases in the number of unofficial disputes, and in trade unions using their strategic position in the economy to maintain the market position of their members.

The quadrilateral of policy objectives associated with the Butskellite consensus became more difficult to reconcile with the approach of the 1970s. The commitment to full employment and the use of Keynesian techniques to influence demand seemed to be insufficient to deal with Britain's balance of payments constraint and the pressures on sterling.

In addition to fiscal and monetary policies other strategies were needed, including a more coherent approach to government intervention in companies involved in exports. There was, therefore, a need to establish a forum where government, employers, and trade unions could discuss future plans for the economy and what shares could be devoted to investment, profits, wages and welfare services. British employers and trade unions seemed to be wedded to the principles of *laissez-faire* and saw government attempts to create forums on pay and prices as unnecessary state intervention.

In the light of the 1980s and the Thatcher government's commitments to the market place, it seems paradoxical to argue that the approach adopted by strategic functional groups during the 1950s and 1960s was to embrace market principles, arguing that wages and prices should be set in the market place with no state intervention in the process of collective bargaining since the bargaining process itself was part of the market context.

The major difference between the Butskellite years and the 1980s was that the governments of Macmillan and Wilson were never likely to abandon Keynesian economics and break with the post-war commitment to full employment; it was because of this commitment, therefore, that governments searched for a policy on incomes and prices. Equally it might be argued that the trade union preference for free collective bargaining also rested on the knowledge that governments would not eschew the fundamental principle of full employment, which in turn meant that the discipline of unemployment had been removed from collective bargaining. Governments were likely to underwrite all wage agreements by increasing demand, a point made very succinctly by Reginald Maudling before he became Chancellor of the Exchequer in 1961:

> I believe that we are still facing the fundamental problem of how a free society can work effectively in conditions of full employment. We have got away from the old, harsh and wrong discipline of unemployment.... However, if that old discipline of unemployment has gone, there must be something to put in its place if we are to have an ordered community consciously advancing.
>
> (Maudling, House of Commons, Hansard: vol. 644, col. 1,095)

In contrast, while business did want government to maintain a high and stable level of demand they also realised that the government's commitment to full employment was making it more difficult for employers to hold the line on wage increases, and thus advocated less government intervention in the economy but more intervention in the sphere of industrial relations to deal with the problem of trade immunities and industrial disputes.

During the years of Conservative governments the trade unions argued that the strategy of these governments was to re-establish market liberal principles. The policies of phasing out rationing, price controls, and farm subsidies meant that the government were creating a climate of *laissez-faire* for profits, prices, and wages and that therefore, in that context, the only available strategy for trade unions was to preserve free collective bargaining. The trade unions, through the TUC, pointed out that the government had both contributed to inflationary pressures and had directed their anti-inflationary strategy on the single issue of wages. The attempt to secure an incomes policy was, therefore, criticised as being socially unjust and unfair since the government were not willing to consider setting ceilings on prices and profits. On their part, the government argued that the attempt to control profits and prices would mean a return to unacceptable forms of state controls. While the CPPI and NIC had failed to gain the co-operation of trade unions, the setting up of NEDC in 1962 seemed to be a more enduring forum as the focus changed from the narrow concern of wages to wider issues of investment, technology, and training.

The Labour government argued that the failure by their predecessors to secure an incomes policy reflected Conservative failure to achieve a more harmonious and more just society. Incomes policy could only survive as part of a wider economic strategy. The commitments by the Labour government to increase expenditures on welfare, to introduce a National Plan to secure a higher rate of economic growth, and to honour pledges on modernisation and technology were seen as setting the context in which trade unions would voluntarily accept the need to moderate wage claims with the government balancing this by putting limits on prices and profits. The problem for the Labour government was that the voluntary nature of incomes policy was seen as not to be working by foreign holders of sterling and that the government did not have a policy to deal with the problem of rising inflation. The government seemed to be making all the concessions while the trade unions were not conceding much in return. The imposition of a pay freeze, devaluation, and the White Paper on the reform of industrial relations, mirrored the conflicts between a Labour government seeking to promote national prosperity and trade unions whose primary concern continued to be the particular interests of their members.

Chapter 10

Disillusionment

The end of Butskellism, and economic policy in the 1970s

INTRODUCTION

Economic policy-making in the 1970s marked the break with the post-war settlement of full employment and the welfare state. The wider economic context created new challenges for the policy makers. The policy of fixed exchange rates agreed at Bretton Woods in 1944, the cornerstone for creating exchange stability during the post-war period, had been replaced in 1973 by countries floating their domestic currencies. The spirit of policy co-operation was replaced by competition and markets as countries used the mechanism of interest rates to deal with the dual problems of inflation and the balance of payments deficits. In addition, the oil price increases in 1973/4 and 1979/80 and the anticipated slow-down of the world economy, produced very different challenges in economic management to the governments of the major industrial countries. Economic policy reflected a series of conflicts and tensions to these challenges, both at the intellectual and the practical levels of the policy process. At the practical level the policy objectives of full employment and the welfare state seemed to clash with anti-inflation policies, the control of public expenditure and levels of personal taxation. At the intellectual level, the battle between Keynesian influences and the criticisms of monetarist economists for winning hearts and minds had spilled over from the academic world to the public sphere. The battle of economic ideas was no longer confined to academic journals between defenders of competing economic models, the ideas were popularised in newspaper articles, editorials and television debates. Economics could no longer be divorced from politics as Keynesian economists became associated with intervention and big government, and monetarism with the market liberal ideas of rational individualism, the market place, and less government.

The policy responses of UK governments in the 1970s can be described at one level as the last attempts to secure an institutional framework for the conduct of economic policy. However, like other previous experiments with liberal corporatist politics, the attempt to implement a Keynesian social democratic consensus seemed to fail not only because of the continued adversarial politics associated with economic policy but also because of the unwillingness of trade unions and employers to become integrated in the policy process. By the late 1970s Britain was described as drifting towards 'ungovernability', pluralist stagnation, and political paralysis. The defeat of the Heath government in 1974 and the demise of the Labour government which ended with the 'Winter of Discontent' in 1979, had reinforced the view that Britain needed a strong government capable of giving leadership without making concessions to narrow and particular interest group politics.

The lessons drawn from the UK experience of the 1970s seemed to be very different from those drawn from the experiences of Britain's European competitors. While in West Germany the response to the oil price increase was to produce a strategy to improve export performance which meant reducing labour costs to improve Germany's competitive edge, the response of the UK governments was to use short-term fiscal policy to slow-down demand. To achieve this objective the West German governments were able to use the existing institutional framework to consult with trade unions and employers' organisations on the issues of pay and prices. Other countries including France, Italy, and the Netherlands also embarked on the German model of concerted action of integrating strategic groups as responsible agents in economic policy-making. In contrast, the debate in the UK seemed to be moving in a different direction. Rather than seeking to integrate functional groups, the argument was that governments in Britain had to break with collectivism and the Keynesian consensus despite the fact that such a political and economic framework had not been established.

POLITICS AND ECONOMIC POLICY

The election campaign of 1970 reflected not only the beginnings of the disillusionment with functional democracy and the tensions between the desires of continuity but also the urgency to break with the past. The election represented conflicting interpretations on the successes and failures of government in the conduct of economic policy in the previous decade. On the one hand, the Conservative Party under the leadership of Edward Heath put forward pledges which seemed to challenge the foundations of the post-war consensus of full employment policies, the welfare state, and the role for government in economic management and industrial relations. The Conservative Party manifesto promised to end subsidies to the nationalised industries, to introduce more selective principles in social policy, to reduce personal taxation and to phase out controls on wages, prices and profits. The Conservative Party also pledged to alter the balance in industrial relations by making trade unions more legally accountable for their actions.

In contrast, throughout the 1970s the Labour Party seemed to be defending the principles of the post-war settlement, of seeking a social partnership with employers and trade unions, and making a case for a more interventionist industrial strategy. Labour continued to favour the picking of winners in technology or manufacturing and to provide subsidies and financial support for key industries as the means to improving Britain's balance of payments. In addition, economic planning and nationalisation continued to be central to Labour's economic strategy to meet the new challenges. In dealing with the problem of inflation, Labour continued to argue that it was a cost-push problem which required intervention, suggesting that a dual policy of price controls and wage moderation was the answer. Labour argued that the control of inflation required a social partnership between government, trade unions, and employers.

Sir Leo Pliatzky, who was the permanent secretary to the Treasury during the 1970s, has argued that it was the Heath government which introduced the market liberal agenda associated with the Thatcher governments of the 1980s:

> in a good many respects its [the Heath government] philosophy anticipated the brand of politics which later came to be associated with Margaret Thatcher. There was the same commitment to restore a market economy, the same aspirations to roll back the frontiers of the public sector. This was the philosophy of Selsdon Man.
>
> (Pliatzky 1982: 98)

Mr Heath had also wanted to reinforce the view that his government had been elected with a clear mandate to break with the past as he made clear in his address to the Conservative Conference:

> we were returned to office to change the course of history of this nation – nothing less...to bring about a change so radical, a revolution so quiet and yet so total that it will have to go beyond the programme for a Parliament to which we are committed.
>
> (Edward Heath, Conservative Party 1970a: 129)

Despite the attempts to embark on a 'quiet revolution', on policies designed to disengage government from the economy, and the pledge not to provide subsidies for 'lame duck' companies, the Heath government became associated (especially after 1972) with the legacy of 'U' turns. Industrial policy decisions were reversed as subsidies to industry, regional grants, and policies to control prices were re-established with the implications for increases in public expenditure. The Conservatives, therefore, went into the 1974 election as the government which embraced market liberal principles, but ended being more interventionist than any other previous government. The enduring economic issues of the previous decades – namely, the failure to combine full employment policies with low inflation, economic prosperity, and policies on incomes and prices – had continued to persist. Like previous governments the Heath government had 'failed' to secure an incomes policy and chose to fight the 1974 election on the issue of 'who governs?', and lost.

However, while some contemporary critiques have argued that Mr Heath ended up betraying the 'revolution', Gamble (1974) has suggested that the Heath government incorporated market liberalism as one plausible strategy as opposed to the view that it represented a shift in Conservative Party thinking. Instead, Gamble argues that while the government did seek to explore the boundaries between the public and the private sectors, the government still

> sought to operate within the constraints of welfare consensus – that is within the explicit recognition of the need to involve organised labour in the running of the state with new priorities for government, notably re-distributive taxation to finance social services, a large public sector and government management of the economy to maintain full employment.

> (Gamble 1974: 210)

The Labour government of 1974, which promised to break with the policies of confrontation and to return to consensus and a new social contract, were also defeated after a series of industrial disputes during the 'Winter of Discontent' in 1979. The economic strategy of the incoming Labour government of 1974 depended on the success of the social contract. The government argued that industrial disruption, the miners' strike of 1973, and the three day week had been the result of the divisive politics adopted by the previous administration. In contrast, the Labour government was to adopt a more conciliatory approach by giving priority to policies which secured more social justice. Wilson argued that if the government showed their willingness to produce a climate of fairness and justice then the trade unions would respond in moderating their wage demands. The Social Contract was, therefore, envisaged to be a plan that was not purely concerned with incomes policy but was rather a contract on social expenditures. These expenditures would be aimed at reducing income inequalities, at the repeal of the 1972 Trade Union Act which would be replaced by reforms giving workers more rights, and also an interventionist economic strategy. However, by 1976, the government found themselves reducing public expenditure in the context of rising unemployment. The social contract was replaced by incomes policy which although successful once again was eventually bound to break down under pressures of income differentials and trade unions wanting to return to collective bargaining free from government direction.

The years between 1970 and 1979 represent a series of paradoxes. First there is the paradox of a Conservative government being elected on a programme of less state intervention and yet ending their term of office being more interventionist and more corporatist. The second paradox is the Labour government, which, despite their commitments on further nationalisation, subsidies to industry, and welfare expenditures, ended their term of office associated with having been the government that declared that Keynesianism was no longer relevant and the introduction of a 'monetarist' dimension into British economic policy. These paradoxes reflected the twin dilemmas of the desire for continuity, but also an urgency to break with the past and to construct a different political and economic agenda to confront the wider economic context where governments could no longer take for granted continued growth in world trade to enable growth in both personal and public consumption.

THE WIDER ECONOMIC CONTEXT: INFLUENCES ON ECONOMIC POLICY-MAKING

Britain's European competitors – including West Germany, France, Austria, and Sweden – had succeeded to integrate trade unions and employers' organisations as social partners in policy-making during the post-war period. In these countries permanent forums and institutions had been established to ensure continuous consultation between governments and strategic economic agents in the process of economic policy-making. In contrast, as outlined in the previous two chapters, British governments since 1945 had failed to produce permanent institutions which would have aided agreements on incomes policies, welfare expenditures, and employment. Instead the British experience had oscillated between statutory wage freezes, voluntary agreements, and breakdown in incomes policy. Furthermore, it was also felt that in the UK trade unions could not be integrated as social partners since the focus of trade union powers had shifted towards decentralised bargains and an informal system of industrial relations and wage drift.

Both the Heath government of 1970 and the Wilson and Callaghan governments were still committed to modernise the UK economy through some form of corporatist politics. They both still believed that commitments to full employment, price stability, and the welfare state could only be sustained by reaching agreements with trade unions and employers on the issues of wages, prices and investment. While the Heath government did make pledges on reducing the role of the state, they still believed that the trade unions and employers had a major role to play as responsible social partners in the modernisation of the British economy. The Labour government, through the social contract, has pointed to a more influential role for trade unions in economic policy-making.

However, while both governments were committed to programmes of concerted action and social partnerships, the context for economic policy-making in the 1970s was very different to that of the 1960s. The 1970s were accompanied by the breakdown of the Bretton Woods agreement and the oil price shocks. The world economy had changed. While the United States had emerged as the dominant economy after the Second World War, willing to use the dollar as the reserve currency, the next thirty years saw the emergence of the Japanese and West German economies with huge trade surpluses against the USA. In this new economic context the fixed exchange rates of Bretton Woods were no longer sustainable. The world economy in the 1970s moved towards floating and competitive exchange rates. The second major difference in the 1970s was the oil price increase of 1973, which not only put increased pressures on Britain's balance of trade but also influenced the economies of the other major industrial nations. Also, the issue of public expenditure and the boundaries between the public and private sectors of the economy were also to dominate economic policy-making. These three issues – the breakdown of Bretton Woods, the oil price increases, and the problem of financing the public sector – changed the context for economic policy-making for the 1970s. The problem for both Conservative and Labour governments was that they seemed to be conducting economic policy using ground rules which no longer seemed appropriate.

The breakdown of Bretton Woods – the implications of a floated exchange rate

While the Heath government might have been willing to operate within the 'constraints of the welfare consensus', both the global and the domestic landscapes were to be very different during the 1970s when compared with the 1960s. At a global level, the early 1970s saw the final breakdown of the Bretton Woods agreement as fixed exchange rates were replaced by a new regime of floating exchange rates. Reliance on changes in interest rates and monetary policies were, therefore, more likely to influence economic policy than policies of fixed exchange rates and fiscal policies. The breakdown of Bretton Woods also represented the undermining of one of the central planks associated with Keynesian economics.

The involvement of the USA in the Vietnam War and the attempt to finance the new expenditures through deficit financing between 1969 and 1972, had increased pressures on the US government to devalue the dollar. After 1945 the US dollar had replaced sterling as the reserve currency so that all currencies were traded against the US dollar. The breakdown of Bretton Woods signalled the unwillingness of the US government to continue to allow the dollar to be the world's reserve currency. Instead, the Americans preferred to return to a system of competitive markets where the US currency could be traded against other currencies without the constant pressures on the US dollar. President Nixon was determined that other countries, including West Germany and Japan who were running trade surpluses with the USA, had to play a more active role in devaluing their currencies. To show that the Americans intended to break with the policy of fixed exchange rates Nixon devalued the dollar and introduced a plan to add tariffs onto imports to the USA. The threat of tariffs and protectionism forced Germany and Japan to enter the Smithsonian agreement in 1972 which included a pledge to devalue their currencies. However, this agreement was short lived as the Americans decided to devalue the dollar yet again in 1973, which essentially meant the breakdown of Bretton Woods.

The major implications of these world factors for UK economic policy were twofold. The first and more immediate problem for the policy-makers was that the conduct of economic policy had to be located in the context of floating exchange rates, which meant that sterling had now to compete with the dollar. UK governments could no longer ignore exchange rate policies, they had to produce policies which ensured that sterling remained attractive to foreign investors even if that meant increasing interest rates to compete with US interest rates, irrespective of what was happening to the domestic economy.

The second implication was that a shift towards floating exchange rates represented a major challenge to the post-war consensus. Changes in UK interest rates no longer reflected changes in UK monetary policy but had to take into account changes in the world economy. This meant that when the American Federal Reserve or the German Bundesbank decided to tighten monetary policy and increased interest rates, then pressure was put on the British government to do likewise to prevent a 'run' on sterling. High interest rates in the UK might, however, have exacerbated problems of inflation and unemployment. The government's commitments to full employment no longer depended on the agenda of wages, prices, and fiscal policies of the previous two decades; now they had to be made compatible with the competitiveness of the currency, exchange rate policy, and interest rates.

A regime of floating exchange rates brought new pressures on the short-term aspects of economic policy-making. While during the 1960s the policies of 'stop–go' had been brought about by a deteriorating balance of trade, and pressures on the exchange rate took shape in the context of a system of fixed exchange rates, the pressures on government to 'devalue' the currency occurred during prolonged discussions between member countries of the exchange rate mechanism. By contrast, under a regime of floating exchange rates, governments had to rely more on interest rates policies and also much wider and more frequent changes in the value of the currency. Under the Bretton Woods agreement, which lasted from 1944 to 1973, sterling had only been devalued on two occasions: once in 1947 from $4.20 to $2.80 and then again in 1967 from the parity set in 1947 of $2.80 to $2.40. Since 1973 the value of sterling against the dollar has been in constant flux, reflecting market sentiments where sometimes the value of sterling had reached a peak of $2.40 (as in 1981) but actually fell to dollar parity in 1983. Equally, changes in the rate of interest have fluctuated between the lower limits of 5 per cent to the higher peaks of 14 per cent.

The oil price shocks and the world economy

The second major factor during this period was the emergence of OPEC, and the implications of an oil price cartel for the world economy and its effect on the British economy in particular. At one level the oil price increases of 1973 has to be located in the context of the breakdown of Bretton Woods. The major impetus behind Bretton Woods was the apparent failure of governments to produce a co-ordinated response to the Great Crash of 1929, the slump in world trade, and the increases in unemployment during the 1930s.

One of the criticisms of the 1930s produced by Keynes was that governments had attempted to regenerate their national economies without evaluating the implications of their national policies on the international economy. The attempt to establish tariff barriers and protectionist policies to benefit domestic industries meant that other countries also responded with protectionist policies which in turn reduced total world trade. The Bretton Woods agreement was more than just an agreement on exchange rates, it also represented a commitment by national governments to produce a forum for policy co-ordination and, therefore, a shift from beggar-my-neighbour policies. The breakdown of Bretton Woods in 1973 also meant the breakdown of this forum.

The absence of a Bretton Woods accord, therefore, added to the problems of the oil price shock in 1973. The non-oil-producing countries – including Britain, West Germany, and Japan – failed to reach any agreement to produce a coherent strategy, when it was obvious that the non-oil-producers were now faced with a balance of payments problem and the threats of deflation and unemployment. Instead, governments in these countries retreated to find solutions within their domestic economies which again resulted in policies which harmed world trade. Britain sought to correct its balance of payments by reducing demand through reductions in public expenditure and also increased interest rates – a policy which was also pursued in the USA and West Germany. High interest rates increased the debt burdens of the new industrial economies which had been encouraged to borrow at low interest rates. Countries in South America (including Brazil and Argentina) and also developing economies in Africa faced with increased debt burdens were forced to redirect a higher proportion of their national income to servicing the debt; this meant less consumer spending and a fall in the aggregate demand for goods manufactured in the Western economies.

There was also a breakup in the influence of Keynesian economists on economic policy-making. The 1970s signalled the retreat of Keynesian influences as economic ideas became an increasingly contested terrain between market liberal and Keynesian economists. There were, therefore, competing explanations on the effects of the oil price increases on national economies. Keynesian economists saw the oil price increases as being both inflationary and deflationary on national economies, while market liberal economists argued that price adjustments would enable economies to absorb the increases without any need for governments to change policies. The Keynesian argument was based on the theme of price rigidities and wage stickiness. Keynesians argued that the oil price was likely to be inflationary. They pointed out that the prices of non-oil-priced goods were not likely to fall to adjust to demand and that instead the response of suppliers was likely to be to reduce output. Since the price of non-oil-priced goods was not going to fall and this was going to be accompanied by an increase in all oil-priced goods, then the effect was also going to be deflationary. Keynesians, therefore, argued that the oil price increase would lead to an increase in unemployment and an increase in the rate of inflation. In this situation, Keynesians pointed out that if governments sought to deflate demand to reduce consumer demand and oil imports then this policy would lead to further deflation and higher levels of unemployment.

According to this Keynesian scenario there was an urgent need to generate a planned approach between the oil-producing countries and the non-oil producers. On the one hand the oil producers were now faced with an excess in savings while the non-oil producers were faced with problems of deflation and unemployment. In this context, governments needed to produce a policy which recycled income and allowed the savings from the Arab nations to be used by the non-oil producers. Such a policy of recycling would have, therefore, allowed for interest rates to fall.

While Keynesian economists argued for policy co-ordination and the re-establishing of a 'new' Bretton Woods, the policy adopted by each nation state indicated the extent to which governments had shifted their priorities towards domestic economic policies. Faced with a worsening balance of payments, West Germany and Japan sought to increase their share of world trade to finance their oil imports. Improving on exports also meant reducing imports and reducing consumer demand which in turn meant higher taxation, higher interest rates, and protectionist policies. In 1978 West Germany, the Netherlands and France set up their own system of fixed exchange rates within the European Monetary System (EMS).

From 1974, , therefore, British economic policy was heavily influenced by the wider economic context. The oil price increases put new pressures on the balance of payments and on the incoming Labour government to reduce demand and, therefore, deflate the economy. Furthermore, the new developments on floating exchange rates, and the high interest rates regimes being followed by other countries to deal with the oil crisis, meant that further pressures were put on sterling and UK interest rates. Britain had also declined to join the EMS in 1978, preferring to retain autonomy over monetary policy.

The problem of overload and the control of public expenditure

The third major concern of the 1970s was the question of how governments aimed to deal with the growth of the public sector in the context of lower growth expectations. While in the 1960s both Conservative and Labour governments had hoped to improve Britain's economic growth performance and had, therefore, 'planned' for the growth in public expenditure to correspond with the growth in national income, the outturns for public expenditure in 1970 were already showing that the rate of growth of the public sector was rising faster than the growth in national income. The problem of the 1970s, therefore, was how governments responded to the slow-down in the rate of economic growth and how they aimed to control the rate of growth in public expenditure when expenditures on pensions and unemployment benefit tended to be demand-generated expenditures?

According to Sir Richard Clarke public expenditure between 1952 and 1971 had increased from 41 per cent of GDP (factor costs) to 51 per cent. The author argued that this rate could not be sustained in the 1970s because

the balance [had] tilted over when the interests of the public as consumers of public services came to be regarded as politically more important than their interests as taxpayers.

(Clarke 1973: 142)

The view of Sir Richard and many others aimed to show that the boundaries between the private and public sectors of the economy had changed to the extent that the size of the public sector was crowding out private sector investment and also endangering individual choice and the freedom of the individual:

I do not think that you can push public expenditure significantly above 60 per cent and maintain the values of a plural society with adequate freedom of choice. We are here close to one of the frontiers of social democracy.

(Roy Jenkins, Speech to the Anglesey Labour Party, January 1976)

While a previous study had suggested that the definitions adopted by Sir Richard Clarke and Lord Jenkins had been unduly alarmist (Mullard 1987), and postulated that the rate of growth in public expenditure had been much slower – public expenditure at market prices had increased from 30 per cent of GDP in 1951 to 36 per cent of GDP in 1970 – the size of the public sector and the financing of public expenditure became major issues of concern in the 1970s. The concern with public expenditure during the 1970s was therefore likely to become a central issue in economic policy-making.

The problem of resource crowding out

The argument that the balance of payments represented a structural constraint was given a new meaning in the 1970s. While in the previous decade it had been argued that Britain was not exporting enough because of its uncompetitive labour costs and low productivity, the work by Bacon and Eltis during 1978 aimed to show that what was actually holding Britain back was the size of the public sector. According to the Bacon and Eltis thesis, the public sector was the non-marketed sector because it did not contribute to exports which meant that it had to depend on the marketed sector to provide taxation. According to the authors, workers in the marketed sector resisted increases in personal taxation to finance the public sector and pushed up their wage demands to compensate for losses in earnings. Furthermore, resources which could have been channelled to the marketed sector had been absorbed by the public sector:

> the increase in non-market expenditure had produced two kinds of adverse effects – higher taxes which have accelerated wage inflation and allowed investment to suffer. A fall in investment has led to a decline in the growth rate of the economy which has led to higher redundancies.
>
> (Bacon and Eltis 1978: 110)

The influence of the Bacon and Eltis argument on government is most probably best reflected in the White Paper on public expenditure in 1975, when the Labour government was seeking to justify a package of reductions in public expenditure:

> the paramount need to move resources into exports and investment makes it essential to contain the demand on resources made by public expenditure. The government, therefore, aims to continue to reduce the public sector borrowing requirement.
>
> (HMSO 1975: 3)

Financing the public sector and the tax burden

In addition to the linkages between resource crowding out and the macro-economic issues of exports and the balance of payments, other arguments on the relationships between the size of the public sector, inflation, and the tax burden also influenced economic policy-making in the 1970s. Central to Mr Heath's 'quiet revolution' in 1970 was that the role of the public sector had to be reappraised and left to do what it did best, which according to the government certainly did not involve using public expenditure to subsidise 'lame duck' industries. Furthermore, Mr Heath also pointed out that the mission of the government was to reduce the burden of taxation, to allow people to keep more of what they earn, and therefore to give individuals the choice and freedom to define their priorities:

> Change will give us freedom and that freedom must give responsibility. The free society which we aim to create must also be a responsible society.... Free from intervention, from interference but responsible. Free to make your own decisions but responsible also for your mistakes. Free to lead a life of your own but responsible to the community as a whole.
>
> (Edward Heath, Conservative Party 1970a)

While the Heath government did not seek to dismantle the welfare state in 1970, it argued that what was needed was a challenge to the attitude of mind, to encourage the enterprise of the individual as the vehicle to improved economic prosperity and to challenge the claims and expectations which had become associated with the politics of intervention and collectivism. From the outset the Heath government abolished the Industrial Reorganisation Corporation and investment grants to industry, and also planned to phase regional employment premiums. According to the government these tasks were best left to the market place and therefore it was argued that such subsidies had to be replaced by tax incentives to firms and individuals.

In challenging the boundaries between the public and private sectors, the Heath government also sought to introduce new principles for the funding of social security benefits by arguing that the government would be selective and target new welfare expenditures rather than continue to provide welfare on the basis of universalism. The government, therefore, introduced the system of Family Income Supplement, aimed specifically at those on low pay, and also introduced rent and rate rebate schemes which were also to be means tested. In contrast, universal benefits including free school meals, subsidised school milk, and low prescription charges were to be phased out. According to the government these plans were to limit the growth of public expenditure from a growth rate of 3.5 per cent as planned by the outgoing Labour government, to a rate of growth of 2.8 per cent per annum.

By 1976 the Labour government were also arguing in favour of the need to reduce the tax burden and keep public expenditure under control. In negotiating the IMF loan, in their Letter of Intent the government agreed to reduce public expenditure and taxation as part of the package to avert the crisis of sterling, and to improve Britain's exports through lower taxation on the individual and on the business sector.

> perhaps not unconnected with our low level of output is that people at work are already highly taxed on their income. I do not believe that it would be right to burden them with the lion's share of taxation. Furthermore, taxation adds to the problem of inadequate financial incentives to work and to invest and this could put our economic recovery at risk.
> (Joel Barnett, Chief Secretary to the Treasury, House of Commons, Hansard: 25 December 1976, vol. 922, col. 1,525)

While the Heath government argued that lower tax thresholds implied increased freedom and responsibility for the individual, after 1976 the Labour government had equally become convinced on the merits of a lower tax burden and the need for increased incentives at work. Both governments seemed to have come to the conclusion that the rate of growth of public expenditure and the implied pressures on the levels of taxation could not be sustained in a context of slower economic growth.

Financing the public sector: the public sector deficit and inflation

The third and more pressing issue for British governments, especially after the oil price increase of 1973, was the question of how to finance public expenditure in the context of a no growth economy? During the era of treble affluence – when there had been continuous growth in the economy which had enabled increases in wages and increases in personal and public consumption – governments did not have to ask voters to make choices between personal and public consumption. The climate of no growth posited a challenge to government and the democratic process as voters had for the first time since 1945 to make choices between personal consumption and welfare expenditures.

During the 1960s, as both governments had pursued policies which were aimed at improving Britain's growth performance and had also planned for growth in public expenditure to correspond with the optimistic forecasts for the economy. The argument in the 1970s was that while the economy had not responded to the expansionist policies when Maudling was Chancellor or to Labour's National Plan, the plans for public expenditure had not been revised to correspond with the actual growth in the economy. However, while the share of public expenditure as a percentage of national income was rising at a faster rate than the growth in national income, the rate of growth in the economy and personal income had facilitated the growth in public expenditure without challenging individual consumption:

For the past 30 years social policy has been the residual beneficiary of economic progress. The Welfare State flourished because the Growth State prospered.... Perhaps for the first time in the history of mankind it was possible to combine public compassion with private self indulgence.

(Klein 1975: 2)

Economic policy-making in the 1970s reflected the tensions between the demands for increased public expenditure but also resistance against increases in the levels of taxation to fund the public sector. Governments could no longer plan for the rate of growth in public expenditure which had been achieved in the previous decade. The context of slower economic growth, the breakdown of Bretton Woods, and the move towards floated exchange rates – together with the increases in oil prices – meant that governments in the 1970s had to seek ways which allowed for the control of public expenditure but did not damage welfare service. Governments had to deal with the implications of public sector deficits and inflation in a context where fluctuations in the exchange rate were likely to be more volatile and de-stabilising for the national economy. Lower rates of growth meant less revenue for the government and, therefore, more pressures on funding a growing public sector by increasing taxes or government borrowing.

While the no growth state generated tensions between taxation and public expenditure, governments were also faced with the dilemma of funding the public sector without resorting to deficit financing. Since economic policy-making became increasingly influenced by monetarist arguments on the relationships between government borrowing, the money supply and inflation, the control of public expenditure became more crucial to the control of inflation. The practice of publishing targets for monetary aggregates including M1 and £M3[1] was launched by the Labour government during the 1977 Budget. The control of the public sector borrowing requirement (PSBR) was now tied more firmly to changes in monetary policy. It confirmed the influence of monetarist thinking on economic policy, while in future City analysts would concentrate on published targets for the money supply to evaluate the government's anti-inflation policies.

The context of deflation and rising unemployment, the pressures on public expenditure, taxation and anti-inflationary measures produced tensions and dilemmas for the economic policy-making process. While the Heath government had promised a 'quiet revolution' and less government in 1970, the collapse of the RB 211 engine at Rolls-Royce, the threatened closure of the Upper Clyde Shipbuilders, and the rise in unemployment to 1 million by 1971, produced the climate for a change in policy. The government was forced to become more interventionist, increasing public expenditure and planning for increased growth and a consequent reduction in unemployment:

With the present level of unemployment I have certainly been prepared to increase public expenditure to help bring it down. I have had two particular considerations in mind. The first is to try to ensure that the expenditure takes place in the areas of high unemployment...with unemployment as high as it has been we have not hesitated to expand public spending.

(Anthony Barber, Chancellor of the Exchequer, *Sunday Telegraph*, 21 November 1971)

However, the increases in public expenditure during the Heath years have also been criticised for being inflationary. Critics of the government, including Enoch Powell and Professor Alan Walters, had argued in 1972 that the increases in public expenditure had contributed to an increase in the money supply and that it was the increase in the money supply which was contributing to the increase in inflation:

It is recognised now that without a corresponding expansion of the money supply inflation cannot continue. Since indisputably money supply is more or less in the control of the government, the means of controlling and if desired of ending inflation, exist.

(Enoch Powell, *Sunday Telegraph*, 18 June 1972)

The governments of the 1970s were, therefore, faced with a new dilemma on public expenditure. While Keynesian economists sought to advocate to both the Heath and Labour governments that it was feasible to reflate the economy through fiscal policies to avoid the deflationary effects of the oil price increases, monetarist economists were also gaining access to the policy-makers. It was during the years of the Callaghan government that ministers started to pay attention to such indicators as sterling M3,[2] indicators which during a previous decade had been nonexistent in economic policy-making:

The most valuable contribution of the 1974–9 government was arguably not in any specific policy at all but in the change of intellectual direction in the latter months of 1976 away from Keynesian economics towards what is known as monetarism.

(Holmes 1985: 182)

According to Keynesian conventional wisdom, the threats of recession and rising unemployment required an expansion of demand yet during 1975 and 1976 the Labour Chancellor produced a series of policy proposals which reflected the extent of the break with Keynesian thinking. While unemployment had reached a new post-war record of 1.3 million, the Chancellor Dennis Healey actually announced a series of public expenditure reductions aimed at public sector investment with housing and road buildings experiencing the brunt of the expenditure cuts. Instead of expanding the economy, the government seemed to be deflating the economy further. Indeed the break with Keynes had been formally announced by the Prime Minister James Callaghan:

> We used to think that you could spend your way out of a recession and increase employment by cutting taxes and boosting government spending. I tell you in all candour that this option no longer exists and insofar as it ever did exist, it injected a higher dose of inflation and a higher level of unemployment. Unemployment is caused by pricing ourselves out of jobs quite simply and unequivocally.
> (Mr (now Lord) Callaghan, Labour Party Conference 1976: 188)

While this speech has been quoted on many occasions, its significance can never be underestimated. The Callaghan speech confirmed a paradigm shift in economic policy-making. After 1976 governments were no longer to be bound to responding to the economic cycle in a mechanical way. It could no longer be taken for granted that governments would use the lever of public expenditure as an automatic stabiliser. According to the new thinking government did not influence the level of employment; that employment was determined in the market place and therefore represented an adjustment to labour market pricing. Furthermore, according to the new doctrine the impact of public expenditure on the economy was that it was inflationary. Thus the role of government had to be the control of inflation through the control of public expenditure.

Outlining what elements constituted monetarism, Laidler (1982) had argued that monetarists would adhere to three general principles:

1 The acceptance of the classical theory of money which implied that the demand for money was stable because it represented the number of transactions for goods and services, these in turn being determined in the goods market. According to the classical view, the demand for money was stable because only changes in the supply side could influence the rate of monetary growth and, therefore, inflation. The main sources of monetary creation were the banks and government. Government increased the money supply through the issues of Treasury bills to fund the PSBR which in turn increased liabilities with the banks.

2 Monetarists were also agreed on the view that the causes and cures for unemployment had to be addressed to problems of rigidities in the labour market, including the influence of trade unions, the levels of social security benefits, and minimum wage legislation.

3 The role of government should be limited to that of controlling inflation by controlling the level of public expenditure, by clearly announcing targets for monetary growth which are consistent with the rate of growth of growth in the economy, and the readiness to use interest rates to regulate the supply and demand for money.

Having painted a broad canvas of the economic context, the aims of the following sections will be to produce an outline of the economic strategies adopted by the Heath government and the Labour governments; to indicate the policy differences to point to the beginnings of a new consensus which was to influence economic policy in the 1980s. While both governments were more prepared than previous governments to adopt a more interventionist approach on industrial, regional and employment policies, they also recognised the need to involve trade unions and employers' organisations in order to produce a more coherent approach to deal with the problems of the balance of payments and wage inflation. What did become very apparent by the end of the period was the unwillingness of trade unions to surrender their rights to free collective bargaining, even if this meant threatening the legitimacy of democratically elected government.

THE HEATH GOVERNMENT

The economic context: the budgetary process

When the Conservative government came to power in 1970, the forecasts for economic growth suggested a growth path of 2.5 per cent per annum with predictions on unemployment at about 550,000, although this was likely to increase because of the tight fiscal stance adopted by Roy Jenkins, the Labour Chancellor from 1968 to 1970. Consumer price inflation was expected to remain at about 5 per cent a year while the government seemed to be inheriting a strong surplus on the balance of payments and a balanced public sector budget. Because of the healthy balance of payments and the trade surplus, Keynesian economists argued that the government had sufficient room in 1970 to immediately embark on a package of reflationary policies directed at reducing taxation and increasing public expenditure. Instead the government seemed to adopt a tight fiscal stance which in turn resulted in the acceleration of unemployment to 1 million by 1971. During 1970 unemployment had been rising at about 4,000 to 5,000 a month, but from the middle of 1971 this accelerated to around 20,000 a month.

In October 1970 the Heath government had published their first plans on public expenditure. According to the public expenditure White Paper *New Policies for Public Spending* (HMSO 1970), the government planned to reduce spending by £300 million in 1971/2 and by £1,600 million in 1974/5. They pointed out that their strategy was to allow individuals to keep more of what they earn and, therefore, generate greater incentives to improve productive effort for individuals, industry and commerce. The government planned to reduce the growth of public expenditure on trade and industry by phasing out subsidies including the regional employment premium and investment grants and also planned to reduce expenditure on public sector housing by reducing council house building and subsidies on public sector rents. The government also cancelled Labour's plans to nationalise the ports. The government also abolished welfare milk subsidies and increased the charges on school meals. Both these policies were perceived as contributing to price increases, but were also seen as confrontational by the trade unions. The increases in charges were considered inflationary, regressive, and divisive. In the meantime, the government reduced corporation tax from 45 per cent to 42 per cent and income tax by 5p.

Furthermore, in addressing the problem of the balance between private and public sectors of the economy, the government produced measures aimed to phase out government, especially in industrial policy. By 1971, therefore, the Regional Employment Premium had been abolished as had the Industrial Reorganisation Corporation and the Prices and Incomes Board. The total cuts package for a five-year period totalled some £1.6 billion. However, this strategy was overturned between June 1971 and November 1971. The sudden rise in unemployment to 1 million, the threatened closures at Upper Clyde Shipbuilders and also the funding of the RB211 engine at Rolls-Royce all seemed to be important causes in bringing about a change in policy.

According to Holmes

> The issue of rising unemployment dealt the killer blow to the Quiet Revolution policy of disengagement from industry. It was the most important single factor in the rescue of UCS although only a marginal factor in the rescue of Rolls-Royce...the upward trend towards the one million mark evoked fears of a return to mass unemployment and social hardships of the 1930s fears that Mr Heath and his ministers regarded as justified. According to one close adviser Mr Heath was emotionally concerned with unemployment – he was constantly talking about the wasteland of unemployment.
>
> (Holmes 1982: 44–6)

In November 1971, the White Paper on public expenditure indicated the extent of the U-turns, the £1.6 billion cuts had been restored, and the government was now actually planning to spend £2.4 billion. As the White Paper stated:

> Since the last White Paper new needs have been identified, such as the rise in unemployment and the collapse of Rolls-Royce – this resulting in a call for higher expenditures in the immediate future and others over a longer period. There is no question here of other needs competing for resources but only of using productive power which would otherwise be idle.
>
> (HMSO 1971: 5)

In one sense the White Paper reflected the presence of Keynesian thinking, the readiness to use fiscal policy to increase demand through the mechanism of public expenditure, especially by using short-term projects such as the bringing forward of naval shipbuilding and house building projects which could easily be turned on or off according to the economic cycle. The government also seemed to accept another Keynesian axiom of redistributing income to those with a high marginal propensity to consume – the government increased expenditure on social security and in particular improved pensions and benefits for the elderly. According to the government the years 1972/3 and 1973/4 were to be the 'lump years' for the increases in public expenditure and that from 1974 onwards expenditure would start to fall.

By December 1972 the extent of the government's U-turn was complete. The focus of the government was on Britain joining the EEC and being able to take advantage of the new opportunities. This meant that industry had to be made competitive in terms of unit labour costs and also on levels of productivity, even if this meant using government to ensure that industry was made more efficient. In this context the government introduced the Industry Act of 1972 which enabled them to provide regional development grants, selective regional assistance, and also funds for projects which provided additional or safeguarded employment. The cost of the industrial policy was estimated to rise from £75 million in 1972 to £454 million in 1974. The government also stopped the threatened closures of Govan and Camell Laird Shipbuilders and also provided funds for the Rolls-Royce RB 211 engine and Concorde. Furthermore, and also consistent with the government's views on European competition, they also embarked on a programme of long-term commitments in the expansion of expenditure in education, piloted through Parliament by the then Secretary of State for Education Mrs Margaret Thatcher. In the White Paper *Framework for Expansion* (HMSO 1971), the government outlined plans to increase expenditure on nursery education; they aimed to reduce pupil–teacher ratios to twenty-one and also to expand opportunities in Further and Higher Education.

Trade union reform and the Industrial Relations Act 1972

By 1970 there seemed to be the emergence of a consensus between the two major parties on the need to reform industrial relations. In 1958 in their document *A Giant Strength*, the Conservatives outlined a series of new reforms to the rules which had guided industrial relations in Britain since the 1906 Trade Union Act. As has already been pointed out in the previous chapter, part of Labour's 'White Heat of Technology' had been the setting up of the Donovan Commission on Trade Unions which had reported in 1968 as was also Labour's response in the White Paper *In Place of Strife* which was published in 1969 only to be withdrawn under pressure from within the Cabinet, by back-bench Labour MPs, and also from trade unions. Both these reviews contained a broad agreement that something needed to be done about the influences of the informal system of industrial relations on collective bargaining, the increases in the number of unofficial disputes and the problems of wage drift for employment and inflation.

While agreement existed on the need to deal with these issues, the means and methods for improving industrial relations varied between the necessity to impose a new legislative framework as was being advocated by the Conservative Party and a voluntary code which became Labour's preferred approach after 1969. While Labour leaders had become convinced that the better solution was for both employers' organisations and trade unions to evolve a voluntary code of practice to deal with unofficial disputes, by contrast the Conservatives had become more convinced on the needs for legislation – especially after what they saw as being Labour's retreat when confronted with trade union opposition. The Conservative manifesto, *A Fair Deal at Work* pointed out that

> There were more strikes in 1969 than ever before in our history. Already in the first three months of 1970 there were 1134 strikes compared with 718 in the same period last year, when the Labour government said the position was so serious that legislation was essential in the national interest. This rapid and serious deterioration directly stems from Labour's failure to carry through its own policy for the reform of industrial relations.... We welcome the TUC's willingness to take action through its own machinery against those who disrupt industrial peace by unconstitutional or unofficial action. Yet it is no substitute for the new set of fair and reasonable rules we will introduce.
>
> (Conservative Party 1970b)

The 1972 Act was based on what Lord Carr called the eight core pillars which as far as the government were concerned were not up for consultation with the trade unions or employers' organisations. Under the new Act trade unions had to register with the Certification Officer and in registering had to submit their union rule book. The rule book had to reflect changes in the handling of disputes including unofficial disputes, ballots, and the closed shop. Furthermore, the Secretary of State (through the National Industrial Relations Court) was now able to compel trade unions to suspend industrial action for a period of up to sixty days if the strike was deemed as harmful to the community or the national economy, and if necessary to be followed by a secret ballot if the dispute had not been resolved. There were to be limits on the numbers of pickets, much stricter rules on secondary action, and also stricter conditions on the closed shops. In future the pre-entry closed shop was to be abolished. The *Rookes* v. *Barnard* case of 1968 had highlighted for the Conservatives the loss of individual rights where closed shop agreements existed. Workers had now the equal right to belong or not belong to a trade union; those who joined a trade union had to join a 'registered' union, strikes which aimed to compel workers to join unions were deemed illegal. Only registered trade unions were to enjoy immunity against civil prosecution when taking industrial action, while a dispute was now defined to exclude inter-union disputes or sympathy strikes. Finally, agreements had to be made binding before the industrial relations court.

Moran (1977) argues that the unwillingness of the Secretary of State to negotiate on any of the central pillars increased the pressures on the TUC to break off the consultation process with the government and to embark on a campaign to make the Act unworkable:

> The events of 13–15 October are of the greatest importance in understanding the final fate of the 1971 Act.... If Carr had not insisted on the indestructibility of the eight pillars, a very different outcome could have occurred. The unions would have negotiated though reluctantly.
>
> (Moran 1977: 89)

The government had originally hoped that the Act could be used as part of the bargain with the trade unions – namely, that an incoming Conservative government would restore free collective bargaining while in return trade unions would co-operate with the new legislative framework. The problem for the government in 1970 was that the Labour government had phased out their statutory incomes policy and replaced this with a voluntary code; but what was more worrying for the government were the new pressures on wage inflation. The hope now was that the new legislation would address the problem of wage inflation directly without an incomes policy, but also in a climate of trade union reluctance to negotiate with the government on issues of industrial relations, pay, or prices.

The Industrial Relations Act remained in operation for two-and-a-half years, but little significant use was made of it. The TUC campaign of non-registration, the secret payments of fines on behalf of the AUEW and the TGWU for refusal to register, and the unwillingness of the CBI to use the legislation, meant that effectively the Act had been put on ice, while the government attention by 1972 had already turned to securing tripartite discussion with the CBI and the TUC on the problems of wage inflation.

Inflation and incomes policy

The increases in public sector charges in 1970 did not constitute any significant attempt to undermine the central concerns of the welfare state or to redefine the boundaries between the public and private sectors. Yet they seemed to be sufficiently important to the government for they increasingly became major obstacles in Mr Heath's successive attempts to secure an incomes policy with the trade unions. Throughout the negotiations of 1972 and 1973, while the trade unions continued to press the government to reverse the charges on school meals, prescriptions charges and housing rents, the government constantly refused to negotiate on these issues because of their political significance. The General Secretary of the TUC, Mr Vic Feather, assessed the importance of public sector charges and their effects on incomes policy as follows:

> The TUC are ready to talk with the government on pay and prices but only on the basis of a delicate balance of policies concerning rents, taxes industrial policy and employment.
>
> (Vic Feather as reported in *The Times*, 12 June 1972)

However, some commentators argued that the government was right to resist the trade union demands and suggested that it was essential for the democratic process that the government should stand by the policies they had put forward to the electorate rather their surrendering their right to govern under pressures of narrow and vested interests:

> The TUC's price for sitting down to talk about incomes seem to be saying that to get agreement there has to be further talks about other policies. Recent policy is seen as socially divisive such a bargain for incomes policy is too politically costly. The government was elected democratically to curb inflation.
>
> (R. Butt, *The Times*, 2 March 1972)

In addition to the increases in charges, the policies of a floated exchange rate brought new pressures on import prices as sterling depreciated against the major European currencies. The rise in import prices accelerated the rate of inflation, which in turn put pressures on earnings and on wage negotiators, making it even more difficult for the government to reach an agreement on incomes while import prices were rising by 16 per cent per annum.

The position taken by the trade unions, therefore, was that government policy had contributed directly to the increases in prices and thus inflation. In this context, to ask the trade unions to moderate wage demands was seen as a further attempt by the government to put a squeeze on living standards. The trade unions, as in the previous decade, argued that incomes policy could not be considered in isolation from other policies on prices and profits; it was in this context that they argued that the restoration of the cuts on public sector charges would indicate the government's williness to negotiate. Critiques on the government side had, however, pointed out that the government had already given too much by virtually surrendering the ambitions of the Quiet Revolution:

> the platform on which Mr Heath was elected in 1970 was not only repudiated but put into reverse. The Quiet Revolution was short lived,

The Industrial Relations Act was put 'on ice'; disengagement from industry was turned into the most active interventionist policy hitherto devised in Britain; the abandonment of statutory incomes policy was the prelude for its return in the most comprehensive peace time form; public expenditure cuts in October 1970 foreshadowed an enormous increase in deficit spending.

(Holmes 1982: 127)

There were three phases to the government's attempts to secure an incomes policy. Phase I, which had begun in 1971 and was known as the strategy of 'n–1', was mainly directed at public sector pay settlements in the hope that government resistance would slow-down the expectations of public sector workers and, therefore, break with the wage price spiral. The government also hoped that by setting an example for the public sector, private sector employers would also resist higher wage demands. The successes of n–1 were only partial, while the government succeeded on defeating the postal workers they had to concede higher wage claims to the miners and power workers in line with the recommendations of the Wilberforce Committee.

The talks on Phase II started in April 1972 and lasted until October, with a voluntary agreement between the ministers and trade union leaders proving difficult to reach. On the one hand, the trade unions wanted the government to control prices and commit more resources to economic growth. The government agreed that they would make commitments on prices and introduce threshold payments of 20 pence for every 1 per cent increase in the price level above the 5 per cent stated by them. However, the government did not seek to make any concessions on the Industrial Relations Act, the charges on school meals, milk rents, and pensions. While the government seemed to be calling for a real partnership, the trade unions felt that the government was not really creating an environment for a partnership. The government had also decided that since import prices were beyond their control, increases in import prices were not to be included with the 5 per cent ceiling. The problem for trade unions was that import prices meant higher food prices. As the talks broke down, the government introduced a statutory wage freeze on 6 November which was to last ninety days.

In April 1973 the government introduced a Pay Board and a new Price Commission. Compared to previous attempts, including the NBPI, the new boards were to have real power on wages and price increases. All firms employing more than 100 workers had to provide the boards with information on wages, prices, and profits, with prior approval being required from the Pay Board for settlements affecting more than 1,000 workers. The government also announced a pay norm of £1 plus 4 per cent. Pay settlements during this phase had actually fallen from 15 per cent to 8 per cent. Furthermore, in 1972 and early 1973 the number of strikes had also fallen dramatically compared to the previous two years.

Phase III, which started in October 1973, was another imposed pay policy as the government and the trade unions again failed to reach a voluntary agreement on wages and prices. In this phase the government reintroduced the concept of threshold payments of 40 pence to be triggered by price increases over 7 per cent. The government aimed to reduce the rate of inflation from 9.2 per cent to 7 per cent over the next year. However, the miners had also submitted a £13 to £15 pay claim which was referred to the Pay Board and rejected as being outside the government guidelines. In early February 1974, the miners balloted for industrial action and received an 80 per cent vote in favour of a strike. Mr Heath, in the meantime, had called for a general election for 26 February on the question of 'who governs?', and lost.

THE LABOUR GOVERNMENTS, 1974 TO 1979

Labour's economic strategy

During the election of February 1974 Labour had pledged to unite and rally the nation with a programme which promised greater social justice and economic renewal. The social contract which had been described as the cornerstone of Labour's programme, sought to provide a coherent approach to social and economic policies. In this context the government made commitments on pensions, housing rents, food subsidies, and education as part of their bargain to maintain and improve the 'social wage', while the trade unions through the TUC agreed to moderate their demands for higher earnings. The economic context, however, was likely to put strains on the social contract. The oil price increase announced by OPEC in 1973 had already put deflationary pressures on economic policy. In December 1973 the Heath government had announced a package of reductions in public expenditure to address the problem of consumption and imports. Labour's programme, by contrast, implied increasing public expenditure and an increase in the budget deficit. In the meantime, economic forecasts predicted slower growth for the world economy as countries sought to deal with their balance of payments constraint through higher interest rates and increased competition for world markets.

An international climate of economic slow-down and the lack of agreement between governments to provide a co-ordinated response, meant that Labour's strategy of making a dash for growth through an increase in public expenditure and deficit financing could not be sustained. As other major industrial countries including West Germany, France, and Japan pursued policies of high interests, pressures were put on sterling as foreign investors moved their capital to countries which seemed to have sound monetary policies, high interest rates, and lower inflation than the UK. These pressures on the exchange rate, in turn resulted in the devaluation of sterling which increased the costs of imports and also inflation. To regain market confidence, the government, therefore, had to produce policies which reduced demand, reduced government borrowing, but increased interest rates. The sterling crisis of 1975 and 1976 meant that the government had to establish special drawing rights through the IMF. Labour's Letter of Intent to the IMF meant the reversal of their programme; instead they embarked on a strategy of public expenditure reductions to reduce the deficit and inflation which had reached an all time high of over 20 per cent. Pressures on sterling increased between March and September 1976. In March, sterling had lost 4 per cent of its value against the dollar which in turn put new pressures on prices. In June the pound had lost a further 10 cents, so that in a period of three months sterling had been devalued by 15 per cent against the dollar.

Between 1976 and the election of 1979, the Labour government pursued a combined policy of reductions in public expenditure and incomes policy. In the meantime, the level of unemployment had increased from 650,000 in 1974 to over 1.5 million in 1978 – the first time that unemployment had broken through the 1 million barrier since 1945.

This was also the period when Keynesian influences were officially downgraded in economic policy-making as both the Prime Minister James Callaghan and the Chancellor Dennis Healey made pledges on the control of inflation through the control of the money supply. The years of the Labour government became increasingly associated with the end of Butskellism and the emergence of the new monetarist consensus as developed by Dennis Healey, the Labour Chancellor, and Geoffrey Howe, the first Conservative Chancellor in the Thatcher government:

> In practice it was not the Conservatives in Government who first denounced Keynes and embraced Friedman. It was not Mrs Thatcher but Jim Callaghan as Prime Minister who declared that we could no longer spend our way out of a slump. It was Dennis Healey not Geoffrey Howe who first put monetarism onto the agenda of British politics and abandoned a Keynesian strategy. Butskellism has come and gone. But with Howe through Healey Howleyism has taken its place.
>
> (Stuart Holland, *The Guardian*, 16 June 1980)

The social contract

The economic strategy of the incoming Labour government had been constructed on the theme of the social contract. Labour, while in opposition, had pointed out that Mr Heath's 'Quiet Revolution' had created an environment of confrontation in industrial relations and divisive economic and social policies. Economic policy between 1970 and 1974 had produced higher levels of inflation, a failure to secure incomes policy, and the enforced shut-down of some industries because of the government's approach to the miners' pay claim. Labour argued that the social contract was at the 'heart of our programme' because it was not concerned solely or primarily with wages, covering as it did the whole range of national policies. The common purpose, as agreed between the trade unions and the Labour Party, was the best way forward to social peace and to ending the miners' strike and the three-day week.

Labour's programme of 1973 represented an interventionist industrial strategy. Labour had made pledges to establish the National Enterprise Board with the aim of taking equity shares in the more successful companies to ensure that these companies became the leaders in Britain's exports performance. Labour also made commitments to take into public ownership shipbuilding and the aircraft industries as industries which were essential to the British economy. There were also commitments on planning agreements with the top 100 companies, and the repeal of the 1971 Industrial Relations Act which was to be replaced by a new Trade Union Act reinstating the rights to pre-entry closed shops, rights against unfair dismissal, rights against race and sex discrimination in the workplace, and also the rights to secondary picketing. These new proposals on industrial relations were seen as essential to the success of the social contract.

The first and most enduring problem facing the Labour government was the oil price increase of 1974. This external shock to the economy had both inflationary and deflationary effects on the British economy and, therefore, was always likely to threaten the principles of the social contract. The problem for the government was whether the pressures on the balance of payments would force them to deflate the economy and the concomitant implications of that for the social contract. On the one hand trade union leaders were likely to come under increasing pressures from their members to break with pay policy in the context of rising prices. The second problem, which was mainly a problem for the government, was how to deal with the deflationary aspects of the oil price increase, the deterioration in the balance of payments, and the pressures on sterling. As part of the social contract the government had made pledges to increase public expenditures, including increasing pensions in line with earnings, rents and food subsidies.

In the March budget the government had announced increases in pensions, food subsidies and housing rents in line with the pledges made during the election campaign, which implied an increase in public expenditure of £2 billion for the year 1974/5. During the first meeting of the TUC/Labour Party Liaison Committee in May 1974, members of the TUC confirmed their support for the strategy adopted by the government and argued that the failure to secure an incomes policy during the Heath years had been due to the unfair and unjust policies. At that first meeting, members of the TUC reinforced their approval of the way the government had sought to meet the pledges made during the election campaign:

> Since taking office the government have demonstrated their commitment to implementing the agreed approach. The General Council of the TUC wish to put on record their appreciation not only of the government's response but also the real contribution made by the affiliated unions.
>
> (The Labour Party/TUC Liaison Committee Meeting, 20 May 1974)

It would, therefore, seem that during this early period of the Labour government there were no disagreements as to what constituted the social contract. Key members of the Cabinet, including the Prime Minister and the Chancellor who were members of the TUC/Labour Party Liaison Committee and trade union general secretaries including Jack Jones of the TGWU and Hugh Scanlon of the AUEW, were obviously agreed that the social contract reflected a holistic approach between economic and social policy. Policies on income redistribution, price subsidies, pension and employment policies, could not be set apart from each other nor could incomes policy be divorced from the government's policies on rent and food subsidies.

The cycle of influence between February and October 1974 had put the spending ministers in ascendancy, partly because the February election had not given Labour an overall working majority which meant that an October election was inevitable. In this context, therefore, electoral politics suggested that it was increases in pensions, food subsidies, and rent subsidies which showed Labour's commitment to their electorate. Barnett argues that this was the period of the 'phoney war' for the government when the Prime Minister seemed to be more intent on winning the next election than generating a longer-term economic strategy to deal with the dual problems of inflation and the balance of payments.

> Instead of cutting public expenditure to take account of the massive oil price increase of 1973 which in our case cut living standards by some 5 per cent, the Chancellor decided to maintain our expenditure plans and borrowed to meet the deficit. This had dramatic consequences for me personally and the country in general.
>
> (Barnett 1982: 23)

By the time Labour had been re-elected in October 1974 with an overall working majority of three, confronting the problem of the balance of payments and sterling had become more pressing – especially with the loss of confidence by overseas investors. The government seemed to have lost the initiative by allowing public expenditure to drift upwards, not only creating problems for funding the increases in the public sector borrowing requirement and also creating problems of confidence in the government and their ability to control inflation. The social contract pointed to in-

creased public expenditure without any commitment by the trade unions
to deliver any form of incomes policy. Incomes policy was to be decided
according to a voluntary code to be established between the TUC and
affiliated unions.

Both the external pressures on sterling and the domestic problems of
funding the PSBR created tensions within the Labour Cabinet between
those ministers who felt that the government had to announce immediate
reductions in public expenditure and to impose an immediate pay policy,
and those ministers who felt that reductions in public expenditure would
result in unemployment and thus jeopardise the social contract. Treasury
ministers including Joel Barnett and Dennis Healey had also come to the
conclusion that in a period when there was no growth in the economy the
government was faced with the dilemma of either increasing borrowing
and, therefore, putting pressures on interest rates and investment or
increasing the levels of taxation. Barnett argued that if the government
attempted to increase taxation then the likelihood was that trade unions
would break with pay policy to make good the income lost through taxation
thus increasing the problem of inflation.

Labour's commitments on public expenditure had been outlined at the
Labour Conference in 1973 in a document called *Paying for Labour's
Programme*. In that document the Party made commitments to maintain
the standards of services and also to increase pensions and social security.
In addition the document made clear that meeting Labour's commitments
depended very much on growth in the economy:

> The cost of maintaining the existing levels of services is going to grow
> very substantially even leaving aside any new commitments. The savings
> on defence, roads and better use of services will not go very far towards
> meeting these commitments. Taxing the rich would only yield a small
> part of the revenue. We shall have to, therefore, rely on economic growth
> to provide the means but it will not be easy even with the most optimistic
> forecasts we should not be able to implement all our commitments.
>
> (Labour Party 1973: 18)

Both Barnett and Healey could, therefore, refer to Labour's programme in
making the case against further increases in public expenditure by arguing
that Britain had entered a period of no growth, while increases in public
expenditure had depended on growth and prosperity. However, spending
ministers, including Barbara Castle at Health and Crosland in Housing,
could equally argue that Labour's economic strategy would be defeated if
the government part of the social contract was not being observed. These
arguments on public expenditure, both within the Labour Cabinet and
between the government and Labour MPs, dominated economic policy-
making from 1975 until the election of 1979. Dissident Labour MPs voted
against the government expenditure plans in 1975 and 1976 which led to

two defeats of the government in the House of Commons, forcing the Prime Minister to use the public expenditure debates as a vote of confidence in the government.

Inflation and pay policy

Immediately after the October 1974 election, the government introduced an emergency budget which phased out subsidies on food and the nationalised industries, which in turn meant higher prices for energy but also higher prices on food and telecommunications. This was Healey's first attempt to regain the initiative on government borrowing. The budget did obviously have an immediate effect on the government's relations with the trade unions and this was reflected in the TUC/Labour Party Liaison Committee meeting of January 1975 when the TUC echoed their worries of these price increases on wages and also the likelihood of a fall in demand and unemployment. In March 1975 Healey announced further cuts to the Cabinet of £1 billion in public expenditure. The Cabinet seemed to be resigned to the inevitable – namely that something had to be done about the rapid increase in the rate of inflation.

Although the social contract was perceived as being central to the government's policy – there were, after October 1974, competing interpretations within the Cabinet as to what policies constituted the social contract. While Michael Foot continued to see the social contract as embracing the whole range of government policies, including fiscal policy, industrial policy, trade union reform and social policy, other ministers – including Reg Prentice, Harold Lever and Roy Jenkins – had developed a much narrower view of the social contract, arguing instead that the trade off depended on the ability of the government to generate economic growth and to maintain full employment and for the trade unions in return to accept the needs for a permanent incomes policy. This group felt that during 1974 the government had already given away too much to trade unions and had received very little in return. The trade unions had still not established a voluntary code on incomes policy:

> the only give and take in the Contract was that the Government gave and the unions took. We did not give in to all their demands for more and more public expenditure in every field from child benefits to pensions, from industrial support to special employment measures, but we did more than we could afford.
>
> (Barnett 1982: 49)

The phasing out of food subsidies and the increases in energy prices, accompanied by the rises in unemployment during April 1975 represented the background for the negotiations between the government and the trade unions to reach an agreement on incomes policy. While the trade unions had previously suggested that the prices of school meals and rents had represented a major foundation to agreeing an incomes policy, now they seemed to be agreeing an incomes policy under more adverse conditions. The readiness to work with the Labour government and the increased awareness for some trade union leaders that it was better to work with a Labour government than threaten another general election, both contributed to the successes of incomes policy between 1976 and 1978. The idea of a £6 flat rate limit which had been introduced by Jack Jones represented the first phase of voluntary incomes policy. Between 1975 and 1977 wage settlements fell from 33 per cent per annum to 18 per cent while price inflation fell from over 26 per cent to 13 per cent. The campaign for compliance by the TUC and the government had obviously succeeded in making rank and file members aware of Britain's economic problems. The second phase of voluntary incomes policy, secured in May 1976, was to last until August 1977 and had changed from a flat rate increase to a percentage increase of 4.5 per cent plus tax reductions. Again, the policy was accepted with little trade union resistance, although there was a call to return to orderly collective bargaining at the end of the agreed period. By the middle of 1977 the earnings index was rising by 8.5 per cent.

In contrast to the Heath government, the Labour government had secured three consecutive years of voluntary pay policy. In one way these years of successful pay restraint did represent the willingness of the trade unions to see the Labour government succeed in dealing with the problem of inflation and the crisis in sterling. The years of incomes policy also showed the ability of trade unions to give leadership to their members to subordinate their sectional interests for the wider common good:

> I believe he [Jack Jones] is the greatest voice in the trade union movement today in favour of what I have always wanted to see: the trade union movement being made socialist. And what is more he is someone who realizes that politicians have to operate in the real world as much as trade unionists do: in the world of the possible.
>
> (Castle 1980: 284)

In one sense, therefore, the period 1976 to 1978 signalled the beginning of trade union acceptance that their attitude to incomes policy was an essential element in economic policy-making. As a result, there was a reluctant acquiescence by the trade unions to demands made by the Prime Minister James Callaghan and the Chancellor Dennis Healey for the continuation of incomes policy in the context of reductions in public expenditure, the phasing out of subsidies, and also rising unemployment.

The sterling crisis of 1975 and 1976 and the intervention of the IMF strengthened the position of ministers who had come to the conclusion that a Labour government could not go for growth alone without other countries pursuing similar policies. The increases in public expenditure and the accompanying increases in the PSBR had made sterling more vulnerable as other countries reduced their public sector deficits and increased interest rates. The Labour government was finding it difficult to fund the PSBR between 1975 and 1976 and, therefore, had to resort to special drawing arrangements through the IMF. The IMF imposed conditions for their loan which included reductions in public expenditure and a commitment to tighter monetary policy. The need to reduce public expenditure, however, was always likely to meet resistance within a Labour Cabinet, especially when some ministers (including Castle, Benn and Crosland) had associated the objectives of social justice and equality with increases in public expenditure. The intervention of the IMF and the government's Letter of Intent, therefore, suspended to a large extent the government's autonomy in economic policy-making. Commitments were made for continuous reductions in public expenditure but also to reduce personal taxation as a means to create incentives and enterprise. The policy of full employment was replaced by the need to curb inflation through tighter monetary control and lower public expenditure. The government's letter to the IMF, sent on 15 December 1976, stated:

> An essential element of the government's strategy will be a continuing and substantial reduction over the next few years in the share of resources required for the public sector. It is also essential to reduce the PSBR in order to create monetary conditions which will encourage investment and support sustained growth and the control of inflation.

Although the government did secure three years of incomes policy despite the reductions in public expenditure and rising unemployment, their accord with the trade unions remained a short-term agreement. The basis of incomes continued to be the willingness of key trade union leaders – including Jack Jones of the TGWU, Hugh Scanlon of the AUEW and David Basnett of the GMWU – to continue to work with the Labour government and use their block votes at both TUC and Labour Party Conferences to ensure the survival of the strategy within the Labour movement. At the end of three years, however, such an arrangement could no longer be sustained especially when Jack Jones, who had been a key supporter of the government and the leader of the largest union, retired and was replaced by Moss Evans who had been elected with a pledge to enforce the return to free collective bargaining.

The fourth round discussion on incomes policy failed to materialise as trade union support for the government fragmented along craft lines and between public and private sector workers. Public sector trade unions came under increased pressures from their members, especially from local authority manual workers and NHS staff, to return to free collective bargaining. In the meantime disagreements also broke between public sector trade unions who wanted the government to restore the cuts in public expenditure and trade unions who represented workers in the private sector and who wanted the government to give priority to reductions in personal taxation.

Although the government did point out that a voluntary code to reduce inflation to 5 per cent had been agreed with the TUC in January 1979, the new agreement could not disguise the break up of the special relationship between the government and the trade unions. The Concordat, in effect, represented the recognition by the government that trade unions were not willing to give a Labour government another year of incomes policy. The return to free collective bargaining meant that some trade unions representing highly skilled workers were aiming to restore differentials, while public sector workers aimed to break with the government's cash limits; both were central to the government's policy on the control of public expenditure. The 'Winter of Discontent', which lasted from January 1979 to March 1979, embodied a series of strikes by skilled workers at Ford's, a tanker drivers' dispute and strikes by local authority manual workers and health service workers.

CONCLUSIONS

The 1970s represented the collapse of the Keynesian social democratic consensus in the UK. The Keynesian social democratic consensus represented both a political and economic agenda for government. Its demise was related to the failure of UK governments to establish both a Keynesian economic and political agenda similar to that established elsewhere in Europe. In Britain the Keynesian consensus had been limited to economic policy which confined governments to defining Keynesianism in terms of fiscal policy and fine tuning the economy by using the budgetary process to influence the levels of aggregate demand in the economy. However, if economic Keynesianism was going to be successful there was always a need to establish political Keynesianism. The commitments to full employment could not be sustained without an institutional forum which facilitated discussions on investment policy, industrial policy or a policy for incomes and prices.

The failure of UK governments to develop a political Keynesian consensus can be explained in terms of what Marcus Olson calls 'common-interest organisations' and their ability to pursue the particular interests of their members without having to take into consideration the wider public interest. The structure of British trade unions reinforces particular and narrow interests as conflicts of interest emerge between skilled workers and manual worker trade unions on issues of wage differentials and strict skills demarcations, and also between public sector and private sector workers. Furthermore, the shift towards decentralised bargaining and an informal system of collective bargaining has again been specific to the

British experience. While Britain claims a more unified trade union structure in that the TUC represents all Britain's trade unions, individual trade unions maintain a high degree of independence which means that even if the TUC does manage to reach an agreement with government there are no guarantees that they are able to deliver their affiliated organisations:

> The Trade Union Congress (TUC) is and always has been, a loose knit confederation of autonomous, often fragmented and ill disciplined bodies, jealous of their own independence suspicious of each other, answerable only to their members and willing to co-operate with each other only on their own terms.
>
> (Marquand 1988: 159)

While trade union fragmentation has made it difficult for UK governments to secure a long-term and enduring incomes policy, the ideological nature of British politics has also contributed to the failure of the Keynesian consensus. While the nationalisation of banking in France had been promoted on the basis of promoting the national interest, in Britain nationalisation still continues to promote ideological differences. Equally, while in West Germany governments have pursued strategies of picking industrial winners in Britain such a policy is described as acting against the interests of the market economy. In West Germany investment in education and the updating of skills are seen as being the responsibility of government; in Britain they are seen as intervention by government.

Both the adversarial nature of economic policy and the fragmentation of interests between and within Britain's trade unions have contributed to the demise of the Keynesian social democratic consensus. The inability to establish a Keynesian political agreement made the Keynesian economic agenda more difficult to sustain. Keynesian influences had to be both economic and political. While arguments about demand management might have been economic arguments the commitment to full employment was always a political argument since full employment was always likely to alter the relationships between employers and workers in the workplace. The commitment to full employment by government implied changes in behaviour in wage bargaining. Employers could no longer leave wages and employment to be decided in the market place and neither could trade unions argue that their role was limited to bargaining with employers on wages. While in other European countries the commitment to full employment and the welfare state was integral to the bargain between government, trade unions, and employers, in Britain the demand for co-operation was always seen as a short-term remedy to deal with an immediate crisis. The problem was that while sterling crises and balance of payments deficits required short-term responses they were also long-term problems which required longer-term solutions.

NOTES

1 M1 is defined as notes and coins in circulation and deposited in bank current accounts.

&M3 is defined as M1 plus funds saved in deposit accounts maintained with clearing banks, in the National Giro Bank, in the Bank of England banking department, and in the discount houses, plus certification of deposit; it excludes non-sterling deposit accounts.

2 M3 is defined as notes and coins in circulation and in bank current accounts, together with funds saved in deposit accounts maintained with clearing banks, the National Giro Bank, the Bank of England banking department, and discount houses, plus interest-bearing non-sterling deposit accounts held by British residents, and other certificates of deposit.

Chapter 11

The economics of Thatcherism

Economic policy between 1979 and 1990

INTRODUCTION: THE CONCEPT OF THATCHERISM

Despite being the most successful Prime Minister this century – no other Prime Minister has won three successive elections since Lord Liverpool – she still lost the challenge to her leadership in November 1990. Although it is too early to write an historical account of the Thatcher years, much has been written about the meaning and nature of Thatcherism. The concept has been utilised at one level to describe the leadership style of Mrs Thatcher, both as Prime Minister and as leader of the Conservative Party. Within this narrow interpretation of Thatcherism, the primary concern has been to analyse the particular impact of Mrs Thatcher on politics and public policy. Biographies have sought to stress the qualities and personal convictions of the Prime Minister and her ability as an individual to give direction to government. Hugo Young (1989) has, for example, argued that the government's commitment to tight monetary policy – especially during the 1981 budget – had been mainly attributed to Mrs Thatcher's personal attachment to sound monetary policy,

> The first quality [of Mrs Thatcher] was a sense of moral rectitude which accounted for the single main achievement that would not have happened without her. This was the attachment to fiscal rigour in the early years, which whatever analysis is made of its consequences was an extraordinary exercise in political will...the determination to pursue the economics of good housekeeping, preached at the knee of her father she constantly invoked and elevated above the merely political to the moral level, came mainly from within her more than anybody else. It was her special contribution.
>
> (Young 1989: 543–4)

In contrast, Thatcherism has also been perceived as representing a set of beliefs which were internally coherent and consistent and which resonated with the British electorate. Stuart Hall has, for example, pointed out that Thatcherism was not limited to an argument about her leadership style and her personal vision on how to restructure the British economy, but also that it promoted a wider agenda on how to reorder British society morally, spiritually, and politically. While Thatcherism could be associated with the rediscovery of the 'spirit of enterprise' and the 'enterprise culture', it also offered a moral vision of the dutiful individual who gives time and expertise freely to the community in voluntary work whether as a governor in a local school or helping to raise funds for some deserving local project.

Mrs Thatcher herself seemed to prefer this wider meaning of Thatcherism:

> We've been working to restore the political system to bring out all that was best in the British character. That's what we've done. It's called Thatcherism.... It's a mixture of fundamentally sound economics. You live within your means, you have honest money, so, therefore, you don't make reckless promises.... It is about being worthwhile and honourable.... And about the family. And about that something which is really rather unique and enterprising in the British character – it's about how we built an Empire, and how we gave sound administration and sound law to large areas of the world.
>
> (Tyler 1987: 251)

According to Mrs Thatcher's personal vision, Thatcherism represents the vehicle which enables the rediscovery of something called the real British character, that is something that all those who are British recognise about themselves and, therefore, share with the Prime Minister and with others who are British. According to Mrs Thatcher the British character is the enterprising individual who seeks to promote individual self-interest with the minimum of state intervention and who in promoting that spirit of enterprise had built an Empire and then proceeded to teach those who were colonised how to govern themselves. The major concern here is not to challenge Mrs Thatcher's interpretation of history but to indicate that Mrs Thatcher's view of what constitutes the real British character is as selective and arbitrary as are other existing and competing interpretations of British history. So although Thatcherism seems to be a concept which had gained ascendancy, there are competing views and interpretations as to what constitutes Thatcherism.

While much has been said about the Thatcher revolution (Jenkins 1987) and the Thatcher economic experiment (Keegan 1983), such questions as how much Thatcherism would there be if there had been no Mrs Thatcher as Prime Minister?, or would the break have come later or not at all?, or would the break have taken the same form with another leader?, allow us to be critical of the assumption that the changes in policy associated with Mrs Thatcher's governments since 1979 were somehow historically inevitable and carried along by irresistible historical pressures. It would be difficult to sustain the thesis that the election of Mrs Thatcher as leader of the Conservative Party and Prime Minister was an inevitable response, for example, to the crisis of British capitalism, without taking into consideration the possibility that events could have turned out to be different. We should keep in mind that Mrs Thatcher's election to the leadership of the Conservative Party in 1975 was not the product of some overwhelming demand for a new free market philosophy but that it owed a great deal to dissatisfaction with the style of the existing leader, Edward Heath, the astute campaign management by the Thatcher camp, and tactical good fortune (Pym 1985):

> I think he [Mr Heath] lost the leadership for reasons that were entirely of his own making and that it is truer to say that he forefeited his claim to the loyalty of the Parliamentary Party than that he was betrayed.... Not only did Ted Heath's attitude ensure he would lose the leadership but it also made it likely that his successor would be someone different. All the front runners, Willie Whitelaw especially, were loyal to Ted Heath and found it impossible to stand against him in the first ballot.
>
> (Pym 1985: 21)

Given that leaders of modern political parties exercise great internal authority and power, the fact that Mrs Thatcher rather than Willie Whitelaw became leader in 1975 is clearly of great significance. As Hugo Young (1989) has pointed out Mrs Thatcher was able to impose on the Party a specific discourse and a set of broad objectives that her rivals for the leadership would probably have shrunk from. However, it is also important to keep in mind that she was no isolated prophet who took the Party by storm. Rather, she emerged from a market liberal faction of the Party which had never been content with the post-war settlement. Other leading Conservatives for example, including Jock Bruce Gardyne, Nicholas Ridley, Nigel Lawson, and John Biffen had continuously indicated their commitment to market liberalism during the years of the Heath government and had actually voted against the government during the policy U-turns of 1972. The fact is that Mrs Thatcher did give greater attention to the market liberal ideas of the Institute of Economic Affairs, The Adam Smith Institute, the Salisbury Reviewers and others, and had their ideas translated into usable political forms by the policy think-tanks (such as the Centre for Policy Studies) established by Conservative Party Central Office. The environment from which Mrs Thatcher has emerged and whose objectives she has sought to pursue (not without considerable tactical flexibility) is more important than the personality cult that has at times attached itself to her name. Gamble argues that:

> what makes the term Thatcherism appropriate to describe what happened to the Conservative party after 1975 is that Thatcher identified herself with the ideas and causes of the New Right and used her position

as Leader to promote the spread of these ideas in a manner which was highly unusual for a Conservative Leader.

(Gamble 1988: 22)

The replacement of Mrs Thatcher as Party leader and Prime Minister confirms the view that the major concern of professional politicians is either to remain the incumbent government or how to become the government. Mrs Thatcher, while being praised by her colleagues as being the best Prime Minister, was increasingly seen as becoming a liability to the Party in winning a fourth term in office.

THATCHERISM: THE RESPONSE TO THE POST-WAR CONSENSUS

One continuing theme to emerge during the previous three chapters has been the various initiatives by UK governments during the period 1945 to 1979 to establish an enduring institutional framework that would facilitate consensus building in the conduct of economic policy. It was also argued that during the 1970s the post-war settlement, underpinned by the twin objectives of full employment and an expanded welfare state, had become more difficult to sustain in the context of rising inflation, a low rate of economic growth, a deteriorating balance of payments deficit, and sterling crisis. The underperformance of the British economy when contrasted to other European economies including France and West Germany, the evident inabilities of British manufacturing industries to take full advantage of the expansion in world trade, and the problems of the trade deficit and repeated crises of sterling, meant that while France and West Germany were achieving a growth rate of 5 per cent per annum the British economy had been growing at just under 3 per cent per annum. The path to UK economic prosperity seemed to be continuously hindered by the balance of payments constraint which in turn had put pressure on the exchange rate and forced government to dampen demand and deflate the economy to reduce imports.

This apparent failure of the UK economy to move towards virtuous growth founded on growing export markets and rising personal incomes, has been attributed to the adverse effects of the stop–go syndrome in economic management. Associated with the problems of stop–go, however, were the problem of what was perceived to be the 'British disease' of low productivity, the problems of wage drift, and the increases in the number of unofficial disputes. The failure of the UK to secure arrangements for a longer-term understanding on the issues of prices and incomes in the context of full employment with employers and trade unions, when compared to Swedish, Austrian, and West German experiments with social partnerships, was seen to contribute to Britain's lack of competitiveness and low growth performance.

The major lessons to be drawn by the policy-makers during the 1970s led to two different approaches to policy. One argument which was embraced by the incoming government of Edward Heath in 1970 suggested that what was needed was to break with pluralist stagnation, which meant breaking with the political consensus of the post-war period. The second interpretation suggested that Britain needed to build better links between industry, trade unions and the government and, therefore, to construct a social contract, to accommodate various interests and to integrate these interests into the policy-making process. However, both the attempt to import a 'Quiet Revolution' by the Heath government and Labour's attempt at a new social contract seemed to be failed 'experiments' by 1979. While by 1972 the Heath government had moved towards corporatism and still seemed to fail to win concessions from the trade unions on the issue of incomes policy, the Labour government – which had made claims of their special relationship with the trade unions – had found by 1977 that despite making major concessions to the trade unions they had also failed to deal with the problems of the balance of payments, sterling crisis, and inflation. The breakdown of the Bretton Woods agreement in 1973, the shift towards floating exchange rates, the oil price increases, rising inflation, and unemployment all seemed to indicate that what was needed was a willingness and conviction by politicians to break with the post-war social democratic consensus.

The election of the first Thatcher government in 1979 and the successive election victories of 1983 and 1987 are seen as confirming the break with post-war settlement and the commitments to full employment, the welfare state, and Keynesian economics. In the context of economic policy-making, the principles of Thatcherism are generally understood as a political practice which comprehensively breaks with the broadly collectivist and the Keynesian political consensus inaugurated by the first Attlee government. The emphasis on anti-Keynesian economic theories is seen as being at the heart of Thatcherism. This has consequently led to the view that the political practice and the policy record of Mrs Thatcher's governments have been primarily concerned with indicating a break with Keynesian economics and replacing welfare collectivism and political corporatism with principles based on individual self-interest and market economics.

However, if the agenda of Thatcherism was to succeed in reversing the problem of economic decline it had to be more than an economic theory, it also had to be a project that transcended the issues of economic failure to generate a much wider debate on the transformation of values, politics, and culture. These interpretations covered a wide spectrum of issues, from an emphasis on the recovery of national sovereignty and international status to the creation of a more disciplined social order and the resolution of a crisis of authority in the British state.

THE THATCHER REVOLUTION AND ECONOMIC POLICY-MAKING

Economic policy-making in the 1980s can be judged as representing a series of paradoxes, being both individualist and yet collectivist. The politics of Thatcherism seemed to advocate both the return to a market economy while at the same time seeming to favour a strong centralising state (Gamble 1988):

> The state must be strong firstly to unwind the coils of social democracy and welfarism which have fastened around the free economy; second to police the market order; thirdly to make the economy more productive and fourthly to uphold social and political authority.
>
> (Gamble 1988: 32)

Thatcherism is perceived to be a crusade for the individual against the monopoly power of the nationalised industries, against the monopoly of local government in the provision of public services, or the monopoly of knowledge of government bureaucracy and professionals. At the same time, however, the government also seeks to undermine the autonomy of local government and local democracy through tighter controls of local expenditures, also removing public services from local authority control if these are seen as challenging the project of Thatcherism (Mullard *et al.* 1990). There seems, therefore, to be little room for pluralism and diversity within the project of Thatcherism. The free individual flourishes only in the context of a powerful state. According to Jonathan Clarke, Thatcherism is seen as confirming the idea of the authoritarian individual who seeks to be free from the meddling of intermediary agencies such as local government, with the prime objective of promoting self-interest but willing to live with a centralist disciplinary state.

The political economics of the Thatcher governments have to be located within the long-term context of economic policy-making, since the concept of Thatcherism formed both a critical appraisal of the post-war consensus and also heralded a vision for the future. Thatcherism represented a twofold criticism of the post-war settlement. First, the Thatcher critique utilised a monetarist interpretation of the post-war settlement in pointing out that the post-war period had legitimised an increased role for government, which had in turn resulted in higher levels of public expenditure, an increase in government borrowing, increases in the money supply, and higher levels of inflation. The view that governments could influence the level of employment or manage the economy was challenged by monetarist economists who argued that governments had actually harmed the UK economy. Monetarists advanced the view that it was necessary to push back the frontiers of the state, and to question the legitimacy of state intervention and the assumption that governments could actually give direction to the economy. Instead it was better to trust the market place and the enterprise of the individual rather than the government. Monetarists argued that governments should make their commitments to the control of inflation by directions on the paths for monetary growth, the money supply, and inflation.

The second influence reflected the views of market liberalism. According to public choice theory those who benefited from the post-war settlement were those who could best organise – namely, those groups who could form cartels or monopolies and, therefore, limit access to their privileged position. Those who benefited were, therefore, those who occupied a strategic position in the economy such as the miners and power workers, who because of their monopoly within the nationalised industries had been able to dictate to government. Accordingly, Keynesianism and the politics of consent implied the securing of the consent of strategic groups often at the cost of the individual citizen who was left on the margins of the political consensus. There was little access within the world of producer groups for the elderly citizen, the self-employed, or for the rights of the consumer. The beneficiaries were producer groups. It was, therefore, essential to the politics of Thatcherism to show that commitments to market principles would also create more equality between individuals and would, therefore, reduce the influence of organised interests. The political market price was unequal because those individuals who were political had the better knowledge and the better access to government. In contrast, the economic market place was more equal because each individual had to be treated as an equal consumer. The competitive economic place does not discriminate between consumers while the political market place discriminates in favour of the political citizen. Public choice theorists argued that the major objective of a liberal government was to depoliticise the economy, which meant the breaking up of state provision of services and the replacement of monopoly by competition policy as the means to greater equality between individuals.

Minford (1980) has described Mrs Thatcher as a political entrepreneur able to respond to the constraints of the market place but also aware of opportunities to bring new ideas into the political market place. The entrepreneur takes the market place as given but only in the short term; in the longer term the entrepreneur seeks to give leadership to the market. While both monetarist and market liberal ideas can be discerned as influencing the economics of Thatcherism it would be misleading to perceive the years of the Thatcher governments as representing a coherent economic policy confined to monetarist and market liberal views on economic management. There is also a need to keep in mind that a major preoccupation of any government must be to remain the incumbent government. No government is therefore likely to confine themselves to one set of economic ideas if these are seen as limiting their freedom of action thus putting their chances of electoral success in jeopardy. It is, therefore, also important to explore the pragmatic nature of Thatcherism and how the government redefined their economic priorities, sometime yielding to certain pressures and willing to learn on the job. The politics of statecraft reflects on 'the art of government' and the abilities of government to recognise both the sources of imposed constraints and the possibilities of autonomy in the policy process. While the concept of Thatcherism implies an ideological realignment and a shift in attitudes from collectivist ideals towards market individualism, the statecraft interpretation of Thatcher years points to the political realignment without the necessity of ideological realignment.

According to the statecraft thesis, the central concern of the government has been the process of constructing electoral majorities, which meant threading together diverse electoral alliances. Political realignment under Thatcherism, therefore, represents the bringing together of diverse interests including the self-employed, home-owners, pensioners, and consumer interests – that is, individuals who had been seen as being at the margin and not considered as important to Keynesian political consensus. The politics of statecraft involved both political and arithmetic calculations which meant the ability to increase electoral appeal without appearing to surrender on political principles:

> Thatcherism is based on arithmetic politics. It relies on the sum of diverse and particularistic appeals; on housing, race, anti-labour or anti-union sentiments, entrepreneurial ethos – but does not represent a unified coalition such as that which lay beneath the Butskellite programme of the Keynesian Welfare State.
>
> (Krieger 1986: 186)

Economic policy-making, according to the statecraft interpretation, refutes the presence of an overall coherent approach but points instead to an ability to add together electoral majorities and to generate policies which benefit electoral majorities. The statecraft approach points, therefore, to a policy founded on political judgements rather than the moral principles which emanate from the political economy of market liberalism. While market liberals accept that markets do fail and that a political agenda for government could be constructed guided by market liberal principles, public policy under Thatcherism seems to be guided by what is seen as the art of the possible. Market liberal economists including Samuel Brittan, the economics editor of the *Financial Times*, have continued to argue during the past decade that the policy of mortgage tax relief was against the spirit of market liberal principles because the policy acted as a subsidy on housing, thus distorting the housing market, prices, and wages. They have advocated that a government guided by market liberal principles would phase out mortgage tax relief and target the exchequer subsidy to lower income groups, Mrs Thatcher's government, however, have maintained their commitment to mortgage tax relief because mortgagors represent a very influential political interest.

In previous discussions (Mullard 1987 and Mullard *et al*. 1990), the author suggested that the various interpretations of Thatcherism could be put into two categories: the fundamentalist/radical perspective, and the sceptical perspective. The radical perspective emphasises that Thatcherism represented a break with the post-war consensus both at the level of economic management and also in the reordering of the British political process. In contrast, the sceptical perspective echoes at one level the criticisms of market liberals such as Samuel Brittan who have argued that the government has shown little commitment to market liberal principles. It also includes those arguments which point to the view that the Thatcher governments, like all governments, are primarily concerned with the politics of statecraft and the winning of the next election, and, therefore, are equally involved in the process of economic management according to the electoral business cycle.

The assessment of economic policy during the Thatcher years, therefore, reflects the tensions between continuity and revolution; between the demands of more individuals and the constraints of the welfare state; between the influences of market liberalism and Keynesian ideas; and between the radical and the statecraft aspects of Thatcherism. The following sections seek to produce a balance sheet between the twin dilemmas of ideology and statecraft in economic policy-making during the 1980s and ask whether the state of the British economy in the 1990s can be explained in terms of a new consensus.

THE ECONOMIC RECORD 1979 TO 1990

A survey of the UK economic landscape in 1990, based on the analysis of economic indicators including growth, employment, inflation, and the balance of payments has led to a plurality of views. They range from claims that Britain has been experiencing an economic miracle since the mid-1980s to claims which seek to suggest that despite Mrs Thatcher's experimentation with the UK economy, the UK is still faced with problems of a balance of payments constraint and higher rates of inflation than its competitors. A study of economic growth in the 1980s, for example, seems to provide different assessments depending on which year is taken as the starting point. If the period 1979 to 1990 is taken into account, then the rate of economic growth during the past decade has still not reached the rates of growth achieved during the previous decade. Taking the recession years into account, the rate of growth achieved over the past decade has averaged 2.5 per cent per annum. However, if the years 1979 to 1982 are left outside the survey then the rates of growth achieved since the mid-1980s would suggest a growth rate of 3 per cent per annum. Indeed, during

Figure 11.1 The anatomy of UK recession, 1990

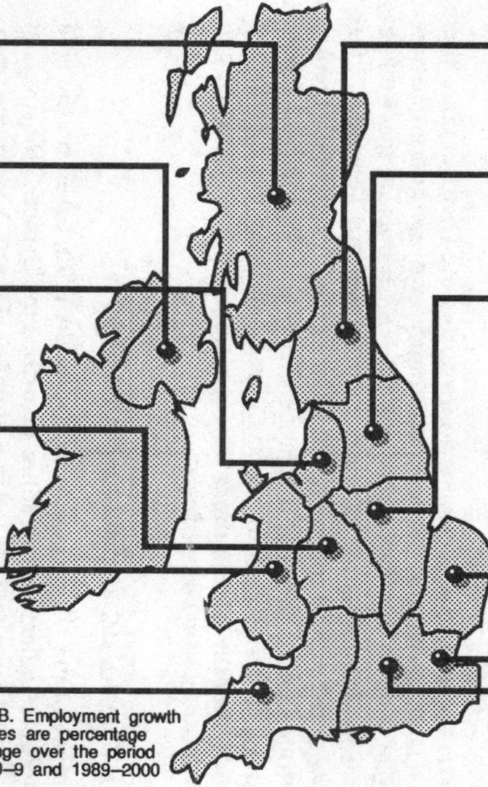

Seasonally adjusted	1989 average	Sept 1990
North		
Unemployment	10.0%	8.7%
Vacancies (000)	10.7	9.5
Employment growth*	-6.6	-6.3
Yorks & Humberside		
Unemployment	7.7%	6.9%
Vacancies (000)	13.3	11.9
Employment growth*	-3.7	-1.6
East Midlands		
Unemployment	5.6%	5.2%
Vacancies (000)	12.9	10.2
Employment growth*	+5.6	+4.4
East Anglia		
Unemployment	3.6%	3.9%
Vacancies (000)	8.3	4.3
Employment growth*	+14.0	+10.5
Greater London		
Unemployment	5.0%	4.9%
Vacancies (000)	23.6	12.5
Employment growth*	n.a.	n.a.
South East		
Unemployment	3.9%	4.0%
Vacancies (000)	71.7	39.6
Employment growth*	+7.6	-0.4

Seasonally adjusted	1989 average	Sept 1990
Scotland		
Unemployment	9.4%	7.9%
Vacancies (000)	21.7	22.6
Employment growth*	-4.2	-4.1
Northern Ireland		
Unemployment	17.6%	13.7%
Vacancies (000)	2.6	4.9
Employment growth*	-2.5	-5.9
North West		
Unemployment	8.4%	7.5%
Vacancies (000)	24.4	20.0
Employment growth*	-5.3	-6.5
West Midlands		
Unemployment	6.6%	5.9%
Vacancies (000)	20.5	13.6
Employment growth*	-3.4	-2.6
Wales		
Unemployment	7.4%	6.6%
Vacancies (000)	13.8	12.1
Employment growth*	-1.0	-2.2
South West		
Unemployment	4.5%	4.6%
Vacancies (000)	18.5	13.1
Employment growth*	+13.4	+4.6

* N.B. Employment growth figures are percentage change over the period 1980–9 and 1989–2000

Source: Financial Times, 21 October 1990

the years 1987 to 1989 UK economic growth has averaged over 4 per cent per annum. The government could claim that the rates of growth experienced since 1983 reflect a stronger economy founded on increases in private sector investment and higher levels of productivity in manufacturing. In contrast to the 1960s and 1970s when government did have to resort to stop–go policies, the rates of growth achieved in the 1980s have been sustainable and durable.

On the issue of inflation the Conservative governments can make claims of bringing the high inflation rates of the 1970s under control. Taking the years 1979 to 1990 as a whole, the year on year inflation has averaged at 6 per cent per annum when contrasted to 10 per cent inflation in the previous decade. However, a year by year study would again reveal that the problem of inflation continues to persist in the British economy despite ten years of Conservative government. The crucial question related to the problem of inflation is whether the government's success vindicates their overall economic strategy. Keynesian economists argue that while between 1981 and 1986 headline inflation did fall sharply from a peak of 21 per cent to 6 per cent, the underlying pressures of wage and price inflation continued to persist. Keynesians have suggested that the low levels of inflation were also highly correlated to an unprecedented increase in the rate of unemployment during this period. Between 1981 and 1983 the rate of UK unemployment had accelerated from 1.5 million to a peak of 3.2 million in 1983, the highest level to be recorded in the post-war period. Keynesian critiques would argue that the discipline of unemployment during this period did moderate wage demands, but with the increases in economic growth after 1987 when unemployment started to fall the rate of inflation had again started to rise to reflect tighter labour markets. Inflation since

Figure 11.2   Inflation as measured by the Retail Price Index 1987–90 (% change on previous year)

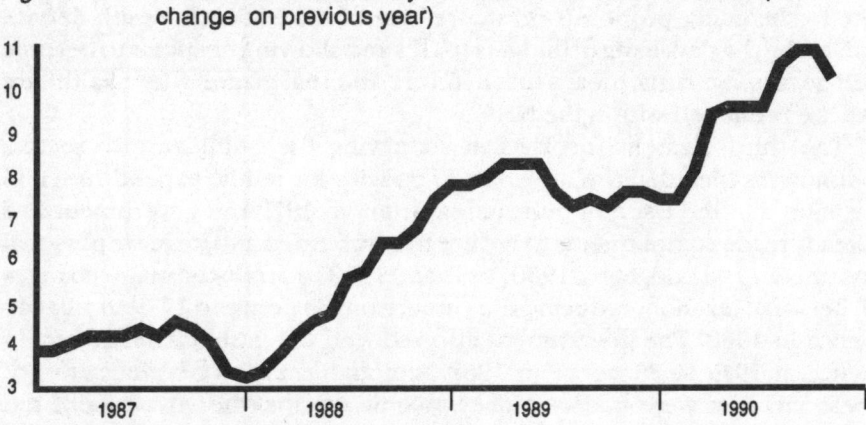

Source: Financial Times, 15/16 December 1990

1988 has continued to rise from 4.5 per cent in 1988 to 9.8 per cent by July 1990. Inflation in 1990 has again become the major concern for the government, despite ten years of high interest rates, tight control over the PSBR, and continued public expenditure restraint.

The government has also claimed that they have permanently redrawn the boundaries between the private and the public sectors of the economy. The programme of denationalisation, which started with Amersham International and British Telecom in 1982, is now near completion. The major utilities of gas, water, electricity and telecommunications would have all been privatised by the end of 1990. Other industries, including British Freight, Rolls-Royce, British Airways, and British Steel have also been successfully denationalised. The 'ratchet' of state ownership and direct government intervention in the economy have been reversed. In future the taxpayers will be free from having to finance the losses of these industries, while the programme of privatisation itself has increased share ownership among individuals thus widening the process of popular capitalism.

In addition to the programme of denationalisation there have also been major changes within the welfare state. Local authority monopoly in the provision of education has been reduced within the context of the 1988 Education Reform Act. Public sector schools can now choose to opt out of local authority control and become grant-maintained schools giving parents more choice in education. Furthermore, under the direction of local management of schools, local authorities have to devolve up to 90 per cent of the education budget to school governing bodies for them to decide the priorities of the school. In housing reform, the 'right to buy' and measures to create more diverse tenancies mean that local government have lost their monopoly in the provision of public housing. The compulsion to submit services such as cleaning and maintenance to competitive tendering also means that local government workers will in future have to compete with private sector workers if they are to win local government contracts. Finally, the forthcoming proposals on the reform of the National Health Service including the devolving of budgets to GPs and allowing hospitals to become self-governing trusts, means that in future 'internal markets' for health care will be promoted within the NHS.

The third element involved in redrawing the public/private sectors boundaries included the direction of policies for public expenditure and taxation. On the issue of personal taxation, in 1979 the government had already made commitments to reduce the tax burden and increase personal incentives. The budgets of 1980, 1983 and 1988 all produced major changes in personal taxation, reducing the surtax from 83 pence in 1979 to a flat 40 pence in 1988. The government also reduced the basic tax rate from 33 pence in 1979 to 25 pence in 1988. Although the major beneficiaries of these changes were mainly higher income groups, the government did achieve the more important objective of eroding the tax base to fund higher levels of public expenditure. Future governments will be faced with the difficult choice of having to increase personal taxation to fund increases in welfare expenditures or postponing expenditure plans.

On public expenditure the government also achieved two major objectives. First, they succeeded in reducing the PSBR and were able to turn a public sector deficit into a repayment of the government debt. While the government had inherited a PSBR of £10 billion in 1979, in 1988 and 1989 they had produced a surplus of revenue over expenditure of some £14 billion in each year. This was Chancellor Lawson's claim to success – the ability to reduce taxation, increase public expenditure, and reduce government borrowing.

The second objective has been to break the link between the growth in national income and the growth in public expenditure. Since the late 1960s the rate of growth in public expenditure had outstripped the growth in national income. In contrast, since 1987 public expenditure had actually grown at a lower rate than national income. While in the early 1980s public expenditure had increased to 46 per cent of GDP by 1989 this had fallen to 38.5 per cent.

In addition to the reshaping of the public sector the government could also claim that their reforms of trade unions have also contributed to the permanent restructuring of industrial relations. As was suggested earlier, part of the Thatcher criticism of the 1970s had been the failure of corporatist politics and the preparedness of governments to surrender their right to govern in the interests of individual citizens and allowing instead for the interests of organised groups to be put at the centre of economic policy-making. Trade unions had been central to the Keynesian political consensus. Mrs Thatcher argued that the trade unions had abused their position in the context of full employment and had forced governments into making concessions which had harmed the economy. The reform of industrial relations represented, at one level, continuity of thinking with previous Conservative governments. The proposals contained in *A Giant's Strength*, issued by the Conservative Inns of Court in 1958 and updated in the Conservative document *A Fair Deal at Work* in 1970, and the 1972 Industrial Relations Act, represented lessons for the Thatcher government of how not to repeat the mistakes of the Heath government. The Industrial Relations Act of 1972 had been a sound piece of legislation but it had tried to do too much too soon and was eventually made unworkable by trade union opposition. Under the Thatcher regime the approach to industrial relations was to be piecemeal, gradual and enduring. Industrial relations in 1990 are now dominated by three major statutes: the Employment Acts of 1980, 1982 and 1988. Trade unions now have to establish a secret ballot before a strike, while workers still have the right to work. The Trade Union Act of 1984 contains the provisions for trade unionists to elect their executive officers every five years by secret ballot. There are also restrictions on pickets outside the place of work, while secondary action has been made illegal as has been the pre-entry closed shop. In future individuals have equal rights to belong and also not to belong to a trade union. Trade union funds are open to sequestration by the courts if they are found to be in contempt of the law.

The long-term effects on trade unions are difficult to assess. While trade union membership did fall sharply from a peak of 13.2 million in 1976 to 10.5 million in 1988, it would be misleading to conclude that the fall in trade union membership can be attributed to changes in closed shop legislation or whether the fall was related to the increase in unemployment during the 1980s. In addition, there is no necessary correlation between trade union strength and total trade union membership. Despite the high levels of unemployment, trade union members in the private sector have continued to maintain their wage levels in line with inflation. It would seem that it has been public sector workers who have experienced a decline in their living standards. Paradoxically it would seem that rather than weakening the position of trade unions, secret ballots have actually strengthened the position of trade union negotiators. In 526 ballots over 80 per cent have been in favour of industrial action.

The third major achievement as far as the government is concerned has been their success in their management of the economy without having to resort to Keynesian economics and corporatist politics. The commitment to market economics and the discipline of monetarism are now seen as central to the Thatcher revolution. On the issue of inflation, the government did not seek to secure consensus with business and trade unions on incomes and prices since this would have worked against the principles of market and non-state intervention. Furthermore, the attempt to secure concessions on incomes policy would have put pressures on the government to increase public expenditure as part of the trade off with the trade unions. The government, therefore, replaced the tools of incomes policy with those advocated by monetarist economists – namely, the control of inflation through reducing the PSBR, monetary targets, and interest rates. Monetarists had argued that bargaining agents required a very clear signal from the government that wage increases would not be accommodated through increases in the money supply; rather, wages would be determined more accurately through market forces without any need for an incomes policy. Unemployment was, therefore, an issue for workers; they had to make choices between higher wage demands or pricing themselves out of the market.

The causes and cures for unemployment and inflation were no longer to be traded off within a Keynesian framework. The commitment of government to the maintenance of full employment enshrined in the 1944 White Paper had already been undermined during the years of the Callaghan government when, despite the rise in unemployment, in 1977 the Labour government did not resort to classical Keynesian demand management. So while Thatcherism cannot be seen as a watershed in marking the break with Keynesian demand management, there were still major differences between Thatcherism and the Callaghan government in dealing with the problems of unemployment. While the Labour government still maintained a firm belief in state intervention, the theme to emerge during the Thatcher years was that unemployment was caused by high wages and workers pricing themselves out of labour markets. The problem of unemployment needed to be resolved in the market place by removing labour market rigidities, minimising bureaucracy, and increasing incentives.

The twin policy objectives of trade union reform and controlling public expenditure were seen as being consistent with the government's 'supply side' economic policies. Keeping tight control on public spending meant releasing finances for tax reductions and thereby increasing incentives to work. Lower taxes would increase take-home pay and increase labour supply, while removing restrictions such as Wages Councils would increase the demand for labour. The National Insurance surcharge was seen as a 'tax' on jobs which the government was also committed to phase out. The Fowler reviews of Social Security in 1986 were also seen as improving supply side policies. This was the Thatcher attempt to deal with what she saw as the 'why work' syndrome. Unemployment benefits and other social security payments had contributed to unemployment duration, since workers could stay longer in between jobs. Furthermore, the levels of benefits had contributed to the poverty trap which meant that there were fewer incentives for workers to move into jobs. Family credit, which replaced Family Income Support, was seen as the government's attempt to remove some of the anomalies of the poverty trap which had forced workers with families to remain unemployed. Family credit was seen as the vehicle for this group's easing their way back into the labour market by making benefits available for those in work according to their family size. Finally, the reform of trade unions was also seen as making the labour supply side less inelastic and more price sensitive.

In seeking to explain the unexpected rise in unemployment from 1.4 million to 2.9 million between 1979 and 1981, the government refuted the argument that the problem of unemployment was related to their management of the economy. Instead ministers sought to point out that most of the job losses had been in the manufacturing sector, where the problem of overmanning had been the most acute. The reductions in subsidy to state-owned industries, including British Steel, British Coal, and British Leyland, meant that these industries had to reduce labour costs and improve productivity. Despite the job losses in manufacturing the government was able to point out that total output had shown high gains in productivity. The increase in unemployment between 1981 and 1982 was seen as part of Britain's adjustment to international markets and that the best way to absorb the unemployed from this sector was to construct an environment where both labour and labour costs were more flexible.

In contrast, some economic commentators, including the Cambridge Group of Economists, Blackaby (1979), and Martin and Rowthorn (1986), pointed out that major closures in steel making, engineering, and textiles represented more than a market adjustment but was actually resembling an accelerated deindustrialisation of the UK economy. The Cambridge Group had argued that the government's lack of concern about the losses in manufacturing capacity was jeopardising the UK economic recovery since in the long run, in the absence of growth in domestic industries, the UK was in danger of not being able to finance its imports. These critiques also pointed to the regional disparities in unemployment, so that while unemployment in the South-east and East Anglia in 1982 was below the national average of 13 per cent, unemployment in Yorkshire and Humberside, the North-east, the North-west and Scotland had increased to an average of 16 per cent of the working population. Plant closure in towns such as Consett and Corby meant that in some areas the unemployed represented over 50 per cent of the working population. As far as these commentators were concerned the blame lay with government policy. The policies of high interest rates had made it more difficult for firms to borrow for investment; high interest rates in the early 1980s had led to a steep increase in the value of sterling which in turn led to a further decline in exports and more job losses. Furthermore, North Sea Oil had turned sterling into a petro currency, which again had increased the uncertainty on the value of sterling and, therefore, was making it even more difficult for industries to plan investment.

The argument that the reform of labour markets would increase access has been criticised because it failed to take into account the issue that those who did experience unemployment tended to be low skilled. What was needed was increased expenditure by government on training and increased investment in individual human capital if the long-term unemployed were to reenter the labour market. The issues of trade union reform and adjustments to the benefit system were, therefore, seen as being irrelevant to those who had lost their jobs in the manufacturing sector. The growth sectors, during the early 1980s, tended to include banking, finance, and new technology. The unemployed, therefore, tended to have no effect on these labour markets, and according to Gavin Davies, City Analyst at Goldman and Sachs, the unemployed might as well have been in Australia. Rather than reducing the boundary between 'insider' and 'outsider' groups in the labour market, government policy seemed to worsen the position of outsider groups. While insider groups of skilled and professional workers experienced increases in wages and higher living standards throughout the 1980s, those with low skills tended to lose their jobs. In the meantime, the growth area for low skilled employment tended to be in the retail industries where most of the jobs were part-time and also low paid.

The second criticism pointed to the problem of labour mobility and house prices. The widening house prices between the North and the South and South-east of England during the early 1980s meant that workers who lost their jobs in the North of England were finding it difficult to get on their bikes and go in search of jobs in the South. House prices in the 1980s had become a major obstacle to labour mobility. While in engineering and new technology employers were reporting problems of filling vacancies in places such as Swindon and Basingstoke, the competition for skilled workers in these areas meant that employers had to offer higher wages to retain their key workers.

In an important study of UK unemployment, Nickell and Layard (1986) have produced an econometric analysis combining both Keynesian and monetarist perspectives as explanatory variables of unemployment during the early 1980s. The main message from this research indicated that while total unemployment had increased by 11.5 per cent during the period 1979 to 1983 the major contributory factor to explain the rise the unemployment was the fall in overall demand. The fall in demand explained over 6 per cent of the total rise in unemployment. In contrast, the analysis of market liberal variables, including the contribution of the benefit system to the rise in unemployment and the trade union effect on labour markets, explained only 2 per cent of the rise in unemployment while the variable of national insurance explained the other 2 per cent. In part, the Nickell and Layard study reinforced the Keynesian argument that the increase in UK unemployment during the early 1980s was mainly to be blamed on the abandonment of Keynesian demand management.

Keynesian economists had pointed out that their economic forecasts had clearly indicated that the policies adopted by the incoming Conservative government in 1979 would lead to an increase in unemployment. Wynne Godley, for example, had predicted as early as 1980 that unless the government did change their fiscal stance that unemployment would rise to 3 million by 1983. Such forecasts were very easily dismissed by both the government and the ascending monetarist economists as belonging to economic models of a previous age. Monetarist economists including Friedman (1980), Laidler (1980), and Minford (1980) in their evidence to the Treasury Select Committee on Monetary Policy, had pointed out that a monetary strategy to deal with the problem of inflation was not likely to lead to any fall in output or a rise in unemployment:

I conclude that (a) only a modest reduction in output and employment will be a side effect of reducing inflation to single figures by 1982, and

(b) the effect on investment and the potential for future growth will be highly favourable.

(Friedman 1980: 61)

When Professor Minford was asked about the effects of monetary policy on employment and growth, his reply to the Select Committee was as follows:

There is no necessary effect on unemployment of cuts in monetary growth. There is no necessary effect.... So I would say that there is no inevitability about large amounts of unemployment resulting from the pursuit of these policies. Indeed the object should be to pursue them so as to minimise as far as possible by pre-announcing, by ensuring credibility, people making mistakes.

(Minford 1980: 35)

Keynesian economists, including Kaldor (1980) and the NIESR (1980) pointed out that the strategy to tighten both fiscal and monetary policies was likely to lead to further deflation, especially in the context of 1980 when Keynesian economists had continued to argue that the oil price increases had both deflationary and inflationary effects on the British economy. As far as these economists were concerned what was needed was for the government to increase demand through fiscal policy to deal with the problem of deflation but also to impose an incomes policy to curb the problem of inflation. Keynesians felt that further reductions in public expenditure and high interest rates were likely to exacerbate the problems of deflation. In April 1981, the letter sent to *The Times* signed by 364 economists suggested that:

there is no basis in economic theory or supporting evidence for the government's belief that by deflating demand they bring inflation permanently under control and thereby induce an automatic recovery in output and employment...present policies will deepen the depression, erode the industrial base of our economy...there are alternative policies and the time has come to reject monetarist policies.

Keynesian economists also argued that the fall in unemployment after 1983 was due to the relaxation of both monetary and fiscal policy by the government. While the government insisted that there had been no policy U-turns from their original strategy, Keynesians pointed out that the reductions in personal taxation after 1983 – together with increases in public expenditure and lower interest rates – had acted on the economy as a classical Keynesian reflation by increasing demand. In contrast, the government wanted to argue that their reductions in taxation, together with trade union reform, have been the major influencing factors on the supply side of the economy increasing incentives, investment, and labour flexibility.

While the government continued to make monetarist statements there was actually a gap between appearance and reality in economic policy-making. Although the government continued to update their medium-term financial strategy, the emphasis on the money supply and interest rates had shifted. After the election of 1983 and the appointment of Nigel Lawson as Chancellor of the Exchequer, adherence to money supply targets became more agnostic as the Chancellor continued to point to the use of other economic levers beside the control of money aggregates to direct economic policy. Nigel Lawson inherited the lowest rates of inflation of just under 4 per cent in 1983 yet for the rest of his period as Chancellor, that is between 1983 and November 1989, inflation continued to edge upwards. The Treasury under Nigel Lawson had changed their economic priorities from the control of inflation to a commitment to growth and the reduction of unemployment, so that since 1983 monetary policy has been relaxed while reductions in taxation and increases in public expenditure were used to increase the level of demand and the rate of economic growth.

After the 1987 election there were further major policy shifts. The first indicator came after the Great Crash in October 1987 when stocks and equities lost over 40 per cent of their value on Black Monday. The Group of Seven (also known as G7) agreed on the need to co-ordinate policies, which meant that for the first time since the breakdown of Bretton Woods in 1973 there was agreement between the major nations to allow interest rates to fall and, therefore, avert competitive interest rates and exchange rates. G7 were agreed that the Stock Exchange crash and the fall in the value of shares would have led to fall in demand and consumption. By allowing interest rates to fall G7 hoped that the rates of growth experienced since 1983 could be sustained. The fall in interest rates in the UK in October 1987 were accompanied by increases in public expenditure announced during the autumn statement of November 1987. The Chancellor Nigel Lawson also announced further tax cuts in the March 1988 budget to fulfil the Conservative pledge of reducing the higher rate of tax to 40 per cent and basic income tax to 25 per cent.

Although there was no actual announcement of a policy change it now seems clear that the Chancellor had also replaced domestic monetary policy with an exchange rate policy of tracking sterling against the Deutschmark around a 3 DM exchange rate. Alan Walters (1990) has recently argued that this was a major policy error by the Chancellor. In moving towards fixed exchange rates at a high rate of interest in 1987, sterling became a very attractive investment to foreign financial institutions which meant that there was a large inflow of capital into the UK which therefore led to the expansion of the money supply, the expansion of credit, and the present inflation. The Chancellor had also lowered interest rates to prevent sterling from rising above 3 DM in 1988, thus stimulating the economy further and increasing the problems of inflation.

The effects of this overall stimulus were not very clear in 1987 and 1988 although some commentators were critical of the 1988 budget as being inflationary. However, it was difficult to criticise the Chancellor for his reflationary policy especially after a decade of high unemployment. The Chancellor had achieved a major objective of his policy as the rate of unemployment started to fall very rapidly. Between 1987 and 1989 unemployment had fallen from a peak of 3 million to just under 1.6 million (from 12 per cent of the working population to 6 per cent). The economy in the meantime was growing at over 4 per cent per annum. However, this rate of growth was difficult for the UK economy to sustain as the balance of payments started to deteriorate in 1988. The expansion of demand was leading to an increase in the rate of imports which were outstripping exports. The forecasts on the balance of payments for 1988 showed a deficit of £14 billion; this was revised to £20 billion in 1989 and £20 billion in 1990. The rate of inflation had increased from 6 per cent in 1987 to 9 per cent in 1989.

Britain's long-term economic problems seemed to be re-emerging in 1990. The balance of payments constraint which had been an obstacle to UK growth in the 1960s and 1970s had again become a problem in the late 1980s. The difference in the 1980s was that Britain had North Sea Oil so rather than importing oil as in the 1950s and 1960s, Britain was an oil exporter in the 1980s which should have meant higher levels of exports to counterbalance imports. In addition the re-emergence of inflation in 1989 and 1990 also seemed to reinforce the view that the government's success on inflation during the early 1980s was mainly due to the rise in unemployment. As the rate of growth in unemployment slowed down and the unemployed became the long-term unemployed, tighter labour markets meant that those in work were able to exert new pressures on employers despite the new climate of industrial relations. Inflation has again become the major priority for the government. Much of the rise in the new inflation has been blamed by monetarist economists on the economic policies pursued by Nigel Lawson since 1987. Fundamental monetarists such as Tim Congdon have for example continued to argue that the problem of inflation is due to government's neglect of monetary policy.

The government's policy on inflation since November 1989 has been to maintain a high level of interest rates. According to the former Chancellor John Major, interest rates were to remain high as long as inflation stayed high, a policy which is likely to be pursued by the new Chancellor Norman Lamont. With Britain inside the EMS attempts to reduce interest rates are now more restricted to changes in sterling value. Fiscal policy can be described as being very tight. During 1988 and 1989 the government have turned a PSBR into a Repayment of the National Debt as revenue to the government has been increasing at a faster rate than public expenditure. The problem of private consumption, however, seems to be more difficult to bring under control. Although since the middle of 1988 interest rates have continued to ratchet upwards from 7 per cent to 15 per cent in 1990, the major impact on consumption has been in the demand for housing as house prices continue to depreciate. High interest rates affect the costs of mortgages but whether the higher mortgage repayments result in less consumer spending continues to be a problem for UK inflation.

The government has been criticised for their use of a single weapon to deal with the problem of inflation. The use of interest rates, while excluding other policy options such as the control of credit and incomes policy is criticised because the Chancellor seems to be refuting other explanations as to the causes of inflation. City Analysts including Gavin Davis at Goldman and Sachs, and economic forecasters at Phillips and Drew and Hoare Govett, have continued to point out that the policy of high interest rates continues to be a blunt instrument in dealing with inflation. High interest rates do not differentiate between curbing consumer spending and invest-ment. So while the Chancellor and the Treasury attempt to control consumer spending through high interest rates, the policy of high interest rates also creates problems of investment. The argument is that the policy could lead to a similar recession to that experienced in 1980 and 1981, and that the gains made on unemployment since 1987 could be reversed. Since June 1990 the rate of UK unemployment has again started to rise at about 5,000 per month.

The question of whether the Treasury is succeeding to achieve a soft landing without pushing the economy into recession remains a major concern for the government as economic indicators continue to yield conflicting interpretations as to what impact interest rates are having on the economy. While CBI surveys and FT reports continue to show a fall in consumer spending, and quarterly comparisons on the balance of trade indicate a slowdown in the rate of the growth of imports – all of which suggests that the policy of high interest rates is having some effect on demand – other surveys on pay settlements and earnings show that pay settlements are continuing to rise which in turn continues to exert pressure on inflation and, therefore, unit labour costs.

ASSESSING ECONOMIC POLICY DURING THE THATCHER YEARS

The macroeconomy

Output, growth and the unbalanced economy

The attempt to assess the impact of Mrs Thatcher's governments on the British economy has to contend with contradictory indicators as to what has been happening since 1979. For example, in citing the theme of productivity as being one of the major achievements of the Thatcher years, economists are not agreed as to whether there had been a miracle and what factors had actually contributed to the increase in UK productivity. UK growth per head between 1979 and 1987 has been estimated at 4.5 per cent per annum in contrast to 2.7 per cent during the previous eight years and the 3.7 per cent improvements among the UK's major competitors. Using the National Institute model to predict productivity gains over the last year eight years, Wren Lewis and Darby (1989) have argued that the NIESR model has helped to explain 38 per cent of the 39 per cent increase. The argument is that the model set up by NIESR was able to explain most of the growth without taking into consideration the Thatcher effect. Muellbauer (1988), for example, has estimated that factor productivity between 1980 and 1987 had increased by 3.15 per cent per annum in contrast to 2.63 per cent between 1959 and 1972, while Phillips and Drew in 1988 have produced estimates to show that labour productivity in manufacturing between 1981 and 1986 had increased by 4.8 per cent per annum and in the service sector by 3.5 per cent per annum. According to these indicators it would seem feasible to suggest that Britain did experience a structural change, achieving a rate of growth of 4.5 per cent between 1982 and 1987. The question, however, is to what extent did these improvements represent a permanent improvement? The OECD (1988) has pointed out that while the employed labour force was falling at about 0.6 per cent a year between 1982 and 1986, the rate of capital stock was increasing at 2.6 per cent per annum over the same period. According to the OECD, therefore, more than 50 per cent of the increase in productivity was related to the substitution of capital for labour. A more permanent improvement in productivity has to show that gains in output are either related to more effective uses of capital investment or the more efficient use of labour inputs.

Increases in output and growth without increases in employment produce an unbalanced economy which tends to benefit those who are in paid employment, particularly in those sectors which benefit from the use of new technologies. Layard has been critical of the argument that companies should continue to reward increases in productivity. His argument is that gains in productivity should be passed on as lower costs and lower prices as a means of widening the benefits of production. There is no reason why the utilisation of information technology and the benefits of production should be limited to those who work in that industry. Lower prices are also likely to benefit the economy because consumers will be able to spend the increases in their income elsewhere in the economy thus improving the levels of demand, output, and employment.

The balance of payments

The question is whether the rising deficits on the current account since 1988 represent the re-emergence of the UK balance of payments constraint and therefore whether they should be interpreted as the new threat to the recent growth. Some economists have suggested that the present deficit is different to that of the 1950s and 1960s in that the deficits accumulated during the Macmillan and Wilson years had been mainly due to increases in demand brought about by government expenditure. In contrast, the deficit in the 1980s can be mainly attributed to private inward investment and consumption. The only threat of the balance of payments to the economy depends on whether overseas holders of sterling continue to have confidence in the government's exchange rate policy. If holders of sterling reach the conclusion that the government will seek to correct the balance of payments by allowing sterling to depreciate then the fall in the value of sterling is likely to create problems of inflation as investors sell their holdings of sterling thus devaluing sterling further; this in turn would mean higher import prices and more inflation. The balance of payments could become a serious problem, then, only if overseas investors lose confidence in the UK economy and shift their portfolio holdings away from sterling. The way the government can seek to avoid a fall in sterling's value, therefore, is to ignore the siren calls of industrialists for a fall in interest rates to improve exports and instead to continue to show their commitment to protect the value of sterling at whatever interest rate is required. Such a policy would contradict the view that sterling might be overvalued. This argument runs counter to the views of market liberal economists who have advocated that the problem of Britain's balance of payments represents a problem of an overvalued sterling and, therefore, what is needed is for interest rates to fall to allow sterling to depreciate.

The problem of wage costs and wage inflation

As unemployment continued to fall in the 1980s from a peak of 3.2 million in 1983 to 1.6 million by January 1990, the rate of wage increases and pay settlements have again become a major problem for the UK despite a decade of industrial relations reform. While unit costs in manufacturing were rising by 1 per cent per annum in 1987, by 1990 these costs were rising at 5 per cent per annum. The tightness of labour markets and the shortages of key workers have put pressure on employers to meet high wage demands to avoid the risk of losing skilled workers. The problem of wage drift outlined by the Donovan Report in 1968 seems to be re-emerging as decentralised bargains are again becoming the norm in wage negotiations. Furthermore, it would seem that issues in pay bargaining such as the going rate have not been replaced by market principles despite the last ten years. The Ford settlement in January 1990 of 10.2 per cent for craft workers was seen as setting the going rate for skilled workers for 1990, as were the bank settlements of 8.3 per cent seen as setting the norm for clerical workers. In 1990, therefore, the issue of wages has again become an issue for the government. It would seem that insider groups of professionals and highly skilled employees are increasingly able to press home their advantage from increases in productivity and skill shortages. Despite the government's commitments to the concept of labour mobility and more open access to labour markets, the wage gaps between unionised and non-unionised workers continue as do the inequalities between skilled and non-skilled workers. The choice for the government as an election approaches will be whether to allow inflation to rise or to use interest rates and a high exchange rate to put pressure on employers, therefore allowing unemployment to rise.

The MTFS was seen as the most explicit commitment by government to a specific economic doctrine. It confirmed the degree of commitment by the Thatcher government to monetarist explanations and policies towards inflation by making clear associations between inflation, the money supply, and the public sector deficit. Within the context of the MTFS it was, therefore, seen that the government had made clear that they proposed to deal with inflation by seeking to influence the rate of monetary growth. The MTFS contained paths for the public sector borrowing requirement (PSBR), the money supply defined as £M3, and inflation. Implicit to the MTFS was the argument that the government should announce to bargaining agents – that is employers and trade unions – how they intended to deal with the expansion of the money supply. This meant that the government would not underwrite wage increases by accommodating increases in the money supply. In future, if companies resorted to borrowing to finance pay increases, they were likely to be confronted with higher costs as interest rates were to be used to reflect the cost of borrowing.

The second element to the MTFS was the control of public expenditure and the reduction of the PSBR. Both bank lending to the private sector and the PSBR were seen as being the major contributors to increasing the money supply and, therefore, inflation. The reduction of the PSBR was seen as being consistent with the government's strategy for the control of the money supply and inflation. Furthermore the PSBR was also associated with financial crowding out in that the higher the PSBR the higher the rate of interest since both the private and public sectors were competing for a fixed amount of savings. A lower PSBR was desirable because it reduced pressures on the rate of interest and, therefore, made it more feasible for the private sector to invest. It also helped to reduce inflation.

One major success for the government has been the reduction of the PSBR. However, the importance that was accorded to the PSBR in the struggle to reduce inflation was seen as being more of a political preference. In January 1980, Nigel Lawson, who was then Financial Secretary to the Treasury, argued as follows on the importance of reducing the PSBR as the path to the reduction of inflation:

Let me start with two simple facts. The first is a statistic. The PSBR is at present about 4.5 per cent of total gross domestic product (GDP) – compared with an average of only 2.5 per cent in the 1960s. The second is an economic relationship. That is, the PSBR and the growth of the money supply and interest rates are very closely related. Too high a PSBR requires either that the government borrow heavily from the banks – which adds directly to the money supply; or, failing this, that it borrows from individuals and institutions but at ever increasing rates of interest which places an unacceptable squeeze on the private sector.

According to Nigel Lawson's thesis both the 'funded' and 'unfunded' elements of the PSBR were damaging to the economy. The funded PSBR led to higher interest rates which then 'crowded out private sector investment, while the unfunded part led to an increase in the money supply and, therefore, inflation. Kaldor (1980), in his evidence to the Select Committee on Monetary Policy, had produced data which indicated that the relationship between the 'unfunded' part of the PSBR and the growth of £M3 had produced a poor correlation, while bank lending to the private sector did produce a more positive relationship. According to Kaldor it was bank lending to the private sector which was the major contributor to monetary growth. He suggested, therefore, that the issue of the

> 'money supply' which is supposed to play such a key role in the sequence of events is really no more than a fig leaf (or at best a smoke-screen)....
> In fact the downward pressure on prices exerted by the money supply is non existent – it is a figment of the imagination. A downward pressure on prices in so far as it exists comes from the loss of price leadership of British firms to foreign producers in the home market and not just in foreign markets which results from the over valuation of the pound, the absence of trade barriers and the rapid fall of the home producers' share in the home market.
>
> (Kaldor 1980: 97)

Kaldor argued that the problem of inflation was still the problem of wage resistance, but rather than the government seeking to secure an incomes policy they had opted for the MTFS which in an indirect way sought to break with wage inflation by reducing the demand for labour. He, therefore, argued that the government's strategy would only succeed in curbing inflation through the creation of unemployment. That would bring trade unions to heel and have a consequent effect on wage settlements eventually. The problem was whether all workers would feel equally threatened by the rise in unemployment:

> If the Government succeeds in its object, it is likely to do so by causing wages to fall behind in the 'weak sectors'. Past experience suggests that

the 'tattered wage structure that would emerge from this process is not likely to be viable and the workers in the disadvantaged sectors will take every opportunity to regain their normal status in the scale of relative earnings.

(Kaldor 1980: 96)

As far as Kaldor and other Keynesian economists are concerned the problems of the present inflation had been predicted in 1980 when they had argued that inflation was due to cost-push factors. The MTFS was seen to succeed only while unemployment was rising, however, once workers felt that the unemployed were not a threat then they sought to restore their earnings by demanding higher pay settlements. Further, as unemployment started to decrease, the problem of wage inflation has reasserted itself.

Whilst since 1980 the government have continued to update the MTFS paths for money supply and inflation, the actual outturns of monetary growth – whether measured as £M3 or M0[1] – have continued to overshoot their targets. Since the recession of 1982 the government has not used interest rates to respond to the problems of monetary growth. The MTFS has, therefore, been seen by some economists as having been abandoned by the government, which is in turn used to explain why the problems of inflation have re-emerged. For these economists, including Congdon (1982) for example, the problem is that the government has shifted from the central principles of monetarism of controlling the money supply.

The resignation of Nigel Lawson as Chancellor of the Exchequer in November 1989 confirmed the extent of his disagreement with Mrs Thatcher and her adviser Sir Alan Walters. They argued that the Treasury should have used M0 as the indicator to decide monetary policy while Nigel Lawson seemed to prefer an exchange rate policy to control inflation. Nigel Lawson had argued that monetary targets had proved to be unreliable indicators on forecasting inflation. His preferred policy was, therefore, to shadow the Deutschmark because of the record of the West German Bundesbank on inflation. The disagreement seemed to be as to what had caused the rise in inflation after October 1987. Sir Alan had indirectly blamed Nigel Lawson for the current inflation when the latter had abandoned monetary policy in favour of shadowing the Deutschmark at around 3 DM, which meant having to devalue sterling and allowing interest rates to fall. Because Sir Alan's views were also seen as reflecting the views of the Prime Minister, the position for the Chancellor became more difficult since it seemed that there was a central disagreement between the Prime Minister and her Chancellor in the conduct of an anti-inflation strategy. Mrs Thatcher's view on the exchange rate was that government cannot buck the market, which indirectly means that government should not attempt to protect the currency. The question whether the problem of inflation was best managed through a tight monetary policy or whether the exchange rate was a better indicator seems to have resulted in uncertainty in economic management during 1989. According to Mr Roger Bootle, UK Economist at Grenwell Montague, the concept behind the MTFS was that policy was going to be conducted according to prescribed rules; however, the downgrading of the MTFS meant that:

> The whole philosophy of conducting policy by a set of rules has been undermined and we are now back to the 60s and 70s when policy was operated by the seat of the pants and relied on judgement.
>
> (Roger Bootle, *Financial Times*, 23 February 1990)

UK inflation and international finance

There is, however, a third argument which goes beyond the Keynesian/monetarist debates as to the causes and cures to the present inflation; it is an argument which takes into consideration the changing financial markets and, therefore, the location of UK inflation in that wider context. The decision by the UK government in 1980 to remove the corset of exchange controls meant that UK finance become more open to outside competition as other financial institutions entered the UK lending market. According to this argument, the increased availability of finance contributed to UK consumers shifting their portfolios into higher levels of credit to finance present consumption, which in turn resulted in an increased level of demand which could not have been predicted by the Chancellor or the Treasury. Furthermore, it would now seem that interest rates will have a more effective role to play in influencing the level of demand. Consumers faced with a high level of credit and high interest rates repayments on mortgages and debt repayments will, in future, have less disposable income to purchase new goods. High interest rates will, therefore, influence consumer demand more directly. The question for the government will be whether workers will seek to compensate for the increases in interest rates by offsetting the increases against higher wage settlements.

While monetarist economists argued that the policy instrument of interest rates was the most effective way to contain the pressure on monetary growth and inflation, it would seem that high interest rates in the present climate could be the cause of recent inflationary pressures. The servicing of debt has become more expensive as mortgage repayments have increased from an average of 15 per cent of disposable income to 23 per cent – the equivalent to an additional 10p on income tax. The argument that increases in the tax burden were likely to be inflationary because workers sought to compensate for reductions in their take-home pay now applies to interest rates.

Microeconomic policy

Supply side economics

Within the context of creating a framework for markets and enterprise to flourish, three major changes in policy might be considered as contributing directly to the structural adjustment to the supply side of the UK economy. The reform of trade union law, the privatisation of major public sector monopolies, and the deregulation of exchange controls could be judged as being part of the government's supply side economics. For example, the programme of privatisation has not only helped the government to reduce the PSBR and also use the extra revenues for tax reforms, but has also ensured that the industries which were privatised did improve on their record of productivity and labour costs. The brunt of the unemployment in the early 1980s was experienced at British Steel and British Leyland. The reform of trade unions is also seen as a major achievement because the legislation will endure irrespective of changes in government. Members of trade unions now accept that there should be ballots before strikes and that trade union officers are elected by secret ballot. Brittan (1988) sees the deregulation of exchange controls as a major achievement because the policy ensured that the UK economy became part of the global network in the inflows and outflows of capital when companies were threatened by mergers and rationalisation as profits and dividends became critical to survival. Brittan suggests that the short termism of the financial institutions provided the impetus for the longer-term prosperity of companies which were threatened by takeovers and closures.

Industrial policy

While both the French and West German governments have maintained an interventionist policy towards their key industries – including coal, steel, and communications – either by providing subsidies or by direct involvement, the aim of the UK government has been to reduce the role of government. Since 1979 government support for industry through the Department of Trade and Industry has been reduced by over £11 billion. Most of the funding directed towards investment grants and regional policy has been phased out. Under the banner of enterprise, the government points to the inward investment by Japanese companies over the last decade as an indicator of success. Industrial policy is seen as shifting from the provision of subsidies aimed at helping large companies towards a policy which seeks to encourage the expansion of small companies by providing funds for enterprise, innovation, and flexibility such as the Enterprise Initiative and Business Enterprise Allowance. The government has also accepted the argument that an integral part of an industrial strategy must be a commitment to training and producing a highly skilled labour force. The setting up of twelve Training Enterprise Councils in 1990, to be managed by industrialists, aims to provide firms with advice on issues of training and the updating of skills of their employees. The government has also made a commitment to provide an extra 50,000 places at Universities and Colleges of Higher Education over the next five years. So although the funding for these measures might appear within the expenditure plans of the Departments of Employment and Education, these initiatives are seen to be an important part of the government's industrial policy. Increasingly, however, with the phasing out of the industrial levy and the closures of the Industrial Training Boards, while relying on a voluntary system of training, the problems of hoarding and bottle-necks for craft workers are re-emerging as companies compete for skilled workers in the context of falling unemployment and tight labour markets. Since training represents a cost to companies, leaving training to the market place seems to confirm two problems of market failure – namely, the problem of externality and spillover effects. As France and Germany continue to outstrip the UK in the training of skilled workers the issue of investment in human capital is likely to become of central concern to the UK economy in the 1990s.

CONCLUSIONS

The study of economic policy since 1979 would indicate that the conduct of policy has contained evidence both of the radical aspects of Thatcherism as well as indicators of continuity and the concern with the politics of statecraft. Those who point to the radical nature of Thatcherism including Holmes (1989), Young (1989), Jenkins (1987), and Keegan (1983) tend to see Thatcherism as reflecting the break with post-war settlement and Keynesian economics. In contrast, those who are sceptical point to the lack of commitment within Thatcherism to market liberal principles despite the language of markets, competition, individualism and enterprise and other discourses which have become associated with the concept of Thatcherism. According to these sceptics (who include Samuel Brittan), the Thatcher government have continued to commit funds to mortgage tax relief, tax relief on pensions, and subsidies to farming interests despite their adverse effects on the market place.

The question as to what constitutes a civilised economy has always been central to those Keynesian economists who have argued that pay, inflation, and employment were inextricably linked and what was, therefore, needed was an informed discussion between strategic participants to construct a policy for price stability, growth, and prosperity. According to these economists, a Keynesian economic strategy went beyond the utilisation of fiscal and monetary levers and that what was equally important were institutions capable of delivering a policy on incomes to deal with inflationary pressures. The question is: Why has the UK been either unable or unwilling to embrace a more civilised approach to pay bargaining similar to that of Japan or West Germany? In these economies a process of consensus building takes place to determine what the economy can afford before the annual pay round gets underway; in contrast, in the UK the primary concern of trade unions has continued to be their commitment to a 'voluntary' system of industrial relations where there is little intervention from the state and where free collective bargaining is seen as central to the role of the democratic rights of trade unions. Trade unions in the UK, therefore, tend to prefer the role of being in opposition rather than being incorporated by government into an overall strategy for the economy.

The Thatcher governments eschewed the concept of the politics of consent and instead sought to produce an economic policy which was guided by rules which applied equally to all individuals. The Thatcher governments were critical of what they saw as the failure of corporatist politics – namely, the process that had contributed to the UK's economic problems of high inflation, rising unemployment, and low growth. The politics of consent produced preferential access to certain vested interests while other interests were marginalised. Within the context of the post-war settlement increases in public expenditure on housing subsidies, food prices, and nationalised industries' prices had become central to the building of the consensus. However, while these subsidies seemed to benefit workers in the public sector, major trade unions and employer interests, they resulted in a higher tax burden and increased government borrowing. According to the Thatcher government, the price of exacting an incomes policy had been too high. Instead, the new government outlined within the MTFS their strategy for dealing with inflation. The priority of the Conservative government was to reduce inflation by reducing government borrowing and using interest rates to maintain control over the money supply. The rate of increase in public expenditure was seen as being at the heart of Britain's economic problems because it had contributed to the inflationary pressures of the 1970s and also to a higher tax burden, which in turn was leading to lower incentives. While the government did depart from any explicit attempt to secure an incomes policy, they still continued to have an implicit incomes policy for public sector workers by imposing strict cash limits on public expenditure. Since 1980 the government has tended to underestimate the rate of inflation which has in turn meant that public sector workers have had to accept lower wage settlements than their counterparts in the private sector. The question is whether the gap in earnings will become permanent or whether there will be a catching up phase as public sector workers seek to restore their position in the earnings table.

The government also seemed resolute – despite the steep increases in unemployment between 1980 and 1982 – not to resort to Keynesian demand management. While the oil price increases of 1979/80 did deflate consumer demand, the government allowed interest rates to rise in line with the commitments outlined in the MTFS. The rise in interest rates, together with the increase in the value of sterling, resulted in a sharp decline of exports markets and an increase in imports. Furthermore, the government also decided to reduce public expenditure. These policy decisions were seen as representing a major break with Keynesian demand management.

Those who argue that Thatcherism represents a radical agenda which broke with the post-war consensus will, therefore, emphasise the reform of industrial relations since 1980, the MTFS, the willingness of the government to live with a high rate of unemployment, the commitment to squeeze inflation out of the economy, and the break with the politics of consent. All of these elements are perceived as constituting a radical departure in economic policy-making – from the attempts to fine tune the economy through macroeconomic policy, to policies aimed at reforming the supply side of the economy. Trade union reform, reforms of personal taxation and the benefit system are, therefore, seen as providing a coherent labour market policy to increase equality of access, mobility and a more flexible labour market. Improvements in productivity over the last decade are judged as confirming the extent to which the government has succeeded in reforming the micro foundations of the economy.

In contrast, those who are sceptical about the radical nature of Thatcherism will point to the government's continued concerns with the political arithmetic of their policies, rather than the morals of a market liberal political economy. Despite the government's rhetoric of phasing out subsidies to powerful vested interests, they still remained committed to the maintenance of mortgage tax relief and other benefits including tax allowances on pensions. Government policies on taxation and social security have made society more unequal, which means that income has become increasingly important in determining people's life chances. Access to health care, and education opportunities are now determined more by people's ability to pay; yet within the context of market liberalism such inequalities will result in the loss of efficiency, especially when a society can no longer explore the abilities of all individuals. The Thatcher government is therefore criticised because of their concern to protect the interests of those groups who are likely to become an electoral majority. It is thus a government which is concerned with protecting the living standards of those who are insiders within the labour market rather than one which seeks to increase access to outsiders. Mortgage tax relief helps most those who are already housed, and it contributes towards increases in house prices which in turn reduce labour mobility. Unemployed craft workers in the North of England cannot compete for job vacancies available in Swindon or Oxford which means that those craft workers who already live

Figure 11.3   How the economy fared in the Thatcher era

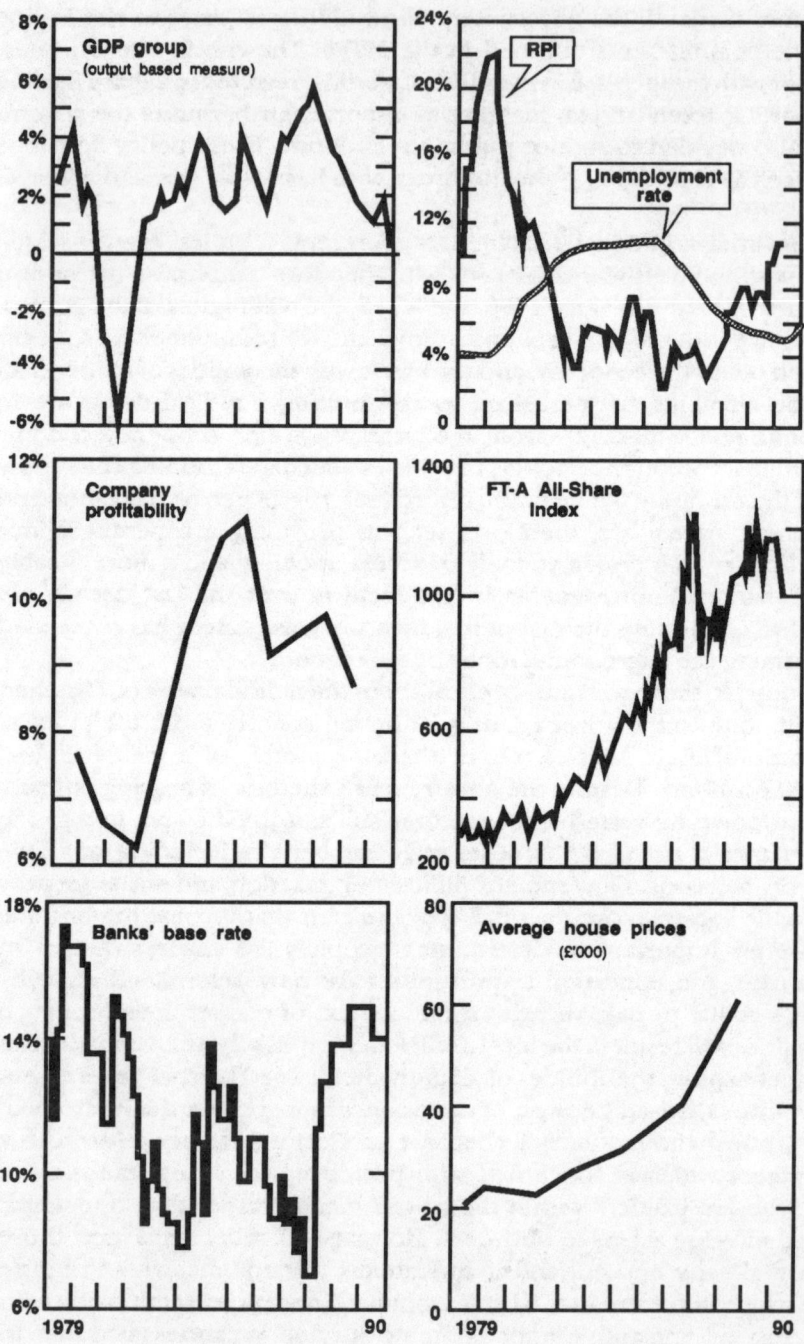

Source: *Financial Times*, 23 November 1990

in these prosperous areas can exert even more pressures on their employers, knowing that there is no real threat from the unemployed.

The view that the government broke with Keynesian economics is also questionable. While the government argues that a tax reduction is aimed at improving incentives, to Keynesian economists tax reductions influence demand. The depreciation of sterling after 1983, the continued reductions in interest rates, and tax reductions all contributed to increase demand and explain why unemployment has continued to fall. While the government might argue that there have been no policy U-turns, keener observers will point to the increasing disparity between the appearances of policy statements and the realities of policies. The government might argue that according to their perspective they have improved the supply side of the economy. Those who are sceptical will point to the effects of policy on the demand side of the economy.

NOTE

1 M0 is defined as notes and coins in circulation and in bank tills, plus the operational balances that banks place with the Bank of England.
£M3 is defined on page 250.

Chapter 12

Conclusions

The options for economic policy in the 1990s

INTRODUCTION: AUTONOMY AND CONSTRAINTS IN ECONOMIC POLICY

Economists might contend that the subject of economics is concerned with the understanding of three crucial questions, these being: how do societies 'organise' themselves to deal with issues of what to produce?, once this is decided, how to produce a good?, and then, for whom should the good be produced? The student of politics, however, will point out that questions concerned with issues of production, allocation and distribution are not just economic questions which require 'rational' economic answers, and will contend that they cannot be separated from issues of political judgement. The debate whether such crucial questions should be left to the market place or whether government should intervene, therefore continues to be a political question. Issues which appear to be economic involve political choice, political judgement, and political calculation; that is, a choice between competing policy options and the relationships between political ideology and policy and also between political principles and the pragmatism of the electoral cycle.

The question of what to produce involves political choice. Governments can use subsidies to influence both investment and levels of demand for certain goods and services, such as tax incentives on unleaded petrol or mortgage tax relief or use tariffs to protect the domestic market from outside competition. The setting of economic objectives also reflects political judgement when they pledge a commitment to a policy of full employment, as it is equally political when they announce that employment is determined by market forces. The comparative studies of Hibbs (1977) and Tufte (1978) have tended to confirm that Social Democratic parties are more likely to make employment their major policy objective while Conservative parties tend to make inflation their central economic objective. Political parties therefore seek to reflect the priorities of their constituents. The commitment to a policy of full employment is politically very different to a policy of curbing inflation since the benefits of low inflation or low unemployment do not affect the same groups of people. While low inflation benefits those with savings and groups on fixed incomes including pensioners, the commitment to a policy of full employment is likely to benefit those who tend to be more vulnerable to unemployment. A policy of full employment also reduces the threat of unemployment and therefore shifts the balance of power away from employers towards trade unions in the wage bargaining process. When in 1980, the Thatcher government declared that inflation was the number one evil, and that the priority of the government was to squeeze out inflation even if it meant subordinating other objectives including the levels of unemployment, the setting of inflation as the major priority represented a political judgement.

At a second level, ideology relates to the question of how economic policy is conducted. While governments might make a commitment to full employment, it cannot be assumed that they have either the ability or the autonomy to steer the economy in such a way as to achieve their declared policy objective. They usually require the co-operation of strategic economic groups and other interest groups to moderate their wages and prices and to make the policy of full employment feasible. The decision to move towards a corporatist politics, which means involving functional groups in the policy process, is a political decision in that some governments do seek to encourage a climate of conducting policy by consensus, while others favour a vision of strong government not making concessions to vested interests but using the authority of being the elected government which serves the interests of individuals.

Third, there is also political calculation in the choice between competing economic discourses. Since there are always competing policy options to deal with the stated policy objective, governments choose between policy alternatives. In making a commitment to squeeze out inflation, the government have a variety of policy options; they can seek to secure an incomes policy to moderate cost-push inflation or use interest rates as a means of curbing demand. There is therefore a process in which economists use their ideas of how the economy works to seek to influence the hearts and minds of government. However, since the major concern of the government is to remain the incumbent government, they are not in the business of committing themselves to one set of economic ideas at the cost of abandoning other policy options. Inevitably, therefore, economic policy is influenced by the electoral cycle, the proximity of an election, and the aim of the government to enter the election on a record of economic competence at least in the short term.

However, while politics does influence economic policy, it is important to emphasise the extent to which the economic context itself is a constraint on political choice. Although governments do have autonomy to give the economy political direction, this does not imply that all economic decisions are political. There is equally a need to be aware of the limits of government in their ability to give direction to the economy. Governments are also involved in producing responses to economic events which are not within their direct control. Chancellors of the Exchequer have no direct influence on the sentiments of financial markets, investment institutions, holders of sterling or other strategic groups. Their main hope is that their objectives are perceived to be creditable policies.

Economic policy-making represents the dual relationship between autonomy and constraint – that is, the continuous voyage between the wider economic context which can both enable and restrain the choice of policy, and the political priorities of government. These 'enabling' and 'constraining' economic factors can both be internal to the national economy and include strategic economic groups such as trade unions, employers' organisations, and other interest groups which are politically important to the government. Other internal constraints involve the workings of government and the tensions that exist between departments of governments, including the continuing battles b .ween the priorities of spending ministers and the Treasury. It also invol.es the dynamics of political parties, the structure and organisation of parties, and the influence of factions within parties. Political parties do not adhere to some coherent ideology, instead they reflect uneasy alliances between diverging interests and it is therefore important to be aware of the ascendency of factions and their impact on political priorities and judgement. Like the Labour Party, the Conservative Party is made up of factions. The election of Mrs Thatcher as leader of the Conservative Party in 1975, confirmed the ascendency of market liberals within the Party, reflecting a break from the dominance of Conservative leaders such as Macmillan, Butler and Heath (and the One Nation Group) who had influenced Conservative Party thinking since 1945. Equally, the challenge of Michael Heseltine to Mrs Thatcher's leadership in November 1990 reflected the re-emergence of One Nation Conservatism as against the market liberalism of Mrs Thatcher and the No Turning Back Group. At present Prime Minister John Major is associated with the thinking of Boyle and Macleod.

In addition, there are external factors which also limit the autonomy of government. The international context and the increased integration of the world economy means that the autonomy of government is increasingly constrained by world financial markets, the movement of finance capital, and goods and services. The phasing out of exchange controls and the impact of international financial institutions on the UK market for savings and borrowing, means that the UK economy becomes more exposed to the world financial markets and governments less able to control domestic money supply. The recovery of the UK economy since the mid-1980s has been partially attributed to the availability of external finance and the willingness of UK consumers to switch their portfolios to a higher level of credit by using the prosperity from the higher value of their property to finance demand for goods and services. So while the government maintained a tight fiscal position by keeping a strict control on their own finances, it became more difficult to control bank lending to the private sector and therefore the rate of monetary growth.

The concerns during the following sections are twofold; the first is the attempt to draw together the relationships between the issues of economic necessity, politics and policy options, while the second seeks to explore the factors which are likely to act as a constraint and also the possible spaces for autonomy for UK government in economic policy-making during the 1990s. The attempt to evaluate the constraints on the UK economy during the next decade depends on the question of whether the British economy did experience a major structural shift over the last decade. Has there been an economic revolution since 1979 so that the underlying economic problems which seemed to besiege all post-war governments have now been resolved? Have ten years of Thatcherism resolved the problems of industrial relations and wage inflation? Also, has Britain's balance of payments been resolved and have North Sea Oil and the increases in productivity in manufacturing turned Britain into a successful export-led economy? Does Britain have the skilled labour force to enable British industry to compete with other major European economies in the production of high quality goods after 1992? Some would argue that the underlying economic problems remain and have actually worsened over the last ten years. Britain today is experiencing a balance of payments deficit of about £20 billion for the third successive year. Economists such as Wynne Godley of the Cambridge Economic Policy Group argue that such a deficit cannot be sustained in the long term. It would also seem that there still is a problem of wage inflation whilst in addition, according to recent studies (Mullard 1991), the move towards a system of voluntary training means that the UK is again faced with problems of skill shortages. Furthermore, Britain is investing less in training and therefore producing fewer skilled workers than either France or West Germany.

THE NATURE OF UK ECONOMIC POLICY SINCE 1945

The study of UK economy policy over the period 1945 to 1975 pointed the extent to which it had been conducted within a Butskellite framework, in contrast to claims that the UK economy had been harmed by an adversarial political system. Instead it would seem that while there continued to be policy differences between the two major parties, economic policy had been broadly conducted within a Keynesian model of demand management, where both Labour and Conservative governments had accepted the principles laid down by the White Paper on Employment Policy in 1944 which stated that, 'The Government accepts as one of their primary aims and responsibilities the maintenance of a high and stable level of employment after the war.'

It would also seem that both governments had accepted to make commitments to the principles of the welfare state as had been outlined in the Beveridge Report of 1942 for expanding the role of government in the provision of public welfare to remedy the problems of inadequate housing and inequalities in health care, and in addition to increase opportunities in education. These twin objectives – to full employment and an expanding welfare state – were therefore to be the foundations of the post-war social democratic consensus and also the framework for economic policy-making.

Furthermore, it can be pointed out that the break with the post-war settlement did not commence with the election of the Thatcher government in 1979. Instead, it can be argued that tentative steps towards the control of the money supply, public expenditure, and the reform of industrial relations had already been taken – first, during the chancellorship of Roy (now Lord) Jenkins with his 1969 budget, and then more importantly by the Labour government after 1976 when both the Prime Minister and the Chancellor Dennis Healey in their negotiations with the IMF and in the budget of 1977 eschewed Keynesian reflationary policies despite the increases in the rate of unemployment. It was also the Labour government which in 1969 outlined proposals for the reform of industrial relations which was followed by the Heath government's Trade Union Act of 1972. There is, therefore, sufficient evidence to suggest that the beginnings of the break with the post-war social democratic consensus had already started in the late 1960s as both Labour and Conservative administrations were becoming increasingly concerned with the UK's problems of accelerating inflation, the continuing balance of payments constraint, and the frequency of sterling crises.

The question of whether the UK economy today is qualitatively different to that of 1979 is crucial to how governments will respond to the challenges of the 1990s. The UK of 1979 was perceived as becoming increasingly ungovernable. The failures of the Heath and Labour governments to deal with trade union resistance, together with the problems of the public sector deficit, public expenditure, and rising inflation increased the pressures on the Thatcher government elected in 1979 to attempt to break with the past. The vision to create an enterprising economy meant reforming trade union law, pushing back the frontiers of government through a programme of denationalisation, and making a commitment to monetarism to deal with the problems of inflation and the public sector deficit.

At the beginning of the new decade it would seem that some of the old economic problems have re-emerged. Despite the reforms in industrial relations and the move towards decentralised pay bargaining, wage inflation has again become a major issue. It would now seem that the fall in inflation during the early 1980s had been mainly due to the rapid rise in unemployment. Both the decline in unemployment and the tighter labour markets, especially for skilled workers, mean that the problems of wage drift and leap-frogging in wage bargaining which had been forecast by the Donovan report in 1968, have re-asserted themselves in the early 1990s.

ECONOMIC POLICY AND THE ART OF THE POSSIBLE

The politics of intervention: issues of nationalisation and privatisation

While there is a strong case to be made on the nature of the consensus and the continuity of policy, there is also a need to keep in mind that economic policy also involves political judgement. The study of the nationalised industries, government subsidies to industry, and industrial policies, high-lights the nature of continuity and also the politics of economic policy. The programme of extensive nationalisation embarked upon by the Attlee government and the denationalisation of these industries since 1979 do not reflect differences of ideologies between the centralism and collectivism of the Labour Party and a liberal and more market-orientated Conservative Party. The logic of nationalising key industries had already started in the UK during the 1930s when the strategy for the rationalisation of industries was central to the industrial policies of the Conservative government. Harold Macmillan in his book *The Middle Way* had already made a Conservative case for state intervention and planning, arguing that governments did not have to choose between intervention and markets. The programme of nationalisation represented more of an attempt to generate new investment in key industries such as coal, electricity, gas and water, where the private owners of these industries were criticised for having failed the nation when the experience of planning for war had led to a general acceptance that state direction of the economy was likely to be effective. There was therefore little Conservative resistance to the programme of nationalisation, and even when the Conservatives did take office in 1951 they only denationalised steel, despite staying in government for the next thirteen years. Equally, it was the Heath government which, under the Industry Act of 1972, attempted to provide funding for investment in key industries, a strategy which was then expanded by the Labour government when they established the National Enterprise Board.

In this sense UK governments were no different to the governments of France, West Germany or Japan where the commitment to 'picking winners' in key industries embraced the nationalisation of economic sectors includ-ing banking, coal, and steel making. Irrespective of whether the incumbent government were conservative or social democratic, interventionist indus-trial policies became the norm in all of the major industrial countries. President de Gaulle found that there was no conflict in pursuing an industrial policy that was good for France which included the nationalisation of French banking and, on the other hand, his party's commitments to a market economy. In Japan also, where politics has been dominated by the Liberal Party, the role of the Ministry for International Trade and Industry (MITI) and its commitment to providing funding for research and development and other subsidies of key industries has not come into conflict with the government's continued commitment to competitive markets and free trade.

The example of nationalisation and industrial policy clearly illustrates that disagreements on policy do not arise from consistent ideological commitments to planning or enterprise but rather reinforce the argument that economic policy is mostly conducted within the context of what can be termed the art of the possible. Most governments have intervened, either directly by nationalising industries or indirectly by providing subsidies or through tariffs, to ensure that domestic demand was met through national industries. Governments have therefore tended to show a continued commitment to industries which are seen as being the foundations of the nation's manufacturing base. Industrial countries with a weakened manufacturing base depend more on imported goods, which in turn act as a constraint on economic growth and prosperity. No government would therefore allow the decline of their national industries because this would reflect the triumph of competitive markets.

While the governments of Mrs Thatcher were closely associated with having halted the upward ratchet of socialism because of their success in denationalising of most of the public utilities, the question of whether the programme of privatisation has been consistent with the objectives of competition policy or expanding popular capitalism is very much open to debate. The denationalisation of public utilities, including British Telecom, British Gas, and British Steel, confirmed the reluctance of the Thatcher government to break up these industries into smaller concerns and increase the number of suppliers. There has always been a tension in the privatisation programme between the priority of succeeding to shift these industries from public ownership and the principles of consumer sovereignty and competitive markets. The urgency to sell public sector assets, however, meant that the government had to ensure that the industries would be attractive enough to induce individual investors and financial institutions who were looking for stable rates of return and low risks in contrast to the uncertainty of the market place. In the end it would seem that the government has been more concerned in selling these industries rather than a commitment to a more competitive and open economy to new suppliers of gas or telecommunications. The individual consumer is still faced by a monopoly producer. The difference is that the producer has shifted from being a monopoly in the public sector to being one in the private sector. The impact of OFTEL and OFGAS as protectors of the consumer is limited by the inability of these regulators to define what is in the consumer interest or public interest, and also whether they control these new monopolies effectively when they are seen as behaving in a way that harms both the consumer and the public.

From the above discussion it would seem that the process of nationalisation and privatisation cannot be located within simple causal explanations. There are no direct relationships between economic ideas and economic policy, or between the influence of political ideologies and policy. It would be misleading to construct an argument which implies that the wave of nationalisation belonged to the age when Keynesian ideas were in the ascendant, while the shift towards privatisation belongs to the age of market liberalism and disillusion with the Keynesian interventionist state. Both the preparedness and the willingness of governments to intervene in the economy pre-date Keynesian economics. They actually parallel the thinking of the mercantilist state and the view of creating a strong nation state and national economy. Furthermore, it would seem that governments in the post-Second World War period have continued to be mercantilist towards their domestic economy while at the same time they have advocated policies of free trade and international competitive markets. In contrast, it was Keynes who criticised the emergence of tariffs and protectionism during the inter-war years and it was Keynesians who urged governments after the oil price increases of the 1970s about the need to co-ordinate the recycling of savings and investment and the reflation of the international economy.

The politics of intervention: choices and constraints of the EMS

The questions whether and when the UK was eventually to join the exchange rate mechanism (ERM) of the European Monetary System (EMS) highlighted the extent to which the decision was both political and economic. The reluctance of Mrs Thatcher to accept the advice of her Chancellor Nigel Lawson in 1987 to join the EMS and the threats of resignation by both the Chancellor and Sir Geoffrey Howe, reflected the pressures and tensions between senior ministers and the Prime Minister on the politics and the economics of the EMS. Mrs Thatcher's position hinged on her vision of sovereignty in economic policy-making and the argument therefore that the EMS represented an external constraint imposed on the UK government's autonomy in dealing with the problem of UK inflation. Those who favoured early entry argued that the autonomy of the policy-makers would actually be enhanced inside a system of fixed exchange rates. These commentators emphasised that the success of the West German and French economies represented examples of governments which committed themselves to a creditable policy of dealing with inflation rather than using economic policy to correspond with their short-term political interests. The argument against the EMS pointed to the loss of sovereignty, especially in making judgements on monetary policy. Once inside the EMS, British monetary policy will be decided by a European Bank that will act like the present Bundesbank, free from government intervention in the conduct of monetary policy. Within the EMS therefore, monetary policy will be de-politicised in the sense that governments will no longer have the autonomy to manage interest rates for electoral advantage. The argument about the loss of sovereignty is seen as being confined to the loss of political judgement.

There is, however, a paradox in that while Mrs Thatcher described herself to be an avowed monetarist her opposition to the EMS and her insistence that monetary policy should remain within the confines of Parliament represented a complete reversal of monetarist thinking. Monetarist economists accuse government of being political, of using borrowing to avoid raising taxation and therefore fuelling inflation. Monetarists want to squeeze the politics out of economic policy-making by ensuring that the central bank is made independent of political interference. Joining the EMS is therefore favoured on the basis that such a policy lessens political manipulation of monetary policy by a British government, which would in turn give greater credibility to the control of inflation.

The timing of the entry and the level of entry was equally a political question. The argument whether entry was to be within a 'wide' band of 6 per cent either way between the bottom and the top limit, and the argument for a narrower band of 3 per cent was both a technical and political argument. Those who advocated a wide band argued that this will prevent speculators who would otherwise be attracted to buy sterling within a fixed exchange rate thus benefiting from a guaranteed exchange rate and high interest rates offered by the UK. The argument is that the inflow of financial capital would increase the money supply and inflation. However, those who favoured a narrow band argue that this will act as a strong discipline against inflation in that exporters will be faced with a high sterling and will therefore be more determined to hold down wage settlements. Furthermore, the wide band approach was seen as a political choice since as sterling is likely to appreciate to the top of the band the government will use this as a lever to lower interest rates to prevent sterling overshooting the top limit of the band and therefore reduce mortgage costs in time for the next election but without having resolved to deal with the problem of inflation.

Joining the EMS to allow interest rates to fall in time for an election is seen as joining the EMS for the wrong reasons. The fall in interest rates and mortgage costs are likely to increase demand at a time when inflation is still rising. Furthermore, the fall in interest rates is likely to lead to new demands for housing which is likely to lead to a new house prices spiral. As the value of sterling falls there will be a surge in exports in the short term, thus reducing the incentive of employers to resist wage inflation.

Britain joined the EMS on 4 October 1990 within the wide band of 6 per

Figure 12.1   Inside the exchange rate mechanism: the twin problems
underlying earnings and unit labour costs

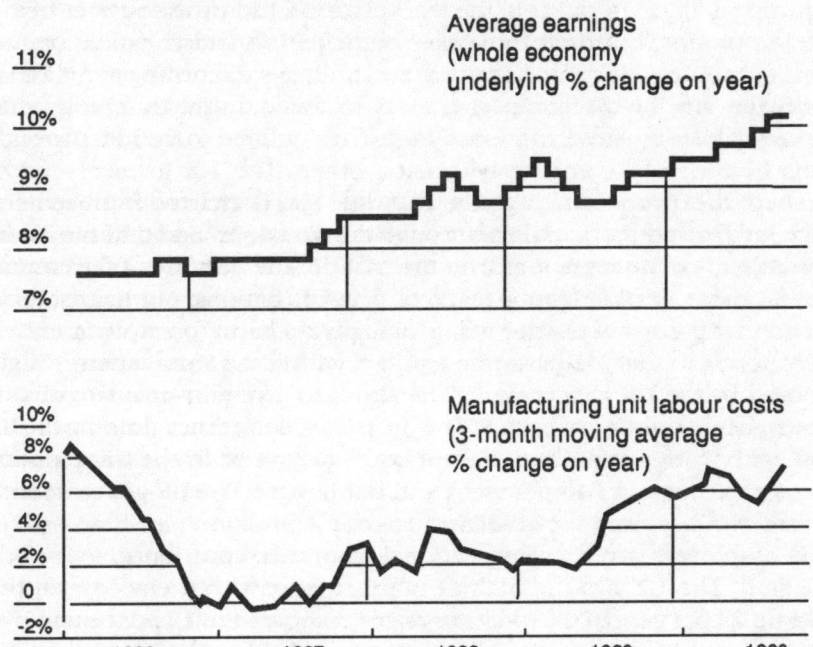

Source: Department of Employment, November 1990

cent against the Deutschmark. The interest rate was immediately reduced
by 1 per cent as sterling moved into the higher band. However, that
optimism was soon to be tempered by other economic indicators which
showed that Britain was entering a recession as wage settlements continued
to put pressure on the rate of inflation. It now seems that the wider
economic context is likely to create new pressures inside the EMS. The UK
does no longer have the choice to devalue sterling by reducing interest rates
to try to boost exports and hence employment. Within the EMS it becomes
more urgent to adjust wage demands if unemployment is not to start rising
to the levels of the early 1980s. However, because of the government's arm's
length approach to incomes policy it would seem that unemployment
would continue to accelerate until workers start to understand the new
disciplines of the EMS.

European charter on social rights

The commitment to a Single European Act for goods and services and labour mobility has also led to arguments about the 'social' dimension to European integration. The idea of a social charter is aimed to give workers in Europe a 'floor' of rights in the workplace, including the right to belong to trade unions, the right to worker participation and consultation, and rights to training, sick pay, pensions, and holidays. According to Ms Papanderou the aim of the social charter is to avoid social dumping where workers, faced by more footloose industries, will be forced to surrender rights in order to compete with each other. The UK government has opposed the proposals, arguing that the social charter represents an attempt to introduce 'socialism through the backdoor' and that Britain has been able to create more jobs over the past decade because of the commitment to more flexible labour markets. The UK government has therefore argued that the social charter would actually do harm to employment.

Proposals to include part-time workers within the social charter is also opposed by the UK government. The aim is to give part-time workers the same rights as full-time workers. The proposals define part-time workers as those who work a minimum of eight hours per week. In the UK, part-time is set for earnings at £46 per week and not hourly. The UK government at present avoids paying social security to over 2.5 million part-time workers while employers avoid paying national insurance contributions for part-time staff. The UK has the highest number of part-time employees; they make up 23 per cent of the total workforce compared to 12 per cent in West Germany and 11 per cent in France. Between 1981 and 1988 the number of part-time workers have increased from 4.5 to 5.5 million in the UK.

In resisting the social charter, UK employment ministers have continuously pointed to the number of jobs that have been created in the UK over the last decade when compared to other European countries. There are now 1.5 million people more in work than in 1979. UK unemployment has fallen from a peak of over 3.2 million to 1.6 million in 1989, the largest fall in unemployment when compared to France and West Germany where the levels of unemployment have remained static at around 2 million. UK ministers have therefore pointed out that the social charter would add to the costs of labour for part-time employees, especially in national insurance contributions, thus reducing the incentive for employers to hire part-time staff. There is also opposition to the concept of industrial democracy and the format for worker participation to be imposed by Brussels. Together with the CBI the government have pointed out that they favour a plurality of formats which might include employee consultation and wider share ownership.

The argument between the UK and the rest of the EC members seemed to be that Mrs Thatcher's government wished to export the Thatcher vision of flexible labour markets to Europe, while other European leaders were equally sure that their own versions of corporatist politics have produced economic success. While the Thatcher government blamed the decline of the British economy on the politics of corporatism and collectivism, the Conservative government of Chancellor Kohl continues to maintain a commitment to the social market economy as developed by the market liberal thinking of Erhard and the social awareness of Adenauer. The West Germans point to the success of their system of industrial democracy, stable industrial relations and the contribution of their version of corporatist politics to deal with problems of wage inflation. In France, the move towards industrial democracy introduced by the Socialist government of Francois Mitterand in 1981 was not overturned by the Conservative government elected in 1984. Worker participation is now accepted as essential to the economic stability of France. While the UK seems to be moving towards a market liberal approach, other governments seem to prefer to keep their options open in order to have a choice between a plurality of policies from subsidies to industries to investment in education and training, from recognition of workers' rights and commitments to market principles, but also to intervene in the economy and to consult with strategic groups when necessary.

FREE TRADE AND PROTECTIONIST POLICIES

Europe: the single market and the emergence of trading blocs

European industry and competition

While on the one hand the concerns of industrial policies and nationalisation are often blurred in the sense that governments can provide indirect subsidies to industries, there are also linkages to be made between the government's commitment to a policy of free trade and policies which are seen as serving their national interests. Despite the commitment to a single European market for goods and labour, arguments continue about the loss of national sovereignty and autonomy. However, both the commitment to European Community and the national interest seem to produce a series of compromises. The attempt to produce a strategic plan for the European Steel Industry is a good example of the conflicts that exist between issues of national sovereignty and European interests. The twenty-two major steel producers, which are represented by Eurofed, accept that there is a need to reduce steel making capacity further despite the major closures between 1982 and 1983. However, they do not agree with the European Commission argument that the best way to reduce that capacity is to liberalise the industry and allow market forces to decide where reductions are made and therefore to end the quota restrictions produced under the Davignon plan. The steel producers argue that under the plan they were able to reduce capacity from 170 million tonnes to 140 million tonnes at the cost of 250,000 jobs in the industry. The steel producers would prefer a planned reduction while the Commission is urging governments to phase out subsidies immediately. In the meantime national governments, faced with a likely increase in unemployment whether in the North of France, Bavaria, Naples or Scotland, are also aware of the political costs in allowing their national steel making industry to decline further in the interests of creating a more viable European industry. In contrast, in the newer industries of information technology and telecommunications the move is towards creating a European-wide alliance capable of meeting the competition from Japan and the USA. In the meantime, therefore rather then urging the liberalisation of the industry European governments have erected barriers to protect their national industries from outside competition.

Agriculture and subsidies

Within the context of the Common Agricultural Policy (CAP), the European Community continues to guarantee prices for European farmers thereby reflecting the electoral strength of small farmers and the readiness of some governments to continue to subsidise their farming industry at the cost of $12 billion a year. It would seem, however, that the subsidies for agriculture will come under increasing pressures during the 1990s, especially from the USA where American farmers are also putting pressure on their government to introduce tariffs and to protect farmers. The Americans see the CAP as creating unfair advantage and therefore argue that it is in breach of the General Agreement on Tariffs and Trade (GATT). European subsidies to agriculture were a major issue of debate at the Uruguay Round in 1987, when European governments did agree to start withdrawing some of the subsidies. In the meantime, the small farmers in France and West Germany expect the protection of their livelihoods to continue to be the priority of their national governments despite the commitment to free trade.

The emergence of trading blocs

While the Single European Act commits European Community members to the creation of a single market, at an international level concern has been expressed that the move towards European union could also be leading towards the construction of 'fortress Europe' which could threaten world trade. The argument comes mainly from the USA and Japan and points to the possibility that while Europe might be moving towards greater mobility of goods and services between European countries the access to European markets for both Japan and the USA will become more restrictive. Recent agreements between the USA and Canada to remove trading barriers and also initial discussions between Australia, Japan, and other South-East Asian countries to release their common interests could point to the emergence of trading blocs in Europe, North America, and South-East Asia. In the meantime, the European Commission seems to be in conflict on two fronts with both Japan and the USA over issues of free trade. On the one hand, the Commission is accusing Japan of dumping practices in setting up 'screwdriver' assembly plants to ensure a foothold in European markets, while on the other, the USA is accusing Europe of violating the GATT commitment to duty-free access because of continued EC payments to domestic oilseed producers.

The problems of Third World debt

Between 1982 and 1988 Third World debt to the major Western economies has increased from $391 billion to $529 billion which means that during the same period the net transfer of resources has switched from a $3 billion transfer in favour of Third World countries to a $31 billion net transfer from the Third World to the Western industrial countries. The commitments to tight monetary policies, high interest rates, and high exchange rates in the USA, UK and West Germany have increased the problem of debt for Third World countries so that about 30 per cent of present GDP being produced in countries in Africa and South America is now being used as debt repayments to Western banks; this means that domestic demand within these countries has to be suppressed to increase exports. The majority of the people within these countries do not have the purchasing power to demand goods being made either in Europe, Japan, or the USA. The awareness that the expansion of world trade depends on increasing the purchasing power of potential consumers seems to be leading countries such as France and West Germany to encourage their banks to move towards debt forgiveness and to relieve some of the debt burden.

The concern with the EMS, the commitment to the European Market, and the problems of world trade, represent some of the major external constraints on UK economic policy during the 1990s and these cannot be resolved by the UK government without the co-operation of other governments. Joining the EMS could provide Britain with the opportunity to deal with the problem of inflation in the context of rules on monetary policies which could be established by an independent central bank. The question is whether the British government is willing to surrender their sovereignty on monetary policy in exchange for a discipline to be imposed from outside the UK. Equally, it would seem that while the social charter extends rights to training and industrial democracy to workers, it might also act as an incentive to UK employers and the UK government to take the issues of training and the updating of skills more seriously. The danger with the free market approach is that training continues to be seen as a cost to the firm rather than investment in the human capital of their employees. While the idea of a European central bank and the social charter might be perceived to be constraints on UK economic policy-making, such constraints might also have a positive influence on the UK economy.

Bibliography

Addison, P. (1975) *The Road to 1945*, London: Jonathan Cape.

Aldcroft, D. (1984) *Full Employment: The Elusive Goal*, Sussex: Wheatsheaf Books.

Alt, J. (1979) *The Politics of Economic Decline*, Cambridge: Cambridge University Press.

Arblaster, A. (1984) *The Rise and Decline of Western Liberalism*, Oxford: Basil Blackwell.

Arestis, P. and Skouras, T. (eds) (1985) *Post Keynesian Economic Theory*, Sussex: Wheatsheaf Books.

Arendt, H. (1961) *Between Past and Future*, London: Faber & Faber.

Argy, V. and Neville, J. (eds) (1985) *Inflation and Unemployment*, London: Allen & Unwin.

Artis, M. J. (1989) 'Wage inflation', in D. Greenaway (ed.), *Current Issues in Macroeconomics*, London: Macmillan.

—— and Lewis, M. K. (1985) 'Inflation in the United Kingdom', in V. Argy and J. Neville (eds), *Inflation and Unemployment*, London: Allen & Unwin.

Bacon, R. and Eltis, W. A. (1978) *Britain's Economic Problem: Too Few Producers*, London: Macmillan.

Bain, G. (1984) *Industrial Relations in Britain*, Oxford: Basil Blackwell.

—— and Elsheikh, F. (1976) *Union Growth and the Business Cycle*, Oxford: Basil Blackwell.

Barnett, C. (1986) *The Audit of War*, London: Macmillan.

Barnett, J. (1982) *Inside the Treasury*, London: André Deutsch.

Barry, N. (1987) *The New Right*, London: Croom Helm.

Bazen, S. and Thirlwall, J. (1989) *De-Industrialization*, Oxford: Heinemann Educational.

Beer, S. (1965) *Modern British Politics*, London: Faber & Faber.

—— (1982) *Britain Against Itself: The Political Contradictions of Collectivism*, London: Faber & Faber.

Begg, D., Dornbush, R., and Fisher, S. (1987) *Economics*, Maidenhead: McGraw-Hill.

Benn, T. (1988) *Out of the Wilderness Diaries, 1963–1967*, London: Arrow Books.

Bhaduri, A. (1986) *Macro Economics: The Dynamics of Commodity Production*, London: Macmillan.

Blackaby, F. (ed.) (1979) *De-Industrialization*, Aldershot: Gower.

Bleaney, M. (1985) *The Rise and Fall of Keynesian Economics*, London: Macmillan.

Borcherding, T. E. (1977) *Budgets and Bureaucrats: The Sources of Government Growth*, USA: Duke University Press.

Bowen, D. (1990) *Shaking the Iron Universe: British Industry in the 1980s*, London: Hodder & Stoughton.

Brandt Report (1980) *North–South: A Programme for Survival*, London: Pan Books.
Breton, A. (1974) *The Economic Theory of Representative Government*, London: Macmillan.
Brett, E. A. (1985) *The World Economy Since the War*, London: Macmillan.
Brittan, S. (1964) *The Treasury Under the Tories, 1951 to 1964*, Harmondsworth: Penguin.
—— (1977) *The Economic Consequences of Democracy*, London: Temple Smith.
—— (1983) *The Role and Limits of Government*, London: Temple Smith.
—— (1988) *A Restatement of Economic Liberalism*, London: Macmillan.
Bruce Gardyne, J. (1984) *Mrs Thatcher's First Administration*, London: Macmillan.
Buchanan, J. (1975) *The Limits of Liberty*, Chicago: Chicago University Press.
—— (1978) *The Economics of Politics*, Sussex: IEA.
Buchanan, J. M. and Tullock, G. (1965) *The Calculus of Consent: Logical Foundations of Constitutional Democracy*, New York: Ann Arton.
Butler, (Lord) R. A. (1973) *The Art of the Possible*, Harmondsworth: Penguin.
Callaghan, J. (1987) *Time and Chance*, London: Collins.
Cairncross, Sir Alec (1985a) 'Economics in theory and practice', *American Economic Review* III, 1128–57.
—— (1985b) *Years of Recovery*, London: Methuen.
Castle, B. (1980) *The Castle Diaries, 1974 to 1976*, London: Weidenfeld & Nicolson.
Cattermole, P. (ed.) (1990) *Contemporary Britain: An Annual Review, 1990*, Oxford: Basil Blackwell.
Caves, R. E. and Krause, L. B. (eds) (1980) *Britain's Economic Performance*, Washington: The Brookings Institute.
Clark, A. and Layard, R. (1989) *UK Unemployment*, Oxford: Heinemann Educational.
Clark, G. and Dear, M. (1984) *State Apparatus*, London: Allen & Unwin.
Clark, J. C. D. (1985) *English Society 1688–1832*, Cambridge: Cambridge University Press.
Clarke, Sir R. (1973) 'Parliament and public expenditure', *The Political Quarterly*, April.
Clegg, H. A. (1960) *A New Approach to Industrial Democracy*, Oxford: Basil Blackwell.
—— (1970) *The System of Industrial Relations in Great Britain*, Oxford: Basil Blackwell.
Coates, D. (1980) *Labour in Power? A Study of the Labour Government, 1974 to 1979*, London: Longman.
Confederation of British Industry (1990) *UK Inflation Performance*, London: CBI.
Congdon, T. Q. (1982) *Monetary Control in Britain*, London: Macmillan.
Conservative Party (1970a) *A Fair Deal at Work*, London: Conservative Political Centre.
—— (1970b) Verbatim Conference Report, London: Conservative Office.
Coutts, K. and Godley, W. (1989) 'The British economy under Mrs Thatcher', *Political Quarterly* 60, 137–51.
Cowling, M. (ed.) *Conservative Essays*, London: Cassell.
Crosland, C. A. R. (1956) *The Future of Socialism*, London: Jonathan Cape.
Crouch, C. (1979) *State and Economy in Contemporary Capitalism*, London: Croom Helm.
—— (1982) *The Politics of Industrial Relations*, London: Fontana.
—— and Marquand, D. (eds) (1989) *The New Centralism*, Oxford: Basil Blackwell.
Dahl, R. (1965) *A Preface to Democratic Theory*, Chicago: Chicago Press.
Dalton, H. (1935) *Practical Socialism for Britain*, London: Routledge.

Davidson, G. and Davidson, P. (1988) *Economics for a Civilised Society*, London: Macmillan.

Desai, M. (1981) *Testing Monetarism*, London: Frances Pinter.

Dornsbusch, R. and Layard, R. (eds) (1987) *The Performance of the British Economy*, Oxford: Clarendon Press.

Dow, J. C. R. (1964) *The Management of the British Economy, 1945 to 1960*, Cambridge: Cambridge University Press.

Downs, A. (1957) *An Economic Theory of Democracy*, New York: Harper & Row.

—— (1965) 'Why the government's budget is too small in a democracy', in E. Phelps, *Private Wants and Public Needs*, New York: Norton Press.

Eichner, A. S. (1979) *A Guide to Post Keynesian Economics*, London: Macmillan.

Elster, J. and Slagstad, R. (1988) *Constitutionalism and Democracy*, Cambridge: Cambridge University Press.

Fishbein, W. H. (1984) *Wage Restraint by Consensus*, London: Routledge.

Flanders, A. D. (1970) *Management and Unions: The Theory and Reform of Industrial Relations*, London: Faber & Faber.

Fox, A. (1985) *History and Heritage*, London: Allen & Unwin.

Friedman, M. (1968) 'The role of monetary policy', *American Economic Review* 58, 1–17.

—— (1975) *Unemployment versus Inflation: An Evaluation of the Phillips Curve*, Sussex: IEA

—— (1977) *Inflation and Unemployment: The New Dimension of Politics*, Sussex: IEA.

—— (1980) *Memorandum on Monetary Policy*, London: HMSO.

—— and Friedman, R. (1985) *The Tyranny of the Status Quo*, London: Penguin Books.

Gamble, A. (1974) *The Conservative Nation*, London: Macmillan.

—— (1988) *The Free Economy and the Strong State*, London: Macmillan.

Gardner, N. (1987) *Decade of Discontent: The Changing British Economy Since 1973*, Oxford: Basil Blackwell.

Gilmour, I. (1983) *Britain Can Work*, Oxford: Martin Robertson.

Grant, W. and Nath, S. (1984) *The Politics of Economic Policymaking*, Oxford: Basil Blackwell.

Gray, J. (1986) *Liberalism*, Milton Keynes: Open University Press.

Green, D. (1987) *The New Right*, Brighton: Wheatsheaf.

—— (1990) *Equality and Freedom*, Sussex: IEA.

Green, F. (1989) *The Restructuring of the UK Economy*, London: Harvester Wheatsheaf.

Greenaway, D. (1989) *Current Issues in Macroeconomics*, London: Macmillan.

Greenleaf, W. H. (1983) *The British Political Tradition. Volume II: The Ideological Heritage*, London: Methuen.

Hall, S. and Jacques, M. (1983) *The Politics of Thatcherism*, London: Lawrence & Wishart.

Harcourt, G. C. (1985) 'Post Keynesianism: quite wrong/or nothing new?', in P. Arestis and T. Skouras (eds), *Post Keynesian Economic Theory*, Sussex: Wheatsheaf.

Harrod, R. E. (1951) *The Life of John Maynard Keynes*, Basingstoke: Macmillan.

Hayek, F. A. (1984) 'Value and merit', in M. Sandel (ed.), *Liberalism and Its Critics*, Oxford: Basil Blackwell.

—— (1988) *The Fatal Conceit: The Errors of Socialism*, London: Routledge.

Heald, D. (1983) *Public Expenditure: Its Defence and Reform*, Oxford: Martin Robertson.

—— (1987) *Models of Democracy*, Oxford: Polity Press.

Heclo, H. and Wildavsky, A. (1982) *The Private Government of Public Money*, London: Macmillan.

Henderson, D. (1986) *Innocence and Design: The Influence of Economic Ideas on Policy*, Oxford: Basil Blackwell.

Henry, N. (1976) *Models of Inflation in the UK: An Evaluation*, London: NIESR.

Hibbs, D. (1977) 'Political parties and macro economic policy', *American Journal of Political Science*, 1467–87.

Hicks, J. R. (1968) *The Theory of Wages*, London: St Martin's Press.

—— (1974) *The Crisis in Keynesian Economics*, Oxford: Basil Blackwell.

Hines, A. G. (1971) 'The determinants of the rate of change of money wage rates and the effectiveness of incomes policy', in H. G. Johnson and A. R. Nobay (eds), *The Current Inflation*, London: Macmillan.

Hirschman, A. (1970) *Exit, Voice and Loyalty*, Cambridge, Mass.: Harvard University Press.

HMSO (1956) *The Economic Implications of Full Employment*, Cmd 9725, London: HMSO.

—— (1961) Council for Prices and Productivity, *Fourth Report*, London: HMSO.

—— (1965) *Machinery of Prices and Incomes Policy*, Cmnd 2577, London: HMSO.

—— (1965) *Prices and Incomes: An Early Warning System*, Cmnd 2808, London: HMSO.

—— (1968) Royal Commission on Trade Unions and Employers' Associations, 1965–1968, *Report*, Cmnd 3623, London: HMSO.

—— (1969) *In Place of Strife*, Cmnd 3888, London: HMSO.

—— (1970) *New Policies for Public Spending*, Cmnd 4515, London: HMSO.

—— (1971) *Public Expenditure to 1975/6*, Cmnd 4829, London: HMSO.

—— (1973) *The Programme for Controlling Inflation, The Second Stage*, Cmnd 5205, London: HMSO.

—— (1973) *The Counter-Inflation Policy, Stage 3: A Statement by the Prime Minister*, Cmnd 5446, London: HMSO.

—— (1975) *The Attack in Inflation*, Cmnd 6151, London: HMSO.

—— (1983) *Democracy in Trade Unions: A Green Paper*, Cmnd 8778, London: HMSO.

—— (1990) Department of the Environment, *Our Common Inheritance: A Green Paper*, London: HMSO.

Holmes, M. (1982) *Political Pressure and Economic Policy*, London: Butterworth.

—— (1985) *The Labour Government 1974 to 1979: Political Aims and Economic Policy*, London: Macmillan.

—— (1989) *Thatcherism: Scope and Limits, 1983 to 1987*, London: Macmillan.

House of Lords (1985) Select Committee on Overseas Trade: Session 1984/5, vol. I, *Report 258–1*, London: HMSO.

Howell, T. R. (1990) *Steel and the State: Government and Steels' Structural Crisis*, Colorado: Westview Press.

Inns of Court Conservative and Unionist Society (1958) *A Giant's Strength*, London: The Society.

Jackman, R., Mulvey, C., and Trevithick, J. (1981) *The Economics of Inflation*, Oxford: Martin Robertson.

Jay, D. (1937) *The Socialist Case*, London: Faber & Faber.

Jenkins, P. (1987) *Mrs Thatcher's Revolution*, London: Jonathan Cape.

Jessop, B., Bonnett, K., Bromley, S., and Ling, T. (1988) *Thatcherism*, Oxford: Polity Press.

Johnson, H. G. and Nobay, A. R. (eds) (1971) *The Current Inflation*, London: Macmillan.

Jones, R. (1987) *Wages and Employment Policy, 1936–1985*, London: Allen & Unwin.

Joseph, K. (1975) *Stranded in the Middle Ground*, London: Conservative Political Studies.

Kahn, Lord (1974) 'On re-reading Keynes', *Proceedings of the British Academy*, IX.

Kaldor, (Lord) N. (1980) *Memorandum on Monetary Policy*, London: HMSO.

—— (1982) *The Economic Consequences of Mrs Thatcher*, London: Duckworth.

—— (1984) 'Keynesian economics after fifty years', in D. Worswick and J. Trevithick (eds), *Keynes and the Modern World*, Cambridge: Cambridge University Press.

Kalecki, M. (1943) 'Political aspects of full employment', *Political Quarterly* 4, 322–31.

Kavanagh, D. (1987) *Thatcherism and British Politics*, Oxford: Clarendon Press.

Keegan, W. (1983) *Mrs Thatcher's Economic Experiment*, London: Allen Lane.

—— and Pennant, Rea R. (1979) *Who Runs the Economy? Control and Influence in British Economic Policy*, London: Temple Smith.

Keynes, J. M. (1936) *The General Theory of Employment, Interest and Money*, London: Macmillan.

—— (1944) 'A note by Lord Keynes', *Economic Journal*, December.

—— (1971) *The Collected Writings: The Economic Consequences of the Peace*, London: Macmillan.

Klein, R. (1975) *Inflation and Priorities*, London: Centre for Studies in Social Policy.

Korpi, W. (1980) *The Working Class in Welfare Capitalism*, London: Routledge.

Krieger, J. (1986) *Reagan, Thatcher and the Politics of Decline*, Oxford: Polity Press.

Kymlicka, B. and Matthews, J. (1985) *The Reagan Revolution?* Chicago: Dorsey Press.

Labour Party (1964) *The New Britain: Labour's Plan*, London: The Labour Party.

—— (1973) *Paying for Labour's Programme*, London: The Labour Party.

—— and the TUC (1973) *Economic Policy and the Cost of Living*, London: The Labour Party.

Laidler, D. (1980) *Memorandum on Monetary Policy*, London: HMSO.

—— (1982) *Monetarist Perspectives*, Oxford: Philip Allan.

—— and Purdy, D. (eds) (1974) *Inflation and Labour Markets*, Manchester: Manchester University Press.

Layard, R. (1989) *How To Beat Unemployment*, Oxford: Oxford University Press.

—— and Nickell, S. (1986) 'Unemployment in Britain', *Economica*, supplement 53, 121–69.

—— —— (1987) 'The causes of British unemployment', *British Journal of Industrial Relations* 16, 287–302.

Levacic, R. (1988) *Supply Side Economics*, Oxford: Heinemann Educational.

—— and Rebmann, A. (1988) *Macro-economics: An Introduction to Keynesian-Neoclassical Controversies*, London: Macmillan.

McCallum, J. (1986) 'Unemployment in the OECD countries', *The Economic Journal*, December, 923–5.

Macmillan, H. (1972) *Pointing The Way*, London: Macmillan.

Malinvaud, E. (1984) *Mass Unemployment*, Oxford: Basil Blackwell.

Marquand, D. (1988) *The Unprincipled Society: New Demands and Old Politics*, London: Jonathan Cape.

Marquand, J. (1989) *Autonomy and Change*, Sussex: Harvester.

Martin, R. and Rowthorn, B. (1986) *The Geography of De-Industrialisation*, London: Macmillan.

Massey, D. and Meegan, R. (1982) *The Anatomy of Job Loss*, London: Methuen.

Maynard, G. (1988) *The Economy Under Mrs Thatcher*, Oxford: Basil Blackwell.

Meade, J. (1984) 'Memoirs of Maynard Keynes', in D. Worswick and J. Trevithick (eds), *Keynes and the Modern World*, Cambridge: Cambridge University Press.

Miliband, R. (1975) *Parliamentary Socialism*, London: Merlin Press.

Minford, P. (1980) *Memorandum on Monetary Policy*, London: HMSO.

—— (1983) *Unemployment: Cause and Cure*, Oxford: Martin Robertson.

Mitchell, W. and Green, D. (1988) *Government As It Is*, Sussex: IEA.

Moggridge, D. E. (1973) *The Collected Works of John Maynard Keynes*, vol. XIV, London: Macmillan.

—— (1976) *Keynes*, London: Macmillan.

Moran, M. (1977) *The Politics of Industrial Relations*, London: Macmillan.

Mosley, P. (1984) *The Making of Economic Policy*, Sussex: Wheatsheaf.

Muellbauer, J. (1988) 'How permanent is the Thatcher effect', *Financial Times*, 16 June.

Mullard, M. (1987) *The Politics of Public Expenditure*, London: Routledge.

—— (1991) 'Study of training in Leeds and Bradford', DES Research, Bradford & Ilkley College.

—— Butcher, H., Law, I., and Leach, R. (1990) *Thatcherism and Local Government*, London: Routledge.

Mulvey, C. (1976) 'Collective agreements and relative earnings in UK manufacturing in 1973', *Economica*, 419–27.

—— (1978) *The Economic Analysis of Trade Unions*, Oxford Martin Robertson.

Muschamp, D. (ed.) (1986) *Political Thinkers*, London: Macmillan.

NIESR (1980) *Memorandum on Monetary Policy*, London: HMSO.

Niskanen, W. (1977) *Bureaucracy and Representative Government*, Chicago: Aldine Press.

Nozick, R. (1984) 'Moral constraints and distributive justice', in M. Sandel (ed.), *Liberalism and Its Critics*, Oxford: Basil Blackwell.

OECD (1988) *Economic Surveys: UK*, London: HMSO.

Olson, M. (1965) *The Logic of Collective Action*, Cambridge, Mass.: Harvester University Press.

O'Morgan, K. (1984) *Labour in Power, 1945–1951*, Oxford: Clarendon Press.

Panitch, L. (1976) *Social Democracy and Industrial Militancy: The Labour Party, The Trade Unions and Incomes Policy 1945 to 1974*. Cambridge: Cambridge University Press.

Pearce, D., Markandya, A., and Barbier, E. (1989) *Blueprint for a Green Economy*, London: Earthscar Publications Ltd.

Peden, G. C. (1985) *British Economic and Social Policy: Lloyd George to Margaret Thatcher*, Oxford: Philip Allan.

Pelling, H. (1985) *The Labour Governments, 1945–51*, London: Macmillan.

Pencavel, J. H. (1974) 'Relative wages and trade unions in the UK', *Economica*, 149–59.

Perkin, H. (1989) *The Rise of Professional Society: England Since 1880*, London: Routledge.

Phelps Brown, E. H. (1977) *The Inequality of Pay*, Oxford: Oxford University Press.

Phillips, A. W. (1958) 'The relationship between unemployment and the rate of change in money wages in the UK, 1861 to 1957', *Economica* 25, 283–99.

Pimlott, B. (1985) *Hugh Dalton*, London: Macmillan.

Plitatzky, Sir Leo (1982) *Getting and Spending*, Oxford: Basil Blackwell.

Pollard, S. (1982) *The Wastage of the British Economy*, London: Croom Helm.

Posner, M. (1978) *Demand Management*, London: Heinemann.

Purdy, D. and Zis, G. (1974) 'On the concept and measurement of union militancy', in D. Laidler and D. Purdy (eds), *Inflation and Labour Markets*, Manchester: Manchester University Press.

Pym, F. (1985) *The Politics of Consent*, London: Sphere Books.

Rawls, J. (1988) *A Theory of Justice*, Oxford: Oxford University Press.

Riddell, P. (1980) *The Thatcher Government*, Oxford: Basil Blackwell.

Robinson, J. (1937) *Essays in the Theory of Employment*, London: Macmillan.

Rose, R. and Peters, G. (1979) *Can Governments Go Bankrupt?* London: Macmillan.

Sandel, M. (1984) *Liberalism and Its Critics*, Oxford: Basil Blackwell.

Sapsford, D. and Tzannatos, L. (1990) *Current Issues in Labour Economics*, London: Macmillan.

Sawyer, M. C. (1985) *The Economics of Michal Kalecki*, London: Macmillan.

Scamell, W. M. (1983) *The International Economy Since 1945*, London: Macmillan.

Schmitter, P. L. and Lehmbruch, G. (1979) *Trends Towards Corporatist Intermediation*, London: Sage.

Scruton, R. (1984) *The Meaning of Conservatism*, London: Macmillan.

Shonfield, A. (1959) *British Economic Policy Since the War*, Harmondsworth: Penguin.

—— (1969) *Modern Capitalism: The Changing Balance of Public and Private Power*, Oxford: Oxford University Press.

—— (1984) *In Defence of the Mixed Economy*, Oxford: Oxford University Press.

Sissons, M. and French, P. (eds) (1964) *The Age of Austerity*, Harmondsworth: Penguin.

Skidelsky, R. (1977) *The End of the Keynesian Era*, London: Macmillan.

—— (1989) *Thatcherism*, Oxford: Basil Blackwell.

Smith, A. (1933) *The Wealth of Nations*, London: Penguin.

—— (1935) *The Wealth of Nations*, London: Dent.

—— (1988) *The Wealth of Nations*, Harmondsworth: Penguin.

Stein, J. L. (1984) *Monetarist, Keynesian and New Classical Economics*, Oxford: Basil Blackwell.

Stewart, M. (1975) *Keynes and After*, Harmondsworth: Penguin.

Therborn, G. (1986) *Why Some People Are More Unemployed Than Others*, London: Verso.

Thompson, G. (1986) *The Conservative's Economic Record*, London: Croom Helm.

—— Brown, V., and Levacic, R. (1987) *Managing the UK Economy*, Oxford: Polity Press.

Trade Union Congress (1990) *A New Agenda: Bargaining for Prosperity in the 1990s*, London: TUC.

Tufte, E. (1978) *The Political Control of the Economy*, Princeton.

Tyler, R. (1987) *Campaign: The Selling of the Prime Minister*, London: Grafton Books.

Walters, Sir Alan (1984) *Britain's Economic Renaissance*, Oxford: Oxford University Press.

—— (1990) *Sterling in Danger*, London: Fontana.

Webster, A. and Dunning, J. H. (1990) *Structural Change in the World Economy*, London: Routledge.

Wigham, E. (1976) *Strikes and the Government, 1893 to 1974*, London: Macmillan.

Williams, P. (1982) *Hugh Gaitskell*, Oxford: Oxford University Press.

Williamson, J. (1984) 'Keynes and the international economic order', in D. Worswick and J. Trevithick (eds), *Keynes and the Modern World*, Cambridge: Cambridge University Press.

Wilson, H. (1971) *The Labour Government 1964–70: A Personal Record*, London: Weidenfeld & Nicolson.

Wootton, B. (1955) *The Social Foundations of Wages Policy*, London: Allen & Unwin.

Worswick, D. and Trevithick (eds) (1984) *Keynes and the Modern World*, Cambridge: Cambridge University Press.

Worswick, G. and Ady, P. (eds) (1952) *The British Economy 1945–50*, Oxford: Oxford University Press.

Wren Lewis, J. and Darby, J. (1989) 'Measuring UK productivity growth', *Economic Review*, June.

Young, H. (1989) *One of Us*, London: Macmillan.

Young, (Lord) H. (1989) *The Enterprise Years: A Businessman in the Cabinet*, London: Clarendon Press.

Index